TELEVISION PRODUCTION

disciplines and techniques

TELEVISION PRODUCTION

third edition

disciplines and techniques

Thomas D. Burrows
Donald N. Wood

California State University, Northridge

Wm. C. Brown Publishers
Dubuque, Iowa

Book Team

John Stout
Executive Editor

Stan Stoga
Editor

Natalie Gould
Production Editor

Julie Anderson
Designer

Carla D. Arnold
Permissions Editor

Carol Schiessl
Photo Researcher

wcb group

Wm. C. Brown
Chairman of the Board

Mark C. Falb
President and Chief Executive Officer

wcb

Wm. C. Brown Publishers, College Division

Lawrence E. Cremer
President

James L. Romig
Vice-President, Product Development

David A. Corona
Vice-President, Production and Design

E. F. Jogerst
Vice-President, Cost Analyst

Bob McLaughlin
National Sales Manager

Catherine M. Faduska
Director of Marketing Services

Craig S. Marty
Director of Marketing Research

Eugenia M. Collins
Production Editorial Manager

Marilyn A. Phelps
Manager of Design

Mary M. Heller
Photo Research Manager

*To our many students who have helped
make teaching the most rewarding of all
professions*

About the Authors

Thomas D. Burrows is a professor in the Radio-TV-Film Department at California State University, Northridge, in Los Angeles. He entered the teaching profession after a considerable career in the broadcast industry. Starting as a disc jockey in his hometown of Tucson, he worked his way up to a position with ABC, Los Angeles, serving as the director of the KABC-TV evening news program and of the nationally syndicated rock music show, *Shivaree*. Subsequently, Prof. Burrows was with KCET-TV in Los Angeles where he received the Christopher, Emmy, and Peabody awards as producer of the PBS series *The Advocates*. As a consultant to ABC Sports in 1984, Prof. Burrows set up a special training program that resulted in the employment of a number of students during the televised coverage of the Olympic Games. He holds a Master of Arts degree from the School of Journalism at the University of Southern California.

Donald N. Wood, professor of Radio-TV-Film, has been teaching at California State University, Northridge, since 1970. He has also taught at San Diego State University, The University of Michigan, and Westminster College (Pennsylvania). Dr. Wood's professional background has been largely in educational broadcasting. He was program coordinator for National Educational Television, area coordinator for the Midwest Program on Airborne Television Instruction, and director of ETV for the Hawaii State Department of Education, during which time he was executive producer of more than eight hundred television productions. Dr. Wood is the coauthor of the textbook *Educational Telecommunications* and author of *Mass Media and the Individual*. He has his M.A. and Ph.D. degrees from The University of Michigan.

Contents

Preface

This third edition of *Television Production: Disciplines and Techniques* is designed as a basic introductory text for a college course in television production. It covers virtually everything that would as a rule be included in such a course.

As the dedication implies, we have deliberately written this text with our students in mind. It is designed as a teaching text—not as a reference book, not as a theoretical discussion, not as a catalog. We have included the technical information that we feel is essential for the beginning student to know, but we have not tried to produce a basic engineering manual. We have centered our discussions and examples on the kinds of equipment that we feel most training institutions will be using— not always the latest state of the art and not always the sophisticated hardware found at network production centers. In fact, we have tried to emphasize the *process* and the *thinking* that go into TV production, not just equipment manipulation. We have touched upon the basic elements of directing but without undue emphasis that would detract from the basic production material.

In short, this text is designed to teach the first-year student what he or she needs to know about audio, lighting, cameras and lenses, the switcher, recording and editing, single-camera production, pictorial elements, on-camera talent, other crew positions, and directing.

We are concerned not only with the *techniques* of TV production (operating equipment and performing basic crew assignments) but also with the *disciplines* of TV production—those intangible professional attitudes and behaviors involving responsibility, self-control, initiative, judgment, respect, and similar attributes. We hope that the reader will bear with us if we continue to return to this theme, but it is true that success in any aspect of the broadcasting field is going to depend more upon one's internalized set of attitudes than upon specific learned skills and techniques.

The text places essential information relating to equipment function and production crew organization within a sequence that is most suitable for broadcast laboratory instruction. We feel strongly that production proficiency (both the techniques and disciplines) can ultimately be gained only through continued involvement in a production operation. Students must have the opportunity to understand the creative process by working at all of the various positions within the crew structure. They must, however, be allowed to come to grips with the complexity of the ongoing production sequence by means of a series of planned gradual steps, each building upon previously mastered concepts and skills.

The two chapters on audio have been retained at the beginning of the book in order to present the student with an early model of the concepts of equipment function and crew organization. It is felt that this sequence of information—with an emphasis upon the audio signal flow—will facilitate a better understanding of comparable elements when they are later presented within the entire combined audio and video operation.

Since the publication of the second edition of the text, the techniques of single-camera production have continued to evolve. The realities of ENG (electronic news gathering) and EFP (electronic field production) are playing an increasingly important role in commercial, educational, and corporate telecommunications. Therefore, this third edition includes additional emphasis on these developments. The chapter on single-camera video production has been updated to include more emphasis on field directing, and this material

(chapter 12) has been moved to immediately precede the chapters on studio directing—giving more coherence to the emphasis on directing techniques in three sequential chapters. Additionally, references to location audio, lighting, camera operation, and other aspects of remote production have been integrated throughout the text.

The reader will also find expanded, clarified, and updated material on all other production aspects throughout the text. Major additions include expanded coverage of lighting (chapter 4), discussion of newer camera developments and color considerations (chapter 5), updated material on videorecorders (chapter 8), a section on computer graphics (chapter 9), and material on the role of the unit manager (chapter 11). Supplemental materials explaining rate cards and production budget planning have been introduced in appendix E.

We realize that many instructors will wish to structure their course units in a manner different from our suggested order. Some may wish to get into cameras before audio or place lighting considerations after basic camera structure and lens design. Others may want to discuss crew positions or basic directing skills earlier than our text does. To this end, we have tried to make each chapter as independent as possible—using appropriate cross-referencing of material.

At the end of each chapter we have included one or more suggested training exercises or class projects. It is strongly recommended that these exercises and projects be carried out—to the extent possible in various facilities—in order to reinforce and adapt the material presented in each chapter. These exercises have been designed to resemble, as nearly as possible, the production realities of the primary types of programming and are structured to permit individualized input by both student and instructor. Production project scripts and materials are provided in appendix D on perforated pages so that they can be revised and used apart from the text in studio exercises.

New to this edition is an *Instructor's Manual* that we hope will be useful to experienced and inexperienced teachers alike. For each chapter it contains a brief summary statement of scope and purpose, sample test questions, and modified versions of the training exercises appearing in the text. For some of the chapters there are additional training exercises as well.

We have had the advice and help of many colleagues and students in pulling this text together. Although we cannot hope to single out everybody who has assisted or influenced us in the writing of the text, we should like to thank specifically those who have made major contributions. In addition to those who have been acknowledged in earlier editions, we especially want to express our gratitude to five of our network colleagues who have given generously of their time and advice in working with us: Dave Dubiel, Truck Krone, Mel Morhouse, Jay Roper, and Bud Untiedt.

We also would like to acknowledge the artistic contributions of Dave McCutheon for his work in redesigning many of the illustrations in this third edition. Brian Wood at the keyboard and Mike Petros at his drawing table also have made many significant contributions. In addition, the many students who have served as our inspiration, our guinea pigs, and our evaluators—working with portions of the manuscript as it was being developed—deserve our deepest appreciation.

Finally, we want to thank our colleagues in universities and colleges across the country who have reviewed portions of the manuscript and have made many valuable suggestions:

Dr. Barton L. Griffith
University of Missouri, Columbia
Dr. Gary Warren Melton
Arkansas State University
John Rosenbaum
Bucks Community College
Professor Doug Trabert
Lake-Sumter Community College
Professor Robert Anderson
Mississippi State University

Despite the support and assistance from our colleagues and students, there undoubtedly are errors to be found. For these, we assume full responsibility.

Except for those otherwise credited, all photographs used in the text were taken by the authors.

TELEVISION PRODUCTION

disciplines and techniques

Introduction to TV Production

1

Electronic camera television production is a fascinating, demanding, and rewarding enterprise—whether done in a studio or on a remote location. There is not only the obvious intoxication of glamour and activity but also the quiet exhilaration of being part of a very captivating and important process of modern communications technology.

Although this text may appear to be concerned primarily with developing proficiency in the technical aspects of television production—the techniques of operating the TV tools and the disciplines of functioning in a television team—another primary purpose should be kept in mind. The most important goal of a college-level production course should simply be that of creating an understanding of the video production process—regardless of one's ultimate vocational objectives.

The realities of television employment are such that while some members of the class may follow a career in production-based positions others will find employment in office-based jobs such as operations, programming, sales, or management. Studio production training will provide a basis, however, for these latter categories of employment as well. Management decisions constantly revolve around what is done in the studio or, of more importance, how efficiently it is done. Sales representatives, scriptwriters, advertising executives, and general managers all must have a grasp of the production techniques presented in this book.

1.1 Techniques and Disciplines

Successful television is dependent upon the premise that every member of the production unit has, over a period of time, developed a set of individual *techniques* and *disciplines* in order to cope with the complexities of various types of programs. Although these two terms do not necessarily refer to mutually exclusive categories, they do describe somewhat differing aspects of the total production sequence.

For their use within the broadcast context, the following definitions of these terms will be utilized.

Techniques refer to specific skills unique to the performance of any single position within the television crew structure. A technique reflects a degree of formal (or possibly informal) training related to production equipment, electronic or otherwise. An audio engineer's ability to select and position microphones for correct balance would be considered a technique. Such a definition, however, does not preclude the possibility of interaction with other crew members. A director's method of using cameras is thought of as a matter of individual initiative and specialized talent—founded upon a few basic techniques and principles of television communication.

At the beginning, it may be easiest for students of TV production to think of techniques as being those particular skills used in operating various pieces of equipment—knowledge of which buttons to push, how far certain knobs should be twisted, and where to connect a given plug, for example.

Disciplines comprise a complete series of procedures that are shared by and relate to the entire production unit. The use of proper voice procedure on the intercom network is a specific example. The thorough preparation and planning necessary before starting out on a remote EFP (electronic field production) recording involves considerable discipline. The interaction of the stage manager, the stage crew, camera operators, and performers in a studio would involve a whole range of disciplines for efficient operation. Disciplines imply a consistency of individual action as well as a consideration for others in the same team effort.

One of the most crucial elements of TV production discipline is that of *responsibility*.

Dependability. A conscientious effort always to do your best. In the complex chain of the television crew there can be no weak link. In any given production situation, the efforts of dozens of persons may be coordinated in an intricate pattern. If one person fails to carry out his or her specific function at the right moment, many precious minutes—or hours—of costly production time can be wasted.

Production discipline also implies many other intangible values and skills. An attitude of *respect* must be acquired—respect for equipment as well as for other members of the production crew. A balanced sense of *initiative* and *self-control* must be concurrently developed—knowing when to jump in with a suggestion or action and when to remain quiet and stick to your own job. Learning how to deal with your own anxiety—how to remain *calm* when the production elements start to fall apart—is another important aspect of developing a sense of television discipline.

To use a simple analogy, when you are learning to drive a car, you may quickly master the separate *techniques* of turning, braking, acceleration, and the shifting of gears. The manner in which you combine these skills to make a left turn in heavy traffic requires the additional element of *discipline*.

As a television-production student you therefore must be concerned not only with the *techniques* of knowing precisely how to use all of the equipment but also with the development of your own sense of production *discipline* so that others will be able to depend upon you with confidence. In fact, one of the most revealing tests of your production capabilities is the answer to this simple question: Do other people want you on their production team? Unless you can answer *yes* to that query, you probably will want to rethink your studio attitudes, your sense of professional discipline and dedication, and your academic and professional goals.

Figure 1-1 What kind of student are you? What is your attitude? What do you hope to get out of this course?

1.2 Development of a Professional Attitude

In talking about abstract concepts such as *discipline* and the development of something called *professional attitude,* it may be helpful to think about them from two different perspectives—first, personal goals and self-image, and second, attitudes toward others.

Attitude and Self-Image

To begin with, you need to ask yourself something about your personal goals (fig. 1-1). *What are your professional aims?* What do you hope to do in broadcasting or film? Do you have specific occupational goals? Are you broadly concerned with doing something socially constructive with media? In any case, what role will education or specific training play in attaining those goals? Then ask yourself *what your immediate learning goals are.* What do you hope to get out of this class? What are you doing to ensure that this will be a constructive experience?

In answering queries such as these, you can come closer to defining a personal value system and a sense of direction. These, in turn, lead to a sharpening of your own sense of professional development and the need for internal discipline. This should help you begin to see specific goal-oriented tasks that revolve around the educational system. You are better able to recognize the need to learn.

You should be able to think in terms of educational course work beyond your immediate TV-production class. What other related academic work do you need? Journalism? Business communications? Political science? Public relations? Management? Communication history? Government regulations? Message design? English? What academic course work is needed in the liberal arts that will help give you a perspective on humankind and your place in contemporary society—an understanding of the *role* of modern telecommunications? Philosophy? History? Foreign cultures? Psychology? The arts? Environmental sciences? You cannot be a successful communicator unless you know something of the content you have to communicate—and unless you understand the environment of the communication process.

When asked what kind of broadcasting student they would like to hire, many top television executives and network officers reply, "Give me students who are intelligent, sensitive, aware of social issues, alert, concerned with human relations, adaptable, and able to solve problems, and I'll teach them the tools and techniques of the business in a few weeks on the job."

In this specific production course, you should begin to realize the need to learn how to understand the telecommunications process, how to use the tools of the communication enterprise. You will start to develop a sense of studio discipline that grows out of an appreciation of the total process of TV production.

One specific discipline mentioned in section 1.1 is the *balance between initiative and self-control*. There are numerous times on any television production when some little thing appears to be wrong. The lighting director is not adding enough back light. The director is ready to take the wrong shot. The stage manager looks as if he or she is going to walk in front of the camera. What do you do in each of these situations? Do you speak up or remain silent? Do you know enough about the total situation to understand what is really happening? Only with enough studio experience and a knowledge of all equipment and all positions can you determine when you should take the initiative to avert a problem and when you should remain in your place because others probably know what they are doing.

Another kind of production self-discipline concerns the problem of *dealing with your own anxieties*. In any television production, various crew members are going to experience differing degrees of anxiety. First, you must accept the fact that some anxiety—some amount of nervousness—is good; it is what keeps you on your toes. People would not be able to turn in a peak performance if they were not a little bit edgy and apprehensive. Second, you will derive some solace from the fact that you are not alone. Every topflight director has gone through the same process, and everyone in your class is experiencing the same sensation to some extent. Third, you should realize that anxiety is born of insecurity—ignorance of specific equipment or procedures. If you are uneasy about a particular assignment or function, make certain you find out what you can about it. Face your shortcomings and fill in your gaps. For example, review the special-effects **bus** of the switcher, or ask your instructor to go over the master control room patching again. With knowledge and experience comes confidence.

Attitudes Toward Others

As you cultivate more confidence and build a positive self-attitude, you will also be able to develop more of a sense of production discipline and an affirmative attitude toward the entire crew effort.

You must recognize the fact that studio television production is emphatically a *team effort*. There is no room in the production process for the lazy and the goldbricker (if you eventually want to succeed in the field). Neither is there room for the braggart and the ego-tripper (unless your uncle owns the station).

A strong sense of discipline and a professional attitude will result in a concern about the success of the program itself. If you are truly interested in the field, then you are, by definition, a *communicator*. In addition, if you are concerned with the communication process, then you want to see the communicative act—the creation of the television message—succeed. You *care* about contributing to a successful communication experience. If the communicative act, the television production, should not succeed, then you care—as a student of the process—to learn why it did not work. You analyze the problems and dissect the mistakes so that you can be part of a successful effort on the next production. If you do not deeply care about seeing the communication process work, then perhaps you should not pursue studies in this field.

As you deepen your sense of professional concern, you will also increase your professional responsibility toward others and toward the production. You will want to make certain that your dependability cannot be questioned. When you are assigned a job, it will be done. When you are supposed to be somewhere (including the start of a lab production), you will be there on time—or earlier.

Another important attribute of studio discipline is *respect*—respect for equipment and respect for other individuals, both **talent** and crew. As explained in the following chapters of this text, by gaining an understanding of the way most equipment works, you will begin to develop some appreciation and sense of *respect for the equipment*. The tools you are working with are not toys; they are not to be mistreated and played with. No professional handles a piece of equipment just to play with it. The tool is there to do a specific job, and that is what it is used for. Remember that the purchase and maintenance and repair of all equipment is limited by a very strict budget—whether in a plush network, a small studio, a noncommercial station, or a university training facility. Once a piece of equipment is broken, two things happen: (1) the studio, or some small part of the studio operation, is out of commission for some period of time; (2) someone, somehow, must pay for the repair of the equipment.

You also show your respect for the equipment and studio by adhering to the established studio policies and regulations. Most studios will have certain operating policies concerning safety rules; supervision of use of facilities; prohibition of eating, drinking, and smoking in certain areas; storage of materials; and so forth. Make certain that you are aware of the specific regulations in the studio where you are working—and follow them.

Respect for individuals is manifest in several ways. Most of the people you are working with in a training situation are learners—as you are. They deserve the same respect and patient treatment to which you are entitled. Unless you feel that you are so superior to your colleagues that you are above evaluation, you have no right to treat others with disrespect. You show your respect—to crew members and performers alike—by being patient and understanding; by offering assistance, when appropriate; and by being genuinely appreciative and congratulatory when a good job is done.

There are several occasions when assistance is appropriate. Two specific instances are in setting up a production and in **striking**—or cleaning up—after a program is recorded. While a show is being set up, some crew members may have relatively little to do—camera operators, recording engineers, projectionists, technical directors, and the like. (Some of these crew members may have specific jobs assigned to them.) People who are free during the early stages of studio preparation should make themselves available to the lighting and staging director or directors to assist in the initial setup.

The same thing is true after the production is completed. Everyone has his or her own area to strike (camera operators coiling cables, audio engineer putting away microphones and cables), but some positions (for example, those of technical director, recording engineers) may be free sooner than others. Whenever these crew members have finished cleaning up their positions, they should assist in the general strike. It is everyone's job to see that the studio and all equipment are restored to their original condition—ready for the next production crew or class. (In unionized shops, of course, one should not cross union jurisdictions to assist someone else. Camera engineers do not handle stage props, and so forth.)

Whether and when to offer assistance often becomes a gray area. Do you move to "save" a fellow student if he or she is about to commit some obvious blunder? (This is related to finding a balance between initiative and self-control.) Do you, as technical director, follow the director's command when he or she tells you to punch up the wrong camera? Do you, as a floor assistant, obey the stage manager when he or she tells you to move an easel stand while the camera is on the air? In a professional, real-world situation you would probably be correct to hold off on executing the given instruction; you would try to save the person giving the instruction by quickly and considerately pointing out the apparent error. In a learning situation, however, you may not be doing the person a favor by saving him or her too frequently. If a director repeatedly makes the same kind of mistake by giving the wrong command and crew members repeatedly save the director by not following the command, are they really helping the director to learn? Or are they just helping reinforce a bad habit? The lab production is, after all, the place to learn by making mistakes—and by seeing the results of those mistakes.

There are many similar gray areas where there is no fast and simple correct response. It is the challenge and excitement of these uncertainties that make television production the stimulating field it is. It is the quick-thinking professional who, because of his or her training and experience and sense of personal discipline, is able to make the right decisions.

1.3 Production Operations

At the outset it will be realized, of course, that there are several different levels of television production. Some TV productions are staged in mammoth studios with millions of dollars worth of equipment and crews consisting of dozens of people. On the other hand, many worthwhile productions are undertaken in tiny, makeshift quarters with a few hundred dollars' worth of equipment and a crew of two or three—or even one. In between these two extremes are most of the typical situations that you are likely to encounter.

Broadcast Categories

The most complex kind of studio productions are likely to be found at *network levels*—both commercial and noncommercial. Figure 1-2 shows a typical network production. (It should be stressed that noncommercial public television operations can—and often do—surpass commercial television productions in terms of program complexities, size of crews, glamour and excitement, and vital production challenges.) Productions at a network level usually will be well budgeted, housed in a large modern facility (although many network productions are still being turned out in older, but handsomely equipped, centers), and have large crews (some productions that originate from several different locations may have hundreds of crew members working in various engineering and production capacities).

At the *station level* of production there is a wide variety of origination complexities. Some commercial network-owned-and-operated stations and some of the major public TV stations will have production facilities that rival the network operations. At the other end of the station spectrum, many smaller stations will have woefully inadequate facilities—cramped studio or studios, small production crews, and older equipment patched together to meet minimal Federal Communications Commission (FCC) broadcast standards (see fig. 1-3).

Another level of professional operations includes *independent production centers*. There are many different kinds of facilities that are not directly connected with a broadcast outlet. Some are major studios producing commercials or independent programs for network-level distribution. Some are smaller outfits that produce a wide variety of commercial

Figure 1-2 Major network studio productions can involve a crew of several dozen engineers, technicians, and production positions. (Photo courtesy of KCET, Los Angeles)

Figure 1-3 Even a small-station production will involve a crew of a dozen or so audio, camera, lighting, staging, and other production operators and technicians.

and noncommercial programming. Many independent companies turn out programming without any studio facilities or production crews of their own; they pull a package together and then go out and rent a studio and hire a crew to do the actual production. Most of the major network entertainment series, for example, are produced by independent production centers—ranging from large Hollywood film studios (Universal, Columbia, Paramount) to major independent television producers (Spelling-Goldberg, Dick Clark, MTM) to specialized packagers (Goodson-Todman, Proctor & Gamble, Children's Television Workshop).

Nonbroadcast Telecommunications

A growing and increasingly important area of production operations is found in nonbroadcast areas. These afford many professional opportunities—with some fields outlined in the following discussion expanding at a rate of 30 to 40 percent a year. For example, over one billion dollars is spent annually on noncommercial programming for industry, government, schools, and religious groups.

The term *corporate video* (or *industrial TV* or *private video*) encompasses all types of telecommunications used for various business and industrial applications—sales training, corporate public relations, employee staff development, administrative and management communication, consumer relations, and so forth. When integrated with computers, laser distribution systems, and satellites, these uses result in some of the most advanced applications of the television medium.

One of the biggest fields of all is *government media*. Local, state, and federal agencies are involved in a myriad of telecommunications projects. The federal government, for example, is probably the world's largest television

and film producer. Military applications, including the Armed Services Radio and Television Network, account for worldwide operations—as does the State Department's Voice of America.

Possibly the most rapidly expanding area is in the field of *medical and health services*. More than 80 percent of the seven thousand hospitals in the country use television and related media for patient education, in-service training (staff development), and/or public and community relations.

Another burgeoning field is in *religious productions*. Although many of the established denominations have long made use of free public-service time offered by commercial broadcasters (*Directions, It Is Written, Christophers*), the greatest use is with the evangelical or charismatic groups. At least five such church bodies operate their own satellite networks. The Christian Broadcasting Network in Norfolk, Virginia, claims to have the most advanced TV studios in the world.

School-level productions are another category to be considered. Thousands of schools, ranging from preschools to medical schools at universities, have television production facilities for various instructional and demonstration purposes. A typical media-center studio is illustrated in figure 1-4. Again, the quality of production facilities ranges from converted broom closets to massive **closed-circuit** (**CCTV**) installations that rival anything seen at the network level. Most college and university facilities used for teaching TV production are probably equipped on a level comparable to that of a local station—barely adequate to do the job, never extensive enough to do everything desired. In the training situation, however, facilities are more likely to be monochrome, using older and smaller vidicon cameras and older helical-scan (nonbroadcast) video recorders.

Figure 1-4 Many closed-circuit audiovisual television installations for schools, corporate video setups, and medical training centers will need a production crew of only two or three persons.

A final major area to be considered is *cable TV production.* Although closely related to broadcast distribution in terms of quality and audience, cable TV represents another whole ancillary field. There are approximately 30,000 persons employed in the cable industry—mainly in sales, management, and distribution. Another completely new field is mushrooming around the cable production companies, however—outfits such as Home Box Office, Showtime, Cable News Network, Black Entertainment Television, the Entertainment and Sports Programming Network (ESPN), and dozens of others. Supplying programming to the cable systems via satellites, these companies—none of which existed prior to 1975—account for a rapidly expanding production market.

An idea of the significance and magnitude of all of these various nonbroadcast production operations can be gleaned by simply looking at respective employment figures. According to United States Department of Labor statistics, in 1980 there were approximately 195,000 people employed in broadcast operations, including both stations and networks. By contrast, it is estimated that about 230,000 people were employed in all of the nonbroadcast areas just discussed (cable, corporate, government and military, medical, religious, and school projects).

Small-Format Television

Although most of us tend to think of television in terms of the professional levels we have discussed—and, indeed, most production courses and textbooks are geared toward this type of production—we should also be aware of an increasingly important phenomenon known as **small-format television** (often referred to as **video**). This term generally refers to nonbroadcast television designed for limited circulation, as well as to cable production and

Figure 1-5 One person serves as audio-engineer-camera operator, while the other half of the two-person small-format team is the on-camera interviewer.

low-power (LPTV) station operations. Many of the topics in this book—such as principles of audio, lighting, theory of camera operation, VTR recording and editing, single-camera production, and pictorial design—apply to small-format television as well as to professional uses.

During the past several years, we have seen a communications evolution (the term *communications revolution* is too much overworked) in the development of smaller, inexpensive television gear. For a few hundred dollars it is now possible to obtain a small, nonbroadcast standard, lightweight, hand-held camera with a built-in microphone and a relatively lightweight portable videorecorder combination (often called a **portapak**). With this basic equipment, a two- or three-person crew—or even a one-person operation—is in the small-format television business (see fig. 1-5).

Small-format television operations are undertaken for a variety of reasons. Most of them could probably be divided into three basic areas: personal recording, community communicators, and video art. *Personal recording* includes several approaches and purposes. Basically, it is concerned with those video uses that are never intended to be seen by a large number of viewers. It may be thought of in part as an extension of home movies—recording family reunions, weddings, the baby's first steps, birthday parties, last wills and testaments, and so forth. It also may include more serious purposes, such as self-evaluation improvement programs, recording marriage counseling sessions, psychiatric training programs, or recording and analyzing an individual's golf backswing. What all of these personal recording applications have in common is that the product is never intended for distribution or viewing beyond a very small handful of participants.

The area of *community communicators,* however, gets into a little more ambitious use of the small-format medium. In this area we have concerned individuals using what is sometimes called "guerrilla television" or "underground video" in order to try to tell a story or get a message across. Equipped with portable cameras and portapak, they will go out and record an event, a social happening, a neighborhood problem. Often dealing with consumer affairs, ethnic problems, or environmental concerns, the community communi-

Figure 1-6 Many types of video-art techniques can be achieved even with the simplest kind of monochrome facilities.

cators offer an alternative to establishment-type channels dominated by government bureaucracy and conventional economic enterprises. Using school closed-circuit systems, community cable TV systems in which large systems have public access channels, and portable video players at community meetings, they try to reach as large an audience as they can.[1]

Another whole category of video usage might be labeled *video art*. This is the intriguing use of video equipment to create artistic images and sounds perhaps entirely unrelated to actual reality. In video art the artist-producer is concerned solely with the artistic elements of composition—balance, mood, tone, intensity, shading, color, harmony, texture, and so forth. The artist may be concerned solely with the creation for its own aesthetic sake, or he or she may want to try to reach as large an audience as possible through any of the community channels. This usage of television may, of course, also be carried into the studio, as illustrated in figure 1-6. Using the variety of professional equipment available for electronic controls, video manipulation, special effects, and signal distortion, the creator has moved far beyond small-format television.

1. For an extended discussion of small-format television, see, for example, Charles Bensinger, *The Video Guide*, 3d edition (Santa Fe, N.M.: Video Info Publications, 1982); Rudy Bretz, *Handbook for Producing Educational and Public-Access Programs for Cable Television* (Englewood Cliffs, N.J.: Educational Technology Publications, 1976); Barry J. Fuller, et al., *Single Camera Video Production* (Englewood Cliffs, N.J.: Prentice-Hall, 1982); Lon B. McQuillin, *The Video Production Guide* (Santa Fe, N.M.: Video Info Publications, 1983); and Michael Murray, *The Videotape Book* (New York: Bantam Books, 1975).

1.4 Production Approaches

One other distinction should be made at this point. This is a distinction that somewhat parallels our discussion of professional and small-format television, although it applies primarily to major professional situations. Students of television production today should be acutely aware of the contrast between *multiple-camera production* and *single-camera production*.

Multiple-Camera Production

Until a few years ago, any discussion of television production dealt almost entirely with multiple-camera production, a category that was concerned primarily with multiple-camera *studio* production. All TV production was presumed to occur in a "real-time" situation in which a 30-minute program actually took 30 consecutive minutes of production time with two or more cameras covering the action and all editing decisions were instantaneously executed as the director switched from one camera to another. Usually this took place in the TV studio, although location or *remote* productions such as political events or sporting contests could be covered wherever the action was taking place. The underlying principle of all multiple-camera productions remained the same, however: several cameras would cover the production from different angles and with different perspectives, with all **editing** (camera switching) being executed while the program was in progress.

During the first decade of popular television, up to the mid-1950s, this meant that all production was done *live*. It actually was happening while the viewers watched. Regardless of the rehearsal time involved, once the program was on the air live—whether it was a drama, musical program, variety show, or wrestling match—the audience watched it at the exact time it was taking place. If the set fell down or the costumes ripped, the viewers saw it all. Although there are relatively few live productions on television today, those production personnel involved in live telecasts—whether a local parade, the news, the Olympics, or a national political event—would readily agree that this is still the most exciting, nerve-racking, and challenging area of television programming. The 1976 debate between Jimmy Carter and Gerald Ford when the audio line went dead for 28 minutes is a good example.

In the mid-1950s, **videotape** recording came into existence. Now it was possible actually to record a program—in its entirety—on videotape and play it back at a later time. It was no longer necessary to present everything live as it happened. It was possible to schedule productions at more convenient times and to go back and re-record a program that had a bad production problem. The era of **live-on-tape production** was born. Most programs—variety shows, talk shows, game shows—were still produced in their entirety but were then recorded for later playback. Many multiple-camera productions, of course, are still produced in this manner today.

Next, in the late 1960s and early 1970s, *electronic editing* facilities became more and more sophisticated. It was now possible to record programs in segments and then piece them together in a **postproduction editing** process. Variety programs were one of the first genre to take advantage of this process. Segments with guest stars could be shot out of sequence; production numbers with costume and scenery changes could be interrupted while the changes were made; programs could be shot in different locations and edited together later. A 60-minute variety-musical program might take all day to record. A 90-minute extravaganza special might take days or even weeks to record and edit together. The principle, however, was still one of multiple-camera recording. Several cameras would be shooting each segment, with instantaneous editing decisions being made with the switcher; and the individual segments could be put together later. This process was carried into dramatic formats also with daytime serials (that always have been produced using video, nonfilm techniques) and some situation comedies (that started using multiple-camera video techniques and postproduction editing in the early 1970s).

Finally in the late 1970s, there evolved the ultimate adaptation of multiple-camera production—using separate videotape recorders to record each camera independently and simultaneously during the continuous performance. This *multiple-camera recording* process allows the director to concentrate on acting and camera work without having to make instantaneous editing decisions. Then at some time well after the production recording, the director can sit down with his or her four or five videotapes of the program and use sophisticated computer-based postproduction editing equipment to put the program together—picking and choosing among the four or five camera angles available at any given moment in the action. Many major network-level productions now regularly use this technique. Although there are increased production costs incurred by the use of three or four extra video recorders and postproduction editing facilities, producers generally feel that the slicker-paced and more polished final program is worth the slight increase in production price. (This multiple-camera recording process was pioneered in the 1950s, using multiple film cameras to record continuous action in the shooting of *I Love Lucy*.) By the mid-1980s, some of the more ambitious 3- to 10-minute music "videos" were using such elaborate multiple-camera and postproduction editing techniques that they were costing as much as a full hour-long variety show had cost just a decade earlier.

Single-Camera Production

By the mid-1970s, however, it was evident that an entirely new television production process was evolving—**single-camera production**. With computer-based editing facilities, it was now possible to put together a very polished studio or location production using only a single electronic television camera. Such an out-of-studio production usually is referred to as a **shoot.** Actually, this evolution had two parallel movements.

On the one hand, single-camera production techniques came about as an attempt to emulate filmic techniques in recording *dramatic* programs. Motion picture films have almost always used a single film camera in the making of dramatic pictures. This method represented the maximum control a director could have over the production elements. Each shot could be carefully staged; lighting could be arranged individually; microphone placement could be worked out for a single camera; actors could be positioned precisely; and so forth. This was an exactitude of control that was never attainable when shooting with multiple television cameras in a continuously running scene. The first experimentation with prime-time, full-length, single-camera recording of television drama started in the early 1970s. As editing devices became more sophisticated, both commercial and noncommercial dramatic programs made more use of this production approach.

As a counterpart to the dramatic uses of single-camera production, *journalistic* applications evolved even faster. With the development of small, hand-held, broadcast-quality video cameras in the 1970s, a new era of **electronic news gathering** (**ENG**) was ushered in. (Professional single-camera ENG techniques are not to be confused with small-format video, described in section 1.3.) Rapid coverage of news had always been hampered by film cameras because of the delay in processing the film. With the advent of small video cameras and portable recorders, however, news footage could be recorded on videotape, immediately edited as needed, and put on the air without delay. Thus, for both dramatic programs and journalistic purposes, the concept of single-camera video production came into its own in the mid-1970s.

By 1980, many other broadcast applications of single-camera *electronic field production* (EFP) were in common usage for local commercials, documentaries, promos, magazine-format productions, location interviews, talk-show segments, videos, and so forth. As the equipment became even lighter and less expensive, other nonbroadcast video programming turned to ENG/EFP techniques; corporate video, medical uses, training materials, government productions, schooling applications, and cable TV were all moving out of the studio and into the field—adopting filmic techniques for video programs.

1.5 A Quick Survey of the Tools and Working Areas

Before getting into any of the specifics of television techniques and disciplines, it may be helpful to have a quick overview of the various elements of TV production. What are the tools you will be using? Where are they usually used? And, generally, how are they used?

Although this book is not to be concerned with the creative processes of writing and producing, it should nevertheless be stressed that the first tool used in any TV production is the *typewriter;* the first working area, the office or den. First and foremost, television is a medium of communication. The tools exist only so that people can attempt to communicate with one another, only so that they can send messages from one point to another. Without that message—without that attempt to communicate—the glamour of television is reduced to a meaningless pile of glittering gibberish.

Once the program is conceived, once the message is designed, you still are not ready to move into the arena of the television studio. Several other working areas come to your attention first. Are there sets to be built? Start in the *scene shop.* Are there props or furniture

to be used? Are there costumes to be obtained? Rummage through the *storage area,* or visit commercial rental agencies where a Louis XIV chair or a coonskin cap can be rented. Are there graphics to be made? Get your order into the *artist's area.*

Many different kinds of TV productions will demand some type of simulated studio rehearsal before you can get into the actual facilities. If there are dramatic scenes to be rehearsed or complicated pieces of stage business that have to be worked out, reserve the *rehearsal hall,* find an empty studio, or use masking tape to mark off the area in the cafeteria.

The television **studio** (fig. 1-7) is, of course, the main center of activity that almost everyone associates with TV production. Whether a converted classroom, a remodeled warehouse, or a million-dollar facility, the studio is where everything is brought together, and the action is frenzied. One of the first things you will notice upon entering a studio for the initial time will probably be the *permanent sets*—the news set over in that corner, the kitchen for the homemakers' program, the discussion set for the noontime talk show. There probably also is a cyclorama or other wall covering stretched out over two or three of the studio walls. Look overhead and you will see one of the key elements of any production—the tools of *television lighting*. The lighting instruments themselves—the spotlights and scoops—are probably hung on some sort of grid or **catwalk** suspended from the high ceiling of the studio. Many different types of lighting are used in various studios. Possibly over in a corner will be the lighting control center, a patching system, and a dimmer board; or these elements may be located in a control room.

Probably the most important tools in the production situation are those electronic pickup devices that can translate the pictures and sounds into electric impulses, which can then

Figure 1-7 Typical medium-sized studio facility. Note the overhead lighting grid and the hanging cyclorama that can be stretched to cover two walls.

be handled electronically as separate elements of the television signal—the **camera** and the **microphone**. The cameras are the most obvious of these devices, stashed away in one corner of the studio. In a simple studio setup, there will probably be two or three small monochrome vidicon cameras mounted on basic tripods. In a large studio, there may be four or five professional color cameras mounted on pedestals, with at least one mounted atop a large crane or boom.

The microphones are more inconspicuous. Stored out of sight until it is time to set up for the production, they will then be connected to cables and plugged into studio inputs located around the studio walls. Some of the microphones are mounted on stands for the announcer or newscasters. One may be attached to a **boom** or **giraffe** where it can be suspended above a performer's head and manipulated by an operator holding on to the other end of the boom arm. Many microphones are designed as **lavalieres** to be worn around the neck. Others will simply be carried in the hands of the performers.

Many productions, of course, do not take place in the studio. They may be **remote** recordings (or **live** broadcasts) from a concert hall, political convention, council chamber, sports arena, main street, or playing field. Once outside the studio, problems are considerably complicated. Extraneous noises cannot be controlled; lighting is inconsistent; background distractions cannot be eliminated. If indoors, the artificial lighting may have to be supplemented by portable television lighting. If outdoors, audio problems may be compounded by wind and crowd noises; lighting conditions may suddenly change; and so forth. The weather may be unpredictable; equipment may fail many miles from the repair shop; and local demonstrators may suddenly decide they want to be on television. Such is the fun and challenge of location productions.

Back in the production center, the next working areas to examine are the control rooms. There may be several different kinds of control areas associated with the TV studio. The first of these may be the **audio booth**, or **control room** (fig. 1-8). This is where all of the sound elements are mixed and handled. The

Figure 1-8 Two audio control rooms: *top,* typical layout with turntables, cartridge machine, and audio console board; *bottom,* darkened control room during production. Audio operator can watch studio production through the large, soundproof glass window as well as on the program monitor, which shows the actual camera shots.

microphone inputs from the studio are terminated in the audio booth, usually in a **patch board**. Then the microphones can be mixed through a master audio board or console. Other audio elements can be added here also—record turntables, audio recorders, sound from a film track, and so forth. The composite sound output can then be either recorded or sent to a master control room where it is mixed with the video signal and recorded onto videotape or transmitted live.

In the **video control room**, or studio booth (fig. 1-9), you will find the comparable video mixing elements. Together with a bewildering array of television monitors of varying sizes and functions, the most important tool you will see is the **TV switcher**. This is the piece of equipment that can select and mix television signals from various cameras and other sources (in much the same way as the audio control board handles the sound sources) and come up with the final composite picture that is the visual half of the entire production. The studio control room may also contain the lighting controls and dimmer board if they are not located on the studio floor.

The next stop on a quick tour will probably be the **master control room** (fig. 1-10). Located a little distance from the studio and control booths, the master control room is the hangout for the engineers. One of the most imposing items you find here will be the **film chain** or **telecine**. This is a complex chain of equipment enabling the mixture of several different sources—such as 8mm and 16mm film and slides—into a multiplexer arrangement of mirrors and prisms that enable the selection of one input at a time to send into the television pickup camera on the film chain. The **videotape recorders** are also located here in the master control room. Depending upon the scope of the operation, this may be quite an imposing array of machines. Finally, and most important, the master control room usually will be the center for all camera-control functions—the generator for the synchronizing pulse that drives all cameras and the individual electronic controls for each camera.

In any modern production operation, another major facility will be the **editing room** or rooms. Possibly located close to the master control room—but ideally not part of it—will be one or more small semiprivate cubicles with complete electronic editing facilities.

If the production area is a remote location—outside of the studio—then the corresponding control rooms also have to be taken outside of the main production center. The audio control, video control, and master control functions will all be placed in some sort of van, truck, trailer, or motor home (fig. 1-11) that can be readily moved from one location to another. Depending upon the scope of the production, all of the control functions may be handled in one small van or they may be housed (in the case of some major sporting events) in several portable buildings that are set up on location several days in advance of the production.

If your quick tour of tools and working spaces includes an actual station, then the final working area (one with which we will not be concerned in this book) is the **transmitter** itself. Usually located on some high ground several miles from the studio operations and connected by a microwave link, the transmitter is the final engineering tool in the complex link that sends out the sounds and pictures of the television portion of the communication chain.

Figure 1-9 Two video control rooms: *top,* the director and the assistant director make shot selections from the smaller camera monitors—the large monitor on the left is the master program monitor, and the large monitor on the right is the preview monitor; *bottom,* the technical director punches the buttons on the switcher to put the selected camera on the air. (Photo courtesy of KABC-TV, Los Angeles)

Figure 1-10 *Top,* The master control room houses the videotape recorders; *bottom,* as well as film projection facilities and all camera control equipment.

Figure 1-11 This remote unit, converted from a large motor home, contains complete control room and engineering facilities for a major production. (Photo courtesy of Learning Resources, California State University, Long Beach; Bob Freligh, photographer)

1.6 *Producing and Directing*

Although most of the emphasis of this book is on the specific production skills concerned with individual positions and pieces of equipment, it is also necessary to introduce the concepts of producing and directing. Keep in mind that in many class productions (as in much of non-commercial TV and small-format professional video) one may function in both of these positions simultaneously—serving in a hyphenated producer-director capacity. The functions of these two postions can, however, still be differentiated.

The **producer** is the one key person who is responsible for pulling the total production together. He or she is ultimately in charge. From the communication standpoint, the producer is the person who determines the communication need, analyzes the potential audience, designs the television message, oversees the general construction and transmission of the message, and is the recipient (target) of viewer feedback and evaluation.

In practice, the producer is in charge of the entire program-making process: conceiving the program, hiring the script writers and other talent, setting up the budgets, dealing with all union and guild problems, taking care of all copyright and other clearance details, looking over the program director's shoulder during the actual production, worrying about legal problems such as libel and FCC fairness requirements, handling details of packaging, and selling the finished product.

In television, budgets and responsibilities are usually broken down into **above-the-line** and **below-the-line** costs. Above-the-line costs include creative and performing personnel such as the producer, associate producer(s), director, art director, writers, musicians, actors, and other performers. The producer is directly in charge of all these related functions, working closely with all personnel involved.

Below-the-line costs include all production and engineering standard costs such as those for the associate director, stage manager, floor assistants, camera operators, technical director, lighting and staging crews, audio engineer, and other engineering positions. Although the producer is broadly in charge of the operation, it is the director who is in direct charge of the production positions, working with them on a close supervisory level.

One way of differentiating between the roles of the producer and the director is to think of the producer as the person who is in charge of pulling all of the elements of the program together prior to getting it into the studio. The director is in charge of everything once the production is at the studio stage—setting up the visual and graphic elements, deciding on the fine points of creative presentations, blocking all action, arranging for technical and production support positions, conducting rehearsals, handling the talent, directing the actual production, and following up on postproduction editing and other concerns.

The **director** generally will be the one most closely associated with the creative decisions involved in the final look and feel of the production—how the microphones are placed and used, how the action is blocked, how the cameras are placed, what actual shots get on the air, the overall artistic design of the visual elements, the timing and editing of the production, and so forth. It is sometimes helpful to think of the director in terms of three different competencies—as planner, as creative artist, and as executor.

As *planner,* the director must be fully aware of all the demands and disciplines of the television medium. He or she must be dedicated to a meticulous preparation of myriad details prior to actual studio production. He or she must be concerned—in conjunction with the producer—with the ordering and reserving of all studio facilities and equipment needed, planning for graphics and special film, requisitioning props and scenery, arranging for crew and engineering personnel. The director must carefully lay out the basic scenic and graphic elements with the art director, lighting and staging personnel, and so forth. He or she must accurately prepare a marked working script and instructions for all other key crew positions—planning all shots and camera transitions well before production time. In short, the director must thoroughly prepare every aspect of the production during the time available before actually getting into the studio.

The director also must function as the *chief creative person* involved in the production. He or she must design the basic creative feel for the production—working with the art director, musicians, actors, lighting and staging designers, and so on. The director must plan the basic audio and visual impression of the program. How will cameras be used? What kind of shots will get on the air? What about the pacing and timing of the program? All of these creative decisions are up to the director.

Finally, the director must function as the actual *executor* of the program—sitting in the control chair and calling the shots during the program. He or she must be calm and cool, authoritative without being irritating, gentle without losing control, responsive without being excessively nervous. Possession of these qualities can be the final test of how well an individual can function under pressure.

Different directors will possess abilities—as planner, as creative artist, and as executor—in varying ratios. Some are excellent methodical planners without being creative; some are creative but tend to fall apart under pressure; some are outstanding at calling shots in the director's chair, but they hate to do the paperwork prior to production. Needless to say, the successful director is the person who can combine all three abilities to the fullest extent. In chapters 12, 13, and 14, we will look at the role of the director in greater detail.

Summary

Television production is a complex and confusing enterprise. Each individual member of the television team must master and demonstrate an exacting combination of *techniques* and *disciplines*—knowing technically how to use all of the TV equipment and being able to interact with all other team members and production elements to produce a successful television program.

This is true whether you are involved with *broadcast operations* (at the network, station, or independent producer level), *nonbroadcast telecommunications* (corporate video, government media, medical TV, religious productions, schooling applications, or cable TV), or with *small-format television* (personal recording, community communication, or creating video art).

Similar techniques and disciplines must be mastered whether you are involved with *multiple-camera* live production (in the studio and on location) or if you are working with *single-camera* filmic procedures (for either dramatic or journalistic purposes).

In any kind of TV-production situation, you must be concerned with a wide variety of working areas and tools of the medium—the typewriter, studio facilities, sets, props and costumes, lighting instruments, cameras and microphones, audio and video mixing areas, the film chain, editing equipment, and various engineering and control facilities. Students in beginning TV production must also be familiar with the jobs of the producer and director. As a producer, you must assume ultimate responsibility for the entire program—from its initial conception to final audience feedback. As director, you are responsible for the specific elements of production—preproduction planning, creative use of the medium, and control room execution of the production. Each position entails its own set of techniques and disciplines.

In chapter 2, we start looking at the specific production elements that make up the sound and picture of the television message. It is often tempting to start first with the video process—the cameras and associated equipment. We prefer, however, to begin with the audio operation for two reasons. First, the audio part of the production is frequently slighted in the treatment of the larger and more complicated aspects of picture production; by beginning with audio we hope to give it the emphasis it deserves. Second, there are several functional similarities between audio and video signal production and manipulation; by studying the audio operation first it is easier to grasp the bigger and more complex picture of the video side of the program in subsequent chapters.

1.7 Training Exercise

Write a brief (five-hundred-word) essay setting forth your own personal professional goals in the broadcasting/film field. What do you hope to be able to accomplish in the area? What specifically do you feel that you will get from this course that will help you to achieve your goals? Can you get any more out of the course? How?

The Audio System: Signal Flow and Technical Control

2

The task of understanding and ultimately operating television equipment becomes much easier if the individual components are seen in terms of the *functions* each piece of equipment is designed to perform. Each item has been developed to ensure that the crew and eventually the director will have the ability to control with split-second accuracy the flow of the numerous audio and video signals available during a production situation.

The **audio** system is an excellent place to start the process of comprehending the basics of television engineering structure. Once audio is understood, the same principles can easily be applied to video. Each audio component has a somewhat analogous counterpart in the video system.

2.1 Technical and Creative Functions of Audio

In many elements that comprise audio and video production, we will see that there coexists both a *technical function* and a *creative function*. It is necessary to meet certain requirements simply to get adequate sound and picture produced (technical function); it then is possible to manipulate these elements for certain aesthetic effects (creative function).

In the audio system, we will be initially concerned with the basic *technical requirements* to reproduce original sound faithfully. That is, we will be involved with controlling signal flow, understanding microphone construction and proper usage, mixing other prerecorded audio sources, and so forth. For the beginning audio operator, the most important job is simply to be able to pick up and reproduce faithfully the actual sound that is being produced as the audio portion of the TV production. How do you control the tools and equipment to do this adequately?

The *creative side* of audio production involves such things as establishing a specific *mood* or *emotional setting* (often with background music or distortion of a normal audio signal), creating an atmosphere of *reality* (with sound effects or certain identifiable voice qualities, such as a telephone conversation), and *enhancing* or *emphasizing* particular sounds or frequencies (to accentuate low tones or high notes). Several of these elements are discussed in this and the next chapter: **mixing** and **shaping** the audio signal (section 2.2); microphone selection and usage, including such considerations as acoustical differences, mike distance, sound balance, audio perspective (sections 3.2 and 3.3); and adding of other sources (section 3.4).

A more detailed discussion of the creative side of audio production, however, is beyond the scope of this book. It involves such specialized topics as musical balance and instrumental characteristics, performing and acting techniques, and advanced engineering concepts. The emphasis in these two chapters, therefore, will be primarily upon faithful technical reproduction of conventional television sound and basic elements of creative control.

2.2 The Seven Basic Control Functions

Each piece of equipment in the studio or control booth can perform one or more of seven basic control functions. If you look carefully at your own audio booth and adjoining studio, you will find that audio facilities are generally designed to move, modify, or otherwise control a signal in these seven ways: (1) *transducing*, or converting sound waves into electrical energy and back again; (2) *channeling*, or routing the sound, sending it wherever necessary; (3) *mixing* two or more sound sources; (4) *shaping* the sound, changing the quality of the tone; (5) *amplifying* the signal; (6) *recording* and/or *playing back;* and

(7) *monitoring* the audio output, listening to and keeping track of the program audio.

In looking over this list, many examples of these functions will probably come to mind from your experience in operating a home stereo and audiotape recorder. In sorting them out, you will come to see that some pieces of equipment can perform more than one function. For example, the speaker that transduces a signal into listenable sound is also obviously a monitor.

Keep in mind that the terminology used to define the various components and their functions may vary somewhat with time and location. There is, however, a basic structure of functional design common to all audio control rooms. Understanding the essential elements of this structure in your own facility is the prerequisite that is necessary to successful operation of the equipment in a production situation.

2.2.1 Transducing

The entire process by which sound (voices, music) is converted into a broadcast signal (electrical information) is referred to as *transducing*. Figure 2-1 shows in simplified form how the transducing element—the microphone components that actually change sound waves into electrical energy—perform this function in a dynamic microphone.

The tone production of a human voice or musical instrument creates pressure waves in the molecules of the air. If these waves are produced at a constant rate of 440 cycles per second, the result is the musical tone of A above middle C.[1] These waves fall upon and

1. The term *cycles per second* (cps) is used as the basic unit of measure for sound pressure waves and, in the past, for electromagnetic waves. In recent years, engineering terminology has for the most part replaced the term *cycles per second* with the term *hertz* (abbreviated Hz) in honor of Heinrich Hertz, who first demonstrated the existence of electromagnetic waves.

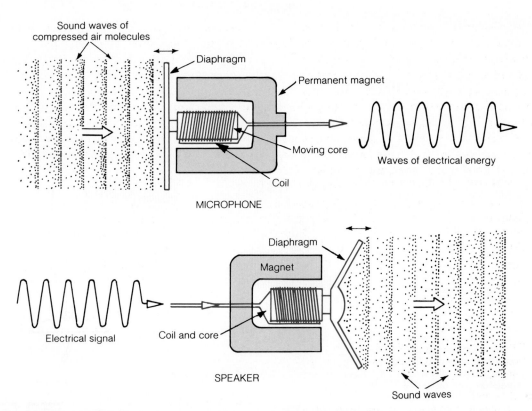

Figure 2-1 Transducing element of a dynamic microphone and corresponding speaker elements.

When sound waves from a voice or musical instrument strike the diaphragm of the microphone, the waves of compressed air molecules cause the attached coil to vibrate. As the coil moves back and forth within the magnetic field of the permanent magnet, a small fluctuating electric current is produced. This minute current, which will be amplified many times, carries the same information as the original sound waves. At the receiving end, when this minute electrical signal reaches the speaker coil it produces fluctuations in the magnetic field that then cause the diaphragm of the speaker to vibrate, creating sound waves that reproduce the original sound picked up by the microphone.

vibrate the **diaphragm** of the microphone and cause the attached coil to vibrate around a part of the permanent magnet. When this coil moves within the resulting magnetic field, an electric current is produced. This signal is now in its new electronic form but retains the original **frequency** pattern of 440 oscillations per second.[2] (A more detailed explanation of wave theory is contained in appendix A.)

The electronic waveform at this stage is said to be an analog of the original sound pressure wave; that is, the wave pattern fluctuations and changes correspond to (or are analogous to) the fluctuations and changes in

2. Actually, the A 440 cps frequency in our example is only the fundamental tone. It is by far the most prominent of many tones that are simultaneously produced when a voice or instrument is sounded. The other tones, which are much softer in volume and occur at higher frequencies, are called "overtones" or "harmonics." Their presence and relative volume are what produce the distinctive quality of any individual voice or instrument. To reproduce any single complete tone accurately, all of these resultant frequencies must be picked up and simultaneously transduced into the electrical signal. A more complete explanation of the overtone series is presented in appendix B.

The original sound waves are transduced into an electrical current that, at the transmitter, is modulated or superimposed over the assigned carrier frequency of the broadcasting station. (By this point, the original signal has been amplified over a million times.) This carrier wave is the specific broadcasting frequency assigned by the Federal Communications Commission—either part of the television channel, or, in the case of radio, a separate part of the electromagnetic spectrum (see appendix A); for example, 690 kiloHertz ("six-ninety on your radio dial"). The TV or radio set then receives this carrier frequency, demodulates (or strips off) the superimposed electrical signal, which is the program information, and the speaker transduces the electrical energy back into sound waves that the ear can perceive.

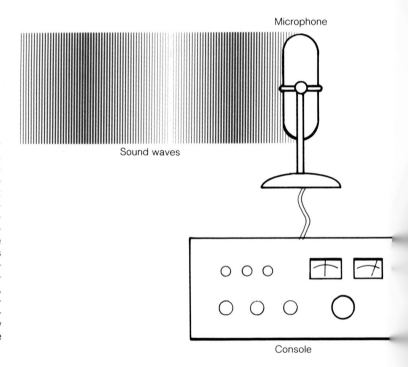

Figure 2-2 Modulation and demodulation in the broadcasting sequence.

the original sound pressure waves. With the newer **digital recording** process, the audio signal goes through another encoding/decoding stage. Using computer technology, the structure of the waveform is further converted into groups of off-on digital pulses. (See the discussion of "digital effects" in section 7.4.) In this digital form, the signal is almost immune from nonsignal *noise* and can therefore reproduce a much higher quality of sound.

Thus far, we have been concerned only with those signal changes taking place within the studio and the audio control room. The signal has been converted or transduced into an electronic pattern, amplified at several stages in its journey, and sent along to the transmitter. The signal is then **modulated** or superimposed within the assigned carrier frequency of the station and amplified more than a million times for transmission into the air. This is still, of course, an electronic signal. The broadcast *carrier wave* makes no change in the molecules of the air through which it passes.

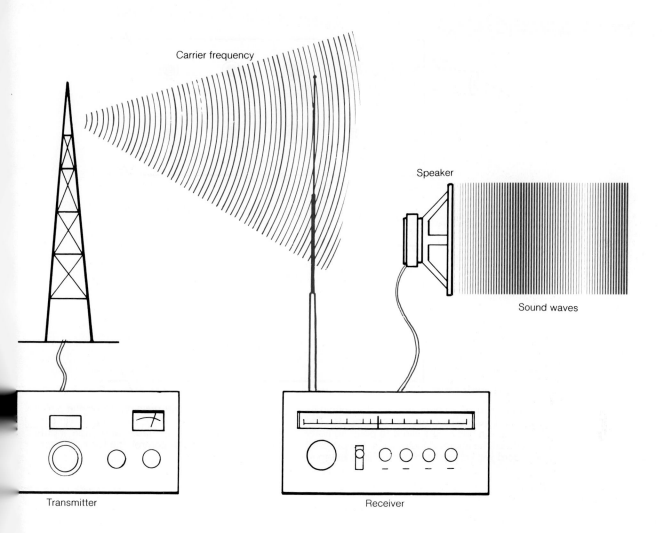

Carrier frequency

Speaker

Sound waves

Transmitter

Receiver

In figure 2-2, we see in simplified form how this modulation phase is but a part of the total broadcasting sequence.[3]

At the receiver, an analogous procedure takes place—only in reverse order. This is called *demodulation*. The relatively weak broadcast audio signal is first removed from the carrier wave (the actual demodulation process), it is then amplified, and it is sent to the speaker of the TV set or radio receiver. The speaker is a transducer something like a microphone with the elements—a coil and a magnet—placed in reverse order. The electrical (audio) signal sets the diaphragm in motion, which pushes against the air molecules, creating the sound pressure waves at a rate of 440 cycles per second, and we hear the original tone of A above middle C.

3. For a simplified explanation of how a carrier wave is theoretically modulated, both by amplitude modulation (AM) and by frequency modulation (FM), see appendix A. For a more detailed explanation, see Sidney W. Head, *Broadcasting in America,* 2d ed. (New York: Houghton Mifflin Company, 1972), chapters 1 and 2.

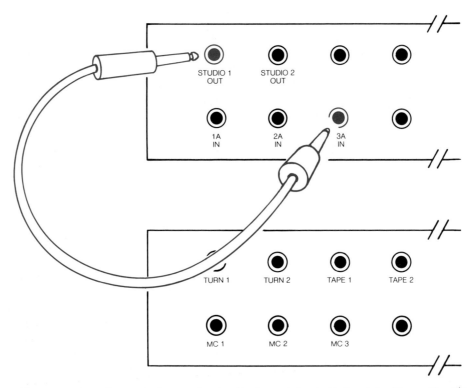

STUDIO 1
OUT

STUDIO 2
OUT

1A
IN

2A
IN

3A
IN

TURN 1

TURN 2

TAPE 1

TAPE 2

MC 1

MC 2

MC 3

Figure 2-3 Portion of a typical patch bay.

The upper row of receptacles are the terminals ("outputs") from studio microphone inputs. The next row down has inputs wired to potentiometer positions on the audio console. Thus, the pictured patch cord will connect the microphone plugged into studio input 1 with position 3A on the audio console. The lower two rows, in this particular configuration, represent turntable and tape inputs (third row) and master control "tie lines" (bottom row).

The cartridge in the pickup arm at the turntable also is a transducer that deserves to be included within this general category. In a way, it is a type of microphone that transforms the vibrations picked up by the needle into an electronic energy form.

2.2.2 Channeling

An audio system contains two main sets of channels or lines designed to allow us to route or send the signal from one point to another. There is the wiring system of the **console** itself, and there is a series of external lines that have been permanently installed to bring outside signal sources, such as a microphone, into the console. The routing device that makes possible the connection of these two systems is the **patch bay** (fig. 2-3).

The signal coming in on a line from a studio mike temporarily terminates its flow at the patch bay, where the round-holed receptacle is called an *output*. Any one of several lines designed to carry that mike signal from the patch bay into the console is labeled an *input* at its patch bay starting point. It is important that you get the input and output concept clearly in mind. A patch cord placed into both receptacles completes the connection—linking the studio line output to the console line input—and the first part of the channeling has been established. The remainder of the journey of the signal through the audio board is largely a matter of clearing a pathway by means of opening a series of switches and **potentiometers (pots),** or volume control faders. Figure 2-4 is a block diagram of a simplified three-input, one-program channel audio system.

However complex an audio system's design may be, it is still only an extension of this basic structure.

2.2.3 Mixing

The primary function of a console board—such as those pictured in figure 2-5—is that of combining and blending the signals from different sources into a balanced whole. This, of course, gets into creative—as well as technical—considerations. Almost every element of the design of the audio board is in some way related to this mixing function.

The process is of value from a production standpoint only when the volume level of each of the incoming signals can be separately controlled. The flow of the signal is so arranged that after each potentiometer is adjusted to a desired level, they are all connected together on a single line called a mixing **bus.** This line is then connected to the final program or line output. Stereo and quad controls on the components in your home operate in much the same manner. The simplified block diagram in figure 2-4 of a three-input, one-program channel console shows the stage in the signal flow at which the mixing of the various signals takes place.

2.2.4 Shaping

The function of shaping—of altering the tonal qualities of the sound—is almost entirely a creative function. The use of the fader as just discussed is an example of one of the methods in which signal quality is altered or shaped. Volume control, however, is only one of many ways in which a sound signal can be changed

to suit a specific purpose. Most turntables and cartridge players (*cart* machines) are equipped with one or more filtering devices to eliminate the high frequency scratch noise of older records. Microphone filters often are built into, or can be patched into, an audio console in order to filter out specified high frequency or low frequency tones or pitches and overtones in order to simulate desired audio situations (the effect of a telephone line conversation, for example).

In addition to filtering devices, well-equipped studios have sophisticated components that can shape audio in other ways—by emphasizing selected frequencies to produce a richer voice or musical quality, for example. An **equalizer** can be used to increase or decrease the levels of different frequencies, thus enriching high or low pitches. A **limiter** might be used to cut off levels when they reach a volume that is too strong. An **audio compressor** can be used to bring low levels up to a certain volume. Echo and other reverberation devices, often used for musical programs or certain dramatic effects, also fall into this shaping classification.

2.2.5 Amplifying

An electronic signal is an organized movement of negatively charged electrons within a wire. Amplification takes place by means of a component's ability to multiply the flow of electrons while retaining the same essential wave pattern. As we saw in figure 2-4, which portrayed the mixing and channeling functions, this process occurs more than once as the signal moves through the system. The signal from a microphone is relatively weak and must be strengthened before it can be mixed with other signals—such as the signal from an audio recorder—that have been amplified before reaching the audio console. Some special types of microphones need additional amplification even before their signals can be carried to the audio patch bay.

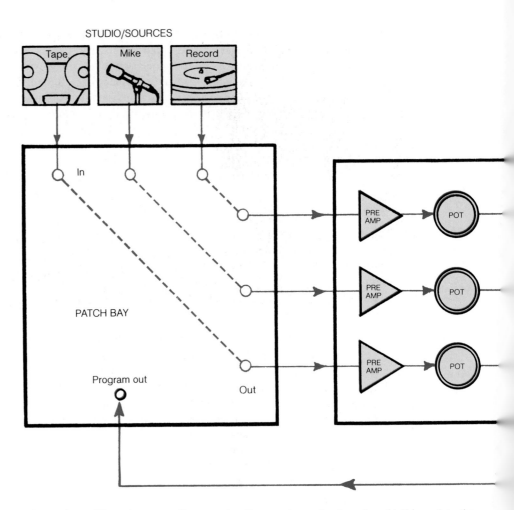

STUDIO/SOURCES

Tape

Mike

Record

In

PATCH BAY

Program out

Out

PRE AMP

PRE AMP

PRE AMP

POT

POT

POT

Figure 2-4 Signal flow of three-input audio system.

This diagram shows three different sources (tape machine, microphone, and turntable) that are plugged into the patch bay. Patch cords (dotted lines) then connect these inputs, through preamplifiers, to potentiometers on the audio console. (In actuality, only the microphone inputs would have to have preamplifiers; see section 2.2.5.) Each pot is connected to a channel selector switch (on-off key) before it reaches the program mix bus. After the three sources are mixed, the combined signal is amplified and the mixed audio is then controlled by the master potentiometer. At this point, the audio is channeled in three directions. Part of the signal is sent to the "volume unit" (VU) meter so that a proper volume level can be monitored visually. The signal is also sent, through a "monitor pot," to the control room speaker so that the sound can be monitored aurally (without affecting the level of the actual program audio). Finally, the "line out" signal is sent back to the patch bay where it is patched to its ultimate destination (master control room, videorecorder, or transmitter).

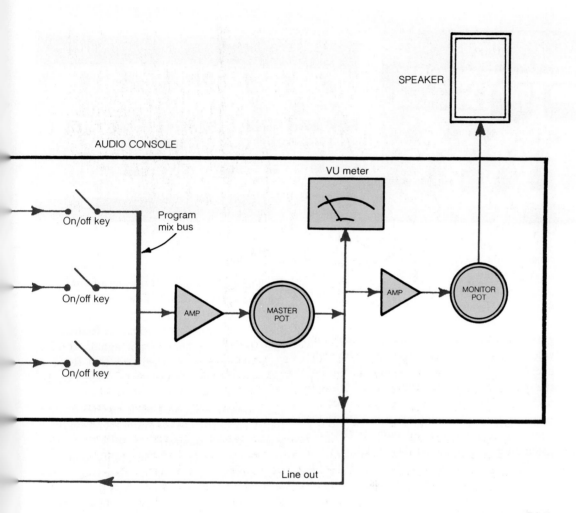

On most audio boards a distinction is made between pots that are designed to have microphones patched into them and pots that are to be used for sources such as audiotapes, records, feeds from videotape recorders, film projectors, and so forth. This is because the microphone positions have a **preamplifier** built in to boost the signal before it can be mixed with other sources. The other electronic sources of audio, such as recorders, already have their signals amplified and are ready for line amplification once the signals are mixed. If one mistakenly patches the already amplified signal from an audio tape machine into a mike channel, the result is a double amplification. This causes a distorted high-level signal when the pot is barely opened.

2.2.6 Recording and Playing Back

The basic functions of the control room record turntables—like audiotape recorders and cartridge machines—need little explanation. A person's own experience with similar equipment in the home serves as an excellent background. The ability to integrate their use in a production situation, however, does require

Figure 2-5 Two audio consoles: *left,* older-style board with rotary knob-type pots; *right,* newer board with slide-faders.

considerable practice in the development of proper operational techniques. Section 3.4 details some specific techniques and applications of audio recorders and turntables.

The audio portion of most television programs is, of course, recorded directly onto the videotape. There is little that the audio engineer has to do other than to make certain that the output of his or her audio console is connected to the videotape recorder (often by patching from the audio board to the master control room) and then to monitor the program audio (by watching the levels).

Playing back prerecorded material for program audio is a different matter. The audio operator has to be practiced in the techniques of cueing up various-sized records and different-speed audiotape recorders. Many audio booths will be equipped with audiotape **cartridge** and **cassette** systems. These playback units (some of which can hold up to ten different cartridges) can be very convenient in playing back sound effects, short announcements, brief musical selections, and the like. (Standard cartridges hold roughly four minutes worth of tape; large-format carts can operate up to ten minutes.) Because each is a continuous tape loop that automatically cues itself, the cartridge is always ready at the push of a button.

2.2.7 Monitoring

For an operator to perform any of the functions necessary to signal flow and control, the audio engineer must have the benefit of some sort of simultaneous information **feedback** of that signal or combination of signals. It takes several components to perform that function adequately. The most obvious of such equipment is the **speaker** in the audio booth, which plays what is being fed out over the program line. In a broadcast situation, there usually is a separate air **monitor**.

One must also have the ability to monitor separately any single sound source from among the several that are being mixed for transmission. This is done by means of a preview or **cue** channel. When the fader for a mike or playback unit is placed in the "cue" position, the sound is heard through a separate bus with its own speaker in the control room. There is generally only one master gain-control pot for all inputs into the cue bus.

The **volume unit (VU) meter** provides another essential informational feedback. In spite of the marvelous structure of the human ear, it is not able to register changes in volume to the same degree that electronic sound equipment can. From an engineering standpoint, this can cause some serious problems.

Within the interacting processes of mixing, shaping, and amplifying, there is a point of increase at which the electronic equipment

Figure 2-6 Two types of VU meters: *left,* on the percentage-preference meter, the upper scale indicates the percentage of proper signal modulation (volume level) and the lower scale shows decibels; *right,* on some professional decibel-preference models, the two scales are reversed, with the decibel reading on top.

ceases to function properly. At this point—which is theoretically 100 percent of the signal strength that can be handled by the equipment—the ability of the components to process the electronic wave patterns accurately begins to break down. The result is a distortion of the signal.

Most VU meters utilize two related scales of measurement to visualize the differing levels of volume on the program line. One of these scales shows signal strength in terms of proper signal modulation. It displays a range from zero to roughly 150 percent—with the area above 100 percent marked in red to indicate the possibility of signal distortion (see fig. 2-6). This scale is most useful during the ongoing production situation (see section 3.3).

During the preproduction setup period of any complicated program, audio inputs from many sources must be pretested and adjusted so that they provide a uniform level of sound volume. During this process the plus and minus **decibel** scale is of considerable importance to the audio engineer. It allows the electronic strength of one signal to be compared with another in terms of a precise mathematical ratio. The VU meter is designed to measure sound in its electromagnetic form within certain specifications of power and line resistance. This

can be considerably different from the way in which one's ear and nervous system react to sound pressure waves coming from a studio monitor.

The trained engineer may put the VU meter to many uses in the process of setting up mikes and balancing various sound sources. For the student, however, it may be sufficient at first to acquire the ability to **ride gain** somewhere between 60 percent and 100 percent of modulation.

And there you have, in a very simplified form, an insider's guide to the audio control room. If this beginning knowledge makes you feel less of a stranger within the confines of the audio booth, it is probably because it is in reality only an expanded version of the tape recorders, cartridge machines, and stereo sets that have become so much a part of our lives.

2.3 Audio Signal Flow

The concept of signal flow is the first of several preliminary areas of knowledge you will need in order to master the techniques and disciplines of television production. This channeling procedure must be understood within a

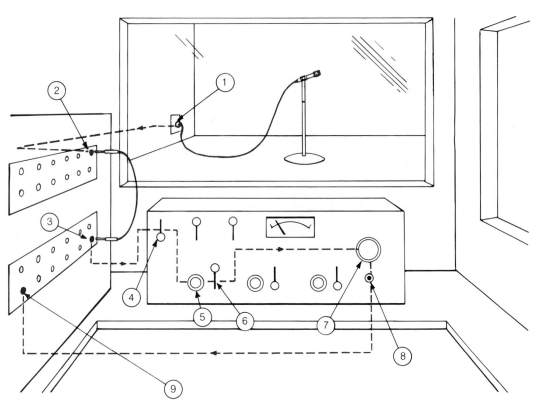

Figure 2-7 Audio signal flow model.

1. Studio microphone input. *2.* Patch bay output (input from studio). *3.* Console input (output from patch bay). *4.* Input selector switch. *5.* Potentiom- eter. *6.* Channel selector or pot on-off key. *7.* Master potentiometer. *8.* Line-out switch. *9.* Program-out patch bay output.

conceptual framework and not as a memorized list of patches made, switches moved, or pots opened. The only way to troubleshoot audio failure is to know each step of the sequence in its proper order.

Figure 2-7 is a typical model of audio facilities. It illustrates the basic steps in the flow of a signal from a studio mike, through a console board, to a line output program monitor. Although equipment design and terminology could differ slightly, the basic sequence of functions should be easily projected into the equipment with which you will be working. Each numbered step is explained in some detail on subsequent pages. As a starting point, a quick review of the block diagram in figure 2-4 may be helpful.

2.3.1 Studio Microphone Input

The microphone, connected to a mike cable, is plugged into a numbered studio receptacle. These inputs either may be gathered together at one junction box or may be spaced at intervals around the studio walls. In some studios, there may even be some input receptacles placed on the ceiling or on a lighting catwalk in order to facilitate hanging microphones.

2.3.2 Patch Bay Output

From the studio input point, the signal travels through a permanently constructed line to an output receptacle at the patch bay, such as the one illustrated in figure 2-8. The number of

Figure 2-8 Typical audio patch bay.

this output corresponds to the number of the studio input. A signal coming through Studio Input #2 is now labeled "studio 2" or "mike 2 out(put)."

Remember that all of the receptacles at the patch bay are either inputs or outputs. One group of these, not of our immediate concern, carries signals to and from the master control room where equipment such as VTR machines and projectors may be located. At this point in our signal flow model, however, we are dealing with those outputs that bring in signals from studio mikes or from turntables and cartridge machines and audiotape recorders right in the audio booth.

In some newer consoles such as those found in network studios and other modern production centers, steps 2 through 4 (patching and console input) have been replaced by an electronic switching unit. By means of this switcher, audio signals from a studio or from **telecine** (VTR and film sound) can be placed into any bus on the board simply by pressing a button.

2.3.3 Console Input

The next step in the flow of our signal is a point of decision whereby we assign that signal to a specific potentiometer for amplification and other related control factors. With our patch-cord already connected to "mike 2 output" (studio) we place the other end into an input that is labeled to correspond with any of the available pot positions designated for mike use. On some consoles it is possible to feed more than one mike line to a single potentiometer position. In such a case we would have a choice of patching into "1a in," "2a in" or possibly even a "3a in" receptacle. These multiple inputs are designed so that additional mikes can be preset for use at differing times during a program.

In some studios, certain audio feeds—mikes, recorders, cart machines, turntables—may be preconnected, or **normalled**, directly into the audio console input lines. For example, Studio Input #2 has its output receptacle at the patch bay ("mike 2 out"). Back in the rack there may already be a wired connection between "mike 2 out" and a line to the

Figure 2-9 Channel selector switches: *left,* rotary potentiometer, or volume control knob, with channel selector switch immediately above the pot; *right,* slide-faders with channel-select "assign" switches—the rotary "pan" knob allows the operator to cross-fade between two or more channels.

console "input 1B." No patch is needed to bring the Studio 2 mike into the "1B input" selector on the board. This *normalled* connection is designed to be overridden, however. If the jack at the end of a patch cord is placed into the "mike 2 out" receptacle, the other end of that cord could then be placed into any other microphone input at the patch bay.

2.3.4 Input Selector Switch

Whichever input line is patched, there must now be a corresponding connection at the **input selector switch** to bring the signal into our mixing "line 1 (pot 1)" example. Although all of these two or three lines could be connected back to microphones simultaneously, they can only be fed into our mixing line 1 one at a time. Your input selector switch may be a two- or three-position toggle switch or several push-button connectors.

On some consoles, optional inputs leading to a single pot and mixing bus can provide for different impedance level inputs (see section 3.1).

2.3.5 Potentiometer

The signal has now proceeded as far as the volume control (called the **attenuator, mixer, gain control, fader, potentiometer** or **pot**). When opened clockwise, the pot (fig. 2-9) acts much like a valve in allowing varying amounts of the amplified signal to pass through. The further the pot is opened, the greater the volume.

On modern electronic audio consoles, the rotary pot has been replaced by sliding faders (see fig. 2-5). With these slide-faders, you increase volume by pushing the fader up, away from you; pulling the fader all the way down cuts out all signals. In addition to greater electronic reliability, there are two advantages to the slide-faders: (1) the audio operator can visually "see" the relative balance of sound or mixing pattern by noting the positions of the various faders; (2) it is possible for the audio operator to manipulate several audio lines simultaneously—one hand can control up to four different faders at the same time, whereas only one rotary pot can ordinarily be controlled single-handedly.

2.3.6 Channel Selector or Pot On-Off Key

Many audio consoles—especially those designed for live radio production—will have two separate mixing buses or channels. They are often labeled as the *program* and *audition* buses, or simply the *A* and *B* channels.

Dual-channel boards can be used to manage two completely separate program lines simultaneously. For instance, the audio engineer can be handling the primary program audio on the *A* channel (using one VU meter), sending the line-out audio up to the master control room to be recorded on the video recorder. At the same time the engineer can be using the *B* channel (and the second VU meter) to record an offstage announcer (who is in a separate booth) on audiotape—to be inserted at the end of the program for the closing credits. Usually the alternate channel can also be utilized to submix several inputs, which are then fed as a group into the main channel.

With a two-bus system there must be some sort of a switch or button that connects the output of an individual potentiometer with one or the other of the channels. Such a switch will also have a "neutral" or "off" position. All switches must be placed to the same channel position in order to mix any group of lines within the console. In a single-bus system, there would only be a simple on-off switch.

2.3.7 Master Potentiometer

All of the combined signals from the mixing bus must pass through the control of the master pot. This is the final volume adjustment point of the mixed signal that is amplified and sent out as the program line output. It generally is left open at a level calibrated by engineering personnel to fit with all other components in the system. This final mixed signal, variously called *program out* or *line out,* is now routed back to a receptacle at the patch bay.

2.3.8 Line-Out Switch

On some consoles, there is one final switch that controls the feed of the mixed program line. As a safety factor, some consoles are designed so that the VU meter will not operate unless this *line-out* switch is activated. Sometimes it is a simple on-off switch. On other boards it is combined with a *remote* or *network* position. This sort of control would enable the operator to quickly switch from a live studio feed to a live network newscast. In many cases, the line-out position would be permanently connected to an input back on the patch bay (fig. 2-7). It is now available as the Program Line Output at a space on the patch panel.

2.3.9 Program-Out Patch

With the signal delivered back to the patch bay, it can now be physically routed from the audio booth anywhere desired. Typically, a patch connection will be made that will send the signal into the master control room where the audio is combined with video on the video recorder. However, the signal can also be patched into any of several other destinations: audiotape recorder, another studio, or directly to the transmitter for live transmission.

2.4 Sources of TV Audio

The previous discussion of audio signal flow represented a typical, somewhat simplified model, based upon the microphone as the audio source. Actually, the audio operator should think in terms of two different categories of audio sources—the *microphone* and other *prerecorded sources*. Each broad grouping has its own techniques and disciplines that must be mastered and practiced.

Microphones

Microphones come in a wide variety of types and sizes, designed for a multitude of specialized purposes. They vary as to *frequency response;* some will pick up low frequencies well, and others respond best to higher frequencies. Microphones differ as to *pickup pattern;* some will pick up everything around them (**omnidirectional**), whereas the performer has to stand directly in front of other microphones (**unidirectional**) to be heard well. Microphones will vary in the technical construction of their *transducing elements*—the way they actually transform sound waves into electrical energy. As a result, some are more rugged than others. Microphones vary in *physical design,* to be used in different ways; some are to be placed in mike stands, some are hand-held, others are worn around the neck or attached to special boom stands.

These different distinctions and differences are discussed in chapter 3. By becoming familiar with the different microphone classifications and characteristics, the audio operator will be able to select the most appropriate microphone for each application. Which microphones should be used for talk shows? Drama? Musical productions? What kinds of mikes are best suited for outdoor (location) productions? Which microphones are used for picking up sound from a great distance? What kind of microphone can be concealed or hidden? These are just some of the considerations that an audio operator has to be ready to think about.

Prerecorded Sound Sources

The basic audio signal flow concept also applies to sound from sources other than the microphone—although the patch starts somewhere other than in the TV studio. The origination of the prerecorded sound may be in the master control or telecine room, or even in the audio booth itself; however, the same basic principles of signal flow apply.

Basically, the audio operator could probably think of prerecorded sound as coming from one of five broad sources: film, videotape, audiotape, cartridges, and records. Although other variations (such as audio cassettes) may occasionally be encountered, these five basic origination media represent the common non-microphone sources of television audio.

Film sound usually will be associated with 16mm film—although some stations and closed-circuit installations may use **sound-on-film (SOF)** for 8mm formats. Thirty-five mm film will seldom be encountered outside of major network operations. Usually the film and its associated sound track will originate in the master control or telecine room—as part of the film chain (see section 11.3). The audio operator ordinarily will not have to be concerned with loading and running the film projector—although several positions may be doubled up in smaller production situations. Once the film projector is properly threaded, the audio pickup will have to be connected to a source on the audio console. As a rule, this is accomplished through the patch bay—typically, from the master control room to the audio control room. The primary jobs of the audio engineer are then correct operation of the board, riding gain, and so forth (see section 3.6).

Although some professional studios still use sound film facilities, very little film is "rolled in" to live or videotaped productions. Generally, the film is transferred to videotape ahead of production time—in order to assure color control and to simplify the actual production situation. Commercials, even though shot originally on film, are transferred to videotape for broadcasting.

Videotape audio tracks are handled—from the standpoint of the audio operator—in a manner similar to the film sound track. Many types of productions will have videotape inserts, in which a short, previously recorded videotape segment is incorporated into the body of another television production. The insert videotape recorder or recorders, like the

Figure 2-10 Production model audiotape recorder.

film projector or projectors, usually will be located in master control or telecine or someplace other than the audio booth. Someone other than the audio operator will be responsible for threading up the videotape recorder and patching the audio line into the audio control room. Again, the primary concern of the audio person will simply be correct operation of the console, getting cues precisely, and so forth.

Audiotape playback, on the other hand, is usually completely in the hands of the audio engineer. The typical audio control room will have one or more audiotape recorders (fig. 2-10). The audio engineer will be in complete charge of making certain the tape is correctly threaded and patched or connected to the audio console. Often the audiotape recorder will be normalled or permanently wired into the audio console (see section 2.3.2). Audiotape frequently is the most convenient medium to use

for prerecording longer segments of program inserts—background music or sound effects, announcements—and for premixing several sound sources. For example, if the production calls for an audio segment that has an off-camera announcer, background music, and a sound effect, it is easier—and much safer—to prerecord that segment rather than to try to mix those several elements during the actual television production.

In playing back audiotape, there are several factors that the audio operator has to watch for. First, the tape speed must be checked. Audiotape can be recorded at several different speeds: 3¾ inches per second (inches of tape travel per second) is the slowest commonly used speed for most recorders (some professional recorders do not have 3¾ ips capability); 7½ is a more common professional recording speed (the higher the tape speed, the better the fidelity of the recording); 15 ips is

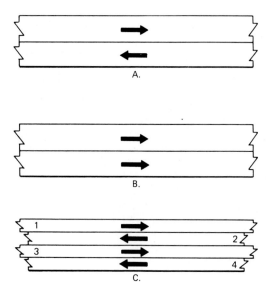

Figure 2-11 Audiotape track configurations.

A. **Half-track monaural.** In monophonic recording, only half of the audiotape track is used for information as the tape is played in one direction. When the tape reels are reversed (the take-up reel being threaded up as the supply reel) and the tape is played in the other direction, the other half of the track is used.

B. **Half-track stereo.** Both tracks are used when the tape is played in one direction. One half-track contains the information for the left channel, and the other half-track is the right channel recording. In this configuration, the tape cannot be reversed and played back in the opposite direction.

C. **Quarter-track** (4-track stereo). In this more common stereo configuration, tracks 1 and 3 are used for left-channel and right-channel information when played in one direction. Tracks 2 and 4 are used for the two stereo channels when the tape is reversed and played back in the opposite direction.

usually used only for high-quality, high-fidelity musical recordings. The audio operator must make certain that the booth audiotape recorder can play back at the correct speed. Second, the track configuration must be checked. Although most audiotape is ¼ inch, various recording configurations use the tape differently. It is possible to have full-track recording (rarely used today), half-track recording (wherein only half a track is used in each direction or both tracks are used for stereophonic recording in the same direction), and quarter-track (or four-track) recording (most commonly used for stereo recording). (See fig. 2-11.) Finally, the audio operator must check to make certain that the supply reel (usually on the left side of the machine) and the take-up reel (which receives the audiotape, usually on the right side of the recorder) are the same size. Tape reels come in several diameters, and if the two reels are different sizes, there is a greater possibility of breaking the tape or spinning the tape off the reel when in either the fast-forward or rewind mode.

Audio cartridge playback was previously discussed (section 2.1.6). As a prerecorded source of sound in the audio signal flow model, cartridge playback would be handled in a manner similar to audiotape. The cartridge player would be located in the audio booth, convenient to the audio operator. Figure 2-12 shows a typical *cart* machine. Since there are no variations in tape speed, track configuration, and reel size, the use of the cartridge is uncomplicated. Also, because the cartridge automatically rewinds itself and is self-cueing, it is very simple to operate.

Records are still a very common source of prerecorded audio, primarily for musical selections and sound effects. Most audio control rooms will have one (ideally, two) record turntable (or turntables) capable of playing records at 45 rpm (revolutions per minute) and 33⅓ rpm. As a source in the signal flow model, the turntables often are normalled into the audio console. The operator needs only to flip the correct input selector switch, turn on the channel selector or on-off key, and the record is on the air. In chapter 3 (section 3.4), we will discuss other aspects of operating these various audio sources—loading and threading

Figure 2-12 Audio cartridge player designed to access nine different carts on three different channels.

audiotape, cueing up records and audiotape, special effects (such as echoes and cross-fading), riding gain, and using the television program monitor for audio cues.

Summary

As an introduction to the audio system, we have been concerned more with *technical* than with *creative* functions. The seven *basic control functions* are modulation (and demodulation), channeling, mixing, shaping, amplifying, recording (and playback), and monitoring. These control functions were traced through the *audio signal flow* pattern: studio microphone input, through the patch bay, into the audio console, through an input selector switch, through the volume control or potentiometer/fader, into a specific channel, through the master potentiometer, out of the board through the line out, and back to the program-out position on the patch bay. This basic audio signal flow applies generally to any sound source—either a *microphone* or various *prerecorded sound sources* (film, videotape audio track, audiotape, audio cartridge, or record).

In the next chapter we will look more specifically at the microphone and consider some basic creative aspects of audio control.

2.5 Training Exercises

1. Make an outline of the equipment found in your own audio facility, using the seven control functions presented in this chapter.
2. Draw a sketch of both the audio patch panel and the audio console in your own facility. This will help you become familiar with the equipment, which will save considerable time as you later operate it.
3. Use the sketch along with the signal flow model in figure 2-7 to trace a signal flow sequence through the equipment of your own audio facility.
4. Compile a list of terms from this chapter that are somewhat unfamiliar. Write out an extended working definition relating to your own facilities. This is an excellent discipline to maintain with every chapter.

Audio Equipment and Creative Production Techniques

3

As stated in chapter 2, the function of a microphone is that of translating the pressure waves that we can hear as music or voices (sound energy) into an electronic wave pattern (electrical energy). Most of what is broadcast, music or otherwise, is an incredible combination of fundamental and overtone frequencies. Imagine, if you will, a hundred-piece symphony orchestra, each instrument of which is producing at any given point in time a fundamental tone and ten or more related **overtone** frequencies—or **harmonics**—that fall within the range of the human ear (see appendix B). A relatively small number of well-placed microphones can do an amazing job of capturing sound. The problem faced in the design of a microphone is that of the accuracy or **fidelity** with which as many as possible of those frequencies are picked up and modulated.

3.1 The Microphone: Function and Construction

In order to be able to appreciate what kinds of microphones are best suited for specific jobs it is necessary to take a quick look at the phenomenon of audio **frequency range**.

Frequency Range

The optimum range of human hearing—from the lowest rumbles to the highest overtones—lies between 20 **hertz (Hz),** or **cycles per second,** and 20,000 cycles per second (Hz). Hearing ability, however, may vary greatly with the individual as a result of inherited characteristics or ear damage.

AM radio, FM stations, and television sound vary in ability to transmit a wide portion of the frequency range. AM transmission is somewhat limited in the broadcasting of music because of the fact that its upper frequency limit until recently was only 5,000 hertz. While an upper limit of 7,500 hertz has

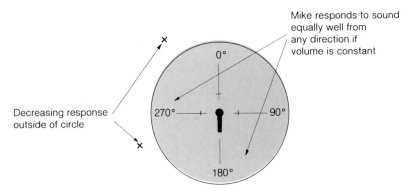

Mike responds to sound
equally well from
any direction if
volume is constant

0°

270°   90°

Decreasing response
outside of circle

180°

Figure 3-1
Omnidirectional
microphone pickup pattern.

now been approved, most AM stations have not yet purchased the equipment necessary for this increased range. High fidelity sound is achieved on FM radio as a result of its ability to broadcast up to 15,000 hertz. The audio portion of the television signal is also received as FM sound with the same theoretical upper limit of 15,000 hertz. Up until the mid-1980s, however, the average home TV set was not equipped to take advantage of the higher frequencies, and as a result broadcasters have not utilized this potential.

There are two related qualities that one looks for in the performance of a microphone. First, it must be able to respond to a wide range of fundamental and overtone frequencies. Second, it must also be able to transduce those frequencies in the same proportion as they occur in the original sound pressure waves. It is the overtones that give a voice or musical instrument its own distinctive quality of tone (see appendix B). A mike's design may vary according to its mode of use, but basically what you pay for is the range and fidelity of sound reproduction.

Microphone Pickup Patterns

Another important criterion in selecting a microphone is its pickup pattern—the area within which the microphone can accurately pick up

sound. Some microphones respond well to sound coming from only one direction; others can adequately pick up sound from all directions. In addition to information concerning the upper and lower limits of frequency response, most microphone manufacturers provide a pickup pattern for each model. It is an attempt to express pictorially the limits of a microphone's response pattern at stated decibel volume levels.

Such information has valuable applications for the trained audio engineer in determining its use. For the production student, the response pattern can be used more simply as an aid in determining the directional qualities of a mike. Such two-dimensional visualization is called a *polar pattern* because it shows the limits of accurate mike response as they would be seen from above. The actual response pattern is in reality a three-dimensional sphere of varying shape.

Figure 3-1 shows an **omnidirectional** (equal from all directions) response pattern. These microphones are also referred to as **nondirectional.** A mike with such a pattern would respond equally well to a sound source placed at any point on a circle (that is, sphere). The actual size of the circumference of the circle would vary with the volume level of the sound source. In other words, the effective range of a microphone can be expressed only in relation

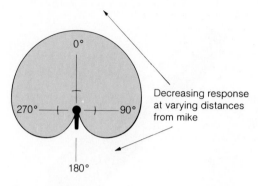

The cardioid, or heart-shaped, pattern represents a microphone that picks up sound primarily from one direction.

Figure 3-2 Unidirectional microphone pickup pattern.

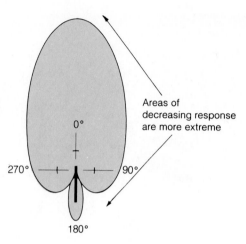

The highly directional microphone is designed to pick up sound, in a narrow response pattern, from relatively long distances.

Figure 3-3 Highly directional microphone pickup pattern.

to a decibel volume level. (Obviously, the microphones in the illustrations have not been drawn to scale with the size of the response pattern.)

Figure 3-2 illustrates a heart-shaped, or **cardioid,** response pattern. Such a pattern is considered as being mainly from one direction, or **unidirectional.** Outside of the pattern area, some of the small **amplitudes** (lower volumes) that constitute the sound source will not be picked up as well as others, if at all. The lesser amplitudes of overtone frequencies, for example, could be those that might be partly lost. The result is an **off-mike** distortion of the original sound.

Figure 3-3 illustrates a pear-shaped, *highly directional* pickup pattern. Specialized long distance, or **shotgun,** mikes operate with this sort of pattern structure. To further increase their sensitivity, they are sometimes used in conjunction with a parabolic dish, which can collect and concentrate a relatively distant audio source and reflect this focused audio beam directly into the microphone.

Standard radio production formats popularized the *bidirectional* microphone pickup pattern. These mikes picked up the sound

equally well from either side of the instrument. This was a desired feature in radio drama and interviews because the speakers-actors could stand on either side of the microphone, facing each other while speaking. Obviously, there is little use for this feature in television production.

Microphone Construction: Transducing Elements

In addition to classification by pickup pattern, the audio operator should be familiar with the basic categories of microphone construction. Depending upon the purposes for which a microphone is to be used, there are several criteria that should determine selection of a mike for a particular job—*durability and ruggedness, frequency response, fidelity, physical use* (whether the mike is to be stationary or movable), *location* (to be used in a studio or outdoors), and *cost*. There are several ways that the actual transducing element of a microphone can be built; these different categories meet different criteria.

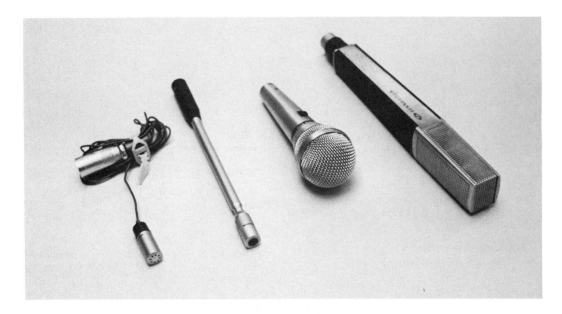

Figure 3-4
Representative studio microphones: *from left to right,* the Sony ECM–16 and the SuperScope EC–12B mikes are both condenser microphones; the larger Electro-Voice 671A and Sennheiser MD 441-U are dynamic mikes.

The **moving coil** or **dynamic microphone** (see fig. 2-1) generally is the most rugged and dependable.[1] It is sturdy and can stand more abuse than other commonly used microphones. It is especially useful for remote and outdoor locations. The moving coil or diaphragm stands up well to moderate shocks and sudden variations in the intensity of sound, and they can be used close to the sound source, which is especially valuable in noisy locations where the announcer or singer must work very close to the mike. The frequency response is good but not as sensitive as other types listed in the following discussion. The dynamic microphone, in its many variations and models, is probably the workhorse of the television industry today.

1. Technically speaking, both the *moving coil* and *ribbon* microphones are "dynamic" mikes because they transduce energy electromagnetically—that is, by some sort of a dynamically vibrating element (either a moving coil or a ribbon) causing changes within an electromagnetic field. However, traditionally, the moving coil microphone has been referred to as a "dynamic" mike. We shall follow this conventional usage.

The **ribbon microphone** (also called velocity mike), by contrast, was the standard of radio production for many years. Its transducing element is a thin strip of metal foil. The mike is generally larger, less mobile, and considerably more delicate than the dynamic microphone. The quality and frequency response are very good, however, and it is an excellent mike for both voice and musical pickup, especially in the lower frequency range.

The **condenser microphone** (whose transducer is a variable *capacitor* activated by sound pressure waves) is also a high-quality, fragile instrument with a very wide frequency range (fig. 3-4). Because the capacitor generates a very low-level signal, it needs a preamplifier; this requires a battery power source either within the mike itself or very near to it, which can be inconvenient at times. The excellent fidelity and wide frequency response, however, make this microphone popular for musical pickup wherever stationary mike placement is possible (for example, for an orchestral string section but not for a rock singer's hand mike). It is considered a superior microphone in professional recording studios. It is also generally the most expensive.

Other types of transducing elements are used for specialized purposes, but none have the quality needed for broadcast usage. The less expensive *ceramic* and *crystal* elements, which translate vibrations from the diaphragm into electrical currents, have neither the fidelity nor the ruggedness needed for professional use. Granular *carbon* transducers are one of the earliest types of microphones. They are still used in telephones but have few other professional applications.

Impedance Levels

In our discussion of the audio console input selector switch (section 2.3.4), reference was made to differing impedance levels. **Impedance** refers to resistance to the flow of an audio signal in the microphone cable. Professional studio microphones are always of the *low-impedance* type. Because there is less resistance to signal flow in the mike cable, the signal can be carried a great distance to the audio console, where it is amplified. Low impedance cables are less susceptible to hum, static, or other forms of outside electrical interference. Professional ½-inch and ¾-inch videorecorders are also designed to work with low-impedance mikes and lines.

However, most amateur and some industrial-level videorecorders call for *high-impedance* mikes. These produce a stronger electrical signal than low-impedance microphones, but the signal deteriorates rapidly because of the higher resistance; therefore relatively short cable lengths must be used with high-impedance mikes. Care should be taken not to mismatch high-impedance and low-impedance microphones, cables, and inputs. Unless a transformer is used, sound distortion will result.

3.2 Microphone Usage Categories

No single, all-purpose microphone has ever been designed. The most expensive microphone would have limitations in some situations. Instead, manufacturers provide a wide variety, each of which may combine a number of qualities suited to differing needs. A tremendous amount of time could be spent classifying the large variety of instruments available. However, it is not necessary for the television student to memorize a long list of microphones and their characteristics. It is of more immediate value if the student clearly understands some general usage classifications under which most mikes can be listed.

Some writers and practitioners have tried to classify microphones into the categories of *on-camera* and *off-camera*—those that are designed to be seen by the audience and those that are to be kept from view. Others have made the distinction between *stationary* and *mobile* microphones—depending upon whether or not the mikes are to be moved during the production. Rather than try to rely upon such clear-cut distinctions, which tend to overlap in practice, we would like to suggest the following three broad functional categories:

1. Hand and/or stand mikes
2. Limited-movement mikes
3. Attached personal mikes

These categories are obviously artificial designations—devised for learning purposes only. (For instance, you will never find a section of a microphone cabinet labeled "attached personal mikes.") These classifications, however, should help you in thinking about the different ways in which microphones can be positioned and used—keeping in mind the positive qualities and limiting factors of each

Figure 3-5 Many hand microphones such as the EV 671A can also be used as stand mikes.

grouping. Also, these are not mutually exclusive categories; there is obvious overlap. Many mikes could fit into two of the groups.

Hand and/or Stand Mikes

Probably the most versatile group of mikes are those medium-sized, elongated instruments designed to work best at a range of 6 inches to 3 feet from a speaker or musical performer (fig. 3-5). Although a few require a fixed mount, most are structured to fit into a holder in a desk (for a news program or panel show) or a floor mike stand (for a performer). The same microphone is used as a hand-held mike for, say, an on-location news event or spontaneous interviews with members of an audience. This category overlaps both the stationary and mobile distinctions, for instance, in the case of a performer who begins a number by using a mike stand (stationary) and then removes the mike from the holder and concludes the number using it as a hand mike (mobile).

Resistance to the rugged handling of, say, a rock music performer is an important quality for such a mike. Most microphones in this category are *dynamic* mikes utilizing the coil and magnet transducer. Many such instruments have a **pop filter** that minimizes the plosive effect of *T*'s, *K*'s, and *P*'s. Such a mike is all the more useful if it is designed to function in the outdoor conditions of news and sports remotes. These mikes require a fairly wide angle of sound acceptance and are usually either omnidirectional or cardioid in their pickup pattern.

Limited-Movement Mikes

The limited-movement category encompasses several different kinds of microphone applications from fixed-position uses to a considerable amount of movement on large **perambulator booms.** Generally, microphones in this category will be larger than those that

Figure 3-6 Two large studio perambulator booms used to cover a drama. (Photo courtesy of KCET, Los Angeles)

are intended to be hand held. Almost always, mikes in this grouping would not be intended for use on camera—they are seldom seen by the audience. As off-camera mikes, they are required to have good pickup qualities at relatively moderate to long distances. Some hand mikes, however, are designed to function adequately as omnidirectional boom mikes.

The label of "boom mike" can cover a wide variety of applications. The big boom, or *perambulator dolly* (fig. 3-6), is a large, three-wheeled movable platform that holds the boom operator and has a long counterweighted boom arm that can be extended and tilted while the microphone itself can be rotated in almost a full circle. It is a large, cumbersome piece of equipment requiring two operators—one dolly pusher and one mike manipulator—and is effective only in spacious studios. They are used

in pairs, for example, to cover the dramatic action in soap operas or to cover guests on a talk show such as *The Tonight Show.*

A smaller boom, similar to that in figure 3-7, would be the *giraffe*—a counterweighted boom arm supported by a tripod on casters that can be operated by one person. Although not as flexible as the big boom, the giraffe can be moved easier and takes up much less floor space. Even though it is thought of as a movable boom, the giraffe is often stationed in a fixed position for an entire production.

Finally, we might consider the use of the **fishpole**—literally a small, lightweight pole to which the microphone is attached. The operator hand holds the pole in order to get the best audio position for any given scene. Although extremely flexible, the operation of this device can be quickly tiring, and it is prone to cause

Figure 3-7 A giraffe, or tripod, microphone boom.

mistakes because of the inexactness in operation (causing boom shadows, dropping into a picture, accidentally hitting scenery, and so forth).

There is today a group of larger and more versatile instruments, all of which have excellent omnidirectional frequency response for instrumental or voice pickup.

When sound must be picked up from an unusually long distance (15 to 20 feet), there are several highly directional specialized instruments that are used. Older versions of the shotgun mikes have a frequency range that is adequate for speech, or the related sound perspective of a sporting event, but not for instrumental music. Recent developments with the condenser shotgun, however, have resulted in a long-range microphone with excellent frequency response.

A special category of the fixed-position microphone would be the **hanging mike.** In certain situations (usually a drama) where it is impossible to mike a speaker in any other manner, it is possible to suspend an overhead microphone—hanging it from the catwalk or lighting grid. As a rule a dynamic microphone with a cardioid pattern would be used. Most audio directors would rely on a hanging mike only as a last resort because there are several disadvantages. The sound source is often fairly far from the microphone; the actor or speaker may be slightly out of position and no adjustment can be made to reposition the mike; the speaker is usually projecting—at best—at right angles to the microphone; and the mike is picking up the sound as reverberations off the studio floor, emphasizing any studio floor noises such as shoes and cables dragging. The result is most often a distant, off-mike quality with considerable ambient noise.

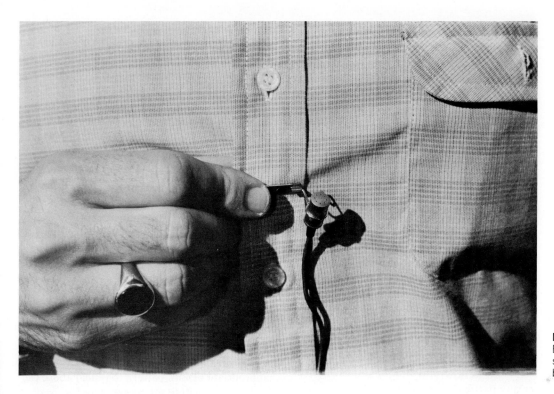

Figure 3-8 The Sony ECM–30 illustrates how small the lapel mikes have become.

Attached Personal Mikes

Television created the necessity for an unobtrusive instrument that could move with the performer. The *lavaliere* microphone (worn around the neck) and the *lapel mike* are the result. Most of the earlier lavaliere models were effective omnidirectional mikes although they were limited to the frequency range of the human voice. Later models can filter out unwanted noise caused by clothing rubbing against the mike. The more recent lapel models have a frequency response more than adequate for instrumental pickup.

Since earlier models tended to be somewhat bulky and obvious, many performers tried to hide the lavaliere under a tie or inside a blouse with a resulting muffled audio quality. Later models are so compact (no larger than a small thimble) that they can be worn on top of clothing unobtrusively, with better audio pickup resulting (fig. 3-8).

The problems caused by mike cords have resulted in the development of the RF (radio frequency) **wireless microphone.** A miniature transmitter—either a part of the mike itself or in a concealed pack—sends an FM signal to a portable receiver that can be placed as far as several hundred feet from the performer. Although these systems have obvious advantages for television production, a propensity for dead spots in the transmission pattern and some limitations in frequency range have been the major limitations to their use. Recent progress with sophisticated receivers, however, has eliminated many of the problems. Ambitiously staged productions and musical videos have made the wireless mike almost indispensable in contemporary programming.

3.3 Using the Microphone

The proper procedures for microphone utilization are largely a matter of the common-sense application of a few simple principles. With this section, we begin to get specifically into the area of the creative functions of audio production. Most successful audio-microphone usage is just an extension of three basic considerations: selection of the correct microphone; microphone placement; and balance and perspective. To these add a considerable amount of experience.

Microphone Selection

In many small stations and university studios, the question of microphone selection may be purely academic. If you have nothing more than a few basic dynamic cardioid microphones, that is what you will use. In most larger situations, however, the audio engineer will have a choice of several different kinds of mikes for any particular production.

First define the audio job to be done. Let's take, for example, the task of picking up a well-tuned concert grand piano. Mikes should be selected on the basis of their known positive and negative qualities. Voice-frequency-range lavalieres and older long-distance shotgun mikes are not going to pick up all of the true tonal quality of the piano. Any of several full-frequency ribbon or condenser stand mikes placed either inside or underneath the instrument can do this satisfactorily. These same mikes placed so that the piano is outside of their pickup pattern would be equally unsatisfactory.

If you are concerned with recording a pop vocal personality, you must take into consideration whether or not the singer is likely to want to use a microphone as part of the performance—as a hand prop. If the singer does, you would want to use a fairly rugged dynamic mike. If, however, the production calls for an off-camera boom mike, then a full-frequency condenser microphone might be used, especially if fidelity to the musical quality is the uppermost concern.

When producing a news program or panel discussion, the full-frequency range of a condenser or ribbon mike is not necessary. Depending upon the "look" of the production, you may decide on either a dynamic desk mike (desk mikes are often subject to considerable table pounding) or lavalieres.

Suppose you are to handle a remote assignment covering a parade or sporting event. You would probably want a rugged, relatively insensitive unidirectional dynamic mike for the narrator-announcer (to allow him or her to work closely to the mike, cutting out as much background as possible) coupled with a highly directional shotgun mike to pick up selected crowd or parade noise as desired. The first task, however, is always the same: define the job to be done in terms of frequency response needed, appropriate pickup pattern, physical abuse the microphone will likely be subjected to, and so forth.

In selecting and positioning microphones correctly for a particular audio pickup, you must be aware of two critical considerations. One is *aesthetic* and the other is *acoustical*. In a dramatic production, the mike should not be seen as part of the picture. Usually, directional long-distance pickup mikes mounted on movable booms are used. In some cases wireless RF equipment may be utilized. On the other hand, if you are working in a news, public affairs, or sports situation, the use of a hand mike is accepted by the audience—as is an occasional camera shot that reveals an operator holding a shotgun mike mounted in a parabolic dish.

Sometimes you must compromise between aesthetic and acoustical needs. In the telecast of a symphony performance, for instance, the quality of sound is very important.

A number of mikes must be placed relatively close to the musicians to assure proper balance and timbre. This is especially true of string and woodwind instruments. An unobtrusive, sensitive microphone placed on a small stand would generally be accepted by the audience.

Microphone Placement

The earlier sections of this chapter have introduced several concepts relating to the selection of the proper microphone for a specific audio task: pickup pattern, frequency response, sensitivity, ruggedness, mounting considerations, and so forth. During this audio setup process, the engineer must also be considering the exact placement of each mike. A microphone that works well at one location may be inadequate in a slightly different position. One must, to use an old adage, "consider the source."

Sound, especially the higher frequencies, diminishes in loudness (amplitude) very rapidly as it passes through the air. This loss directly relates to the amount of energy it takes to propel the pressure wave through the molecules of the air. The rate of drop-off is scientifically described by the *Inverse Square Law*. Although this text is not the proper place to attempt to describe all of the principles of physics involved, the operating concept is easily understood: *as microphone-to-source distance is doubled, the loudness is reduced to one-fourth.*

Therefore, if you have an audio source (voice) giving you a constant level of sound 1 foot from a microphone, and then you move the mike back to a distance of 2 feet, the loudness of the sound hitting the microphone will be only ¼ as loud as it was when the mike was 1 foot from the source. Similarly, if you again double your distance and place the microphone 4 feet from the source, you will reduce your loudness level to ¼ of what it was at 2 feet (or ¹⁄₁₆ of what it was at 1 foot).

Putting this principle into simple operational terms, suppose you have done a microphone-level check (measuring a performer's voice loudness prior to going on the air in order to determine where to set your pot level) with a person who is seated 1 foot away from a desk mike (see section 3.5). Once the program starts, however, if that person then decides to lean back just 1 foot farther to be more comfortable, you have lost close to 75 percent of that person's volume! On the other hand, if you have a performer working 10 feet from a long-distance directional microphone, and that person moves 1 foot backward, there will not be much of a noticeable difference (the performer has only increased his or her distance by ¹⁄₁₀).

You must remember, however, that each microphone has its own pickup pattern involving distance and sensitivity, and outside of that pattern the quality of sound will rapidly deteriorate.

Acoustical considerations for microphone placement can be thought of in terms of two interacting factors: *audio direction* and *microphone distance*. Audio direction refers to having the source (voice or musical instrument) squarely in the path of the directional pickup of the mike—with the audio source aimed directly at the microphone. If the audio source is not in the directional path of the microphone, or "on the beam," then the resulting pickup will be off-mike. This results in a hollow, distant effect similar to being too far away from the microphone.

The audio operator must be constantly aware of *microphone-to-source* distance as it relates to *sound-power wave distortion*. If, for example, two actors are playing a dramatic scene, they will face more toward each other than out to an "audience" area. The audio operator must work closely with the director so as to determine the various speaking positions of the actors as they move about the set. An all-too-common error in the above situation is

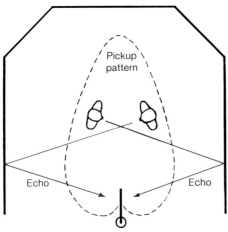

Although the two actors are standing "in the pattern" of the directional mike, their voices will be picked up with a hollow "off-mike" quality because they are not facing toward the mike; they are directing their voices away from the microphone.

Figure 3-9 Incorrect placement of directional mike between two performers.

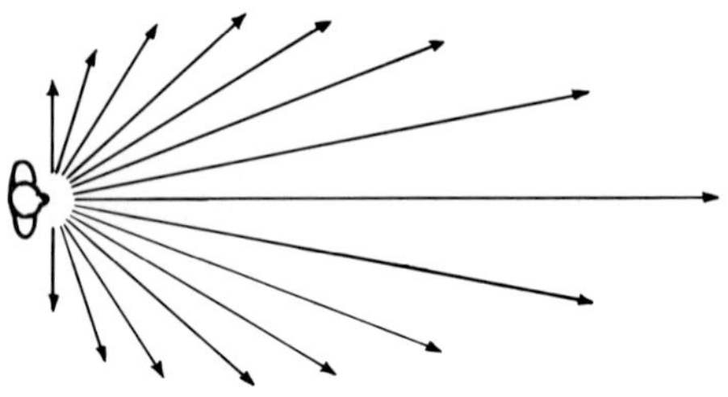

Figure 3-10 Sound pressure waves decrease rapidly in intensity except those projected straight forward.

Figure 3-11 Correct placement of directional mikes.

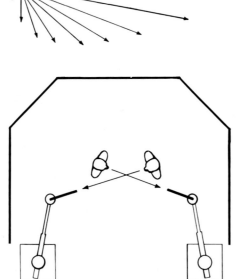

In order to achieve optimum audio pickup from two actors facing each other, it is necessary to use two directional microphones; a separate mike is placed directly in the vocal path of each actor.

to place one directional mike in the "audience" area in an attempt to pick up both voices (fig. 3-9).

At first glance, the actors would seem to be within the pickup pattern of the directional mike. One must keep in mind, however, that each sound source has a *projection* pattern, which is somewhat similar to the pickup pattern of a microphone. With the human voice, the shape of the mouth and lips tend to focus the strongest pressure waves in a relatively narrow channel as represented in figure 3-10.

When mikes are placed at a side angle (45° or more to the direction of the direct sound pressure waves), the result is a considerable drop-off in audio level and in "presence." If one attempts to turn up the amplification at the pot to compensate for this loss, one will also begin to hear the reflected echo sound waves coming back from the set and walls of the studio. The result is an "off mike" distortion of the original sound. While these reflected echoes are always a part of any sound pickup—contributing to the effect of natural room "presence"—they should be heard only in their natural proportion to the primary sound waves.

The proper placement of microphones for a two-person conversation is shown in figure 3-11. Using two mikes, the audio operator must position one mike directly in the path of each voice to pick up the best and most direct voice quality. If the two persons move about the set during the conversation, then the perambulator dolly would be a necessity. The boom arm is extendable and the angle of the mike can be changed to keep the proper distance and mike direction in relation to the actors.

The correct distance from source to microphone is at once a fairly simple and obvious matter and, at the same time, a highly complex study. Depending upon the type of microphone and the audio quality desired, the optimum speaking distance may be anywhere from a few inches to several feet. A typical shotgun directional mike might give fairly good audio pickup as far away as 10 or 15 feet. Because of the pickup patterns, speakers should generally work closer to an omnidirectional mike than to a unidirectional mike. Under good studio conditions, with a normal speaking voice, the announcer or talent should work about 1 foot away from an omnidirectional mike and up to 2 feet away from a cardioid mike. These are only rough rules, of course, and much depends upon such factors as studio conditions, specific microphone characteristics, and vocal qualities.

Balance and Perspective

In establishing the overall sound quality, you, as the audio director, must also give consideration to the subjective factors of how various sources balance each other and sound in perspective to each other. No frequency response chart or VU meter can replace the human ear in determining the final sound of a program.

Getting the right proportion of volume levels from different sources is necessary. Are the musical instruments balanced? Is there too much piano for the vocal group? Are all of the panelists speaking at the same apparent level? Can a proper balance be achieved simply by adjusting volume levels with the faders, or should microphone placement be altered?

This last question gets into the area of audio **perspective**—an especially important concept in dramatic audio. Actors should appear to have an audio **presence**, or proximity that matches their video distance. The tighter a shot (the closer a character appears to camera), the closer a person should sound; as a character gets farther from camera, the more distant his or her voice should become. Thus, as two characters move in relation to each other on the screen, their audio perspective should change also. As a person walks out of a scene, his or her voice should appear to get further off-mike; as a person looms larger on the screen, we should get the feeling of more presence. An extreme close-up shot often calls for an exaggerated audio intimacy—a stream-of-consciousness technique suggesting a stage whisper or aside to the audience.

This audio presence cannot be achieved simply by adjusting volume levels with the pots. Microphones have to move in relation to the actors. Either the actors walk farther away from the microphones (to achieve audio distance) or the mikes, on booms or fishpoles, have to be moved away from the actors. Care must be taken to ensure that video distance and audio presence do not unintentionally contradict each other. Many an amateur dramatic effect has been ruined by using a hidden microphone concealed near a doorway in the rear of a set; the player then bids an emotional adieu only to have his or her audio presence increase as he or she walks away from the camera.

3.4 Adding Other Audio Sources

Up to this point we have been concerned entirely with the microphone as the source of television audio. We now turn our attention to other sources of prerecorded sound (as outlined in section 2.4).

Patching Audio Sources

All prerecorded audio sources generally come from one or two locations—either the audio control room or the telecine (the master control room). Those playback machines located in the audio booth (audiotape recorder, record turntables, cartridge player) either will be normalled (permanently wired) into the audio console or will be patched through the audio patch bay in the booth. Those audio sources coming from the telecine or master control (film projectors, videotape players) will probably be fed into the audio booth through some sort of external patching arrangement.

In many studio operations, the master control room has a patch bay similar to the one in the audio booth, except that the master control room patch bay has inputs not for microphones but for audio outputs from videotape recorders and film projectors. These audio outputs (and there often are two audio tracks per videotape recorder) can be fed to each other and to other terminals in master control and/or they can be connected to **tie lines**. The tie lines are used to connect the master control room with other key locations, such as a transmitter or the audio control room. It is these tie lines that are used for sending audio signals from the audio booth to master control (for example, the program audio from "line 1 out") where the audio can then be recorded on videotape recorders or sent out to the transmitter via further patching. Similar tie lines are used for sending various audio signals (for example, from film projectors and VTR machines) from master control to the studio audio booth for mixing into program audio.

Once the prerecorded audio sources are patched or normalled into the console, they then follow the signal flow as explained in section 2.3. The correct input selector switch for each source must be flipped on, the channel selector (pot on-off) key must be set, and the pot or fader is then used to control the volume. Like microphone levels, the volume level or gain of prerecorded audio should be adjusted to peak at close to 100 on the VU meter. Riding gain on prerecorded audio *should* be somewhat easier than riding gain on live microphones, because the prerecorded audio has already gone through a mixing and recording process and should be set at a fairly constant level.

Cueing Procedures

A crucial aspect of using prerecorded audio of any type is getting the sound **cued up** to exactly the right starting point so that the correct sound is available precisely when the director calls for it. Except for the audio cartridge, which cues itself automatically, this means that the audio operator is going to have to get the sound cued up at the correct spot.

For purposes of a detailed explanation, it would probably be most worthwhile to look at the specific procedures involved in cueing up a phonograph record. Although the layout of audio booths—the relationship of audio console and turntables—varies considerably, the following steps can be adapted to any situation:

1. Place the potentiometer in the **cue**, or **audition, position**. With a knob-type pot, this will be all the way to the left. With a slide-fader, this will be all the way to the bottom of the scale. This particular pot is now connected only to the cue audio system, which has its own speaker.

2. With the turntable power off, place the needle in the outside groove of the record. Lightly place your fingertips on the inside label of the record. Turn the record clockwise until the first tone is heard. (Most turntables are equipped with a felt pad that allows the record and the felt to move independently of the turntable surface.)

3. Stop the record at the first tone, now move it in a counterclockwise direction one-quarter of a revolution and stop. If the record is not backed up in this manner, it will **wow** as it comes up to speed when it is put on the air.

4. With your free hand, immediately take the fader (pot) out of the cue position, being careful to leave it at the "0" volume-level position. (More than one TV audio operator or beginning disc jockey has been blissfully unaware that the record he or she thinks is on the air is being heard only on the cue speaker.)

Figure 3-12 Cueing a record.

5. Just prior to playing, gently lay your fingers on the record. (With the slightest jolt, the needle will jump out of the groove.) Use your other hand to switch on the turntable power. This is called *slip cue*, because the turntable is now up to playing speed while the record is being held in readiness (fig. 3-12).

6. At the proper command, the record is released and the pot is brought up to the desired level. The one-quarter turn now allows the felt to grip the turntable and bring the record up to playing speed. At this point, the timing of the operator is very critical. If the pot is already opened when the record is released, we will hear scratches prior to the first tone. If the operator is a fraction of a second late in opening the pot, the first tones will

be *upcut*. This means that the beginning of the record either will not be heard at all or will be played at a very low level.

7. As soon as the record starts, you should immediately glance at the VU meter to see if any further adjustments in level are necessary. It is a good idea—prior to the actual production—to check the level of the opening section of any record to be used during a production situation. This *cannot* be done when cueing a record because the VU meter does not monitor any signal on the cue system.

If your turntable is equipped with a non-slip rubber mat, then the record must be started from a dead-stop position. In this case, a half revolution is suggested in order to bring the turntable up to playing speed to prevent a wow.

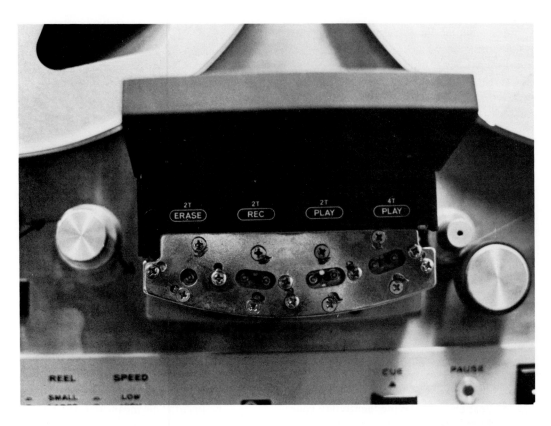

Figure 3-13 Stereo audiotape recorder. This recorder has four heads: an erase head; a record head; and two playback heads, depending upon the track configuration desired.

In working with videotape and film projection, the audio operator probably is not involved with loading the playback machine or concerned about the cueing process at all. This is usually handled by an engineer in master control or the projection-film chain area. The playback engineer will have the VTR machine or film projector threaded and cued up according to the film or videotape leader or footage counter, which indicates exactly how far before the desired sound and picture the machine is set. The primary job of the audio operator is simply to check his or her signal flow (input selector switch, channel selector key) and be ready to bring up the volume when directed to do so. In most studio situations, the audio booth will be equipped with a TV-line monitor. This enables the audio operator to see the actual TV program as it is being put together. Thus, the operator can get a visual cue for the videotape and film inserts—which reinforces the direct cue from the director—and time his or her audio starts accordingly.

In working with audiotape, however, the audio engineer has the responsibility for threading and cueing. Threading the audiotape recorder is a simple process, as long as you carefully follow the threading diagram. Always check to be certain that the audiotape has not been incorrectly wound on the reel, that the magnetic side of the tape (usually dull) is threaded so that it comes in contact with the playback head of the recorder, and that the base (usually the shiny side) is facing away from the heads.[2] The audio recorder has three or four heads arranged in a row—the erase head, the record head, and one or two playback heads (fig. 3-13).

2. On most modern *video*tape, the oxide or magnetic side of the tape is the shiny side.

In cueing up the audiotape, the principle is the same as for cueing records. Once the first tone is heard (with the pot set in the cue position), the supply and take-up reels should simultaneously be turned backwards by hand so that the first tone is about 2 inches from the playback head. (For tape recorded at 3¾ ips, it need only be about 1 inch; for 15 ips recordings, it should be closer to 4 inches.)

Mixing and Other Techniques

When two or more sound sources are mixed together—microphones and prerecorded sources or some of each—the audio operator must rely upon his or her ear to be sure that the balance is correct. Recorded music may vary considerably in volume within the space of 20 or 30 seconds of playing time. For this reason, the operator must be careful not to let a sudden increase in the volume of background music distract from what is being said. Unless otherwise occupied with cueing records or tapes, most audio engineers keep their hands right on the pots or faders in order to ride gain, constantly adjusting to even small changes in the input level.

Occasionally the audio mixing can be rather complex. Sometimes several microphones will have to be *potted down* (faded out) simultaneously while a prerecorded announcer on audiotape is started. This can be accomplished on a dual-channel board if one of the channels has been converted (or can be switched) to a submaster; then the several microphones can be put on the submaster by means of the channel selector switch and controlled with one submaster pot.

At other times, there may be constant balancing and readjustment of several sound sources—say, background music on a tape, sound effects on a turntable, and two different microphones. Dramatic continuity may call for a **cross-fade** or **segue** between different musical selections. A cross-fade is a transition whereby one sound (musical record) is faded out while another is faded in, thereby effecting a temporary overlap of the two musical selections. A segue is similar except that the first sound is completely faded out before the second one is brought in. Both of these procedures call for the simultaneous control of two different turntables.

Continuous sound effects can be achieved with audiotape by **looping**. With a **reel-to-reel** player, a single tape loop can be spliced together and played continuously, which will give you several seconds of a background sound. With an audio cartridge player, you can remove the stop-cue and the entire cart loop will keep repeating.

Occasionally the audio operator may have to make some fast switching for special effects. Filters are often used to simulate a telephone conversation, for example. If the picture changes in the middle of one person's dialogue on the telephone (that is, if we are looking at John talking on the telephone and then the picture changes to Susan listening to John), we must instantaneously have a corresponding change in audio in order to maintain the proper sound perspective. Watching the TV-line monitor, the audio operator must make certain that we perceive the filter effect (to simulate the other end of the telephone conversation) when the picture changes from the speaker to a reaction shot of the listener.

Finally, mention should be made of echo effects. Even without fancy reverberation chambers and special devices, a simple echo effect can be achieved in most control booths with just one audiotape recorder. It is necessary only to patch and connect the tape recorder for simultaneous recording and playback. That is, the *line out* from the console must be patched into the *audiotape in* as well as the *audiotape out* being fed back into the console. Then by introducing an independent audio source, say a microphone from the studio, this source is recorded on the record head of the tape recorder and, as it passes over the playback head a split second later, fed back into the console. It can then be mixed—through the pot controlling the audiotape playback—with the original sound coming directly from the studio microphone. The result is the original sound, followed a split second later by a recorded version of the same sound. Depending upon the level of the audiotape playback pot, this effect can range from a very slight echo suggestive of a large hall or cave to some very bizarre futuristic electronic distortions. When using this procedure, however, the operator must be careful to ride the gain on the master pot very closely; as the reverberation is increased, the feedback effect greatly amplifies the master level very rapidly.

3.5 Production Techniques

We are now approaching the point where you should be ready for your first production exercise. It may be helpful at this juncture to emphasize the difference between single-camera film techniques and the immediacy of a continuing process inherent in a multiple-camera TV production (see section 1.4), for this distinction generally shapes the nature of television production and determines the roles of the crew members.

Television and Film Production

Conventionally, live studio television seeks to achieve the nonstop production of entire programs or at least complete segments of programs. Film technique, especially as used in dramatic motion pictures, involves the shooting of multiple takes of short 10- to 20-second segments. These are usually shot totally out of story sequence. Much of the art of filmmaking lies in the later painstaking editing process. In live television, the director is doing all of the editing as the program progresses. What you see (on the line monitor) is what you get. With advances in technology, however, the two processes are gradually coming to resemble each

other more and more. Various TV sports and public affairs programming borrows heavily from the film genre for its videotape editing techniques. The simultaneous use of three film cameras employed on several MTM productions is like live television, although there is a later editing process.

Television's primary virtue is that it is able to capture the reality of a continuing performance or event in real time, not a stop-and-go recreation of time. In the arts, this is an important ingredient of the creative process, especially for the performer. It is also essential to sports, news, and some public affairs programming.

Television's ability to function within the "real time" continuum, however, places considerable demands upon all of the crew members. Before beginning your initial class production exercise, you should be aware of the intercommunication network, the elements of vocal command procedures, and some audio setup procedures.

The Intercom Network

The system by which all production elements are brought together at the precise moment that they are needed in a program is the intercommunication network, or **intercom network**. Also known as the **P.L.** (for private line), this is, in essence, a closed-circuit audio network that connects all primary production and engineering personnel by standard telephone **headsets** that have an earpiece and a small microphone or mouthpiece. Thus, the director can talk to the **stage manager,** or **floor director**,[3] without the conversation being picked up by any microphones; the technical director can talk to camera operators; the audio engineer

---

3. The terms *stage manager, floor manager,* and *floor director* are used interchangeably in this text. Used in different parts of the country, by different kinds of production centers, they all refer to the chief crew member on the floor—the director's surrogate for the studio stage.

can give commands to the boom operator; the associate director can check with the video recording engineer; and so forth.

Of course, with everyone trying to communicate with everyone else, the system would result in absolute and continual chaos—without a measure of discipline and self-restraint by all involved. Ordinarily the director predominates, and the system is at his or her disposal at all times; when the line is clear—or when the director specifically assigns the P.L. to some high priority function—the appropriate crew members have access to the system. In some large systems, separate P.L. networks may be set up for engineering and production personnel. Thus, the video engineer and technical director can carry on a conversation without interfering with the director and floor crew.

A double headset system also might be used by the audio personnel. This enables the audio director and boom operator(s) to hear the P.L. with one earpiece and to monitor the program audio with the other earpiece. This is invaluable for a boom operator who is following a fast-moving piece of dialogue among three people, for instance; he or she can directly monitor the balance and perspective being picked up while manipulating and adjusting the boom position.

The **studio address (S.A.),** or **studio talkback** system, is another link in the production crew intercommunication network. The S.A. talkback microphone in the control room (and there may be a parallel system out of the audio booth) enables the director to activate a special studio speaker so that he or she can talk to everybody in the studio, regardless of whether or not they are on P.L. headsets. (The S.A. speaker automatically cuts out the regular program microphone input to guard against any unintentional feedback, which could damage the audio system. Needless to say, the studio talkback should not be used while microphones are activated during a program.) Part of the discipline of the television director is knowing when to use the S.A. (to communicate efficiently and quickly with the whole crew and all talent simultaneously) and when to rely on the floor manager (to interpret and carry out direct orders and implied threats).

The total intercommunication system is further extended—to the performing talent during the production—by the hand and arm signals of the floor manager. This is the pantomime system by which different directions can be given to persons while they are on camera without having to vocalize any commands and thereby possibly unintentionally getting these directions picked up as part of the program audio. (See appendix C for illustration of basic hand and arm signals.)

Vocal Command Procedures

At this stage, you also need to be aware of the vocal commands that are used to direct the entire production. Over the years, television production has evolved a system that separates commands into two phases—preparation and execution. The *commands of execution* are those cues that directly affect what goes out over the line monitor. "Take camera one" and "Cue the announcer" call for an immediate action at a precise point in time. For a crew member or performer to be able to respond with this immediate action, however, he or she must be given adequate preparation time to be mentally ready and/or physically prepared to perform some action or operate the equipment. For this reason, all commands of execution must be preceded at some point by a related *command of preparation.* Figure 3-14 shows how the commands fit into the time frame of the production sequence for a simple audio exercise. (The commands and timing indicated in figure 3-14 are designed to be used with the commercial/production exercise in appendix D-1.)

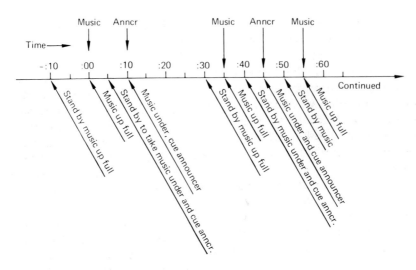

This chart shows the commands to be given in a simple commercial announcement. The commercial starts at ":00" with music; the announcer reads the first copy starting at ":10" (10 seconds); music comes up full at ":35"; the second announcer starts at ":45"; music comes up full at ":55"; and so forth.

Figure 3-14 Time frame for a simple audio production.

The term **standby** (for announcer, music, record, and so forth) is probably the most functional preparatory command for your present needs. *Cue* is quite often used to begin a command of execution. Sometimes just the term *music* or *announcer* can be used as the command of execution. Complete voice command procedure for a total television production is, of necessity, somewhat more complicated than what we have presented here; other commands will be discussed in conjunction with the explanation of video-switching procedures (section 7.5).

Audio Setup Procedures

Finally, prior to the initial class audio-production exercise, we should outline some basic steps in an audio setup. During any production setup, the audio assistants will follow the audio engineer's instructions as to which studio inputs to use and where to set up the mikes. This is an important introduction to the concept of position responsibility within the chain of command. By the same token, it is the director who has the ultimate responsibility for the operation.

The person in charge of audio should first go through the entire signal flow process mentally before giving any instructions. If a mike does not work, it is he or she who must initiate a step-by-step signal flow checkout. To gain the most from any training exercise, it is suggested that all patches and mike cords be unplugged and redone with new input numbers as each new director takes over.

Once the mikes are all working, the audio operator should get a **level** from each of the performers. Different voices vary considerably in strength. Using the VU meter, the audio operator can find an optimum position on the potentiometer for each voice. This is an average or middle position between the highest and lowest movements of the needle. The highest points or peaks should only occasionally exceed the 100 percent modulation position of the meter.

Summary

As part of the *technical* requirements for audio production, it is important to know something about *microphone construction*—frequency response, pickup patterns, construction of transducing elements (dynamic, ribbon, condenser, and other types), and impedance levels. These factors determine the way different microphones can be physically handled—as hand or stand mikes, limited-movement mikes, and attached personal mikes. Getting into *creative* considerations, the audio director must be concerned with the way microphones are utilized—*selection* and *placement* of the mikes, and *audio balance* and *perspective*. In adding other prerecorded sound sources, the audio operator must also be familiar with *patching* from different areas, *cueing* techniques for various media, and *mixing* procedures. In preparation for our first audio-production exercise, the audio operator must also understand basic television production procedures, the *intercom network, vocal commands,* and the *audio setup* operations.

In the next chapter, we turn from audio to video considerations as we look first at lighting requirements and techniques.

3.6 Training Exercises and Class Audio Project

Class Exercises

1. Prepare a list of all of the microphones that are available for use in your own facility. Using the manufacturer's specifications, if available, describe the specific design qualities for each, as well as any limitations that should be noted.
2. Go through a live demonstration for each mike, showing the pickup pattern and range of frequency response. Listen carefully for the distinctive differences in sound quality occurring in each of the basic types of instruments.

Class Audio Production Project (Appendix D-1)

This audio production exercise is in the form of a radio commercial. It is designed to develop the techniques and disciplines needed to set up microphones and mix two announcers with music. Although one mike could be adequate, it is suggested that two stand or desk mikes be used for the exercise. This use will provide more practice in setup, patching, and operational techniques. The mikes should be placed at least 3 feet apart and side by side so that both announcers can see the stage manager's signals. The announcers should work about 12 to 18 inches from each mike.

First of all, consider the production elements that must fit together in a precise sequence for the initial portion of the commercial script. First establish the music, which is then faded under (that is, at low volume, below the announcer's voice but still audible) for the announcer who speaks for 25 seconds. The music is then brought up again for 10 seconds, then under again as the second announcer speaks for 20 seconds. The music is brought up again, and the first part of the commercial is completed. Figure 3-14 illustrates the production time frame.

It looks simple, and it really is, just as long as the two announcers and the audio engineer are able to coordinate their actions. For this, some sort of director is needed. In most smaller audio operations, the audio engineer would serve this function. As preparation for later, more complicated television production exercises, it is suggested that a separate person act as director.

TV Lighting Equipment and Techniques

4

Television production consists basically of two elements—audio and video. Chapters 2 and 3 dealt with audio. Chapters 5 through 9 deal specifically with different aspects of the television picture. (The rest of the book is concerned with putting it all together.) Before we can look at how cameras and lenses work, however, it is necessary to spend some time looking at that physical phenomenon that makes all vision possible—light! Without light there would be no video. And without good lighting there would be no good video.

4.1 Types of Light: Incident and Reflected

Light comes to us in two somewhat different forms. There is light that comes directly from a source such as the sun, a light bulb, or a candle. This is called **incident light** and, as important as it is, tells us little beyond the fact that we are looking at a light source.

We see as a result of a second kind of light, which has been reflected from and, as a result, altered by the surface of a material substance. It is this **reflected light** that transmits information to us regarding our environment. The brain has been conditioned to respond to this information as perceived by the eye.

As children, we constantly reinforced our developing visual sense by touching the objects in our immediate environment. We were, in effect, programming our computerlike brain so that we could "believe our eyes." Looking out on the world, we see a series of flat planes and curved surfaces occurring at various angles. The reflected light from these diverse surfaces comes to our eyes in differing intensities—depending upon the position of the incident light sources. Our brain learns to translate these variations of light and shadow into the concept of shape and texture.

Take as an example the instructor's desk in a classroom. The dimensions of the top of the desk are defined for us by the uniform intensity of the light reflected from all points of its surface. The light reflected from the side of the desk is of a different intensity, possibly somewhat of a shadow; this tells us that these side surfaces are at a different angle from the top and indeed are the sides of the desk. Other features, such as drawer handles and the legs, are defined by the shadows that the light source "molds" around them.

Reflected light also tells us much about the *texture* of a surface. The even, shiny quality of light reflected from the desk top denotes a hard, uniform surface. Cloth would be much more light absorbent. We can perceive the texture of a heavy cloth material by the many tiny shadows created by the design of the weave.

Illumination for video production, as we shall see, is an art that involves the proper use of lighting equipment to control the light that is reflected *from* the subject *to* the camera. It is the way we shape and control this reflected light that determines what the TV camera perceives as a picture.

4.2 Lighting Objectives: Basic Illumination

When the lighting director (L.D.) sets out to design the lighting plan (section 4.6) for any type of video production, he or she must think in terms of two interacting concerns. On the one hand, there are important considerations that grow out of the *artistic* or *creative needs* of the program. These will be examined in section 4.3. On the other hand, the L.D. knows that the creative aspects of lighting must exist within the larger context of *general illumination,* which is necessary to meet the technical needs of the camera system. These two categories—basic illumination and artistic concerns—correspond to the basic technical and creative functions as introduced in section 2.1.

The term that is usually used to refer to this general or primary illumination is **base light.** The first consideration in providing base light is simply to make sure that there is sufficient illumination so that the cameras can operate. Like the human eye, unless there is a minimum amount of light the camera cannot "see." However, modern cameras can function with a relatively small amount of light. Therefore, our main concerns with base light are achieving a consistency of brightness and maintaining color quality on all cameras on all shots.

Base light should not be thought of as a separate planning entity. It is, rather, the sum total of specialized and general lighting used throughout the set. A specialized artistic effect, light falling on a performer, may also illuminate parts of the set and thereby contribute to the total base light effect. To accomplish an even base light the L.D. must take into consideration two technical aspects of the lighting conditions—whether artificial or natural (sunlight)—*intensity* (contrast ratio) and *color quality* (color temperature).

Contrast Ratio

Intensity, the first of these factors, has to do with the complexities of the video camera pickup tube and the way it reacts to differing degrees of brightness within a single picture. For example, in an evenly lit living room scene on a wide shot, the colors are correctly balanced and the detail of the picture is clear. Now, as we introduce into this shot a person wearing a white raincoat who fills the left-hand quarter of the frame, several rather drastic things happen. The camera's *automatic gain control* (AGC), which maintains an overall brightness level, reacts to the introduction of the very bright area by decreasing the intensity of the rest of the picture. Without any changes in either the lighting or the camera controls, the right-hand three-quarters of the picture will suddenly become much darker. The colors will have a somewhat muddy tone, with the details of the set obscured. The raincoat will be an out-of-focus blur and the person's face a dark spot. Stated in simple terms, the acceptable range of contrast between the brightest and the darkest elements of the picture has been greatly exceeded. The light level, which was previously sufficient for a picture, has been "compressed" by the introduction of an overpowering amount of light.

The human eye can accept a *contrast range* of up to 100 to 1. A somewhat conservative but safe figure for television would be nearer to 30 to 1—or even 20 to 1. This means that the brightest elements within a picture should not be more than twenty or thirty times as bright as the darkest elements.

When elements reflect greatly varying amounts of light (such as the raincoat and the person's face in our example), the problem is even more critical. It is then referred to as a contrast ratio between the two elements. As a rule, lighting directors should try to avoid a contrast ratio of more than about 20 to 1. The picture generally will look better if an extreme ratio is avoided.

While the relative size and degree of brightness of the raincoat in our example is somewhat extreme, the basic principle of contrast range and contrast ratio is an important one to observe when lighting any set or, more important, the people within that set.

There is a very common error that often occurs as students are learning lighting techniques. The faces in the picture may seem too dark, so to solve the problem, more and more light is added to the set, which falls upon the face and on the background. The problem usually is that there is already too much light being reflected from a light-colored background in relation to the light reflected from the face. The problem is compounded if there is too much back light hitting the hair and shoulders (section 4.5).

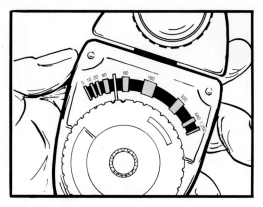

Although construction may vary from model to model, most light meters register light falling on the meter in terms of footcandles (ftc).

Figure 4-1 Light meter scale.

Light Meter. The human eye is much less sensitive in detecting differences of light intensity than a video camera. The relatively narrow range of what is acceptable to the camera as an adequate light level is difficult to judge with the unaided eye. For this reason, all lighting for television should be done with the aid of a **light meter.** Using the **footcandle (ftc)** as a unit of measurement, the meter visually indicates the intensity of light coming from the direction in which the meter is pointed (fig. 4-1).[1]

The intensity of television lighting can be measured in two different ways. We can find out how much *incident* light is falling upon a subject by holding the meter very near the subject and pointing it toward the light source. This incident light measure tells us how much light arrives at a given point. Equally important is the *reflected* light reading, which tells us how much light is reflected from the various surfaces of the subject into the camera lens. For this reflected light reading, point the

1. One footcandle is the amount of light that would fall upon a surface placed at a distance of 1 foot from an established theoretical source approximating the brightness of one candle.

An incident light meter "reads" in footcandles the actual amount of light coming from the light source. A reflected light reading indicates the amount of light reflected back from the surface of the subject being lit.

Figure 4-2 Incident and reflected light readings.

meter directly at the subject from the perspective of the camera. The meter should be held close to the subject, but care must be taken to avoid blocking the light source. Obviously these two methods of measuring light (incident and reflected) will result in two greatly varying readings (fig. 4-2). These two different types of readings are used for different purposes.

For the most part, the light meter is used to measure incident light as it comes from the source. The L.D. first adjusts the strength of individual lighting instruments and then uses the meter from different points in the set to find *hot spots* where overlapping projection patterns have caused the intensity to exceed the average level. These readings, however, do not tell the whole story.

Depending upon the texture and color of a surface, only a percentage of the original source light is reflected into the camera. A light green knitted dress might reflect 30 to 40 percent of the illumination falling upon it, whereas a black knitted dress might reflect less than 10 percent. A white vinyl jacket, on the other hand, might reflect well over 90 percent. Different elements of the set also may have large variations in reflected light bounced back to the camera. These reflected hot spots coming from the set or the performers must be measured by reflected light readings with the meter pointed toward the subjects at close range.

It is these reflected light readings that can tell the L.D. when the contrast ratio for a given camera has been exceeded. If the contrast range is too great, either the bright hot spots must be toned down or the darker areas must have more light. Because reflected light readings are only a small percentage of the power of the original light source, the L.D. may wish to use a second, more specialized, meter with a magnified scale so that the variations are more visually apparent.

In summary, it should be noted that the overall level of base light can best be determined by a direct incident light meter reading. On the other hand, the contrast ratio can be determined only by a comparison of reflected light readings from the brightest and darkest elements in the picture.

Color Temperature

One other factor must be taken into consideration when working with base light for color television. This is the phenomenon of *color temperature*. You have probably noticed that different light sources may have slightly different color tints. A fluorescent bulb gives off more of a bluish light compared to the reddish light given off by an incandescent tungsten bulb. When working with monochrome cameras, the color temperature of different light sources has little effect on the picture quality. In color television, however, the pickup tube is very sensitive to the color temperature of various kinds of light sources.

The color temperature of light is actually measured on a scale known as the Kelvin scale; different light sources are calibrated in degrees Kelvin (K). The redder the light source is, the lower the Kelvin temperature; the bluer a source, the higher the Kelvin temperature. A color temperature between 3,000 degrees K and 3,200 degrees K is considered to be the ideal white light for color television. This is about the range of incandescent bulbs. Most color television lighting is designed to fall within the range of 3,000 degrees K to 3,400 degrees K.

If a light with an ideal Kelvin temperature (say 3,200 degrees K) is used on a dimmer, however; its color temperature will decrease

as the lighting instrument is supplied with less and less voltage (see section 4.6). Thus, a light may give off a perfect white light when operated at full intensity; but when the light is brought down on the dimmer, the subject being lit gradually takes on a reddish tint. This color distortion is not readily perceived by the naked eye, but the color camera is very sensitive to any drop in color temperature over a couple of hundred degrees Kelvin. This is a common error that beginning lighting directors make. Once you have determined that a specific lighting instrument is the correct color temperature (most lighting sources designed for color television are rated at 3,200 degrees K), make certain that you do not lower the voltage of the light by using it on a dimmer (section 4.6) at a setting lower than "8" on a 10-point scale.

Shooting in an outdoor setting where sunlight becomes a major source of illumination necessitates an added awareness of Kelvin temperature. Depending upon haze and cloud conditions, color temperature readings can range from 4,500 to 12,000 degrees K. In these situations, video cameras must be adjusted for the abundance of bluish light (section 5.2). One of the main problems with outdoor shooting occurs as the sun moves across the sky or weather conditions change. Scenes shot during different parts of the day will have differing color values and may not edit well together.

4.3 Lighting Objectives: Creative Purposes

As a creative or artistic factor in video production, lighting can be said to have four main purposes: (1) to define the shape and texture of physical form, and by extension, to create a sense of depth and perspective within the elements of the set or location; (2) to imitate the quality of light characteristic of a situation or setting in reality; (3) to establish and enhance the psychological mood of a performance or setting; and (4) to focus attention upon a single performer or aspect of the production and thereby separate that subject from any feeling of relationship with setting or location.

While this last concept usually has a specialized application, the other three purposes should be thought of as principles that can be simultaneously applied within a given production situation. The same light that gives shape to a person's features can also provide mood and, at the same time, relate to the setting itself (for example, a beam of sunlight coming through a window and falling on the heroine's face). At first glance, it might seem that some of these purposes apply only to dramatic productions. This is not necessarily true. These principles apply to all types of programs from game shows to live news remote transmissions.

Perspective, Shape, and Texture

When a light source is placed right next to a camera, the light waves reflected back into the lens will be of a generally uniform quality. This effect is called *flat lighting* because the illumination has "filled" the hollows and curves that are the distinguishing features of the subject. When the light source is moved so that the beam comes from a different angle, the resulting shadows "etch" the features so that the eye can perceive depth and texture. The camera system functions best when there is an exaggeration of contrasting light values within the video picture. The art of creating the illusion of depth on a flat video tube is largely a matter of accentuating the illumination patterns that we utilize in the normal process of vision.

The experienced lighting director knows that it is the manipulation of shadows, rather than bright spots, that can most effectively add form and texture to any object. Light coming from the side or rear of an object will throw shadows in certain shape-defining ways. Extreme side lighting (at right angles to the camera position) will emphasize textural quality by exaggerating shadows, making any object look much rougher than it would otherwise appear.

The heightened sense of perspective that is necessary to the video picture is simply an application of this basic concept in the context of the entire set. Performers and foreground objects can be separated from the background when the angle and intensity of the light beam are adjusted to create a slight "highlight" effect (section 4.5).

Reality

Light operates on our conditioned responses in other equally important ways. We all have tuned in to the middle of a television play and watched a series of close-up shots. We usually, either consciously or unconsciously, are aware of being indoors or outdoors and of the time of day by the quality of light on the actor's face. It is probably outdoors and near noontime if the light is relatively bright and there are definite shadows under the eyebrows, nose, and chin of the actor. The scene may have been shot inside a studio, but the *imitation of reality* is a product of the lighting.

Other specific shadow and lighting effects suggest certain kinds of realistic situations. Shadows of venetian blinds or prison bars cast on the rear wall of a set help to suggest a particular locale. Other **off-camera** lighting effects help to pinpoint a setting: a low-angle flickering light indicates a campfire or fireplace; a continually flashing red light indicates the presence of an emergency vehicle. Other effects help to further the dramatic narrative: a shaft of light coming from under a door of a room previously unoccupied indicates the presence of an intruder; a flashlight probing around a darkened room helps reveal evidence of a struggle.

Lighting from unusual angles or sources can give unnatural or symbolic effects; for example, lighting from a low angle usually results in a foreboding, sinister appearance.

Figure 4-3 Sinister lighting effect.

Mood

Similarly, the psychological *mood* of a performance or production can be reinforced by the quality of light and its abundance or absence. Comedy is bright; **high-key lighting** is used, which gives an intense overall illumination with a fully lit background. Situation comedies, game shows, and big musical numbers in a variety program would rely on this kind of lighting to establish a light-hearted mood.

Conversely, tragedy or fear are communicated when the area surrounding an actor is dark or dimly lit. **Low-key lighting** refers to selective illumination that highlights only the necessary elements of a picture: usually the background is dark, extreme lighting angles may be used, and only part of the picture is disclosed. Again, specific dramatic moods may

be reinforced by special effects: a flashing neon sign outside a sparsely furnished hotel room suggests a seedy part of town; lightning flashes create an eerie mood; lighting from a low angle tends to give a character a sinister, unnatural appearance (fig. 4-3).

Focus of Attention

When an extreme contrast exists between the light on a subject and the light falling on the visible background area, the eye is drawn to the subject. The most obvious example would be the use of a *follow spot* on a performer in a musical or variety show. Another variation of this technique would be **limbo lighting** where the subject is placed "in limbo" against a softly lit **cyclorama** or some other nondescriptive, neutral background (section 9.2).

Figure 4-4 Typical cameo lighting: figure against a dark background.

Figure 4-5
Representative silhouette lighting: dark figures against a light background

Another way of achieving focus of attention is with **cameo lighting,** where the performer is lit but the background is completely dark (fig. 4-4). A **silhouette** effect—with the performers kept in darkness but outlined against a brightly lit background—may be desired for a dance routine or other special situation (fig. 4-5). A single shaft of light may be used to accent a contestant in a suspenseful climax of a game show. The host of a documentary may be accented with a strong back or side light. Subtle lighting highlights may be used in many other dramatic and nondramatic settings in order to control focus of attention.

So, above and beyond the necessity of using enough base light for basic illumination, the lighting director also must plan creative lighting in order to add shape and texture and perspective, heighten the illusion of reality, create and enhance a specific mood, and focus attention.

4.4 Types of Lighting Instruments

A visit to a commercial supplier of theatrical and television lighting equipment can be a dazzling experience in every sense of the word. There are hundreds of highly specialized pieces of equipment either on display or in the catalogs. One sees a range of instruments designed for the largest studio set as well as the newest lightweight portable gear for EFP and ENG uses. In section 4.5 we will examine the basic studio lighting techniques as a way of establishing a foundation for all video illumination. These principles will be adapted to small-format and EFP production in section 14.4. An understanding of lighting technique is made easier by the fact that most lighting instruments fall into one of two basic categories—the controlled-beam **spotlight** and the diffused-beam **floodlight.** (Many lighting professionals use the term *hardlight* to refer to spotlights, distinguishing it from the "soft" light of a floodlight.)

Controlled-Beam Spotlights

The classic controlled-beam spotlight illustrated in figure 4-6 is the workhorse of studio lighting. The spotlight is used wherever a highly directional beam of light that can be shaped and focused is desired. Its chief characteristic is the ability to throw a spot of light on any particular area or performer. It is commonly referred to as a **Fresnel** (pronounced without the *s*) although each manufacturer will have a different name for it.[2] Figure 4-7 shows the characteristic structure of the Fresnel lens.

In addition to the distinctive lens structure, the other distinguishing feature of the

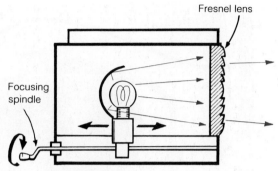

Fresnel lens

Focusing spindle

By turning the focusing handle or spindle, the bulb-reflector unit can be moved toward the lens or back to the rear of the housing. When in the forward position, the spotlight beam is "spread" to cover a relatively wide area. When moved to the rear of the housing, the beam is more narrowly focused, or "pinned," on a smaller area.

Figure 4-6 Focusing mechanism of the Fresnel spotlight.

Plano-convex lens

Fresnel lens

The plano-convex lens and the Fresnel lens have the same surface curvature, enabling them to share identical focusing characteristics. However, by using a succession of concentric ring-shaped steps—with the surface curvature of each concentric ring being congruent with the same relative surface of the plano-convex lens—the weight and bulk of the Fresnel lens is substantially reduced, which also cuts down on the heat buildup

Figure 4-7 Design of the Fresnel lens.

spotlight is the movable assembly that allows the illuminating unit (bulb and reflector) to be transported back and forth between the rear and the front of the instrument.[3] With the bulb

2. The lens generally used in the instrument has a series of raised concentric rings on the outer face that help to dissipate the tremendous heat buildup in the enclosed structure. Augustin Jean Fresnel was a nineteenth-century scientist who did important research into the nature of light.

3. The focusing mechanism described here (and pictured in fig. 4-6) is moved forward or backward by turning a crank or focusing spindle. Other spotlights accomplish this by means of a focusing ring or ring focus, or (on smaller quartz instruments) by a horizontal focusing lever.

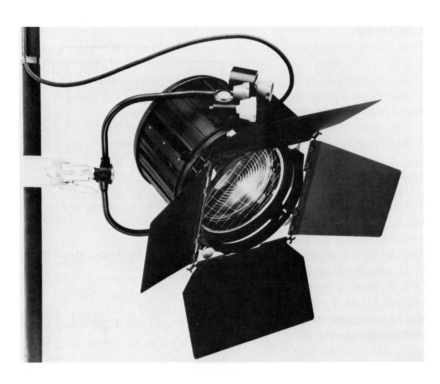

Figure 4-8 Fresnel spotlight. (Photo courtesy of Strand Lighting)

in the rear "pinned" position, the light rays are focused in a narrow beam of high intensity—spreading no more than, perhaps, 10 degrees. As the bulb is moved forward in the housing, the beam becomes "spread" and its intensity is diminished. In the full-forward spread position, the beam forms approximately a 60-degree angle.

The models most generally in use range from 500 watts to 10,000 watts. In a 2,000-watt instrument (commonly called a "junior") a spotted (pinned) light will produce an intensity of 600 footcandles when measured at a distance of 25 feet. In the fully flooded (spread) position, the intensity of the same instrument drops to roughly 60 footcandles—but the light now covers an area six times larger in diameter. Fresnel spots are also classified by the diameter of the lenses. The most common studio sizes are the 6-inch, 8-inch, 10-inch, and 12-inch models.

Some newer lights are designed to be fully adjustable from the floor with a long pole. The 2,000-watt, 8-inch instrument in figure 4-8 has knobs located on either side of the yoke and on the lower assembly that can be engaged by a connector on the end of a matching pole. The light can be spotted and flooded, adjusted up and down, and moved sideways back and forth without the crew member having to climb a ladder.

The **ellipsoidal,** or **leko,** spotlight shown in figure 4-9 gains its name from its fixed reflecting mirror at the back of the unit. By means of its tube shape and focused lens (either Fresnel or **plano-convex**), it projects an intense directional beam that is well defined at its edge point.

The beam can be further shaped by movable metal shutters (also known as *cutters*) located inside the lamp housing, behind the lens.

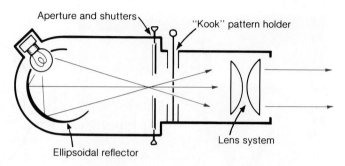

Aperture and shutters

"Kook" pattern holder

Lens system

Ellipsoidal reflector

Light rays are reflected from the ellipsoidal reflector and focused through the aperture. At this point the shutters can be partially closed to shape or narrow the beam of light. Special cucalorus patterns may also be inserted at this point to project hard-edged shadows. The beam is then further focused through the lens system and projected as a sharp directional beam with a well-defined edge.

Figure 4-9 Lens system of the ellipsoidal spotlight.

Figure 4-10 Ellipsoidal spotlight. *Left,* ellipsoidal spotlight (photo courtesy of Strand Lighting); *right,* example of a shadow pattern cast by a "cookie" inserted in a leko (ellipsoidal) spotlight.

At this point—where all the reflected rays of light are in sharp focus—there is also a place to insert a patterned metal design cutout. The shadow of this **cucalorus** or **cookie** or **kook** is then projected to add visual interest to large, plain background surfaces. Some common kook patterns include prison bars; arabesques and Moorish motifs (fig. 4-10); venetian blinds; crosses, squares, and other geometric designs; cloud patterns; and so forth.

Because it throws a very harsh beam, the ellipsoidal spot is rarely used as the basic instrument in lighting a person or object for television. It is to be used strictly as a special effects light.

Figure 4-11 The basic scoop. Scoops are designed for both incandescent bulbs and for quartz lighting. Popular sizes for most television studio applications are the 14-inch and 16-inch diameters (photo courtesy of Strand Lighting). Drawing indicates the diffused pattern of the reflected light rays.

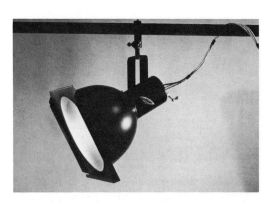

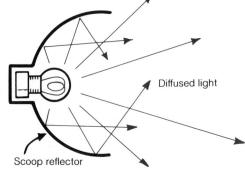

Diffused light

Scoop reflector

There are several other varieties of fixed-beam spotlights. One popular type is much like an auto headlight with the lens, bulb, and reflector built together as a single unit. This *internal reflector* spotlight is common as a portable source of light, or—as a *clip light*—it often is used to fill in and highlight areas that are otherwise not adequately lighted.

Another type of portable spotlight is the *external reflector* model, which is a highly efficient quartz lamp in a small housing with no lens. Although not as controllable and precise as a Fresnel spot, this model is lightweight, easily moved (often with a clip-on attachment or a lightweight tripod), and is more than adequate for most remote lighting assignments.

Floodlights

When we examine the specific techniques of lighting (section 4.5) we shall see that the effects of the focused-beam spotlight are balanced by the use of a somewhat lesser amount of softer light from a different angle. The purpose of this light source is to soften and thereby control the shadows that are created by the angle of the focused spotlight. When a number of *floodlights* are used in a set, the effect is a soft diffused light that eases the harshness of the shadows.

To help achieve the shadowless effect of a large source area, the floodlight does not use a lens; it will probably have a diffusing reflector, which has the effect of spreading out the source; it may use a soft-light bulb with no exposed filament at all; and it may use a **scrim**—a soft, spun-glass filter or other translucent piece of material in a rigid frame, attached to the front of the instrument (see section 4.6).

The classic model for a floodlight is the half hollow globe structure known as a **scoop** (fig. 4-11). Its large reflecting area is made of a light-diffusing material that spreads the illumination in a nonfocused scattered pattern. Floodlights built in a rectangular shape are known as **pans** or **broads** (fig. 4-12). Some of these have controls that allow for an adjustment of the degree of spread. Their square shape makes possible the additional use of blocking devices known as **barn doors** (see section 4.6). A 2,000-watt floodlight will have a pattern of illumination that is more than twice the area of a 2,000-watt Fresnel spotlight in the maximum spread position.

When a series of pans are constructed in a continuous side-by-side row, they are called **strip lights** (fig. 4-13). They are most often used—frequently with colored **gels**—in lighting the background **cyclorama** (**cyc**, pronounced "sike") or other large set surfaces. Each individual lamp will typically be from 500 to 1,000 watts.

For larger studio productions, huge multibulb instruments such as that pictured in figure 4-14 may be used. Such an 8,000-watt "super-softlight" may either be mounted on a

Figure 4-12 The *pan* shape of the reflector or the *broad* beam provided is the source of the name that describes the lighting instrument. *Left,* pan mounted on a floor stand (photo courtesy of Mole Richardson); *right,* ColorTran 1-K broad with barn doors.

Figure 4-13 Strip lights.

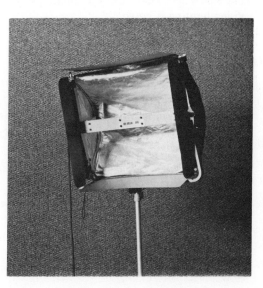

Figure 4-14 Super Softlights. *Left,* in this 8-K *super softlight,* there is no direct light from the eight 1,000-watt quartz bulbs; all light is reflected by the large curved surface (photo courtesy of Mole Richardson). *Right,* the Lowel Softlight 1500 has two bulbs that bounce light off the canvas reflector impregnated with foil for a diffused light.

floor stand or hung from a lighting grid (section 4.6). The eight 1,000-watt bulbs can be separately controlled in order to produce a variety of intensity levels. The bulbs are positioned so that only diffused light is sent out from the large reflector.

Today, most spotlights and floodlights are designed to use the **quartz** bulb (also referred to as a *globe* or *bottle*). The term "quartz" is applied to a variety of quartz-iodine, tungsten-halogen, and similar illumination sources of bulbs that have largely replaced the incandescent bulb. The advantages of the quartz bulb are that it is smaller, longer-lasting, more efficient (producing more illumination per watt), and does not darken with carbon deposits as it gets older. It does, however, tend to lose some of its Kelvin temperature as it ages—producing a slightly yellowish light.

This brief review of lighting instruments barely suggests the number and variety of equipment that is available. In the past decade, leading manufacturers have developed a whole new generation of highly efficient, light-weight, and portable lighting systems. This section has been presented to provide a practical background for an understanding of the principles on which all stage, film, and television lighting is based.

4.5 Fundamental Lighting Concepts

As noted in section 4.3, creative lighting is largely a matter of careful control of the effects of both light and shadow.

Three-Point Lighting

The specific techniques through which these effects are accomplished can be easily understood by examining the classic lighting setup borrowed from motion pictures. It is known as *three-point lighting* because it involves the use of three different light sources—the **key light,** the **fill light,** and the **back light.** Each has a separate effect upon the subject being lit since the three lights differ in relative angle or direction (or apparent source), level of intensity, and the degree to which they are either focused or diffused. Taken together, the cumulative effect is that of a balanced and aesthetic unity—what Rembrandt called a "golden triangle" of light. Figure 4-15 illustrates how the three sources are used in a typical situation. This three-point lighting arrangement provides not only the *base light* but also meets the *creative purposes* of form and texture, reality, mood, and focus of attention.

It is important to keep in mind that our three-point lighting model is an ideal, based upon a concept that was developed for film production where a *single* camera shoots the subject or subjects from one angle only. Each shot could be separately set up and lit. The ways in which this underlying concept is modified to apply to multiple-camera, continuous-action video production follow. (Single-camera EFP video production, of course, can come closer to the filmic model of separate setups with balanced three-point lighting carefully plotted for each shot; see section 14.4.)

Key Light. The primary, most important illumination in any lighting plan would be the *key* light. It is the apparent source of the light hitting the talent and provides the majority of the light that is reflected into the camera lens (see fig. 14-17). Almost invariably, a spotlight is used for the key light; its strength and directional beam emphasize the contrast of light and shadow, defining the shape and texture of the subject. It is the use of the key light that brings out the features of the face and illuminates the eye itself.

While more extreme angles can be used to produce special dramatic effects, the optimum result is achieved by placing the key off to one side of the face of the subject, coming in at an angle between 30 and 35 degrees. (If the key

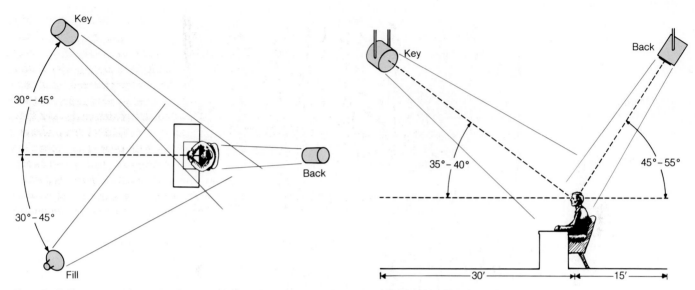

The key light and the fill light should normally be placed approximately 30 to 45 degrees from a line drawn straight in front of the talent (with the fill being more directly in front of the talent). The back light should theoretically be directly behind the talent, at a steeper angle than the two front lights.

Figure 4-15 Three-point lighting.

light is placed directly in front of the talent, the result is a flat, washed-out appearance with no shadows, no sculpting or molding of the face.) The height of the key will depend to some extent upon the facial contours of the talent. It should be placed high enough to produce a slight shadow under the chin and nose, yet it must be low enough to get the light directly into the eye socket itself. (If the talent has deep-set eyes and the key light is at too steep an angle, the result is simply two dark shadows under the eyebrows.) A good rule of thumb is that the key should normally be placed at a 35-to-40-degree angle above the vision line of the subject.

In setting all lights—but especially the key—you must consider carefully the angle of the light hitting the subject as it relates to the intensity of the light being reflected back into the camera lens. In terms of the basic laws of optics, *the angle of incidence equals the angle of reflection,* or reflected light bounces off of a flat surface at the same angle as the incoming light hits the surface.

If you have a light source projecting a beam perfectly perpendicular to a flat surface, that beam will reflect directly back upon itself. However, if you raise the light source so as to create a 30-degree angle above the perpendicular, as in figure 4-16, then the reflected beam will bounce back downward at a corresponding angle of 30 degrees. If the subject being lit has a rough texture or uneven surface, the reflected light will be diffused and this angle is not important. However, if you are lighting a smooth and relatively polished surface (such as vinyl or even oily skin), this angle can become very critical.

Applying this principle to the way light is reflected from the face of a subject, you can see how the relatively smooth (and sometimes oily) surfaces of the forehead and nose can create shiny, highly reflective, hot spots as light is bounced back directly into the camera lens.

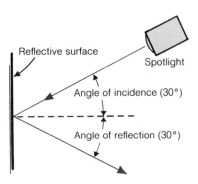

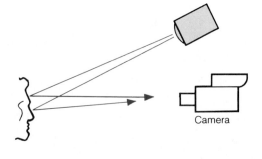

Figure 4-16 Angles of incidence and reflection.

Basic laws of optics tell us that the angle at which the rays of light hit a flat reflective surface (angle of incidence) will equal the angle at which the reflected rays (angle of reflection) bounce away from the surface. Therefore, if the reflective surface (talent's shiny forehead or gleaming nose) is normally sloped, the reflected light from the spotlight may well be bounced back directly into the camera lens causing an unwanted highlight or glare. Close coordination between the lighting director and makeup personnel is necessary to avoid this problem.

Figure 4-17 Subject with key light only.

This same effect may occur many times over within a large set with its various angles and planes. Similarly, productions using studio graphics mounted on cards may have trouble with reflected glare—unless a dull matte surface is used or the cards are properly angled to reflect the light away from the camera lens (section 9.5).

Fill Light. In order to "fill in" on the dark side of the face or object being lit, some sort of *fill* light is needed. It should come in at an angle on the side opposite from the key. Ordinarily a floodlight (such as a scoop or broad) would be used, although a spotlight in its *flooded* position often can be effective. In any case, a soft diffused light is desired. (See figs.

Figure 4-18 Subject with fill light only. Note the spill on the background cyc.

Figure 4-19 Subject with balanced key and fill lighting.

4-18 and 4-19.) It is used simply to soften the shadows and give some illumination to the otherwise dark side of the talent. Fill light should not be as strong or as directional as key light; it should not compete in creating shadows or countering the shaping qualities of the key.

In much color television production, a great amount of fill light is used to achieve a consistently even *wash* of illumination over the entire set. In this application, the fill light comes close to serving the same purpose as base light (see section 4.2).

Figure 4-20 Subject with back light only.

Figure 4-21 Subject with balanced three-point lighting (key, fill, and back light).

Back Light. As the name implies, *back* light comes from behind and above the subject. A spotlight is virtually always used so that the light can be directed and focused like the key. The back light falls upon and, as a result, accentuates such features as hair, shoulders, and top surfaces of set elements. (See figs. 4-20 and 4-21.) This highlighting effect separates the talent from the background, adding to the illusion of depth within the total picture.

Without adequate back light, the subject appears flat and tends to blend in with the background—as in figure 4-17.

Back light requirements will vary with the color of the subject, the background, and the desired effect. Hair color and texture are especially crucial. For example, blondes require relatively little back light. Their natural hair color separates them from the background. Also, tightly curled hair generally needs extra back light because it does not reflect light well.

Auxiliary Light Sources

There are several other terms that refer to more specialized types of lighting. Two of these are actually variations of key and back light. A *side light* is a key that hits the subject on the side of the face—usually at about eye level. A **kicker** is basically a back light that works at an angle (maybe 45 degrees from dead center) instead of directly behind the subject.

One of the most important additional sources of illumination is the **set light** or **background light** (not to be confused with the *back* light). This is the major source of lighting for the cyclorama or background set behind the performers. In addition to helping fill in the overall picture (basic illumination), background lighting can give form and texture to the setting, provide a sense of reality, or suggest mood (creative functions). Set lighting can tell the audience whether it is an indoor or outdoor locale, in daytime or evening. Specific locations can be suggested by certain kinds of window effects or cookie patterns in the ellipsoidal spot (venetian blinds, prison bars). Mood can be reinforced with high-key or low-key lighting. Colored gels on a plain cyclorama can help to establish mood on a color production.

In one function or another, most types of lighting instruments can be appropriately used for background lighting. Floodlights (scoops or strip lights) are often used for general illumination of a cyclorama or flat space. Spotlights can be used to highlight certain areas or present dramatic lighting effects (for example, strong diagonal slashes of light or selected low-key elements). And, of course, the ellipsoidal spot can be used with a variety of cucalorus patterns for various shadow effects. (See figs. 4-10 and 9-14.)

Other special lighting effects depend upon careful background lighting. A good *silhouette* demands an evenly lit background, balanced from top to bottom as well as from side to side. A good *cameo* effect, on the other hand, requires a complete lack of any light hitting the background; front lighting must be carefully controlled to make certain that no spill is reflected onto the set behind the talent.

The background lighting must also be balanced with the three-point subject lighting to ensure that no undesired semi-silhouette effect is attained. As mentioned in section 4.2, if the background is too strongly lit, the faces of people in front of the background will tend to go dark by comparison.

Actually, in any moderately complicated lighting setup, the illumination is coming from many directions and angles. In addition, the subjects—the persons being lit—will be moving within the set. The concept of key, back, and fill lights should be used as a guide, not as a rigid set of rules. Auxiliary lighting and special effects will be added as needed for certain creative purposes. The important consideration is that the lighting director be totally in control of the *direction, intensity, quality* (harsh shadows or diffused), and *color* (if applicable) of light falling upon performers and set.

Multiple-Camera Lighting

As mentioned earlier, the concept of three-point lighting was developed for the motion picture single-camera technique. With this approach, every shot has its own lighting setup. When the subject and camera are moved, the lighting is changed. Detailed care can be taken to sculpt the face and other features of the subject with the key light, blended with back and fill lights.

With television's multiple-camera formats and continuous-action productions, lighting directors found it difficult to adhere to the pure disciplines of classic three-point lighting. In a game show or variety program, for example—shot from three or four cameras (and possibly even more angles)—the participants and performers move unpredictably all over the set. The solution to this situation is to create a base light *wash* throughout the entire set. The result is a "flat" but practical lighting job.

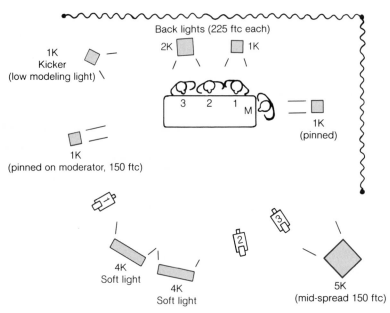

Back lights (225 ftc each)

1K
Kicker
(low modeling light)

2K   1K

1K
(pinned)

1K
(pinned on moderator, 150 ftc)

4K
Soft light

4K
Soft light

5K
(mid-spread 150 ftc)

Figure 4-22 "Plan A" lighting plot.   Modified three-point lighting plan designed for participants primarily addressing the audience.

Some situation comedies shot with electronic multiple-camera techniques have had substantial success in overlaying the concept of three-point lighting within a flat-lit set. Working together, the TV director and lighting director can select points within the scene where the actors will remain in place for a period of time; in these spots careful three-point lighting can be used for close-ups. When portions of the scene contain physical movement, the action is picked up by the cameras on wider shots (section 6.2)—so the flat lighting will not matter as much. Close-ups are kept to a minimum in the areas lit by flat lighting. It is a compromise, but it works fairly well.

Daytime serials ("the soaps") that crank out an hour a day of multiple-camera production are hard pressed to do much in the way of delicate lighting; but using the above technique, they do manage to achieve an overall satisfactory lighting effect. Since productions of all types operate within tight budget limitations, lighting directors never have all of the time and crew they need to do a perfect job.

They simply do the best they can with what resources they have. But in all video production, three-point lighting—with its potential for texture, depth, modeling, perspective, and focus—remains the standard against which all lighting work is measured.

Different Production Approaches.   As a way of examining some of the problems of multiple-camera lighting—as well as their solutions—look at the example of a four-person discussion program such as the one suggested by the "Frame of Reference" script in appendix D-3. The participants are seated in an L shape with the host on the camera-right side. This arrangement allows the host to keep eye contact with the three guests while leading the discussion.

If the nature of the format is such that the three guests will tend to speak straight out to an audience area behind the camera 2 location, and the host will often address the viewers by means of camera 1, then you can use the "Plan A" lighting plot as shown in figure 4-22.

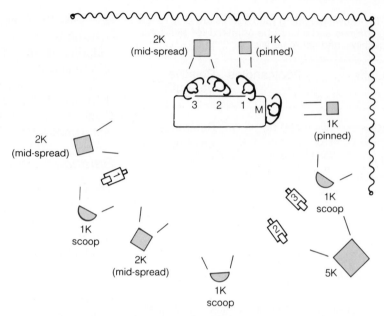

Cross-key lighting may be appropriate when participants are involved in considerable give-and-take head-turning discussion.

Figure 4-23 "Plan B" lighting plot.

In this plan, you would be using a modified three-point lighting setup.

If, however, your program is such that the guests for the most part turn to each other and to the host during the course of the discussion, then the "Plan B" lighting arrangement (fig. 4-23) would be more appropriate—utilizing a *cross-key* lighting technique.

Three-Point Lighting. In the "Plan A" plot, the key light is provided by the 5-kilowatt Fresnel-type spotlight, which is spread so that it covers all four participants. Its angle will create slight shadows on the faces of the three guests. It should be tilted so that its light also falls on the cyclorama in the background. Fill light is provided by the two 4-kilowatt *softlights* (see fig. 4-14) from the camera-left side.

One possible problem would be that when guests 1 and 2 occasionally turn to their right to speak to guest 3 (on the camera-left side) they would have only fill light on their faces—from the angle of camera 1. This problem can

be solved by placing a spotlight *kicker* from over their right shoulders to provide a "modeling" light effect. To do its job properly, this controlled-beam light should be hung as low as possible, but not so low that the head of one guest would cast a shadow on the side of another guest's face.

The host is covered by a pinned spot from a slightly different angle from the camera 1 shooting perspective. This gives the host's face some shape and definition. The host's fill light comes from the two *softlights*.

The back lights are located as indicated on the lighting plot (fig. 4-22). Their intensity should be adjusted to take into account the relative back light needed by blondes and brunettes—as well as light or dark clothing around the shoulder area. Check the light falling on the cyclorama to be sure that its quality is even behind all camera shots. Problems can be solved by placing additional scoops or broads to fill any dark spots.

The following lighting ratio figures are only rough guidelines and should be adjusted for skin tone, clothing, and set materials.

Light	Footcandles	Relative Strength
Key	150 ftc.	Reference point of 1
Fill	75 ftc.	½ of key
Back	225-300 ftc.	1½ to 2 times key
Background	75-115 ftc.	½ to ¾ of key

Figure 4-24 Ratio of key, back, fill, and set lights.

Cross-Key Lighting. On the other hand, if the discussion program is expected to be such that most of the conversation will take place with participants facing each other, then camera 3 (and possibly camera 2) would be moved farther to the right so that most camera shots will not be profiles of the people speaking. The participants—especially guests 1 and 2—now need to be lit from two divergent camera angles (as they will be facing both to their right and to their left at different times). One solution to the situation is *cross-key* lighting as illustrated in figure 4-23. Most lighting directors would consider this "Plan B" approach a compromise at best.

Cross-key lighting can usually be accomplished with spread spots from four different positions. Some additional fill light should be used to soften the keys and to make sure that the cyc is evenly lit. There still may be unflattering shadows on both sides of the noses (resulting from the relatively harsh controlled-beam spotlights hitting the subjects from opposite directions). This effect is known as a *butterfly.*

There is a variation of *wash* lighting that can solve the butterfly problem. You simply fill the entire set from all angles with illumination from a number of floodlights and *softlights.* There are no harsh shadows remaining. You

have solved the "butterfly" problem, but the trade-off is that you now have no modeling or sculpting at all—all of the faces are completely flat. An adequate lighting job, however, has been accomplished in a relatively short period of time—a compromise at best. Good, strong back light is especially important with this type of wash lighting.

Balanced Lighting by Ratio

The first thing a lighting director must do in creating a three-point lighting pattern is to decide on the relative strengths of each of the source lights. There are some basic guidelines that lighting directors use in making their preliminary plans. Figure 4-24 shows an average ratio of key, back, and fill lights that can be applied in most basic lighting situations. The footcandle figures represent incident meter readings that would be made at the point where light strikes the subject.

The key light, being the primary light source, is given the reference point of 1. Other light sources are then adjusted in relation to the strength of the key. The back light is typically up to 1½ the strength of the key. And the fill is roughly ½ of the strength of the key.

Such ratios are only guidelines, of course. Once the lights are turned on, the lighting director can then check the shot through the camera monitor and get a better picture of the reflective qualities of the subject and the rest of the set. The final lighting decisions have to be based upon many factors, such as color and shading of the object being lit, texture and shade of the background, the illusion of reality, and the desired mood. Particular care must be taken with skin tone and hair. Too much light on the hair and shoulders can cause the face to look relatively darker than it naturally would be. If any picture elements appear out of balance they should then be checked by reflected light meter readings.

Of the three fundamental light sources, the back light is the most difficult to measure and to work with. Achieving the desired effect of highlighting the hair, shoulders, and so forth, calls for considerable intensity. Because of the steep angle of the typical back light, much of this intensity does not reflect into the camera. The direct incident meter reading, therefore, will seem quite high in relation to the effect on the picture. Because it is usually much closer to the subject than the key light, the wattage needed in the back-light lamps will often be less than that used for the key lights.

The light falling upon the background, which usually has its own independent sources, also consists of some contribution (*spill*) by both the key and fill lights. For this reason, it is sometimes difficult to predict background light level accurately in the initial plan. The reflective quality of background materials varies considerably. The same amount of incident footcandles falling upon a light-colored cyclorama and upon dark wood paneling will produce considerably different amounts of light reflected into the camera.

As we have stated, during the process of lighting setup, the basic lighting balance is achieved by means of incident light reading. When the performers are in place, there must be a final adjustment process that should utilize a more accurate set of reflected light readings. The footcandle readings will, of course, be on a much lower scale, but the same basic ratio will apply. Again, however, the final suitability of a picture should never rest with an arbitrary ratio and a light meter. Ultimately it comes down to how the picture looks on the monitor to the director and the lighting director.

Economy of Lighting

Frugality in the use of lighting instruments is an important consideration. Good lighting technique is often as much a matter of knowing when to take out or dim lights as it is of knowing how to add lights to a set. The modeling and texturing effects of a few well-placed key lights are easily wiped out by adding too many lights from too many directions. As newer cameras are developed that require less light for basic illumination, it is possible to be more artistic and creative in the use of selective lighting—as long as you maintain the even base light needed for color production.

Another important consideration is the manipulation and control of unwanted shadows. Although facial and textural shadows are desired for modeling and dimension, many kinds of shadows are undesirable and distracting. An obvious example is the shadow of a microphone boom on the set behind the performers. Other examples are the shadows often cast by other performers, by large props, or sometimes by the camera itself. Many a beginning lighting person has tried to counteract these unwanted shadows by adding more light to the shaded area—trying to "burn out" the shadow. In essence, what this does is throw the overall lighting intensity out of balance, producing hot spots for the camera. The correct solution is to eliminate the shadow—either by moving or repositioning the object casting the shadow (such as raising the boom arm) or by moving or controlling the light source (for example, by lighting from another angle or by masking off part of the light with barn doors as outlined in section 4.6).

4.6 Studio Lighting Procedures

Having looked at some of the basic television lighting requirements and concepts, we are ready to consider the actual techniques and procedures involved in lighting a television setting. Several of these aspects also involve practice and discipline in the execution of specific lighting functions—for example, in the precise preparation and use of lighting plans and plots and in careful observance of all safety precautions.

Figure 4-25 Two types of lighting ladders: *left,* ladder with four free-wheeling casters, must be steadied by an assistant on the floor; *right,* the ladder with a tricycle steering arrangement and a lockable wheel can be operated by one person.

Mounting Lighting Instruments

The first concern should be the way that the lights are actually mounted or supported. How are they to be positioned and held in place? Basically, there are two ways—by hanging them from above or by mounting them on a *floor stand.*

Hanging Mounts. Most television studios are equipped with a **lighting grid** for mounting lights above the staging areas. This facility gets the lighting instruments up at about the right height for most applications and leaves the studio floor uncluttered for camera and talent movement, microphone placement, and various set elements. Most studios have some sort of pipe grid or batten system upon which the lights are actually suspended. The pipe grid is a rigid permanent arrangement of pipes a foot or two beneath the studio ceiling; the lights are fixed directly to the pipes by any one of several kinds of hanging devices. The counter-weighted batten system, on the other hand, allows the battens to be raised or lowered by some sort of counterweight system so that lights can easily be worked on from the studio floor.

After lights are hung in the right position, final adjustments (**trimming**) have to be made at the operating height, even on a counter-weighted batten. Some of these might be accomplished with a *light pole,* which can be inserted into the ring-focus mechanism on some spotlights to adjust the spot-flood position of the bulb-reflector unit. Some larger studios will have a *catwalk,* which allows lighting operators to move around on a permanent scaffolding to reach most of the lights from above. In most studios, however, some sort of special movable *lighting ladder* is used that allows lighting personnel to climb up to any instrument for final adjustments and focusing. Two types of studio ladders are pictured in figure 4-25.

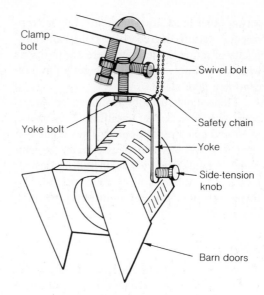

The C-clamp holding this Fresnel spotlight to a pipe grid has four adjusting screws or bolts.

Figure 4-26 C-clamp.

Lighting instruments may actually be connected to the grid or batten with a variety of fastening devices. Many are simply placed into position with a **C-clamp,** which connects the light firmly to the grid but allows for no vertical adjustment of the instrument (fig. 4-26). A *sliding rod* and a **telescope hanger** are two arrangements whereby a light can be attached to the bottom of a long rod that can be positioned at varying heights on the grid or batten. The **pantograph** is a scissors-like spring-counterbalanced hanger that allows lights to be pulled down or pushed up quickly and easily to any level. This is the most convenient arrangement for rapid adjustments and easy positioning of lighting instruments.

Floor Stands. In many kinds of studio arrangements, the suspended lights often have to be supplemented by lights mounted on floor stands. Although too many floor stands would tend to clutter the studio floor and get in the way of other production elements, they do represent a certain degree of flexibility and simplicity of setup. Sometimes there are positions where it is simply impossible to get a light except on a floor stand.

Floor stands usually are mounted on tripods with casters that facilitate easy movement and quick repositioning. They come in a variety of weights and sizes capable of handling many different kinds of lighting instruments. Of course, for location productions (wherever supplemental lighting is needed), the portable floor stand is indispensable.

Lighting Control

The video camera system is extremely sensitive. Optimum performance is possible only when illumination is kept within certain carefully prescribed limits. The lighting director must work within the following four separate yet interrelated parameters in order to achieve the artistic and technical purposes of lighting:

1. The level of intensity
2. The degree of focus or diffusion
3. The shape of the projected beam
4. The color quality

After the initial setup is completed the lighting director, working with the director and video control operator, makes a continuing series of adjustments throughout the rehearsal period and prior to the final take. There are a number of mechanical and electronic controls that are utilized during this process.

Intensity. We have already described the way in which the beam from a Fresnel-type lamp can be spread in order to lessen its intensity and at the same time cover a much wider area. It must be remembered that the fully spread beam has only a small fraction of the intensity of the strength of a pinned beam.

Inverse Square Law. Whether a beam is focused or diffused, there is another factor that has important implications in terms of intensity. Although it is not easily apparent to the naked eye, variations in the distance between a source light and the subject create large differences in intensity.

The same *inverse square law,* which determined for us that sound from a given source drops off in ratio to the square of the distance from that source as the distance is increased (see section 3.3), also applies to the rate at which light strength decreases with distance. Figure 4-27 gives an indication of how critical a move of even 10 feet can be at shorter distances. It must also be noted, however, that the *rate* of drop-off is not as critical when distances from the lamp to the subject are relatively long. We can examine the impact of this effect by considering two very different lighting examples.

Let us assume we have a news crew doing an interview at night. The only source of light is a *clip-on* spotlight attached to the camera itself. The meter gives us an incident reading of 200 footcandles on the subjects at a distance of 10 feet. Using figure 4-27 as a rough guide, we can figure that if our subjects move back 5 feet, we will have a reading of less than 100 footcandles. The loss of half of the available light will make a severe difference in the quality of the picture the camera can produce.

On the other hand, let us look at a typical studio situation. We have a camera that gives us our desired picture with 200 footcandles. And, because we are working with powerful lights, we are getting that reading on our performer at a distance of 40 feet from the lights. Now, if our performer moves backward 5 feet, we will lose less than 20 footcandles. Examination of figure 4-27 will reveal how the rate of decline diminishes (per unit of distance) as the distance is increased.

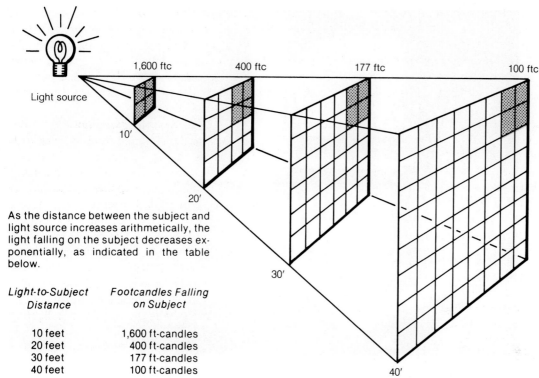

| 1,600 ftc | 400 ftc | 177 ftc | 100 ftc |

Light source

10′

20′

30′

40′

As the distance between the subject and light source increases arithmetically, the light falling on the subject decreases exponentially, as indicated in the table below.

Light-to-Subject Distance	Footcandles Falling on Subject
10 feet	1,600 ft-candles
20 feet	400 ft-candles
30 feet	177 ft-candles
40 feet	100 ft-candles

Figure 4-27 Inverse square law applied to television lighting.

If we expand our last example and think in terms of a large studio drama production shot from multiple camera angles, we can see why such a production would have a number of lights hung at distances of 30 to 40 feet. The longer source-to-subject distance provides for forward and backward stage movement without fear of substantial light level changes—and at the same time the lower vertical angle (fig. 4-15) helps to assure that there are no shadows in the eye sockets.

The Dimmer Board. Located at some distance from the actual lighting instruments—either in a corner of the studio or in some control room—is the patching and control equipment. In any kind of sizable studio operation, this is centered around the dimmer board. Although dimmers vary tremendously in construction and operation, they all function on the same general principle: by controlling the amount of power that flows to the lighting instrument, the lamp gives off more or less light. Two types of dimmer boards are shown in figure 4-28.

Patching and dimming equipment is, in many ways, analogous to the patch panel and console in the audio control booth. Apart from the creative considerations, we are concerned with power flow instead of signal flow. There is a basic routing system for getting power to a light.

This equipment varies greatly from one studio to another in both sophistication and capacity. It would serve little purpose, therefore, to attempt to describe all of the possible techniques of patching operation that would follow the many individual designs. This is best learned from the specific construction of the equipment in your own studio. As a frame of

Figure 4-28 Two types of dimmer board installations. (Top photo courtesy of KCET, Los Angeles)

reference to that process, it may help to consider some fundamental functions common to all lighting control equipment.

When a light on a grid has been connected to the nearby numbered line or grid outlet, the electrical power to turn on that light is available from two different sources in most studio setups—either a nondimmer circuit or a dimmer circuit. If no intensity control over the lamp is needed, a patch is made from the grid outlet or *load circuit* to a numbered nondimmer circuit and turned on at the switch or circuit breaker. This connection is normally referred to as a *hot patch*. If intensity control is called for, the patch is made from the load circuit into the dimmer board for a controlled power source. Here the circuitry may vary according to the design of the board.

In most boards, multiple units of lights can be connected into a single dimmer circuit. There is, of course, a definite limit to the amount of power that can be fed to any one circuit. This limit must be ascertained and always observed.

As mentioned in section 4.2, when there is a reduction in the amount of current being supplied to a bulb filament, there is a corresponding lowering of the Kelvin color temperature of the light. Care must be exercised so that key and fill lights are not dimmed into the yellow or red ranges. Because back lights do their job of separation without reflecting as much light directly into the lens, they can be dimmed into the yellow range without as much apparent effect.

Selection of Instruments. Our final note on intensity is one which should seem obvious, but it is one that is all too often forgotten in the pressure of production activity. The lighting director must choose the *correct* instruments and the correct *number* of instruments to do the job at hand. Frequently, lighting crew personnel will spend time trying to adjust a 2 kw (2,000-watt) spotlight when a 1 kw or even a 500-watt unit might be more

Figure 4-29 Lighting scrims: *top,* half scrim; *bottom,* full scrim. (Photos courtesy of Mole Richardson)

suitable. Similarly, the use of too many instruments can enormously complicate the process of achieving proper light levels. Or you might be trying to spread one spotlight too thin when you really need separate instruments to cover the areas needed.

Focus and Diffusion. There are several ways by which diffused light is created and controlled in order to keep it in its proper perspective in relation to the focused key light. The primary control factor is that of adjusting intensity through some of the methods described earlier. Placement is also very important. The best diffused light is achieved by using several instruments placed at differing angles.

There are also several devices that are important to the lighting director's toolbox. The most commonly used pieces of equipment for these purposes are either attached to the front of the instrument or mounted in front of it.

A *scrim* is a wire mesh shaped to fit the front of the lighting instrument (fig. 4-29). It works by scattering the beam and cutting back

Figure 4-30 Foil reflector. The two-sided reflector is an invaluable part of all outdoor location shooting. The partitioned foil-leaf side (shown) produces a soft diffused light. A smooth silver-paper surface on the other side produces a brighter, more intense light. (Photo courtesy of Mole Richardson)

on intensity. Scrims are used to soften a spread Fresnel light. To further soften scoops, pans, and broads, a clothlike opaque filter made out of spun and pressed fiberglass is used. Available in three thicknesses, it greatly cuts down on the intensity and projects a soft, almost shadowless light.

When shooting outdoors, using the sun as a key light, a *foil reflector* is often used to provide a relatively diffused fill light (fig. 4-30). It can also be used to provide a key light with the sun serving as the back light.

Shape. If lighting directors had to work with only the large raw beam projected by most instruments, then their work would be difficult indeed. Fortunately, there are a number of shaping devices that are used to modify and block parts of the beam.

One of the main difficulties is that of controlling the overlap of multiple light sources, which produces high-intensity hot spots. The most common solution to this problem is achieved through the use of *barn door* shutters, which are attached to the front of a spotlight (see fig. 4-8). Used in pairs or sets of four, these hinged plates can provide an adjustable edge to the beam. By moving the shutters, both the height and width of the projected light can be limited. Most assemblies can be rotated to provide maximum adjustment. In a "leko" or ellipsoidal lamp, the movable shutters are inside the instrument (adjusted with outside handles) in order to provide an even greater definition to the projected pattern (see fig. 4-9).

There are times when the lighting director needs to create a small area of reduced intensity *within* a projected beam. For this a *flag* or *gobo* is used. These are rectangles of varying size either made of metal or of frames covered with black cloth. They can be hung from the lighting grid or mounted on a floorstand in a position to block out the light to a specific area (fig. 4-31). One use, for example, would be to cast a slight shadow on the forehead and top of the head of a person with thinning hair who otherwise might appear almost bald under bright lights on a close-up shot.

Occasionally, an added amount of light must be pinpointed at a particular area of the set. If barn doors cannot project quite as precise a pattern as needed, then a *top hat* or *stovepipe* can be used to do the job (fig. 4-32). Inserted in the same frame designed to hold the barn doors, the top hat—which ranges in size from 4 inches to 1 foot—can reduce the spotlight's beam to a smaller, clearly defined circle without increasing the intensity of the spot.

The *cucalorus* (the kook or the cookie, as it is often called) is a cutout design that, when placed in front of a spot, projects a pattern upon a cyclorama or large set surface. Ellipsoidal spotlights are designed so that smaller metal kooks can be inserted into the instrument housing by means of a "dipstick" (see fig. 4-9).

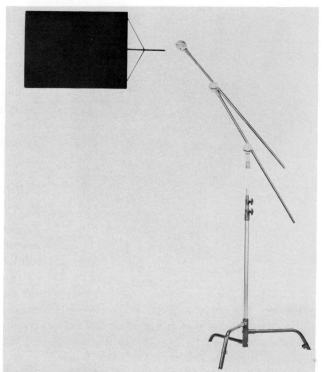

Figure 4-31 Flag. Flags are used to block the light on specific areas of the performer or set. With their stands and extension arms, they provide an important final control over illumination. (Photo courtesy of Mole Richardson)

Figure 4-32 Top hat with several adaptor rings to control the size of the light allowed to hit the set. The top hat, or stovepipe, is another blocking device that provides a more precise light pattern. (Photo courtesy of Mole Richardson)

Figure 4-33 Gel holder on a scoop. Frames that hold a gel filter in place are designed for all types of floods and spotlights. (Photo courtesy of Mole Richardson)

Color. There are occasions when a set or other production location is simply too dull and drab for attractive pictures with sufficient color contrast. It may be that more "warmth" from red-brown earthtones is needed. Or possibly the "cool" effect of green and blue is desired. To solve this problem, variously colored *gels* are used to add color to the setting and occasionally to the performers' clothes and fleshtones. The gel is a thin transparent celluloid material, available in a wide variety of colors. The gels can be cut to fit a specially designed holder that slides into the same frame that is intended to hold the barn doors on a spotlight (fig. 4-33).

In using gels, the lighting director must work carefully with both the video control operator and the makeup artist. The effect of projecting three or four different colors onto a set can be subtle but must be carefully controlled. Since the camera system tends to pick up and accentuate red, you should be especially cautious with its use. Because most normal makeup is in the reddish range, too much light through a red gel will greatly exaggerate fleshtones (see section 10.5). Light from a green gel, on the other hand, has an unflattering effect on most persons—especially on those with darker complexions.

One of the most effective applications for gels is that of using them with strip lights to color a cyclorama. A wide variety of color combinations and effects are possible. A continually changing dawn effect, for example, can be created—with the background shifting from a deep violet through various reds and pinks to a light blue.

Safety Precautions and Disciplines

Safety is the responsiblity of everybody connected with a television production. Any unsafe situation can be avoided by using common sense and observing basic precautions. Part of the discipline of television production is the habit and attitude of "thinking safety." Every crew member, whether or not part of the lighting team, should be disciplined to think always in terms of avoiding or correcting hazardous conditions. *Think overhead.* Are all lights, mounts, and other equipment securely fastened? When heavy equipment is moved or repositioned overhead, is everybody warned and the area below the equipment cleared out? *Think electrical.* Is all equipment turned off before moving or inspecting it? *Think hardware.* Has the item of equipment been thoroughly checked out and is it ready for use? Has everything been connected? Tightened? Tested?

Whenever a lighting assistant is moving or trimming lights, there should be at least one person steadying the ladder from below. The person on the ladder should always carry a wrench (secured by a band or tie around the wrist to prevent dropping it on persons or equipment below) to tighten any lamps that have become loose from excessive turning. When making any adjustment on any lighting instrument, the safety cable or cord should always remain fastened, securing the light to the pipe or grid.

When changing the direction of a light, always loosen the thumb screw (swivel bolt) first. Do not mistake it for the bolt holding the lamp hanger to the clamp, as loosening that bolt will detach the lamp from the lighting grid.[4]

When moving a light (clamp, hanger, and housing), always make certain that there are no people or equipment below the area in which you are working. Be certain the power to the lamp is off. Just because no light is being emitted does not mean that there is no power coming to the cord. Damaged lights, burnt-out bulbs, and short circuits are all potential dangers. Again, be sure that the power is off at the lamp's new location before plugging it into the grid outlet or load circuit. When moving an instrument from one location to another, the safety cable is always the last item to be unfastened, and it is the first thing to be hooked up when the instrument is repositioned.

When moving or focusing lights, do not look directly into a light. A light that measures 200 ftc at 30 ft may approach 100,000 ftc at the source. Studio lights are bright enough to permanently damage or even blind the naked eye.

A 2,000-watt lamp creates a dangerous amount of heat. After being on for only a few minutes, most studio lamps are hot enough to cause serious burns. Most studio lamps have handles. Use them! Lighting technicians should also be furnished with heavy-duty asbestos gloves. Special caution must be used when adjusting barn doors, as they are directly in the path of the light source at only a few inches and absorb a large amount of heat.

Before moving a lamp, whether a large studio model or a small portable light, let the lamp stand for 10 to 15 minutes. This will help the lamp cool, help prolong the life of the filament, and also lessen the possibility of lamp explosion or burn-out from the shock of moving.

Preproduction Planning

One final note about production *discipline* from the standpoint of lighting procedures. In lighting—as in every aspect of television production—it is imperative that as many details as possible be taken care of before walking into the studio for the production setup and rehearsal. Every minute counts in the studio. You cannot afford to start your planning once you reach the studio.

The lighting director must use a lighting plan or **light plot.** This plan will be worked out well in advance of the actual studio setup time. It will include a schematic layout of the primary staging areas and the lighting requirements for each one. It should indicate each lighting instrument to be used and the intensity ratios among the various instruments. Often there is space for additional notes. Here the director will indicate which lights are to be placed together on dimmer circuits or what kinds of lighting effects will actually be used on the air. Figure 4-34 represents a sample lighting plan for a simple talk show. Study also the examples used in figures 4-22 and 4-23.

In many production situations, the lighting director will also prepare a more detailed set of working instructions—a worksheet that lists, for each instrument to be used, the description of the light (spot, scoop); its size (500 watts, 2 kw [kilowatts]); the staging area it is to cover; its function (key, kicker); the grid outlet or load circuit it is to be plugged into; the dimmer or nondim circuit it will be patched to; and so forth. Again, the detailed preparation at this point will save valuable minutes of studio setup and rehearsal time later. The disciplined production person knows the importance of thorough **preproduction planning.**

4. The most common type of lamp hanger is the C-clamp (see fig. 4-26). There is a bolt that holds it to the lighting grid and a bolt that holds the light holder to the C-clamp. This bolt (yoke-bolt) should *never* be loosened. To turn a light, there is usually a thumb screw in the side of the clamp. Make note of this when studying lighting in your own studio.

Producer/Director:_____

Production Title:_____

Lighting Setup: (Date)_____ (Time)_____

Air/Recording: _____   _____

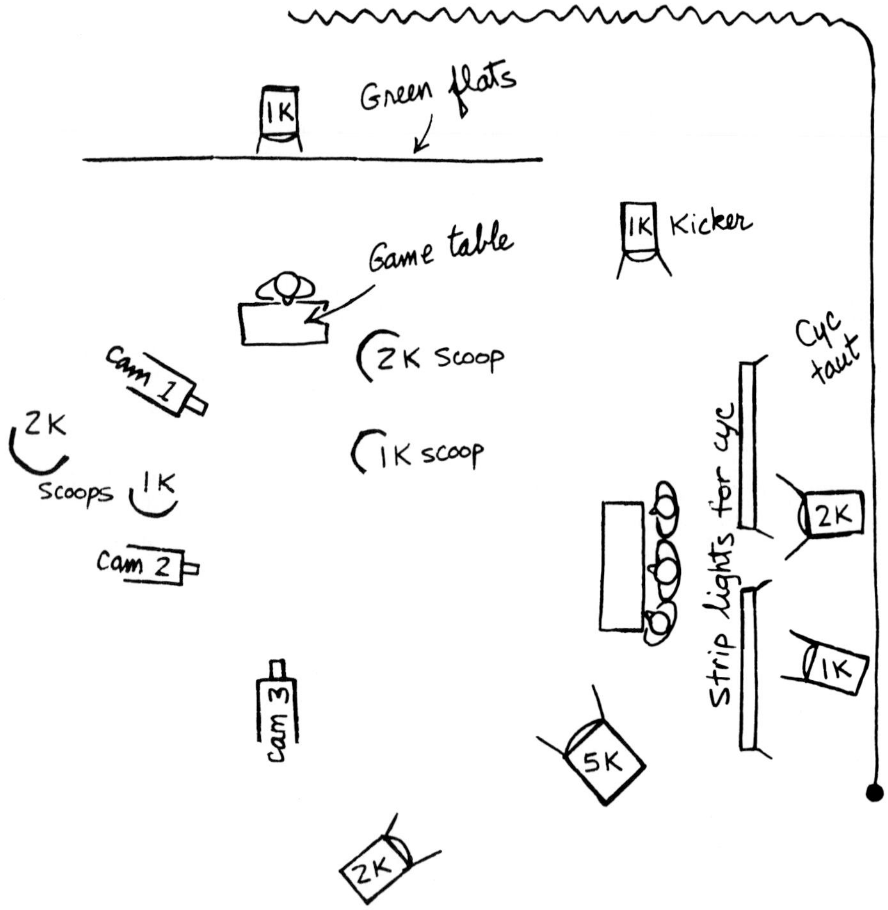

Figure 4-34 Sample studio lighting plot.

The director of the television production would fill out a light plot on a form similar to this. Although the symbols are not to scale, these instructions indicate generally how the director envisions the production from the lighting standpoint: where the talent will be, how the numbered cameras will be positioned, and basically what lighting instruments would be used. The lighting director could then take this lighting plan and devise a more detailed lighting worksheet for the lighting crew to follow.

Summary

As with audio considerations, lighting directors must be concerned both with technical (*basic illumination*) needs and with creative purposes. In addition to establishing the correct amount of *base light* (usually determined by an *incident light* meter reading), the L.D. also must work within an acceptable *contrast ratio* (established by *reflected light* meter readings) and maintain the correct *color temperature* (3,000 to 3,400 degrees Kelvin).

The creative lighting objectives include perspective and molding *shape* and *texture,* establishing a feeling of *reality* (or nonreality), creating a *mood* or emotional setting, and *focusing attention.* All of these functions are accomplished with *spotlights* that have a highly directional focused beam and/or with *floodlights* that give off a nondirectional diffused light.

Lighting a typical subject involves standard *three-point* lighting (key light, fill light, and back light). *Auxiliary sources* such as a side light (or a kicker) or background light may also be incorporated. When working with *multiple-camera lighting,* certain modifications and compromises in the ideal three-point lighting concept have been accepted—such as *cross-key* lighting.

As a starting point, lighting directors sometimes use a *basic ratio,* with the back light strongest, then the key light, and the fill being the weakest source. Complete studio lighting procedures also include knowledge of various *mounting devices* and—most importantly—various approaches to *lighting control* (intensity, focus and diffusion, shaping the beam, and color control). Finally, we must be concerned with essential *safety precautions* and the discipline of thorough *preproduction planning.*

All of the lighting considerations, of course, are but a means of creating the picture that will be picked up by the camera and its lens system. Camera/lens structure and camera operations are discussed in the next two chapters.

4.7 Training Exercises

Illustrate, on camera, the modeling effects of light upon the structure of the face by means of the following demonstrations:

1. From a straight-on position in line with the camera, direct a single key light upon a subject's face from angles of 60, 45, and 30 degrees from the horizontal. Note the generally uncomplimentary effect of shadows under the eyebrows, nose, and chin at the steeper angles.
2. Set the key at a 30- to 35-degree vertical angle, straight-on to the subject's face. Start with the camera position exactly in line with the direction of the light. Then have the subject slowly turn his or her face to the right. Have the camera make an arcing movement in the same direction, keeping a full-front face shot. Stop both of these movements at regular intervals, observing how the shadows created by the

various lighting angles model the shape of the face. Note how the lines of the subject's forehead, nose, cheek, and so forth, are much more definite than with straight-on front lighting.

3. Set up a basic key, back, and fill light structure. Alternately take out and then put back one or even two of these basic light sources. This is most effective when the lights are on dimmers and the process is done gradually. Experiment with the various footcandle ratios among the three light sources by means of dimmer control.

4. With the basic key, back, and fill setup, use different subjects so that the variations created by hair, skin color, and clothes can be noted.

5. Using a mirror and a flashlight for a light source, experiment with the optical principles equating the angle of reflection with the angle of incidence. Hold the flashlight at eye level and shine it directly into the mirror. Raise the flashlight above your head, point the beam downward, and note where the reflected beam hits you on your body. How do the reflected angles change as you vary the angle at which the flashlight beam hits the mirror?

Camera Structure and Lens Design

5

With this chapter, we begin a look at the video system. It is a complex chain that includes lenses, cameras (and their mounts), camera control units and a synchronizing generator, a switcher, possibly an editor, usually a video recorder, and (ultimately) a transmitter. The next four chapters will be concerned with various components in this system.

5.1 Video Signal Flow and Control Functions

Just as we discussed the audio system in terms of audio signal flow, so also would it be helpful to think in terms of the **video signal flow** for the picture part of the television production. The same seven basic control functions introduced in section 2.2 can be applied to the video system. Figure 5-1 illustrates in simplified form the basic units in the video signal flow.

The first step, *transducing,* is accomplished by the camera itself. The camera, like the microphone, is a **transducer** that receives physical energy (light waves) and transforms it into electrical energy (video signals) that is suitable for electronic distribution. Although considerably more complex than the microphone, the camera performs this same basic function.

The video signal is then *channeled* directly or indirectly into the video switcher. Although no patch bay is as obvious as that in the audio system, cameras nevertheless can be patched or connected to different inputs in the switcher or to other points in the master control room.

The switcher (chapter 7), like the audio console, is the heart of the video signal flow. Here is where all video *mixing* occurs. Camera pictures can be selected and combined in a variety of ways.

Some amount of video *shaping* also can occur at the switcher. This function, however, is controlled primarily through the **camera control unit (CCU).** What most people think of

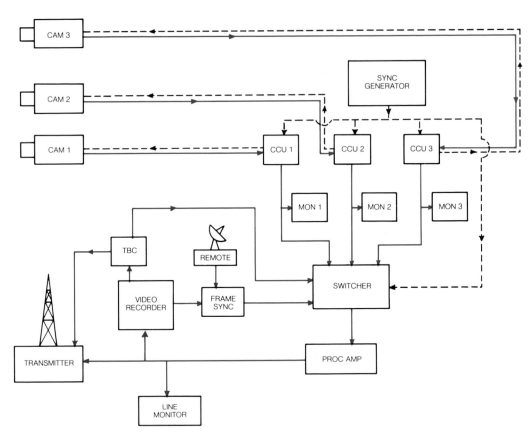

Figure 5-1 Diagram of the video signal flow.

A portion of the synchronizing ("sync") pulse (dotted line) is sent out from the sync generator to each camera control unit (CCU) and on to each camera—keeping all cameras in perfect synchronization. The complete sync pulse is also sent to the switcher. Simultaneously, the picture information (solid line) flows from each camera to the CCU, where the video signal can be shaped and altered. The composite signal (picture plus sync pulse) is then channeled into the switcher, with the picture information also being displayed on the video monitor for each camera. (In the diagram, from the CCU on through the rest of the system the solid line represents the composite signal— picture plus sync pulse; the dotted line is omitted for the sake of simplicity.)

From the switcher, the composite signal can be sent, through a process amplifier, on to the line monitor, to a videorecorder, and/or to the transmitter. A videorecorder also can be used, of course, as a picture source—sending its recorded program material through the time-base corrector (TBC) and on to the switcher or to the transmitter. Remote sources (satellite feeds, microwave links) also can serve as inputs to the switcher, flowing through the frame synchronizer that conforms the sync pulse with the other composite signals.

as the camera is actually only part of a much larger unit known as the **camera chain.** Most of the equipment necessary for the control and shaping of the video signal is not located at the camera itself but at a separate point under the supervision of the video control operator. (On newer and simpler cameras—variations of the vidicon—controls are preset and do not need continual adjusting or attention.)

The *amplification* of the video signal occurs at several different points in the total system. Wherever the signal is distributed any significant distance through the various camera cables, *distribution amplifiers* are used to boost the signal periodically. Our simplified diagram (fig. 5-1) does not attempt to show all of the points where distribution amplifiers would be placed throughout the system.

Various types of video recorders (chapter 8) are used for **recording** and **playback** of the television signal. Usually, the signals recorded by the video recorder would include both the video and audio information for the entire TV production.

As with amplification, *monitoring* takes place at several different points within the system. In any regular studio production, the camera operators will have a camera monitor to enable them to see what they are picking up with their cameras. The most conspicuous display of TV monitors is in the control room, where the director has a monitor for every camera and other video source being used in a particular program. In the simplest of studio operations this would involve three or four monitors. In ambitious network productions dozens of monitors might be used in a single control room.

Control Components

The video signal is much more complex than the audio signal. It takes roughly six hundred times as much "information" to produce a video signal than to produce sound to cover the same period of time. Consequently, the picture is vulnerable to a number of disruptive influences within the system itself. There must be several specialized components that monitor, adjust, refine, and stabilize the picture throughout the video signal flow. The sophisticated pieces of equipment are introduced here in order to provide a reference point for the remainder of chapter 5—although some aspects of their technical nature will not be covered in detail until later chapters.

Sync Generator. In order to coordinate the functioning of all components in the video system, the **synchronizing generator** creates the sync pulse, a series of timing pulses that locks together all elements of the video signal at every stage of production, switching, recording, editing, transmission, and reception. This sync pulse has often been called a system of *electronic sprocket holes* that keeps everything coordinated in a lockstep pattern. This series of timing pulses is based upon the basic 60-cycle alternating current used in the United States and in many other countries using the NTSC television system.[1]

Proc Amp. It is the job of the **process amplifier** to take the *composite video signal* from the switcher—color, brightness, and synchronizing information—and then stabilize the levels, amplify the signal, and remove unwanted elements or *noise*.

TBC. Video signals from videotape recorders often will have synchronizing pulses that have been slightly altered or have deteriorated during the recording and playback

---

1. In 1941, the United States adopted the recommendations of the National Television System Committee (NTSC) which defined the basic 525-line, 30-frame format described in the following sections of chapter 5. This NTSC system—still the standard for North and South America and Japan—is one of three different formats used by various countries throughout the world.

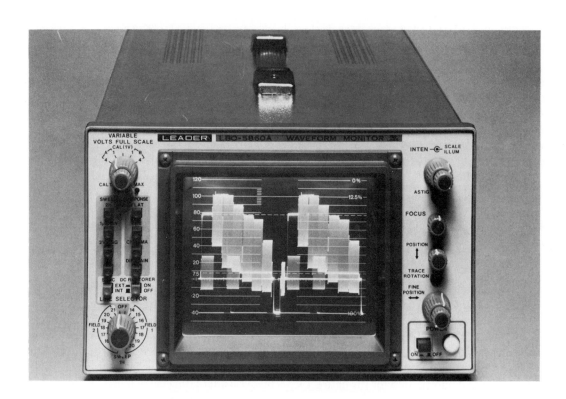

Figure 5-2 Waveform monitor.

process. The **time-base corrector** takes these signals, encodes them into a digital form, and then reconstructs an enhanced synchronizing signal for playback and editing purposes (see section 7.4).

Frame Synchronizer. A relatively recent and sophisticated piece of equipment, the **frame synchronizer** (and "field synchronizer") takes video sources from outside of the studio control or video recorders, compares their sync pulses with studio sync, and adjusts the differences between the two. The signals are put through a digitalized phase prior to output. Satellite and other out-of-studio feeds can thereby be coordinated through the studio switcher.

Oscilloscopes. In addition to the components that have an ongoing automatic function in shaping the signal, there are components for adjustments that can only effectively be a matter of operator judgment at the camera control unit. Two of these pieces of equipment are visual read-out monitors, which provide the feedback for continuous picture control.

The **waveform monitor** (fig. 5-2) is a type of oscilloscope—a cathode-ray tube that depicts changes in electrical information by means of a visual line display. It shows the varying amounts of bright and dark elements in a picture. Like an audio VU meter, it allows the operator to keep the brightest elements in a picture from exceeding the 100 percent level of what the video system can properly handle.

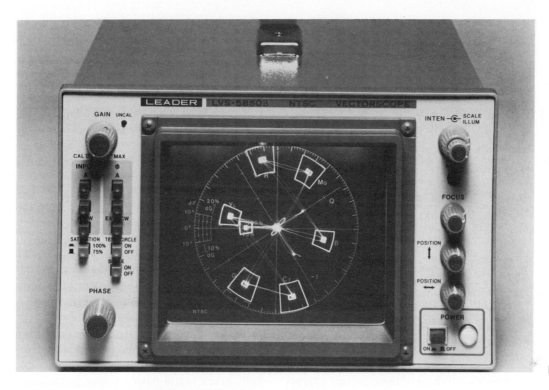

Figure 5-3 Vectorscope.

By adjusting the picture controls, the operator can keep the light-to-dark ratio in balance.

The **vectorscope** (fig. 5-3) is a similar type of scope. It shows the individual levels for the three primary colors and the three complementary colors in the picture (see section 5.2). The lower the amount of red in a picture, the closer to the center of the monitor the glowing red dot will be.

Color Bar Generator.   One other control element to be mentioned here would be the **color bars.** The color bar generator sends a standardized pattern of vertical colored bars through the switcher. This is used to calibrate the color values and adjustments on all cameras, video recorders, and monitors. The color bars are also recorded at the beginning of a video recording so that the playback machine can be matched to the color levels at the time of the recording.

5.2 The Color Video System

At the heart of the entire television operation lies the camera **pickup tube**—the miraculous refinement of the cathode-ray tube that can transform (transduce) visual pictures into electrical signals. Although there are some rather good industrial-level cameras that utilize a single-camera-tube system, most professional cameras have three pickup tubes—one each for the *red, green,* and *blue* components of the picture. These are the three primary colors that exist in light.

Three Variables of Video Color

Through the process known as *additive* color, the three camera tubes (each one picking up a different primary color) can combine their signals to produce a wide range of color (**hue**), vividness of color (**saturation**), and brightness

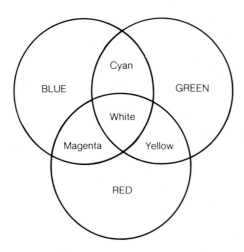

Where any two of the three primary colors (red, green, blue) overlap, they form a secondary color—cyan (green-blue), magenta (blue-red), or yellow (red-green). Combinations of varying intensities of the three primary colors can produce all possible hues. All three primary colors in a balanced proportion produce white.

Figure 5-4   Color chart.

(**luminance**). All three of these factors interact to contribute to the quality of any video color. (See also the discussion of these variables in section 9.1.)

Hue.   The concept of "hue" refers to what we normally would think of as the actual tint or *color* base itself—red, brown, orange, and so forth. Figure 5-4 lays out the three primary colors and shows how any two of the primary colors can be combined (in the overlapping areas) to produce the three complementary colors—*cyan* (blue-green turquoise), *magenta* (reddish purple), and *yellow* (combining red and green).[2] The full range of hues is obtained as the proportions of colors are changed. For example, a proportion of more red and less green produces hues in the reddish-brown range.

2. A color plate showing these colors can be found in any standard reference work such as any basic encyclopedia article on "Color."

When light waves of all three primary colors are added together in the correct proportions, the resulting effect is white. White is not the absence of color; it is the presence of all colors! If you have trouble accepting this physiological phenomenon on faith, prove it to yourself. Take a close look at a picture on your own color TV set with a strong magnifying glass. The result should astound you. What you perceive from a distance as "white" actually is composed of very vivid red, green, and blue bars (stripes, or dots) surrounded by black borders!

Saturation.   The intensity or vividness of a color is described in terms of "saturation." Basically, this indicates how pure a color is—how far removed it is from a dull grayish shade. A vivid kelly green, for example, is more heavily saturated than a grayish olive green—even though they may both have the same brightness value. In terms of the primary colors, the kelly green would have a strong green signal with just a small amount of red to give the slight yellowish cast. The olive green, on the other hand, would contain less green and more red. But both signals could consist of the same amount of voltage or total video energy.

In television pictures, therefore, saturation is inversely related to apparent "grayness"—and even "whiteness." A pure blue color, for example, can have a little red and green added to make it "grayer." If more red and green are added, the result will be "whiter"; the effect is to appear lighter on the TV screen but less saturated. So, the stronger the blue hue in this mixture, the more saturated the color is.

Brightness.   In opaque colors, "brightness" (lightness) or "value" refers to how much white is present in any given hue. In television terms, however, brightness can better be thought of as the strength or intensity of the electric signal. It is the opposite of "dimness."

Figure 5-5 RCA TK–41 camera. For years, image-orthicon cameras such as the TK–41 were the workhorses of the broadcast industry. The *diameter* of these larger I-O tubes was about the same as the *length* of the modern vidicon tubes. (Photo courtesy of RCA)

Starting with the same pure blue signal we had in the saturation example, its brightness is diminished as the strength of the blue signal is decreased. No red or green is added to the picture (which would decrease its saturation), but the blue itself is *diminished* (which decreases its brightness).

One way that brightness is affected, of course, is by lighting. If we have a light blue chair in a set (light-colored, but low in saturation because its "blueness" has been diminished by adding a little red and green to give it some "whiteness"), it can be either bright or dark, depending upon how much light falls upon it. Therefore, our light blue chair may be relatively low in brightness if it is not well lit, and a darker grayish blue chair (also low in saturation) may be brighter if it is well lit. Simultaneously, a brilliant royal blue chair (heavily saturated) may be dark (low in brightness) if not in a lighted area.

This variable also relates to the *luminance* video signal which is discussed in the following material.

Camera Pickup Tubes

The **image-orthicon (I-O)** tube was the first practical camera tube developed. For many years, models such as the venerable TK-41 (fig. 5-5) were the standard of the professional industry. During the 1960s, however, the **vidicon** tube was developed and soon found its way into most applications formerly reserved for I-O cameras.[3]

3. The first pickup tube developed was actually the **iconoscope** tube developed in the 1920s. It was never put into extensive use, however, as it was very insensitive to light, requiring large amounts of illumination to give a decent picture.

Figure 5-6 RCA CCD–1
camera. The model is
holding one of the three
chip-like silicon-based
"charge-coupled devices"
that have replaced the
camera pickup tubes in the
foreground. (Photo
courtesy of RCA)

The vidicon is smaller and more rugged, and it can generally withstand a higher contrast ratio (section 4.2). A major operating benefit is that it is more stable; it warms up relatively fast and requires little operator attention. One other major advantage of the vidicon tube is that it is less expensive and lasts longer than the I-O tube. Thus, vidicon technology became the standard of both commercial and noncommercial television.

During the past few years, many refinements and improvements in the basic vidicon design have resulted in a wide range of advanced tubes—many of which operate at very low levels of illumination. Sophisticated models such as the **Plumbicon®**[4] and the **Saticon®**[5] can function effectively at light levels of less than 50 footcandles.

The newest innovation in television pickup devices is the RCA CCD-1 camera in which each of the three tubes is replaced by a **charge-coupled device (CCD).**[6] These are small silicon memory chips that produce the color and brightness parts of the video signal. Figure 5-6 shows the size of the CCD compared to the tube it replaces. Among its features are the elimination of both *image lag* (the smearing or streaking of white areas of the picture when the camera is moved across the scene) and *burn-in* (a type of "image-retention" where the tube remembers the image of a picture it has been focused on and superimposes a negative image of that scene over succeeding shots).

One major advantage of the CCD camera is its ruggedness and durability; the manufacturer states that the chip simply will not wear

4. Plumbicon® is a registered trademark of N. V. Philips.

5. Saticon® is a trademark of Hitachi.

6. Introduced by NBC at the 1984 political conventions, the CCD cameras were praised for their ability to function with very low light levels and to pick up fireworks without any burn-in or image lag.

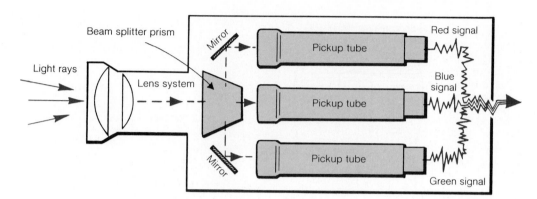

By means of a special color-separating prism, incoming light is split into its red, blue, and green components. These three separate images are then reflected by mirrors into their designated pickup tubes. (In the diagram, the red image is reflected into the top tube, the blue light rays are passed into the middle tube, and the green light is reflected into the bottom tube.) The tubes themselves, of course, do not discriminate among the colors; each tube just generates an electronic signal corresponding to the light information reaching it through the beam-splitter prism and mirrors. The three separate video signals (one carrying the light information for each color) are then transmitted and eventually recombined (at the receiver) to re-create the full-color picture.

Figure 5-7 Diagram of a color camera beam-splitter prism.

out under normal use. In spite of its thumbnail size, the CCD performs the same basic job that the cathode-ray camera pickup tube does. It changes a focused image of light into a sequenced electronic signal that can be recorded, edited, transmitted, and converted back into a visual image by the TV receiver.

Structure of the Camera Tube.

In a three-tube camera, each tube is identical. They are labeled red, green, or blue because each tube is designated to pick up only one of the primary colors. The glass prism **beam splitter** (fig. 5-7) filters out and directs just one designated color to each pickup tube.

To illustrate how the pickup tube works, let us look at, for example, the "blue" tube in a camera. The action starts with an image, focused by the lens, entering the beam splitter where the blue light energy or "information" from the picture is separated out and sent to the blue tube. Here the blue information falls upon a screen—called the **target**—at the front of the tube.

The target has two functional layers. The first is a very thin *conductive* layer that allows the **photons** (elements of light energy) to pass through it and land on the next layer. This second layer of the target is a *photoconductive* element; this is a type of grid that contains over 200,000 individual photosensitive dots, or **pixels** (a term popularized by computer reference to the *pic*ture *el*ements). Each individual dot, or pixel, reacts to the light energy (photons) striking it by *lowering its resistance to the passage of electrons*. This is a crucial concept for understanding how the next phase works—the scanning process.

On the target the pixels are arranged so that there are over 400 of them on a horizontal line, and there are somewhat over 500 horizontal lines from top to bottom of the target.[7] In the 525-line NTSC format, some of the top and bottom lines are used for information other than the picture video. (See fig. 5-8 for an extended illustration of the entire process.)

7. In the CCD-1 there are 403 pixels in each horizontal line and there are 512 horizontal lines that are used for picture information.

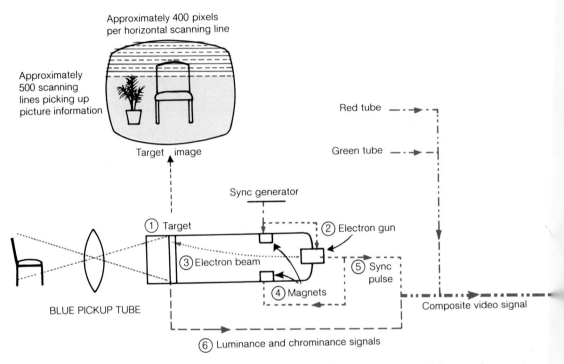

Approximately 400 pixels per horizontal scanning line

Approximately 500 scanning lines picking up picture information

Target image

Red tube

Green tube

Sync generator

① Target
② Electron gun
③ Electron beam
⑤ Sync pulse
④ Magnets

BLUE PICKUP TUBE

Composite video signal

⑥ Luminance and chrominance signals

Figure 5-8 Simplified diagram of the vidicon pickup tube and the home receiver tube.

As the incoming image is filtered through the beam-splitter prism (fig. 5-7), the light corresponding to one particular color (blue, in our example) falls on the target (*1*) of the pickup tube. At the rear of the tube, an electron gun (*2*) emits a beam of electrons (*3*) that is pulled back and forth (and up and down) by a ring of deflection coil magnets (*4*). The magnetic impulses sent to these magnets are controlled by the synchronizing pulses (*5*) created by the synchronizing generator. As the scanning beam is pulled across the target, some of the electrical energy (electrons) are allowed to pass through the photoconductive layer—depending on the amount of light that has fallen on the target. This minute electrical signal, which corresponds to the light reflected into the lens from the object in front of the camera (a blue chair in our example), then releases a small electrical current that forms the luminance and chrominance signals (*6*) that define the picture. As these signals are added to the sync pulses, we have a composite signal that—when combined with the signals from the red and green tubes—is ready for broadcast.

The Scanning Process. The focused image falling upon the mosaic-like target produces no effect unless the target is energized by an electrical charge. This is accomplished by means of a scanning process that, in a precise continuing sequence, "reads" the electrical charge on each pixel (which corresponds to the amount of light hitting the pixel) and translates this into a minute electrical signal.

This process starts when a component called the **electron gun** at the rear of the tube shoots out a stream of electrons that passes through the magnetic field of a ring of **deflection magnets** located just in front of the gun. The effect of the magnets is to divert or deflect the electron beam in a critical back-and-forth and up-and-down scanning pattern. It starts by scanning the pixels on the photoconductive layer of the target from left to right along the top or first horizontal line.

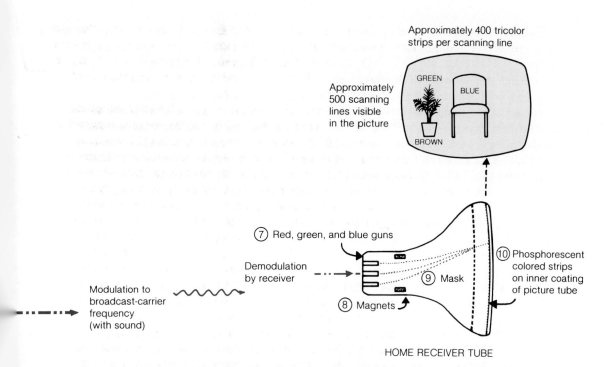

Approximately 400 tricolor
strips per scanning line

Approximately
500 scanning
lines visible
in the picture

GREEN

BLUE

BROWN

⑦ Red, green, and blue guns

Demodulation
by receiver

⑩ Phosphorescent
colored strips
on inner coating
of picture tube

⑨ Mask

Modulation to
broadcast-carrier
frequency
(with sound)

⑧ Magnets

HOME RECEIVER TUBE

At the receiving end, the picture and audio information is stripped from the carrier wave (demodulated) and the blue, red, and green information is sent to three electron guns (*7*) in the rear of the kinescope or picture tube. Each color gun shoots out an electron beam, which varies in intensity corresponding to the strength of the electron signal initially created by the vidicon target. This electron beam also is directed back and forth (and up and down) by a ring of deflection coil magnets (*8*) controlled by the same sync pulses that created the original picture. Thus, the scanning beam re-creates the picture information for each color in the same pattern and at the same intensity as the signal from the camera. Each electron beam is precisely aimed through a mask (*9*) that directs the stream of electrons at the face of the tube with pinpoint accuracy. The electrons bombard the tiny phosphorescent "dots," or *pixels,* on the inside of the tube—usually arranged in vertical bars or strips of the three primary colors (*10*)—making each one glow with an intensity that corresponds to the original picture signal. As the various red, green, and blue pixels are combined in varying intensities, the original image is re-created at the rate of sixty fields every second.

As the scanning electron beam hits each pixel, some of the energy (electrons) will be allowed to pass through the photoconductive layer and land on the conductive layer. The number of electrons passing through is proportional to the quantity of photons landing on each pixel; the greater the light energy (number of photons) is, the lower the resistance will be, and therefore the greater the number of electrons passing through and landing on the conductive layer.

These electrons from the scanning beam that get through to the conductive layer are then "drained off" through a wire, and they become the electrical current that is the **video signal,** which corresponds to the image being picked up by the camera tube.

After the beam scans one line, it is momentarily turned off by a **blanking pulse** and pulled back to the left side of the tube by the **horizontal synchronization pulse.** Simultaneously the scanning beam is pulled down to the *third* horizontal line, which it then scans.

Sequentially, the electron beam continues to scan all of the *odd*-numbered lines on the target.

When the bottom odd-numbered picture line has been scanned, the camera tube has produced a top-to-bottom (and left-to-right) picture **field.** Because only half of the lines have been scanned (picking up information from only half of the pixels on the target), this field represents only half of the total video picture. And it has taken only ¹⁄₆₀ of a second to scan this field!

Now a **vertical synchronization pulse** sends the electron beam back to the top of the picture to start the scanning process all over again. This time, the *even*-numbered lines are scanned to produce another "half picture" field. These two fields—the odd-numbered lines and the even-numbered lines—make up the total picture that is referred to as a **frame.** Thus, there are 30 full frames per second. This pattern of combining the two fields into one frame is called **interlacing.**

The basic pattern of the electron beam is similar to that of your eyes reading across a line of type on a page and then jumping back to the left side of the page and starting on the next lower line—525 lines per page, 30 pages per second! The resulting electrical message is the video signal that has just begun its long and complicated path.

Luminance and Chrominance Signals. In examining how the video picture is put together, it is also necessary to understand something about the concepts of *luminance* and *chrominance* signals.[8] These phenomena can best be examined by looking at our earlier

studio example of the light blue chair. Because of the beam splitter, the blue tube will pick up the primary image of the chair.

Energized by the scanning beam electrons, the blue tube pixels react to the image of the chair focused on the target by initiating the sequential electrical message that corresponds to the chair's image. The video signal will vary as the light and dark areas of the chair are scanned. This is the **luminance** signal, and as it reacts to the differing levels of brightness in the picture, it is, in effect, defining the shape of the chair. In fact, if you were to look at the television picture on a monochrome monitor, it is this luminance signal that would be giving you the black-and-white picture.

At the same time, each tube is also reacting to the saturation or *chroma* of the chair—whether it is a grayish blue or a bright blue. The grayer or less saturated the color is, the more that some of the subtleties and tones will be picked up by the red and green tubes. It is this blending of the saturation of each of the three primary hues that provides the basis for the **chrominance** signal.

In actuality, any pure hue (the blue in our example of the chair, for instance) would be virtually impossible to find. Most colors have some tints of other hues embedded within the color; our blue chair will have some green or red (or both) light in its hue—even though it might not show up as a distinguishable aquamarine or purple cast. So our blue chair also would have some of its qualities being picked up by the green and red tubes.

As mentioned earlier, some portable cameras—by utilizing an ingenious system of multiplexing and combining signals—use only one pickup tube for color pictures. Even though both the luminance and chrominance information can be integrated this way, the resulting picture is generally not as rich as that produced by the three-tube cameras.

8. In most video systems the luminance and chrominance signals are combined as they leave the tube. In the ½-inch Sony Betacam format, however, they are recorded as two separate signals. Some ¼-inch (8 mm) systems do the same thing.

The mixing of the several colors does not take place in the camera chain, of course. Strictly speaking, what the camera system does is to *separate* the colors. In fact, the colors—the luminance and chrominance signals—remain distinct entities (even when combined within the composite video signal) throughout the entire switching, recording, editing, transmitting, and receiving process. Your TV set at home even displays separate pinpoints of distinct primary hues as the individual red, green, and blue phosphor dots, strips, or bars are illuminated. It is only when these microscopic pinpoints are interpreted by our brain that the miracle of "color" is perceived.

The Receiver Picture Tube

Just as the radio speaker resembles the microphone (the speaker's components are in reverse order of the microphone's signal flow), so the TV set's picture tube is the mirrored analog of the camera pickup tube.

As the camera is picking up the picture—and during the subsequent channeling, mixing, shaping, amplifying, and monitoring of the picture—the signal remains in a "pure" line *video* format. Switchers, studio monitors, recorders, and editors all process this line level signal. For the picture to be transmitted, however, the audio signal must be added, and then the video and audio information must be converted to a **radio frequency** (**RF**) signal. It is this RF signal that can then be modulated onto a **carrier wave** that can be broadcast on a radio frequency in the electromagnetic spectrum.

The first task of the home TV set is to strip off the audio signal and then demodulate the picture information. Then each of the red, green, and blue guns in the receiver or **kinescope** tube shoot out a stream of electrons. This electron beam, like the scanning beam in the camera pickup tube, is controlled by a ring of magnets that deflects and controls the beam to reproduce the left-to-right and top-to-bottom scanning pattern initiated in the camera.

In most TV sets, the electron beams pass through a **masking plate** that focuses the electrons as they strike the designated phosphor pixels on the inside glass of the picture tube (fig. 5-9). This inner coating can be either in the form of triad groups of red, green, and blue dots or in the form of tiny, vertical, phosphorescent strips of the same colors. At the synchronized scanning rate of sixty fields (thirty frames) per second, the electron beams reproduce the video picture essentially as it was originally picked up by the camera tube.

Like the image picked up by the camera, the picture displayed on the receiver screen never exists as a completed frame, even for an infinitesimal fraction of a second. The TV frame does not have a discrete existence the way a frame of motion picture film does. What we have is the linear tracing of a point of light moving at an incredible rate of speed. At any given micro-second, one "half picture" field is always at some stage of the continual scanning process—with elements of one image overlapping the previous picture.

But because of the phenomenon of *persistence of vision* ("visual lag"), the brain perceives this incredibly rapid series of light flashes as a moving picture. The human eye tends to retain images for a split second after the image has been removed. If about fifteen or more separate images per second are flashed before the eye, human perception will cause them to blend together, thus creating the illusion of motion. This persistence of vision is what makes simulated moving pictures possible—on film as well as on the face of a television tube.

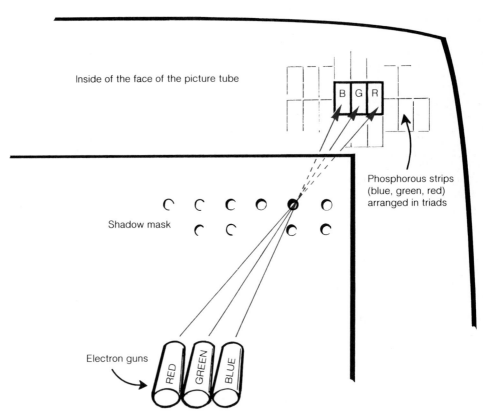

Inside of the face of the picture tube

Phosphorous strips
(blue, green, red)
arranged in triads

Shadow mask

Electron guns

RED GREEN BLUE

Figure 5-9 Shadow mask
for color receiver.

Most color receivers utilize a shadow mask, a thin metal sheet perforated by tiny holes. These carefully aligned dots or slots ensure that as each of the three electron beams is pulled across the face of the tube in its scanning pattern, it will hit only those phosphor strips colored to correspond with its designated electron gun in the rear of the tube.

5.3 Lens Characteristics

In conjunction with the camera pickup tube, the single most important element in the whole pictorial process probably is the lens. As illustrated in figure 5-8, it is the lens that focuses the picture upon the face of the pickup tube. A good lens can help the cheapest vidicon camera produce a sharp, clear picture. An inferior lens can turn the best Plumbicon camera's picture into blurred trash.

Shortly after its introduction in the early 1960s, the **zoom lens** became standard equipment on virtually all studio television cameras. For most types of video production this will likely remain true in the future. Indeed, most TV-production students will probably never see a **fixed-focal-length lens** on a television camera. The zoom lens, however, because of its numerous lens elements, can never be as optically perfect as a fixed-focal-length lens designed for a specified magnification.

Ironically, the introduction of **high-definition television (HDTV)** may well set the stage for a return to limited applications of the fixed-focal-length lens. Those who have seen an HDTV demonstration, with its incredibly sharp picture resolution, cannot help but be impressed with its potential for both theatrical

Figure 5-10
Demonstration of Sony's HDTV (high-definition TV) system. Note the 3 by 5 aspect ratio and the lack of discernible scanning lines in this monitor picture.

and industrial applications.[9] (See fig. 5-10.) In order to take advantage of the HDTV higher picture quality, it may be practical to utilize the better optical characteristics of the fixed-focal-length lens. (The Sony HDTV camera comes equipped to accept a variety of fixed lenses, ranging in focal length from 11.5mm to 56mm.) This possibility may lend some added importance to our preliminary study of lens function in which the fixed-focal-length lens will serve as our model.

The characteristics of **focal length, focus, *f*-stop,** and **depth-of-field** are all simpler to grasp with a non-zoom fixed-length lens as a reference. It is much easier to comprehend the concept of a **long lens** compression of a picture or a **wide-angle lens** giving a greater depth-of-field if one visualizes the actual length and

9. In the past few years both CBS and Sony have held public demonstrations of their HDTV prototypes. Both systems use a wide-screen format and a scanning system of over 1,100 lines. Compared to the NTSC 525-line system, the HDTV picture is astonishingly crisp and lifelike.

angle of the lens. In fact, any serious still photographer who has worked with fixed-focal-length lenses will find it much easier to understand what a zoom lens can do—and why—than the photographer who has only worked with a zoom lens. Therefore, this section will deal with lens characteristics using the fixed-focal-length lens as a reference point. Section 5.4 will deal specifically with the zoom lens.

Focal Length

The *focal length* of a lens is measured from the optical center point of the lens (when it is focused at infinity) to a point where the image is in focus. This focus point would be either the film in a film camera (movie or still camera) or the surface of the pickup tube in an electronic camera (fig. 5-11). Focal length is measured in either millimeters or inches (25 millimeters is approximately equal to 1 inch). The lenses used for 35mm film cameras are the same lenses that were used on most of the earlier professional image-orthicon cameras, and therefore provide a convenient reference

FOCAL LENGTH

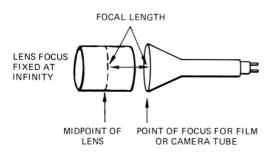

LENS FOCUS
FIXED AT
INFINITY

MIDPOINT OF
LENS

POINT OF FOCUS FOR FILM
OR CAMERA TUBE

With the lens focus adjustment set at infinity (on adjustable lenses), the focal length is measured from the center of the lens to the point where the subject image is in focus on the surface of the pickup tube.

Figure 5-11
Measurement of lens focal length.

point. Lenses used on earlier large vidicon cameras, on the other hand, are comparable to those used with 16mm film cameras.

Lenses of differing lengths are used so that more or less of a scene can be included in the picture. *The longer a lens is, the narrower its viewing angle will be, the less you will be able to get in the picture,* and therefore *the larger individual subjects will be.* Conversely, a short focal-length lens will give you a wider viewing angle, thereby allowing you to get more in the picture, but individual subjects will appear smaller than normal.[10] This *law of lenses* is illustrated in figure 5-12. Long lenses, therefore, can be used to obtain closer views of

10. Because the face of the camera pickup tube is not processing *all* of the picture information passed through the lens, which is a circular scene, there is an apparent difference between the horizontal and vertical angles perceived by the camera. The electronically scanned picture is four units wide and three units high. The perceived angles, therefore, have the same 4:3 ratio. A 1-inch focal length vidicon lens, for example, will have a horizontal angle of about 27 degrees and a vertical angle of approximately 20 degrees. For most planning purposes, the horizontal angle is the most commonly used.

objects. A long **telephoto** lens can get a relatively close-up view of an object from a great distance. On the other hand, a **short** (or wide-angle) **lens** will tend to increase distance and make things look farther away than they are. This fact can lead to distortion of distance.

A long lens (or a long-lens setting on a zoom lens) will *compress* distance. Two objects that are far apart from each other and at a great distance from the camera will be brought closer to the camera with a long lens, and consequently will seemingly be brought closer to each other. A common example is the baseball shot of the pitcher and batter as seen with an exceptionally long telephoto lens from center field. Although the pitcher and batter are about 60 feet apart, the camera is perhaps 400 feet away. Thus, the two players are brought much closer to the camera, and consequently, the distance between them is apparently compressed; on the home screen they may look as if they are only 10 or 15 feet apart.

On the other hand, a wide-angle lens (or a short-lens setting on a zoom lens) will *exaggerate* distance for exactly the opposite reason. The shorter the lens, the further apart objects appear to be spread. Small studios can be made to look immense by use of a wide-angle lens. The apparent force of a punch thrown at the camera will be greatly exaggerated with a wide-angle lens; if the person throwing the punch is only 4 feet from the camera, and the punch brings the person's fist 3 feet closer to the camera (so that the fist stops 1 foot short of the lens), the person's arm has covered a great amount of viewing space by moving only 3 feet. The distance is exaggerated. Figure 5-13 illustrates how two lenses—one **narrow-angle** and one **wide-angle**—will vary the apparent distance between two persons.

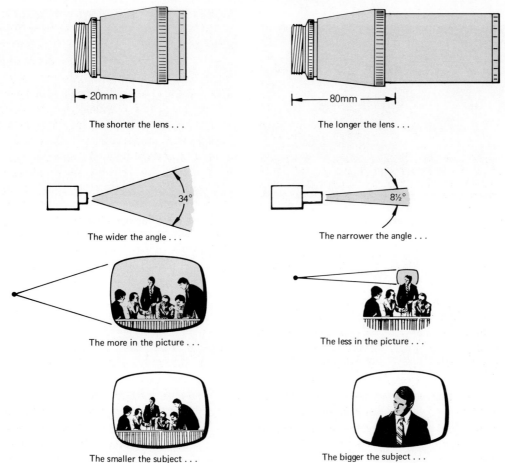

The shorter the lens . . .

The longer the lens . . .

The wider the angle . . .

The narrower the angle . . .

The more in the picture . . .

The less in the picture . . .

The smaller the subject . . .

The bigger the subject . . .

Figure 5-12 Law of lenses.

In discussing the length of various lenses, it should be noted that the size (diameter) of the camera pickup tube will affect the apparent size of the picture obtained with a given focal-length lens. Because the older I-O camera had a larger surface area on the face of the pickup tube (either 3-inch or 4½-inch diameter) than the smaller vidicon and Plumbicon variations (which range from ½-inch to 1¼-inch diameters, with consumer models down to ⅓-inch), a 25mm vidicon lens might result in a picture approximately the same size (or focal length) as a 50mm I-O lens—although the 50mm lens is about double the actual physical length of the smaller vidicon lens.

Two subjects viewed simultaneously through different sized lenses. The monitor on the left shows them as seen by a narrow-angle lens; note how close they appear to be. The right-hand monitor shows the same subjects as seen through a wide-angle lens; note how the short lens exaggerates the distance. The woman and man are actually about 7 feet apart.

Figure 5-13 Comparison of long and short lenses.

Lens Length	Viewpoint
10 mm	Extreme wide angle
25 mm	Wide angle
40 mm	Normal
100 mm	Narrow angle
200 mm	Extreme narrow angle (telephoto)

Figure 5-14 Standard vidicon studio lenses.

Figure 5-14 lists the relative viewing angles of common sizes of larger vidicon lenses (or settings on a zoom lens), compared to the normal perception of the human eye.

Focusing Characteristics

Many fixed-focal-length lenses will have two adjustable rings. One will be the *f*-stop, or aperture opening, and the other will be the focusing ring. This focusing ring, which is common to all who have worked in still photography, can be adjusted anywhere from a few inches to infinity. In most television studio work, however, this adjustment is seldom used. The reason for this is that most older black-and-white TV cameras, which were designed to be used with fixed-length lenses, made the focusing adjustment by moving the pickup tube within the camera. This adjusts the distance from the lens to the surface of the tube, thus handling most ordinary focusing jobs within the studio. This physical movement of the pickup tube was accomplished by turning the focusing knob or handle on the side of the camera.

On color cameras, however, it is impossible to move the three pickup tubes back and forth. Therefore, all focusing is accomplished by the focusing ring on the lens and/or by rearranging the lens elements in the zoom lens. This adjustment is usually accomplished by remote control from the rear of the camera—often on the **pan handle.**

The f-Stop Aperture

As we mentioned when discussing lighting and contrast range (section 4.2), the television camera has a relatively narrow range of light tolerance as compared with the human eye. All camera lenses, therefore, have an adjustable **diaphragm** (or *iris*) that can open or close the *aperture*. This lens opening is strictly to control the amount of light, within acceptable limits, falling upon the surface of the pickup tube; in no way can it affect the size of the picture the lens will pick up. (The size of the picture is strictly a function of the lens diameter and its relationship to the focal length of the lens.)

The size of the **aperture,** or lens opening, is given an *f*-stop number. Because of the complicated formula by which the *f*-stops are determined and identified, *the lower the f-stop number the larger the lens aperture,* and *the higher the f-stop number the smaller the lens aperture.* For instance, *f*-22 is typically the smallest aperture found on most television lenses. The widest opening usually may be anywhere from *f*-1.4 to *f*-3.5, depending upon the structure of the lens. (Longer lenses generally cannot "open up" as far as shorter lenses; they cannot let in as much light. More light therefore is needed when using long lenses.)

The most obvious application of *f*-stop adjustments is to enable the production technicians to adjust to varying light sources. If you are working under very poor lighting conditions, it might be advisable to open up to *f*-2 or even *f*-1.4. On the other hand, if you are working under extremely bright conditions (perhaps outdoors on a sunny day), you might want to "stop down" to *f*-11 or *f*-16.

Depending upon whether one is moving up or down the graded scale of *f*-stops, the amount of light permitted to enter the lens is either doubled or cut in half with each *f*-stop change. Let's take, for example, a given amount of light entering a camera with the lens set at *f*-5.6.

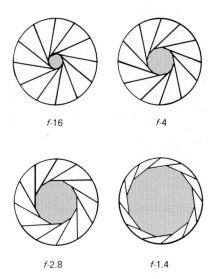

Each time the *f*-stop number is doubled or halved, the amount of light allowed through the lens is decreased or increased by a factor of four. For example, *f*-2.8 allows only one quarter as much light through the aperture as *f*-1.4. But *f*-2.8 allows twice as much light to pass through as *f*-4.

Figure 5-15 Diagrams of various *f*-stop openings.

By stopping down to *f*-8, the opening is made slightly smaller so that one-half as much light is now entering through the lens as with the *f*-5.6 opening. Conversely, moving from *f*-5.6 to *f*-4 doubles the amount of entering light (fig. 5-15).

One word of warning about *f*-stop adjustments should be stated at this point. Generally speaking, the camera operator should not routinely think of the *f*-stop as a means to compensate for bad lighting. Bad lighting or uneven lighting should be handled by correcting the lighting, not by tampering with the camera adjustments.

Of course, with most modern cameras there is an automatic iris control that continually adjusts the aperture opening to the lighting conditions. If it is necessary to control the *f*-stop manually (for specific darkened or purposely overexposed effects) this "auto setting" must first be defeated (turned off).

The depth of field of a lens can be increased by altering any one of three different variables:

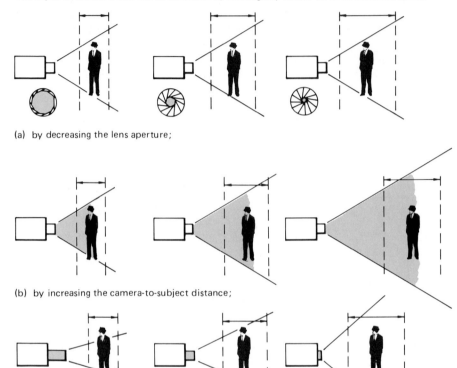

(a) by decreasing the lens aperture;

(b) by increasing the camera-to-subject distance;

(c) by decreasing the lens focal length.

The depth of field of a lens can be increased by altering any one of three different variables:
(a) by decreasing the lens aperture,
(b) by increasing the camera-to-subject distance,
(c) by decreasing the lens focal length.

Figure 5-16 Depth of field.

Depth of Field

One final consideration at this point is the depth of field of a lens on a particular shot. Depth of field refers to *the distance between the nearest point at which objects are in focus and the farthest point at which objects are in focus.* In a typical shot, objects close to the camera will be out of focus and objects too far away may be out of focus; the middle ground where objects are in focus is referred to as the depth of field.

Three different factors interrelate to determine the depth of field: the f-*stop* (the smaller the lens opening, the greater the depth of field), the *distance from the subject to the camera* (the greater the camera-to-subject distance, the greater the depth of field), and *the focal length of the lens* (the shorter the lens, the greater the depth of field). Figure 5-16 illustrates these three variables.

Of these three factors, however, the only one that really gives you much flexibility is the f-stop. The camera-to-subject distance and the lens focal length are both related to the size of picture. You cannot alter either of these two variables without drastically changing your picture. In other words, if you have a given medium shot that you do not want to change, and you want to increase your depth of field, you cannot increase your camera-to-subject distance (by moving the camera back) or you cannot decrease your lens focal length (by changing to a shorter lens) without changing your picture to a long shot. The only option left, therefore, is to stop down to a smaller lens opening; to compensate for that factor you will need to add more light to the scene.

Occasionally, beginning students arrive at the conclusion that the ideal lighting situation is one in which the lens can be stopped down to the smallest possible opening—thereby attaining the greatest depth of field (area of focus) possible. This, however, may not always be a desirable aim. First of all, for aesthetic reasons, the director may not want the background in focus, as it may detract from the foreground action of performers. Or the opposite may be true: the director may want the foreground to be out of focus (for example, he or she may be shooting through some defocused leaves of a tree) in order to concentrate on the action in the background. This is referred to as **selective focus**—when either the foreground or background is deliberately kept out of sharp focus.

In order to achieve these effects, it is necessary to have a shallow depth of field—a wide-open aperture. This, of course, necessitates low-level lighting. Depending upon the exact lighting conditions, the camera operator may have to defeat the "auto setting" of the automatic diaphragm.

Occasionally, for dramatic effect, the director may want the camera operator to **pull focus** to shift a shallow depth of field from a foreground object to the background, or vice versa. This also can be accomplished only with a wide-open aperture. For example, the director may want to open on a tight close-up shot of a half-empty glass close to the camera with the background out of focus; the camera operator could then change the focus (without otherwise altering the shot at all) to focus on the figure lying on the sofa while the foreground glass goes blurry.

Other factors may also necessitate a deliberate shallow depth of field. Perhaps the dramatic setting calls for low-key lighting, which means you have to operate with the lens aperture opened up. Another consideration is simply that of creature comfort; high-key lighting—solely for the sake of working with a greater depth of field—may not be worth the toll it takes on the performers working under the more intense lighting for a prolonged period.

5.4 The Zoom Lens

For the most part, television cameras have never been operated with just a single fixed-focal-length lens. From the beginning of studio productions, professional cameras were designed for what was termed a "complement" of lenses. Three to five lenses needed by a specific camera for a given production would be selected and mounted on a rotatable **lens turret** as shown in figure 5-17. Thus, a typical studio complement of I-O lenses might include a 35mm, a 50mm, a 90mm, and an 8-inch lens. The camera operator would simply spin the turret and any one of the several lenses could be immediately positioned in front of the pickup tube. A facile and experienced camera operator could *rack* to any one of the four lenses and have it in focus within a second or two. The practical limitations for multiple-camera live (or live-on-tape) productions are obvious; but this arrangement could be used again if fixed lenses with their inherent higher optical quality are to be utilized in single-camera EFP "film style" HDTV productions.

Figure 5-17 Lens turret on an older image-orthicon camera. Any one of the four different fixed focal-length lenses can be rotated into the "taking" position in front of the pickup tube. (Photo courtesy of Jerry Hughes)

The development of the *zoom* lens has allowed camera operators and directors to achieve rapid and continuous adjustment of the focal length of the lens and consequently to control precisely the size and framing of shots. It has changed the way in which directors approach visual continuity. In addition to giving the director and camera operator a wider range of lens lengths that are immediately available, the zoom lens also facilitates very smooth on-the-air movement.

This **variable-focal-length** zoom lens is essentially an arrangement of gears and optical elements that allows the operator to shift the lens elements—moving them back and forth in relation to each other. This achieves varying focal lengths by changing the theoretical center point of the lens. Although zoom lenses will vary greatly with price and manufacturer, those lenses designed for professional and industrial levels all share some of the same basic characteristics.

Lens Ratio. For most production situations, a 10-to-1 magnification ratio is common. On a typical lens this would result in focal lengths ranging from, maybe, 10.5mm at the wide-angle position to 105mm at the *zoomed in* high-magnification or "long lens" position. Figure 5-18 provides some indication of the range of shots available with a 10-to-1 ratio lens. Smaller vidicon cameras might be equipped with just a 6-to-1 zoom lens, giving them the limited flexibility of, say, a 12.5mm-to-75mm range. For sporting events and other outdoor public events programming, zoom ratios of 30-to-1 and greater are not uncommon.

These two views represent the extreme focal lengths of a 10 to 1 zoom lens: *left*, zoomed "out" to the shortest focal length (widest angle); *right*, zoomed "in" to the longest focal length (narrowest angle).

Figure 5-18 Range of a zoom lens.

Movement Control. Virtually all zoom lenses will have some sort of motor-driven zoom mechanism. Less expensive models may have only one or two rates of speed. This does not give you much artistic control over the effect you may want to achieve. Therefore, professional lenses usually will have *variable speed* controls. Generally, professional zoom lenses also will provide an optional manual zoom control lever for those times when only the human touch will suffice. It should be noted, however, that serious damage will result if the manual lever is engaged while the power zoom control is in operation.

It is this ability to obtain smooth on-the-air zoom movement that gives the director production flexibility when using zoom lenses. It is possible gradually (or quickly) to **tighten up** a shot, going smoothly and slickly from a **long shot** to a **medium shot** to a **close-up.** This simulated movement is much safer and easier to handle than trying to move the camera physically. In addition, there are many occasions—especially on remote location productions—where it is simply not possible to move the camera. The movement of a zoom is not the same as the movement of **dollying,** however, and this distinction can make a subcon-

scious difference in the reaction of the audience. (This area is discussed in section 6.1.)

Focusing. On all zoom lenses, the focus control is the slip ring located farthest toward the front of the lens. This ring is usually adjusted by remote control when cameras are set up for studio use. Staying in focus can be a problem with zoom lenses. As cameras are moved to different positions on the studio floor, there are constantly changing distance relationships between the camera and the various subjects. Each change necessitates checking to be sure that the lens is set for a "zoomed in" close-up shot—before it is needed. If it is not set, the operator coming from an in-focus wide shot may zoom into an out-of-focus close-up.

To preset your focus, zoom in all the way to the tightest shot you can get and adjust the lens focus. Now, zoom back slowly and check to make sure the subject is in reasonable focus throughout the entire length of the zoom. If not, the only slight adjustment you can make is with the zoom lens focus.

As long as you have a few seconds and you are sure that the talent is not going to move or

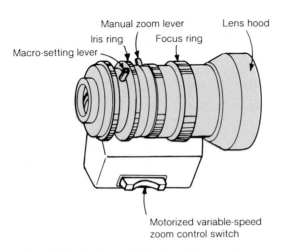

Manual zoom lever   Lens hood
Iris ring   Focus ring
Macro-setting lever

Motorized variable-speed
zoom control switch

In addition to the motorized variable-speed zoom control switch, adjustments on the lens include the macro-lens setting, the iris (*f*-stop) setting, the manual zoom lever, and the focus ring.

Figure 5-19 Diagram of typical zoom lens.

the director is not suddenly going to ask you to get a shot of something at some other distance from the camera, you should be able to get the zoom focus preset. But problems do occur—especially when you quickly have to get the unexpected shot that you were not prepared for.

On some lenses this problem has been solved by allowing you to make a *flange-focal-length adjustment* each time the lens is attached to the camera (fig. 5-19). This keeps all points of the zoom in focus.

Macro Lens.   This special adjustment has become a standard focusing feature of most of the newer lens units. In the **macro** position, one can take extreme close-ups of printed material or small objects at distances of 2 inches or less from the lens. The procedure will vary with individual equipment, but the rather sensitive process of such delicate focusing is usually handled by adjusting the manual zoom lever and not the focus ring.

Iris.   As outlined in section 5.3, the iris (*f*-stop) position has an important relationship to picture focus. If incorrectly set, it can also

greatly affect the quality of color in the picture. In a studio situation where light values are fairly constant, settings will stay within a narrow range. Operating instructions for each camera usually will provide optimum **lux** or *footcandle* levels as related to an *f*-stop setting.[11] For example, on many lenses an *f*-4 setting would be proper for a 200 ftc. reading.

Also, as mentioned earlier, on many lenses there is an automatic control that reacts to incoming light and continually adjusts the *f*-stop as light values change. Some manufacturers provide a *temporary automatic* feature that allows the lens to hold any *f*-stop position set by the automatic sensor.

One reason for overriding this automatic diaphragm setting would be to achieve a *selective focus effect* with a shallow depth of field. This is because the "auto setting" simply reacts to light; it cannot comprehend any desired artistic effect. Another reason for overriding the automatic setting would be to select the features that you want correctly exposed when there are both extreme bright and dark elements in a picture. If you are shooting someone against a bright blue sky, the auto setting is going to adjust to the vast expanse of the light sky, and you are going to get the person in silhouette—which is fine if that is the effect you want. However, if you want to see the features on the person's face, then you are going to have to manually open up the *f*-stop (to a lower *f*-number) to correctly expose the relatively dark face—and thereby deliberately overexpose the bright sky.

On the other hand, when shooting outdoors, light values often can change drastically—as camera angles are changed, as shadows appear, and as sun and cloud patterns

11. The *lux* measurement is based upon an amount of candle light falling upon an object from the distance of 1 meter. While not completely accurate, footcandle readings are often multiplied by 10 to get a rough lux measurement, (e.g., 40 ftc. = 400 lux).

Figure 5-20 Sony DXC 1820 camera. Note the settings for the built-in filter disc.

interplay. Under these conditions, the automatic iris can make the production much easier.

Color Temperature Conversion Filters.

Professional cameras designed for both studio and field production usually have a built-in filter system to compensate for Kelvin temperature differences between indoor and outdoor lighting. Located just in front of the beam splitter (section 5.2), this filter component is an integral part of the optical system within the camera. As an example of how this works, the Sony DXC 1820 has a rotating disc of four filters (fig. 5-20) for different lighting conditions: (1) iodine lamp and sunrise and sunset; (2) bright outdoor; (3) cloudy or rainy; and (4) white fluorescent. It is interesting that sunrise and sunset have the same color temperature as artificial quartz-iodine light. This has to do with the angle of the light rays and the filtering effect of the atmosphere at those two times of day.

One should also carefully follow the instruction book that comes with each camera, as some filters will screen out more total light than others. For instance, in the DXC 1820, outdoor positions 2 and 3 allow one-half as much light to get through to the target as setting 1. This means that *f*-stop settings for indoor or outdoor shooting must be carefully adjusted with the filter position in mind.

5.5 Operator Control Adjustments

Teaching institutions that have professional or industrial-level cameras possess sophisticated items of equipment having a number of controls that make possible high quality pictures. On the other hand, misuse of those controls will greatly diminish picture quality and even cause permanent damage to the equipment. Each class should establish a definite policy as to which controls on the camera (or CCU) are for student adjustment and which are to be handled only by the instructor or trained staff personnel.

Those controls relating to zoom operation described earlier would normally fall within the realm of student control. Such controls should be checked for correct settings as part of camera set-up. On the camera itself, however, there are several controls that, although they may not be designated for student operation, should nevertheless be understood so that settings can be checked for proper positions and levels prior to camera operation.

White Balance. The white balance control establishes the correct color balance to produce a pure white. In a studio situation where all illumination is produced by lights having a consistent 3200 degrees Kelvin temperature, it is possible to do most production work with the **white balance** switch at the factory-established *preset* position. If, however, a camera is to be used for field production where Kelvin temperatures are constantly changing, the white balance procedure must be understood and utilized.

The alternate white-balance switch position on most cameras is labeled *auto,* which simply means that the camera will automatically accomplish the necessary adjustment process as follows. In this mode, with a white card filling the lens image, the camera color system senses any excess of either red or blue light and within a few seconds adjusts accordingly. The white card serves as a neutral reference point so that the camera can judge the balance between red and blue in the light source(s).

To get the proper adjustment for flesh tones, the white card must be placed exactly where the subject's face will be for the shot. In field work where a change in the camera-to-subject angle may introduce a new light source, a new balance adjustment may be necessary. On some cameras there are additional

fine control adjustments that permit the operator to subtly tint with additional amounts of red or blue without having to go through the entire balancing procedure.

Video Output Level Selector. Many cameras have an **automatic gain control (AGC),** which automatically adjusts video levels to compensate for differing light conditions. However, other cameras have a **video output** control, which allows the operator to adjust to some degree for low light levels. The "0 db" position is established by the manufacturer as the standard level of video output for the camera under prescribed lighting conditions. The term *decibel* (db) has been borrowed and slightly altered from its audio derivation; but as with audio, each 6 db increase means that the amplified signal is doubled. This control should never be thought of as a way to make a badly lit picture look good. All it can do is make the bad picture look a little brighter.

Viewfinder Indicators and Controls. In addition to the previously discussed camera controls, the viewfinder itself will have controls and visual indicators. On some cameras the **tally light,** which tells both the operator and the talent/subject that the camera is feeding the switcher, will also light up to indicate that the white balance adjustment in the camera has been completed. On those cameras designed for field use, there may be several **warning lights,** which indicate *low battery power, insufficient lighting,* or *abnormally high setting of the gain control knob* that is causing excessive drain on the battery.

It should also be noted that the **brightness** and **contrast** controls are only for the viewfinder adjustment; *they do not have any effect on the video output of the camera.* Operators who are unaware of this basic fact can be a menace to any proper camera set-up procedure. Such uninformed operators may take one look at their incorrectly adjusted viewfinder picture and—assuming that the camera settings are wrong—begin to mess up a perfectly good camera output by changing the *f*-stop, filter setting, and gain controls. The viewfinder controls—like the camera controls themselves—should be adjusted only while the operator is in headset contact with the person (usually the instructor or technical director) who is in charge of camera set-up in the video control center.

Other Controls. Some cameras have several additional control units that—while not necessarily complicated—are best suited to an individualized-study approach. Such items as the **fade time control,** the **negative/positive selector,** and the **phase control selector** all have clearly marked "0" or neutral positions. The beginning student should be made aware of these *off* positions in order to be able to confirm their negative status during the process of learning camera operations.

Summary

As with audio techniques and lighting considerations, a discussion of camera characteristics and operations could also be broken down into technical aspects and creative concerns. The sections dealing with the camera tube, the receiver picture tube, the lens characteristics, and the zoom lens have been concerned largely with *technical matters.*

The *video signal flow* can be seen as parallel to the audio signal flow. The same functions apply to both audio and video control: transducing, channeling, mixing, shaping, amplifying, recording (and playback), and monitoring. Additional sophisticated *control components* are added to the video system—sync generator, proc amp, time-base corrector, frame synchronizer, waveform monitor, vector scope, and color bars.

The color video system is concerned with accurately rendering three color components—*hue, saturation,* and *brightness.* The transducing function is identified largely with the *camera pickup tube*—the vidicon and its variations. The three principles that led to the development of the television system are *persistence of vision, electrochemical conversion,* and *scanning.*

The three-tube color camera splits the incoming light into the three primary colors of red, green, and blue—each one being channeled to its own pickup tube. The image falls on the *target,* where it is *scanned* by an electron beam sweeping back and forth, and generates both a *luminance* and a *chrominance* signal. The *receiver picture tube,* which can be thought of as the mirrored version of the camera pickup tube, is driven by the same sync pulse that keeps all elements of the video production-distribution-reception system locked together.

Mechanical and optical considerations of the fixed-focal-length lens include consideration of the *focal length, focusing characteristics,* the *f*-stop *lens aperture,* and *depth of field.* Although the zoom lens has several advantages pertaining to *flexibility in selecting focal length* and the facilitation of *smooth movement,* it also has some potential drawbacks relating to focusing characteristics. Operating considerations of the zoom lens include *lens ratio, movement control, focusing, macro lens setting, iris control,* and *color temperature filters.*

There are several other camera controls that students should be familiar with, although they would not necessarily be authorized to make such adjustments without explicit approval and supervision: *white balance, video output level,* and *viewfinder picture adjustments,* among others.

5.6 *Training Exercises*

In order to familiarize yourself with the cameras and focusing characteristics of the lenses in your own studio, work through the following projects:

1. Draw a schematic diagram of the video signal flow in your studio and control rooms. Physically locate components such as the sync generator, camera control units, proc amps, and time-base corrector. Draw in their positions in relation to cameras, monitors, switcher, recorders, and so forth.

2. With a trained staff engineer on the P.L. intercom at the camera control unit, show how the camera picture on the studio monitor is affected when CCU controls such as automatic black level, chroma, and video gain are maladjusted. Experiment with camera-located controls such as the iris setting, filters, and focus. Run through the white balance procedure. Then deliberately change the color in the light source; show that picture on the monitor; then run the white balance procedure again and show the corrected results.

3. Experiment with varying depth-of-field conditions and different focal-length lens settings. Position and adequately light two classmates about 10 feet apart in an almost straight line with the camera—similar to figure 5-13. Using a long lens setting (zoomed in all the way), how close can you move in toward them and keep them both in focus? Try the same with a wide-angle lens setting (zoomed back all the way). Keeping the foreground subject the same relative distance from the camera, how does the size and camera-to-subject distance of the background person change as you vary the focal length? Keeping the focal-length setting constant, vary the light levels and *f*-stops accordingly. How close can you get with the lens opened wide (low-key lighting)? How close can you get with a smaller aperture (high-key lighting)?

4. Demonstrate the zoom ratio of the cameras in your studio—using measured horizontal distances on a wall or against the cyclorama. Using the macro lens setting, determine how small a portion of a printed page you can use to fill the camera shot. Note critical focus problems. How much depth-of-field do you have?

Camera Operations and Production Techniques

6

Camera work is the result of the interaction of four elements of movement, functioning either in combination or singly: the angle and magnification changes made possible within the *lens* itself; changes in the *direction* a camera can be pointed or aimed; *elevation* changes achieved through the utilization of the **camera mount;** and changes of *camera position* accomplished by the movement of the mount itself.

6.1 Camera Movement

The first of these four elements—the angle and magnification characteristics of the lens—was introduced in the last chapter.

Movement of the Zoom Lens

The development of high-quality zoom lenses considerably changed the shooting patterns used on all types of television programs. Prior to this, directors and camera operators had to be well versed in what eight or so basic fixed lenses could produce in terms of angle, magnification, and other optical qualities. Some directors were noted for plotting angle and distance for each shot with a military precision. The result was often excellent television. Unfortunately, this process meant that much of a camera's usable "air" time was lost in simply getting to and from specific locations and in rotating the turret to the correct lens.

With the zoom lens, of course, much of this lost time was regained. The camera operator always has the lens in position, and it is relatively easy to adjust the variable-focal-length zoom control (on the air as necessary) to obtain the exact viewing angle desired. With this ease of operation, however, also comes the tendency to get lazy and careless.

In the hands of a director and/or camera operator who is inexperienced, indolent, or both, the use of a zoom lens often results in dull, unimaginative camera work. It is easy to

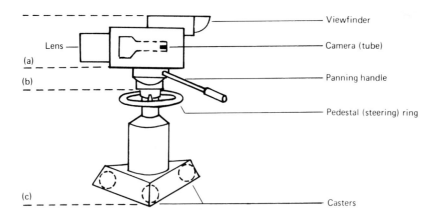

(a) **Camera Head** includes the camera tube and electronics, the viewfinder for the camera operator, and the lens.
(b) **Camera Mounting Head** with the panning handle that controls pan and tilt movements.
(c) **Camera Mount** pictured is a "studio pedestal" with the steering ring and enclosed casters.

Figure 6-1 Three basic parts of the camera.

fall into the trap of assuming that it is always possible to get a decent shot from any camera position at any time. Good camera work, however, requires that the director and camera operator always plot out each shot as carefully as possible, whether using a lens turret or a zoom lens. A large part of successful camera production *discipline* is related to this careful preplanning process. When truly creative people are involved, the zoom lens provides a versatility that amply compensates for the few limitations of the instrument.

The beginning camera operator soon begins to feel familiar with the production terminology. When the lens is *zoomed in,* the angle of the shot is made narrower and the degree of magnification is increased. The effect is that the viewer is *pulled in* to the subject. The reverse is true when the lens is *zoomed out.* The viewer is *pulled out* from the subject.

An important consideration with any zoom movement is that of making sure that the lens focus is preset. The correct procedure for presetting the zoom lens (so that the subject is in focus from long shot to close-up) varies with individual camera design, the ratio of the zoom range (i.e., the relationship of the widest angle to the narrowest angle), the distance from the camera to the subject, and whether the camera is monochrome or color. General instructions were mentioned in section 5.4; specific directions are usually included as part of a camera's performance specifications.

Camera-Head Movement

The second type of camera-lens movement—changes in the direction a camera can be pointed or aimed—is accomplished by the use of the **camera mounting head,** or **panning head.** This pan head is used to attach the camera itself (with its system of lenses and the camera viewfinder) to the camera mounting or support. Thus, there are essentially three basic parts to the complete studio camera setup—the camera itself; the mounting or panning head; and the camera mounting (fig. 6-1).

The camera mounting head allows two kinds of movement: **panning,** which is a horizontal movement of the camera, by rotating the camera mounting head; and **tilting,** which is a vertical movement of the camera, by pivoting up and down.

There are two types of camera mounting heads that are most often used in professional studio operations. The *cradle head* balances the camera on a rocker mechanism that assures a fairly good balance of the camera during most panning and tilting moves. The *cam head* uses two cams, one placed on either side of the head, to provide even better balance than the cradle head and to enable the camera a greater range of movement in tilting.

It should be noted that all instructions for a change in camera direction are given in terms of the camera operator looking toward the performance area. A new picture subject would be identified as being *camera right* or *camera left* of the operator. Thus a *pan right* or a *pan left* is a horizontal move of the lens of the camera in that same direction (fig. 6-2).

For vertical movements, *tilt up* and *tilt down* are used to denote a change of shot framing in those respective directions (fig. 6-3). Although some directors may use the word *pan* to refer to a vertical movement, this usage can result in some momentary confusion on a busy intercom line and is not recommended.

Camera Mounts

Of the four types of camera-lens movements mentioned in the introductory paragraph of this chapter, the last two—camera elevation and camera position—are both dependent upon the camera mount.

The simplest and least expensive camera mount is the **tripod.** This three-legged stand usually is fastened to a dolly base consisting of three casters. The casters either can be allowed to rotate freely, facilitating quick and

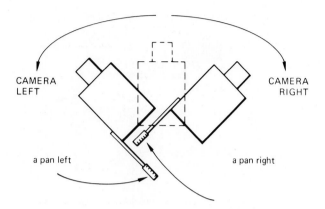

In order to pan the camera in a given direction, the panning handle must be moved in the opposite direction. Thus, in order to execute a "pan left," the camera operator has to move the panning handle to the right.

Figure 6-2 Camera panning.

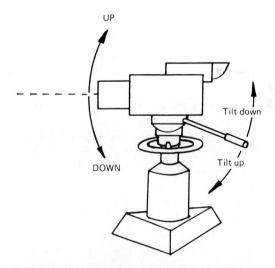

In tilting the camera up or down, only the camera head is pivoted. The camera mounting head (panning head) is not physically moved up or down with the camera mount.

Figure 6-3 Camera tilting.

Figure 6-4 Camera mounted on an adjustable tripod.

Figure 6-5 Camera on a compressed-air pedestal mount.

easy movement of the camera in all directions, or can be locked into a nonmovable position, which results in a steady camera unit for straight-line movement.

The tripod illustrated in figure 6-4 has a crank-operated pedestal that can be used to raise and lower the camera—although not smoothly enough to be used on the air. Most tripods, however, have no means of elevation adjustment other than the laborious process of mechanically adjusting the spread of the tripod legs. Thus, there is no real way to achieve any elevation repositioning during an actual production. The tripod, however, is lightweight and most models are readily collapsible. This makes the tripod a desirable camera mount for most remote productions.

A much more flexible type of camera mount is the *pedestal*. The simplest version is the lightweight *field-studio* pedestal. There are a couple varieties of this mount, which is basically a cross between a tripod and the heavier counterweighted studio pedestal. The field-studio pedestal, with its three larger casters, can be maneuvered like a tripod. Its distinctive feature is the central pedestal that can be raised or lowered, either by a hand crank or with compressed air. Although this method of camera elevation is not normally smooth enough to use on the air, it does allow for relatively quick elevation positioning of the camera between shots.

The counterweighted studio pedestal is a much more flexible and maneuverable studio mount. It has two main features: a thick central pedestal containing the counterweight (compressed air) system that enables the camera operator to raise or lower the camera smoothly on the air; and a steering ring that can control all three casters in a synchronized manner so that smooth on-the-air camera movements across the studio floor can be achieved (fig. 6-5). This ease and the steadiness in camera movement have made the studio pedestal a popular workhorse in many studio situations.

Left, crane adapted for field use, designed to be pulled along special tracks for trucking movements; *right,* special truck-mounted crane for following Olympics bicycling events. (Photos courtesy of ABC Sports)

Figure 6-6 Crane-mounted cameras for Olympics coverage.

Inherited from the film industry, the **studio crane** is the largest and most flexible type of camera mount. Although camera cranes come in a variety of sizes, they all have two elements in common: everything (including a seat for the camera operator) is mounted on a large four-wheeled crane base; and the camera itself is mounted on a boom arm, or tongue, that can be moved vertically or laterally without moving the crane base (fig. 6-6). Even though the studio crane provides the ultimate in smooth and flexible camera movement—for instance, the camera can be elevated from as low as 2 feet off the studio floor to more than 10 feet high with the larger cranes—it does have the drawbacks of being relatively large and bulky and of requiring more than one camera operator. For these reasons, studio cranes are seldom seen in medium-sized studio operations.

Camera-Mount Movements

There are several different ways in which the entire camera and its mounting can be moved about the studio floor. One of the most obvious

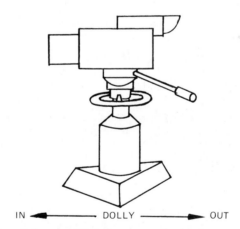

IN ◄――――― DOLLY ―――――► OUT

In a dolly movement, the camera is simply moved closer to or farther from the subject.

Figure 6-7 Camera dollying.

is moving closer to or farther away from the subject; this is referred to as **dollying** the camera (fig. 6-7). When a camera with a lens turret of several fixed-length lenses was used, the physical movement toward or away from a subject was an important movement option for the director. It was the only way to get closer to or farther away from the subject without changing lenses.

Figure 6-8 Comparison of dollying in and zooming in.

Dollying In: *top,* as the camera dollies past the foreground objects (or persons), the viewer is physically transported closer to the primary subject. The viewing angle is not changed; therefore, the viewer arrives at the subject with a relatively wide-angle view that exaggerates the distance between foreground and background objects. Note how the prisoner's head becomes larger in proportion to the background objects—the pine trees and the gallows are relatively unchanged while the cactus is completely lost behind the prisoner's head. The camera obviously is very close to the prisoner.

Zooming In: *bottom,* as the camera zooms in to the primary subject, the viewing angle is narrowed down to exclude the foreground objects (persons). However, since the resulting picture has a relatively narrow viewing angle, the distance between foreground and background objects is compressed, resulting in less depth in the picture. Also, the relationship among the picture objects remains unchanged. Note how the association among the pine trees, the noose, the prisoner, and the cactus has remained the same; they have all increased in size to the same extent, resulting in a "flattened" perspective. Obviously the camera has not moved.

For the most part, the zoom lens has eliminated the need to rely extensively upon the *dolly in* and *dolly out* movements. There is a subtle difference between the types of movement, however, and a dolly is still preferred to the zoom for certain effects. The dolly movement physically moves the viewer past foreground objects, changing the relationship of various objects in the picture; the viewer's angle of vision remains the same, but physical elements are changed. With the zoom, on the other hand (as illustrated in fig. 6-8), the viewer's physical relationship with all objects in the picture is not altered; however, the viewer's angle of vision is narrowed down to exclude unwanted material; thus a sense of concentration is achieved without physically moving the viewer.

Lateral movement of the camera and its mount is known as **trucking.** A change of picture is accomplished as the camera *trucks right* or *trucks left* because the camera moves sideways without panning to the right or left (fig. 6-9).

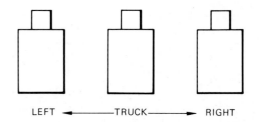

LEFT ◄———————TRUCK———————► RIGHT

In a trucking movement, the camera and mount are moved laterally without any adjustment of the camera mounting head.

Figure 6-9 Camera trucking.

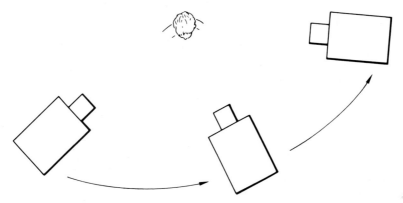

As the camera arcs to the right, the camera operator also has to pan left in order to keep the subject centered in the picture.

Figure 6-10 Camera arcing.

It should be noted that both trucking and dollying movements are difficult to accomplish with a long focal-length lens or with a zoom lens that is zoomed in to a narrow angle. The slightest unsteadiness during the camera movement is exaggerated because the long lens, while magnifying the subject, is also magnifying the shaky camera movement. To a lesser extent, the same problem is apparent with panning and tilting movements. Generally, *the longer the lens, the more difficult any kind of camera head or camera-mount movement is going to be.*

A valuable camera movement is the **arc,** which is a combination truck and pan. As the camera circles, or arcs, to one side of the subject, the camera head is rotated so that it always points at the subject (fig. 6-10). The resulting picture maintains the same subject and the same sized shot, but the perspective or shooting angle changes as the camera movement is executed.

While the tripod mount does not allow for any on-the-air adjustment in the elevation of the camera, most studio camera pedestals are designed to facilitate a smooth change in camera height. In this case, the word *pedestal* is used as a command verb as the camera operator is asked to *pedestal up* or *pedestal down.*

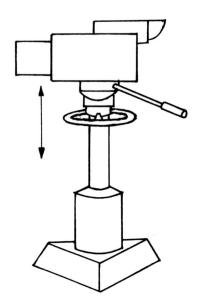

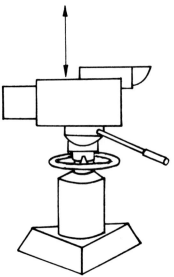

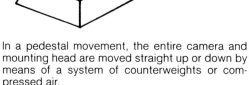

In a pedestal movement, the entire camera and mounting head are moved straight up or down by means of a system of counterweights or compressed air.

Figure 6-11 Camera pedestaling.

While such elevation changes may be limited to roughly 2 to 4 feet, this subtle change can be quite effective, especially at close quarters (fig. 6-11). The pedestal movement can be thought of as a vertical equivalent to the truck. If the camera head is held stationary during a pedestal movement, then the picture subject will change as the camera is moved vertically. If the camera head is tilted during the pedestal movement (in a vertical analog to the arc shot), then the same subject can be kept in the frame while the angle and perspective will change.

In larger studios where the crane mounts or **crab dollies** are used, other movements are also possible. **Craning,** or **booming** (up or down), involves raising or lowering the crane or boom arm. The effect is similar to a pedestal movement, except that much greater vertical distances can be covered. A **crab** shot (left or right) is similar to a trucking shot, with the entire crane or crab dolly being moved sideways. One different kind of motion is the

tongue move. With a large crane, the boom arm or crane can be tongued left or right in a lateral motion (while the base remains stationary).

6.2 Camera Perspectives

Before getting into specific camera operations, the beginning camera operator should be aware of the different ways that cameras can be employed in a television production.

The Viewpoint of the Camera

Generally speaking, the television camera can be used to represent one of three different perspectives: *reportorial* (or *presentational*), *objective,* or *subjective.*

Reportorial (Presentational) Perspective.
The reportorial viewpoint describes those uses of television when a presenter or reporter is speaking directly to the audience through the

camera. The speaker establishes eye contact with the camera and talks directly to the lens. This approach is most often seen in newscasts, instructional TV lessons, sermons, some variety acts (for example, stand-up comedians), some political talks, demonstration programs, and so forth. Camera work in this kind of situation usually calls for a relatively close shot of the speaker—unless he or she has something to display or demonstrate for the camera. Basically, the aim of the camera work is simply to give the viewer a reasonably comfortable look at the person speaking.

Objective Perspective. The easiest way to visualize the use of the objective perspective in television is to imagine the camera as an eavesdropper. The camera is standing back, taking an objective look at what is going on. No one is addressing the camera directly; the camera is just an observer of the action. This type of camera work constitutes the bulk of what we see on television: it includes virtually all drama, most variety and musical performances, talk shows and game shows (except when the host or announcer is directly addressing the audience through the camera), sporting events, and similar productions. Camera techniques vary tremendously for objective production. A wide variety of panoramic shots, quick reaction shots, leisurely camera movement, and rapid camera transitions are required for differing formats. Virtually all of the techniques discussed in the rest of this text are applicable to objective camera work.

Subjective Perspective. Subjective-perspective camera use takes on special meaning when applied to dramatic productions. It refers to those occasional moments when the playwright-director wants to place the viewer in the position of an actor. The camera actually becomes (usually for only a scene) a participant in the drama. It interacts with other players, and it views the world from the individual perspective of the character it is representing. The camera, as the actor's eyes, is in the front seat of the car for the chase sequence; it is in the boxing ring, squaring off against the champion; it is trapped in the burning building, flames licking at the lens; it is drowning, with the waves lapping over the top of the camera-actor. These obvious filmic applications can also be applied—in a less sensational manner—in many types of studio television drama: the haggard hero looking in the mirror, the defocused glaze of the alcoholic lapsing into a coma, the scattered glances of the paranoid in a strange room, the intimate gaze of a lover seducing the camera, and so on. The subjective camera is a specialized technique, one that can have substantial impact when used judiciously. It also is a technique that requires the utmost in precision and concentration from the camera operator.

These three perspectives are intermingled in many television productions. The newscast mixes reportorial and objective perspectives as the newscaster turns from the camera to interview an in-studio guest. The drama mixes objective with subjective techniques, and a touch of the reportorial-presentational is thrown in as an actor turns to make a comment directly to the audience. The talk show jumps back and forth as the host and guests turn from their conversation with each other to talk directly to the viewer. As the camera operator is aware of these varying perspectives—and the production effects appropriate for each one—it is easier to achieve good camera work.

Field of View

At this point, the camera operator should be familiar with the various terms designating the size of the shot desired, or the **field of view.** Generally, most television shots can be related to three basic descriptions.

EXTREME CLOSE-UP
(XCU)

CLOSE-UP
(CU)

MEDIUM SHOT
(MS)

LONG SHOT
(LS)

In addition to these basic shots, many other designations and modifications are possible, such as the ''extreme long shot,'' the ''medium long shot,'' the ''medium close-up,'' and so forth.

Figure 6-12 Basic television shots.

The Long Shot (LS). The long shot would be far enough away from a person that the entire body and quite a bit of the surroundings would be included in the shot. Often, the face of the person would be indistinguishable at this distance. If the person is so far away that he or she is hardly identifiable as a specific individual, then the shot can be labeled an *extreme long shot* (ELS or XLS). The label *wide shot* is used to denote a picture that encompasses the larger, external aspects of the program at a particular point in time. This **establishing shot** relates those people involved in a program not only to each other but also to the setting and circumstances of that program. The establishing shot is frequently used at the beginning of a program to establish the general locale or setting for the program or scene to follow. It also is often used as a closing shot to signal to the audience that we are pulling back from the action, out of the drama, as it comes to a close. Thus, the wide shot is generally used to communicate the broader elements that make up a program. Figure 6-12 illustrates the various fields of view.

The Medium Shot (MS). All of the shot designations are, of course, relative. What is a long shot for one dramatic segment may be considered a medium shot in another situation. Generally, a medium shot of a person would include most of the body, perhaps cutting the talent off slightly above or below the waist. The medium shot is probably the basic shot in standard television production. It is used to convey much of the dialogue in a drama and most of the action in talk shows, game shows, variety programs, and many other studio productions.

The Close-Up (CU). On the other hand, the close-up shot— with its sense of physical intimacy—can probe the individual and personal aspects of what a program is communicating. The eyes and facial expressions provide an important insight into the full meaning of a person's words. In many dramatic situations—as well as in many reportorial-presentational circumstances—the closeup is reserved for moments of high intensity and deep emotion. The close-up is usually defined as a shot consisting of the head and top of the shoulders of a subject. Of course, a close-up shot may be of objects other than a person; it may be a close-up of some item being demonstrated or of some picture being examined. Again, the term is relative. If even a tighter shot is desired—say of just the eyes or of the eyes, nose, and mouth of an individual—then the shot would be labeled an *extreme close-up* (ECU or XCU).

The process of alternating between the long shot and close-up aspects of a program is possibly the most important element in the communicative language of both film and television. This basic principle was discovered by pioneers such as Edwin Porter and D. W. Griffith during the early days of the motion picture. They realized that by moving the camera into a closer position they could accomplish what is automatically done by the eye and the mind. While the scope of human vision is almost 180 degrees, we immediately isolate and particularize the focus of our attention to a single person or object when the brain is motivated by a stimulus such as motion or sound. Cutting from a wide-angle to a close-up camera shot is much the same process, except that the distance factor is greatly reduced by lens magnification.

6.3   Picture Composition

Much has been written on the subject of picture composition and the related concepts that deal with the cumulative effect of a series of picture images. As in the motion picture, the main concern of television is usually the human element. Sets, props, and graphic arts have an important auxiliary function, but it is people we watch—the movements of their bodies and the expressions on their faces. When one considers the viewer sitting at some distance from a 19-inch or 21-inch screen, the positioning of those faces and bodies assumes a critical importance.

As we discuss the following elements of framing, headroom, lead room, composition, and balance, keep in mind that these various "rules" that have evolved as part of the grammar of the medium should be considered *guidelines*—not federal regulations. Once the rules have been mastered, they exist to be modified or broken with proper justification and basis—dramatic motivations, artistic considerations, and so forth.

Framing

Television directors (borrowing somewhat from their older film cousins) have developed a simple terminology to describe to the camera operator the basic dimension of a shot. The scope of a shot is described in terms of that portion of the body that is to be cut off by the bottom edge of the picture. Thus a *full, knee, waist,* or *chest* shot quickly communicates the required *framing* of a person in the picture. Equally expressive are the terms **single** or **two-shot,** which describe the number of people to be included in the shot. For closer face shots, the precise terminology may vary somewhat with the individual director.

Other descriptive labels have evolved to specify certain kinds of desired shots. For example, an **over-the-shoulder shot (O/S),** as illustrated in figure 6-17, might be called for in a situation when two people are facing each other in a conversation (such as a dramatic scene or an interview program). This means a shot favoring one person (who generally is facing the camera) framed by the back of the head and shoulder of the person with his or her back to the camera.

Headroom

An important discipline for all camera operators is that of consistently maintaining an adequate amount of **headroom.** This term refers to the space between the top of a subject's head and the top of the frame. When this distance is not observed, the results can be somewhat distracting (fig. 6-13).

It is especially important that headroom distance be uniform among all of the cameras on any production. A helpful guide for shot consistency is to place the eyes of subjects at

WRONG   WRONG

CORRECT

Figure 6-13 Correct headroom framing.

the point of an imaginary line approximately one-third of the way down from the top of the picture. In close-up shots, the framing is best with the eyes slightly below the line. In wider shots, they would be slightly above the line (fig. 6-14).

There is a very good technical reason why headroom distance is carefully watched by camera operators and directors. Due to several factors, most home television sets lose up to 10 or 15 percent of the picture area at the outer edge. As a result, framing that would appear to be adequate on the studio monitor will actually result in a **cropping** of heads or graphic art lettering on the home receiver.

Lead Room

When speakers or performers directly address the camera (reportorial perspective), they generally are centered in the frame, unless there is some foreground object or over-the-shoulder visual effect to be included in the frame. When subjects are speaking to one another, however, as in a dramatic presentation or a public affairs panel discussion (objective perspective), the framing is much more attractive if there is an added amount of **lead room** or *talk space* in the side of the frame to which they are speaking. By the same token, a distracting, crowded effect is created if the framing is such that the face of the subject is placed too close to the frame edge (fig. 6-15).

The concept of lead room applies even more strongly to moving subjects. If a person is moving laterally across the screen, it is important to allow lead space in front of the person (fig. 6-16). Lead the talent; do not follow.

Depth Composition

Television is a two-dimensional medium. In order to simulate some feeling of depth, the director and camera operator can manipulate certain elements in pictorial composition. The feeling of depth is enhanced if some familiar background is used; it helps to give a feeling of scale or perspective. If a plain or abstract background is used, the viewer has no yardstick against which to gauge the distance from the subject to background.

Foreground objects can add significantly to the feeling of depth. By framing some nearby objects off to one side of the picture or along the bottom of the picture, the subject in the background is placed in greater relief. Care must be taken, however, not to force an unnatural effect for its own sake—as this will undoubtedly appear contrived to the viewer.

Whenever possible, depth composition can be achieved with the arrangement, or **blocking,** of talent. If several people appear in a scene, try to arrange them so that some are closer to the camera than others. Nothing is deadlier than three or four people stretched out in a straight line, all equidistant from the camera.

As a general rule—with many exceptions—the longer a shot is, the more headroom it should have.

Figure 6-14 Correct headroom on different sized shots.

BAD   BETTER   BEST

The camera operator should always intuitively give talent additional space in the direction in which he or she is looking.

Figure 6-15 Proper lead room or "talk space."

BAD   CORRECT

Whenever a person is moving across the screen, the camera operator should anticipate the flow of movement, always giving the talent additional lead room to move into.

Figure 6-16 Proper lead room for a moving subject.

The over-the-shoulder shot (*left*) generally presents a more dynamic, interesting, and aesthetically pleasing picture than the flat double-profile two-shot (*right*).

By shooting the person behind the desk from an angle (*left*), a more inviting and vigorous effect can be achieved than with a formal head-on flat shot (*right*).

Figure 6-17 Depth staging.

Even with only two persons, an over-the-shoulder shot as a rule is prefered to a flat two-shot of a double profile (fig. 6-17).

A feeling of depth can also be achieved by careful use of angles. If a shot calls for someone to be sitting behind a desk, the camera can get a much more interesting shot by trucking right or left and shooting the desk and subject from an angle (fig. 6-17). Of course, the dramatic context might call for a formal head-on shot of a judge or stern employer.

Balance and Other Considerations

There are many artistic elements to be considered in composing an aesthetically pleasing picture: balance, tone, unity, rhythm, proportion, line, mass, and others. It is beyond the scope of our discussion to try to treat these elements in this book.[1]

A few words about **balance,** however, would be in order. Many beginning camera operators try to achieve a pleasing composition by striving for **symmetrical balance.** They

try to place the most important element directly in the center of the picture and/or try to balance picture components with equal elements equidistant from the center. This kind of mechanical balancing can lead to very stiff, dull, formal pictures.

A more dynamic kind of composition is **asymmetrical balance,** wherein a lightweight object some distance from the center of the picture can balance a heavier object closer to the center (similar to a seesaw with a light person at the end of the board balancing a heavier person seated close to the center). (See section 10.1.)

Another way to avoid centralization of picture elements is to think in terms of the **rule of thirds.** Imagine the television screen divided horizontally and vertically into thirds. If major pictorial elements were placed at the points where the lines intersect, the result would be a more pleasing balance than if perfect symmetry were achieved (fig. 6-18).

Movement

A final consideration of picture composition is the temporal and fluid quality of the medium. Since an important element of television is *movement* of one kind or another, pictures rarely remain static for any period of time. Even in a discussion program, the guests will turn their heads as the conversation shifts to

1. For a full discussion of all of the elements of picture composition, see Herbert Zettl, *Sight Sound Motion: Applied Media Aesthetics* (Belmont, Calif.: Wadsworth Publishing Company, 1973). See also Gerald Millerson, *Effective TV Production,* 2d ed. (London: Fokal Press, 1983).

another person. In large musical or dramatic production, the set and other background elements must be taken into consideration. For these reasons, proper composition involves a constant process of adjustment and an exercise of discretion in matters of balance and proportion.

6.4 Operating Techniques

At this point, the beginning camera operator should feel ready to start working with the cameras. A few words about some operating procedures—especially some safety precautions—should, however, be mentioned first.

Safety Procedures

There are several simple basic standard rules that every camera operator should always follow.

1. Put on your headset; make sure you are in contact with the control room before doing anything else.
2. If your camera is equipped with **lens caps,** check with the video engineer before removing them. Always ask for "permission to uncap." Unless you get this permission from the director or someone else in control, assume you are not yet authorized to use the camera.
3. Virtually every studio camera has provisions on the camera mounting head to lock the pan and tilt mechanisms. The pan and tilt locks should always be securely engaged whenever the camera is not in use. Release the locks, making certain you have a firm grip on the panning handle. Although all mounting heads should be balanced so that the camera head will not lurch forward or fall backward when

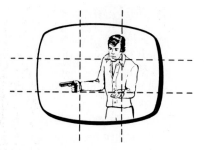

Note how the two main focal points—the face and the hand holding the gun—are located at the intersections of the thirds.

Figure 6-18
Asymmetrical balance and the rule of thirds.

unlocked, it is conceivable that something could go wrong and the camera could be damaged. Once you have the pan and tilt heads unlocked, *never let go of the panning handle* without first locking the mounting head!

4. In all camera operations, always be alert to the possibility of an accident that could result in the camera falling over or off its mount. Check all tripod leg adjustments; make sure the camera mounting head is securely fastened. Be especially careful, with lightweight tripods, of the possibility of tipping over the whole camera mount (for example, by stumbling over a camera cable).
5. Never stand on the camera cable. The **coaxial cable** consists of numerous individual strands of wire. Any unnecessary pressure on the cable can break some of these fragile wires.
6. After the production, reverse the procedures you followed in setting up the camera. Lock your pan and tilt heads before doing anything else. Cap up your lens and remove your headset.
7. Return your camera to its storage area and coil your cable in a figure-eight pattern.

Operating Hints

Aside from these rules, there are several operational techniques that will help you in most studio situations. Check to see exactly what procedures are followed in your studio.

Camera Setup (Prerehearsal). Even before you are ready to set up your camera, see if you can help with other studio preparations. Can you be of assistance during the early stages of lighting and staging setup? In union studios, of course, this is not allowed; but in many university, industrial, and educational closed-circuit operations, all crew members are expected to assist in all positions. Always be ready to help out wherever needed. This is part of the *discipline* of a successful team member.

With the consent and assistance of the video engineer, check out all connections, locks, adjustments, and controls on your camera. Make sure everything is in working order. Do not try to adjust the specific camera controls on the back of the camera (except for viewfinder adjustments) without explicit guidance or permission from the supervising engineer (see section 5.5). Check your *f*-stop, but do not change or adjust it without higher authority.

Most camera mounting heads have adjustments that will apply a variable amount of drag or resistance to the pan and tilt controls. Depending upon the explicit production requirements, you may want your pan and tilt controls rather loose and free or you may want them tightened up. Adjust them accordingly.

Rehearsals. In general, do not abuse the PL intercom (section 3.5). Quite a few production positions will be using the same line. Use it for speaking only when absolutely necessary. Use it for *listening* all the time. You never can be sure when the director or an engineer will have to get you to react instantaneously.

During the early technical or blocking rehearsal, familiarize yourself as thoroughly as possible with the production and your role in it. Make certain you have floor assistance wherever and whenever you need it—someone to handle your graphics, someone to pull your cable in a difficult move. If you are working a boom or crane camera, make sure you coordinate all moves with your camera assistants. Practice all transitions and difficult moves; practice starting and stopping your pedestal and trucking moves; go over your different dollies. If you are using a zoom lens, make sure you know what all of your on-the-air zooms will be. Preset your focus for your various zoom movements. (Depending upon your position and the camera-to-subject distance, each zoom will have its focus preset differently.) Make sure you have plenty of cable to handle every move you may need to execute on the air.

On-the-Air Production. In general, be extra alert. Be prepared for anything. Anticipate the worst. (Your camera cable may tangle; your zoom lens may jam; your camera may get caught in a microphone cable.) Assume nothing. Again, this kind of alertness and sense of anticipation is what separates the disciplined professional from the "I'll get by" dilettante.

Prepare and anticipate all of your moves. Preset your zoom lens every time you get on a new long shot (and you should then be ready to zoom in, staying in focus, if called upon to do so). Make certain you are zoomed out all the way (to a wide-angle position) before attempting any camera moves (such as dolly, truck, arc, pedestal). If you are using a free-wheeling tripod, be certain your casters are set, all pointing in the correct position, before trying any camera-mount moves.

Always be ready for your next shot. Use your **shot sheet** (section 13.4) if the director is working from one; otherwise, anticipate your next shot based upon the rehearsal. Every camera should be equipped with **tally lights** on the front of the camera (for the talent) and by the viewfinder (for the camera operator); these indicator lights tell you when the camera is actually on the air. Watch your tally light; break to your next shot as soon as you are off the air—but not before.

If you are shooting an **ad-lib** or a semi-scripted program, do all you can to help the director. Anticipate shots the director may want. If you have the director's prior permission (or command), then "fish" for good shots. Do not, however, try to dictate to the director what shot to take. In many panel or interview programs, the director will not want you to move from your basic shot; do not presume to know more about the program than the director; stay with your assigned shot until you receive other orders. Watch the talent for signs that will telegraph any moves on his or her part. When the talent leans forward, shifts feet, looks toward the next set element, be ready to move with the first step or the rise from the chair. Again, anticipate; be alert.

At this point, you should be ready for your first camera assignment.

Summary

Camera movement can be divided into four classes: (1) movement of the lens (*zooming*); (2) movement of the camera mounting head (*panning, tilting*); (3) elevation and lateral movement of the camera mount (*pedestaling, tonguing, craning* or *booming*); and (4) movement of the entire mount—tripod, pedestal, or crane (*dollying, trucking, arcing, crabbing*). A zoom resembles a dolly except that when dollying, the viewer is physically moved while the viewing angle does not change; when zooming, the viewing angle is narrowed and there is not the same feeling of movement.

There are three different camera perspectives that can be employed: *reportorial* (the camera is addressed directly); *objective* (the camera is an eavesdropper); and *subjective* (the camera is an actor). The field of view of a camera can be thought of as consisting of long shots, medium shots, and close-ups—with quite a few variations and combinations.

In determining picture composition, shots are labeled descriptively—such as full shot, knee shot, waist shot, chest shot, single, two-shot, three-shot, and over-the-shoulder shot. Headroom and lead room (talk space) are two important framing considerations. The illusion of depth in a television picture can be enhanced with proper background considerations, foreground objects, blocking of talent, and use of staging angles. Asymmetrical balance, which is generally more interesting than symmetrical balance, can be partially achieved by using the *rule of thirds*. Picture composition also has to be achieved in movement—as television is a temporal medium, constantly changing.

Before operating a camera, there are several safety procedures that the camera operator should follow. There also are a number of operating hints that the camera operator should be aware of during the set-up period, during the rehearsals, and during the actual production.

Once the production crew member has mastered camera operation, the next step is to tackle the video switcher. Chapter 7 deals with the way camera outputs are selected and/or mixed to become the program video.

6.5 Training Exercises

1. Write a two-page analysis of how picture composition and camera movement were used during a 30-second or 1-minute television

commercial that exhibited more than the usual slick or banal application of these disciplines. Choose one you have already seen several times.

2. Set up a class practice session during which every member of the class has an opportunity to practice all of the lens and camera movements outlined in this chapter: lens movement (zooming or rotating a lens turret); panning and tilting; pedestaling (if your studio has studio pedestals); and camera-mount moves (dollying, trucking, arcing); plus crane movements if your studio is so equipped.

3. Stage five or seven class members in a manner similar to figure 6-8. Practice both a dolly in and a zoom in. Carefully note the differences. What are the emotional effects or subjective feelings of each movement? For what purposes would you use a dolly? A zoom?

The Switcher: Disciplines of the Technical Director

7

As outlined in section 5.1, the video signal flow can be traced in a pattern parallel to the audio signal flow. At the heart of the video signal flow system is the control room video switching unit—the **switcher.**[1] This video switcher, much like the audio console, has three primary functions. First, it is a *channeling,* or routing, device that can select a video source from any of several different cameras for signal output on the program line. Second, it is a *mixer* (the British term for the unit is the *vision-mixing desk*) that can combine different video sources by means of **superimpositions, keys,** and other **special effects.** Third, the switcher also can be thought of as a *shaping* device, because some of the effects possible with the switcher do substantially alter the quality or shape of the video signal.

At the networks and top production houses, switchers are in use that carry these traditional functions to new levels of electronic wizardry. At this level the switcher is more often referred to as a **special effects generator (SEG).** When used in conjunction with a number of specific function modules, the unit can create and execute a wide range of video displays and transitions. The ultimate shaping device is the **digital video manipulator (DVM),** which takes the basic video signal and breaks it down into a series of digital pulses (see section 7.4). It is this digital legerdemain that enables us to achieve the eye-dazzling computer effects that have become common in the past few years.

---

1. The term *switcher* is confusing because it is commonly used to refer both to the piece of machinery (the video switching unit) and to the operator who pushes the buttons (the switcher who does the switching). To avoid confusion, in this text we shall follow industry practice and refer to the switching unit operator as the **technical director,** although the student occupying this position obviously is not a technical *director* in the professional sense of the word.

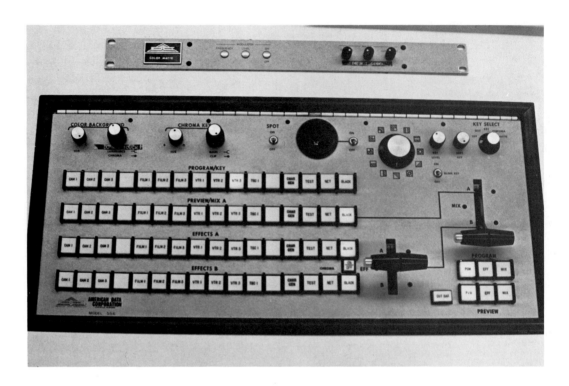

Figure 7-1 Relatively simple switcher with two effects buses.

One of the most frequently used effects is that of a continuous movement (animation) of lettering or other elements of a *graphic.* In addition to familiar **dissolve** and **wipe** transitions, the picture can be made to **fold over,** which gives the effect of the turning of a page. Instead of a simple corner wipe with a separate picture in any given quarter of the frame, the **squeeze zoom** can reduce the whole frame to occupy the designated quarter-frame and at the same time fill the remainder of the screen with a new picture.

The graphics that one sees on television are less often the work of an artist with pen and brush than they are the electronic product of a creative artist-technician working with a **character generator** and/or a SEG computer graphics package (see section 9.5). The display of a ballplayer's still picture and sports statistics is designed days in advance and programmed into the unit for instant retrieval at game time.

The "smart switcher" allows the operator to preprogram effects such as dissolves, wipes, tumbling cubes, flipping pages, and shrinking inserts. Effects that include timed transitions—such as an exact 2½-second (75-frame) wipe—can be similarly programmed into the switcher's microprocessor for later precise execution. The digital technology that makes this possible is discussed in section 7.4.

7.1 The Principle of the Switcher

The switcher in a network television studio is indeed an impressive instrument. With its multiple rows of buttons, switches, levers, and lights, it is quite a formidable piece of machinery. Despite all of its complexity, however, it operates on exactly the same fundamental principles found in the simplest units. Figures 7-1 and 7-2 illustrate two types of switching units.

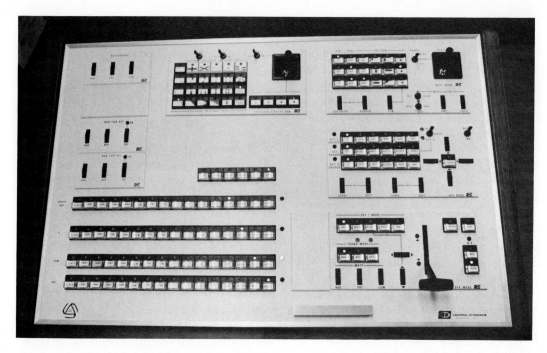

Figure 7-2 More complex studio production switcher.

While most educational institutions cannot afford special effects generators capable of performing the most complex video effects, it is important to keep in mind that certain primary functions and their related operating principles are common to all switching units. When these basic functions are clearly understood, the well-trained student can master the equipment found in professional studios without difficulty. Differences in board configuration and capacity can be readily grasped if one is well grounded in the basics. Thus, this chapter has been written to treat switcher function and operation as generalized concepts that can be applied to the switchers found in most university studios.

Basically, the switcher can be thought of as a sophisticated *connection panel*—a means of taking video signals from several cameras and other sources (film chains, video recorders, remote feeds) and selecting those to be sent out as the *program signal,* or "program line out." There are two identical **banks** of buttons—identified in figure 7-3 as the *A*

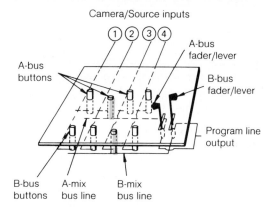

On the *A* bus, camera 2 is punched into the mix-bus line. On the *B* bus, camera 3 is punched into the mix-bus line. Thus—depending upon the positions of the fader arms—either the *A* bus (camera 2) or the *B* bus (camera 3) will provide the program line output.

Figure 7-3 Cutaway schematic drawing of two-bus switcher.

bus and the *B* bus. Each camera (and other source) has an input line that is fed to a button on the *A* bus and simultaneously each source is connected to a button on the *B* bus. There is also a **black** signal sent to a button position on each bus; this signal contains just the synchronizing pulses—no picture information—so it can be used whenever the switcher is to send out a blank (or black) picture.

Running beneath each row of buttons (out of sight within the switcher) is a **mix-bus** line. This functions much like the program mix bus in the audio console (fig. 2-4). When one of the camera/source buttons is pressed, the signal from that camera (or other source)—for example, camera 2 on the *A* bus in figure 7-3—is connected to the mix-bus line. Only one signal source can be connected to a given mix-bus line at a time; the buttons are self-cancelling so that when a button is pressed, that action releases the previous connection. Therefore, each mix-bus line can have one camera signal punched into it at any given moment.

Each mix-bus line is then connected to a lever that functions just like a fader-potentiometer on the audio console. Each **fader arm** controls the amount of video signal flowing through the bus. When the *A*-bus fader is activated, the signal from the *A* bus is sent out the program line. When the *B*-fader arm is activated, the signal punched up on the *B* bus becomes the program output. The two fader arms are usually designed so that they can be physically locked together. In this manner when one fader is activated, the other will be automatically deactivated. Thus, when both fader arms are pushed up toward the *A*-bus position, the *A* bus will be activated and the *B* bus will be dead; when both faders are pulled down to the *B*-bus position, the *B* bus will be sending out its signal as the program feed and the *A* bus will be inactive. By keeping the two fader arms locked together—moving them up and down simultaneously—we will always

have one bus activated (sending out the program signal) while the other bus is dead.

The simple switcher we have just described is the heart of every video switching unit regardless of how complex the equipment may be.

7.2 Cuts, Dissolves, Fades, and Supers

Moving pictorial expression utilizes two basic methods of changing from one image to the next. There is the direct cut, or **take,** in which the picture is instantly replaced by another; and there is the **dissolve** in which the picture is, for a varying but brief period of time, blended with the subsequent image. All fancier forms of electronic transitions—such as the wipe, the defocus, numerous pattern wipes, and digital-based transitions such as the foldover and squeeze zoom—are but extensions of the dissolve.

Figure 7-4 illustrates the way in which either a **cut** (take) or a dissolve can be accomplished. With camera 1 pressed on the *A* bank (or bus) and both fader levers together in the *A*-bank position, the switcher would be feeding the picture on camera 1 to the program line. If the director wanted to instantaneously replace the camera 1 picture with the picture from camera 3, he or she would have the technical director simply press the camera 3 button on the *A* bank. The result is an immediate cut or take to camera 3.

If, for any one of a number of dramatic or aesthetic reasons, the director wanted to momentarily blend the images of two cameras in a transition, he or she could utilize a dissolve. Figure 7-4 shows the switcher set up for a dissolve from camera 1 to camera 2. With camera 1 punched up on the *A* bus and camera 2 on the *B* bus, camera 1 is on the line because both levers are in the *up* position, so all the video signal is coming through the *A* bus (camera

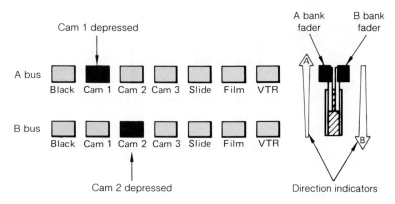

The arrows of the two fader-arm direction indicators show where the fader must be in order to activate its respective bus. Thus, the *A* fader must be **up** to activate the *A* bus; and the *B* bus is activated when the *B* fader is **down**—at the widest part of its direction indicator.

Figure 7-4 Simple television switcher.

1). But as we begin to move both levers downward, we are decreasing the video signal from camera 1 on the *A* bank at the same rate that we are adding power to the picture (camera 2) on the *B* bank. When both faders are at the bottom position—fully activating the *B* bus and cutting out the *A* bus—we see only camera 2. But for a brief period we had the two camera pictures overlapping during the *dissolve* transition.

For years motion picture directors, working in the dramatic idiom only, used the *lap-dissolve* to denote the passage of time or the physical distance of one scene from the next. With the advent of television as a medium for many idioms—such as music, news, sports, documentaries, and so forth—the dissolve is often used in these program types as a connecting device.

If the director wishes to blend two images together and hold them in combination for a specific period of time, the result is termed a **superimposition** or, more often, a **super.** This is accomplished simply by holding the two fader levers midway between the *A* bus and the *B* bus, thus providing partial video display from both of the two buses (each with a different camera picture punched up).

Another type of video move—usually indicating a major program transition from one segment to another—is the **fade,** which is simply a dissolve using black in place of one of the cameras. Thus, a *fade in* to camera 3 is actually a dissolve from black to camera 3. A *fade out* is conversely a dissolve from the camera on the air to black.

When two pictures are *in super,* the brighter elements of both pictures dominate the resulting combination and the darker elements tend to disappear. An obvious question might be, Why not separate the faders—activating both buses—and have the full value of both pictures? The best answer is that the resulting two-picture video level is usually far in excess of what the video control system can handle. The effect is a *blooming* (or white domination) of the brightness scale of the picture. In a super, however, where one picture has a weak brightness scale (such as the name card that is all black with white letters), it is

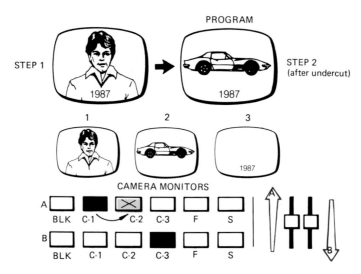

Figure 7-5 Undercutting while in super.

In this diagram, we have camera 3 supered over camera 1. By punching up camera 2 on the A bus—replacing camera 1 with camera 2—we have "undercut" to a new super, camera 3 over camera 2.

possible to cheat somewhat and slightly separate the faders to reinforce the weaker video signal. In this case, a prior word to the video operator is advised.

When two cameras are supered, it is possible to replace instantly either one of the pictures with any other signal source available on the switcher through a process called an **undercut.** As an example, in step 1 of figure 7-5 we have set up a super with camera 1 on the A bus, camera 3 on the B bus, and the faders in the midposition. In step 2, by simply pressing the camera 2 button on the A bus, the super instantly changes to camera 2 and camera 3 instead of cameras 1 and 3.

If the two cameras are supered and the director wants to fade to black, the faders can be simultaneously *split* in those directions that kill their respective signals (in our illustration, moving the A fader down and the B fader up). Thus both cameras would be faded out at the same time. For the most part, however, it

greatly simplifies the process of learning the switcher operation if the faders are always locked together.

The usual method of fading to black is to use the black position on the inactivated bus as another camera and dissolve to it. For instance, in figure 7-4, if the director called for a fade to black, we would first have to punch up black on the B bus. Then we would move both faders down to the B-bus position. In actuality, we would be fading out the A bus with camera 1 on it while we are simultaneously fading in the B bus with black (nothing) punched up on it.

Monitors

In describing the undercut procedure illustrated in figure 7-5, we showed what would appear on each of the three individual camera monitors and what would appear as the final super on the program line monitor. By this point in our study, most students will have become aware of a series of monitors in the video control room.[2] There may be up to a dozen different monitors, each performing an important individual function. Every video source will have its own monitor. Each studio camera, film chain (or telecine camera), and video recorder will have a small individual monitor. Other monitors, in a larger station operation, will include a network monitor (to indicate the actual network **feed**); an off-the-air monitor (a regular TV receiver tuned to the station's transmitter); one or more remote monitors (which can be used for a variety of auxiliary inputs, including more on-location microwave feeds); and so forth.

In addition to the smaller monitors (they may range typically from 7-inch to 12-inch tubes), there are a couple of other large monitors. The most crucial of all is the **line monitor.** This is the monitor that shows the actual picture coming out of the switcher that is being sent to master control for live transmission or video recording. The line monitor performs the final picture monitoring function in the video signal flow model (section 5.1) and is analogous to the master audio speaker-monitor. This monitor, the one the director must be constantly aware of, serves as the final check on the program picture content.

The other large monitor in most control room configurations is the **preview monitor.** This is ordinarily set alongside the program monitor in an equally prominent spot. It can be used to preview anything the director wants to see. (Again, recall the audio previewing capability of the cue position on the audio console, section 3.4.) Typically, the preview monitor is used to preview special effects or supers. Usually these shots will take some amount of adjusting before they are set up exactly the way the director wants them, so the preview monitor can be used for these special previewing purposes.

7.3 Preview and Preset Switcher Functions

The switcher model that we have discussed up to this point—with two rows of buttons and one set of faders—would severely limit any but the simplest of productions. With just two more banks we can greatly increase the versatility of the switcher.

Program and Preview Buses

To accomplish the previewing function, we need to set up additional switching buses to feed the preview monitor. With only two mix buses there is no way to have a preview of a super—even if we had a second monitor to preview it on. One of the two mix banks must carry a full-strength picture signal. We cannot, at the same time, have our fader levers set in the midposition.

In figure 7-6 there is added a **program bus** that is, in effect, the final source of what goes out over the program line. When the *mix* button on the program bus is pressed, the program line is fed whatever has been set up on the two mix banks. The program signal would be a super if both faders were set at the midpoint (and each mix bus had a different camera punched up); the program signal would be a single camera (with the program mix button pressed) if the fader arms were at either the *A*-bank or *B*-bank position. (On the other hand, if the program mix button was *not* punched up—as in figure 7-6—then whatever camera button was engaged—camera 2 in the case of figure 7-6—would be the program signal.)

2. The video *monitor* is distinguished from the regular television *receiver* in that the monitor is usually a high-quality unit with the ability to reproduce fine detail. It receives a direct, unmodulated, video signal, as opposed to a modulated radio-frequency signal (see sections 2.2.1 and 5.1). Thus, there is no audio and no channel-selection capability.

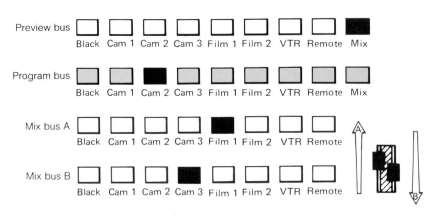

Preview bus — Black, Cam 1, Cam 2, Cam 3, Film 1, Film 2, VTR, Remote, Mix

Program bus — Black, Cam 1, Cam 2, Cam 3, Film 1, Film 2, VTR, Remote, Mix

Mix bus A — Black, Cam 1, Cam 2, Cam 3, Film 1, Film 2, VTR, Remote

Mix bus B — Black, Cam 1, Cam 2, Cam 3, Film 1, Film 2, VTR, Remote

Figure 7-6 Basic four-bus television switcher.

In this illustrated example, camera 2 is punched up on the program bus and is therefore being sent out directly to the program line. The preview bus has "mix" punched up, which puts the *A* and *B* mix buses in the preview mode. On these two buses we have film camera 1 selected on the *A* bus and camera 3 on the *B* bus. With the fader arms split between the two mix buses, we have both buses partially activated. Thus, we have a super of film 1 and camera 3 being adjusted on the preview monitor while camera 2 is being sent out on the air.

If, as in figure 7-6, we also have a **preview bus** with an identical mix button—and that bus only sends a feed to the preview monitor—then we can have that preview of an upcoming super. In the simplest use of the term, we have a chance to *preset* (view and adjust) the super as well as to *preview* it.[3]

With this switcher layout, figure 7-7 illustrates how the preset and preview modes work in operational terms. With the switcher set up as in figure 7-6, the monitors appear as in stage 1. Camera 2 is feeding the program line through the program bank. Cameras "film 1" and 3 are in super on the mix buses and are feeding the preview monitor because "mix" is punched up on the preview bank. The super can now be adjusted by manipulating the fader arms of the mix-bus *A* (film 1) and mix-bus *B* (camera 3) until the desired balance is

achieved. Then, in stage 2, we "take cameras 3 and film 1 in super" by simply pressing the program mix button.

In executing this operation we have utilized the concepts of preview and preset and also employed a basic switcher principle of moving the continuing program feed from one area (bus) of the switcher to another. This principle of moving the program feed around to different banks of the switcher (or special effects generator) assumes much more importance as one works with switching units of more complex design. For now, however, let us look at another application of the basic four-bus switcher.

The monitors in figure 7-8 start out with the same set-up as in figure 7-6 (and stage 1 of fig. 7-7), with camera 2 on the program bus (and monitor). In this instance, however, we want to cut first to the shot of the sports car and then gradually fade in the super of "1987." First, we cut directly to camera 3 on the program bank (stage 2). The command "set up

3. In many professional studios, there may be another preset monitor separate from the standard preview monitor that allows the technical director to view and adjust special effects as differentiated from the viewing of an upcoming shot.

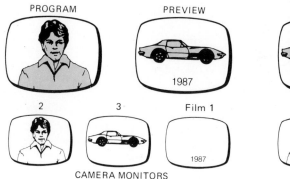

Stage 1: With the switcher set up as in figure 7-6, camera 2 is on the program monitor while a super of camera 3 and film 1 is preset on the preview monitor.

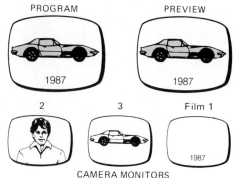

Stage 2: After adjusting the super (of camera 3 and film 1), the super is taken by simply pressing the mix button on the program bus.

Figure 7-7 Taking to a preset super.

super of camera 3 and film 1" tells the technical director to adjust the super of film 1 (bus *A*) over camera 3 (bus *B*) by moving the fader arms to achieve the desired balance. He or she will note where the levers are positioned and then move them both down to bus *B*. By punching up *mix* on the program bank, the technical director has now rerouted the camera 3 signal from a direct feed through the program bus to a program feed going through bus *B* and the fader arms. The picture being sent out over the program line—camera 3—has remained unchanged. When the director wants to gradually fade in the super of film 1 (stage 3), he or she slowly pushes the fader arms back up to the previously noted desired (preset) positions.

Adapting to Individual Switchers

There are dozens of models of switchers in use throughout the industry. It would be futile to attempt to list the specific features and bus configurations of each of them. Some switchers have no permanently designated preview bus; any one of several different banks may be set up to serve preview functions. On some

switchers, the preview function may be automatically transferred to the deactivated bank; for example, with mix levers at the *B* bus (on a standard four-bus switcher) the upcoming shot on the *A* bus is shown on the preview monitor; then—after a dissolve to the *A* bus— the preview monitor automatically "flip-flops" to show whatever is on the *B* bus. In more complex boards that use a *take bar*, this flip-flop feature may operate between the *preset* and *program* banks. The variety among switchers becomes even more overwhelming as the special effects generators (SEGs) become increasingly sophisticated and complicated.

By carefully reviewing the examples outlined, by concentrating on the fundamental concepts of *bus functions* and *preview/preset operations,* and by studying the analogy to the audio board, the student should be able to adapt these principles to any switcher. Keep in mind that professionals—especially those who free lance at a variety of facilities—go through a similar process quite often. As long as one can trace the video signal flow, one can figure out how any switcher or SEG works.

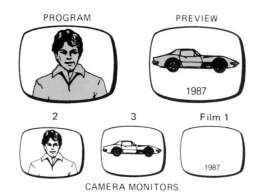

Stage 1: With the switcher set up as in figure 7-6, camera 2 is on the program monitor, while a super of camera 3 and film 1 is preset on the preview monitor.

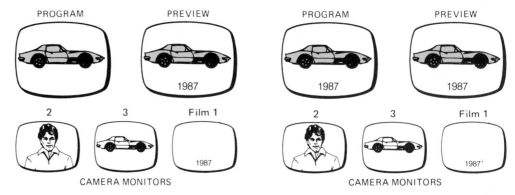

Stage 2: Camera 3 is punched up directly on the program bus (and monitor), while the super of camera 3 and film 1 is adjusted. When the desired balance is achieved, the positions of the fader arms are noted; then both levers are moved down to mix bus *B,* and the "mix" button is pushed on the program bank. The line feed (camera 3) remains the same. (We have just gone from a direct feed of camera 3 through the program bus to a feed of camera 3 through mix bus *B.*)

Stage 3: On command from the director, the fader arms are brought up to the preset positions, and the super of film 1 over camera 3 is accomplished.

Figure 7-8 Fading in a preset super.

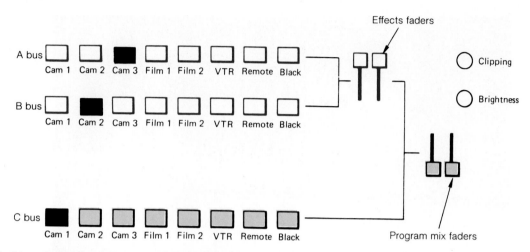

In this switcher the *program mix faders* determine the picture that is the program feed. An effect (super, key, split screen, corner insert) can be set up on the "effects" banks (*A* and *B* buses) using the *effects faders,* which can be mixed (dissolved) with the *C* bus. In the example, camera 1 (going through the *C* bank) is on the air, and the switcher is prepared for a dissolve to camera 3 (on the *A* bank—or, if the *key mode* has been activated, we may be set for a dissolve from camera 1 to a key of camera 2 over camera 3).

Figure 7-9 Multiple-function-bus switcher.

Multiple Function Banks

Key and **wipe** effects are now standard on even the most basic types of production switchers. (These fundamental electronic effects are discussed in more detail in section 7.4.) The variety of moving design transitions based upon the principle of the wipe may number as many as several dozen on more elaborate units. The concept of the key, which along with the label of **matte** is variously applied to a number of related video effects, involves replacing a portion of a background picture with a solid keyed image (for example, white title lettering) from another camera source. As opposed to the ghostlike double image of a conventional superimposition, the key results in an opaque design being stenciled into the background image to form a solid mosaic.

On some switchers, these effects are generated only through banks that have been designated solely for that purpose. In less complicated switching consoles, either one or both effects may be created through buses that can be operated optionally as basic mixing banks.

One operational example of how *mix* and *effects* functions can be operated from the same banks is a basic three-bus SEG in which one bank may be the primary mix bus while other banks are designated as **effects buses.** In figure 7-9 we have illustrated a three-bus configuration with the lower bus (*C* bank) functioning as a mix bank. As such, it assumes the properties of a home-base bus, from which we can dissolve to the *A* or *B* bank picture in the usual manner, or from which we can dissolve to an *A* and *B* banks effects combination of two picture sources as produced in a key or a **split screen** (see section 7.4).

Let us first look at how we would set up a simple dissolve from the *C* bank to the *A* bank. With this three-bank structure we must designate the *A* bank as the other operative bus in the dissolve by placing the *effects levers* in

Figure 7-10 Corner insert. This effect may either be used as a transition from one camera to another or it may be used to hold two pictures on the screen for a period of time.

the upper *A*-bank position. We can then make the *C*-to-*A*-bank dissolve by moving the *program mix levers* from the lower (*C* bank) to the upper (*A/B* banks) position. (If the effects levers were in the *B*-bank position the dissolve would have been to that bus.)

By putting the program mix faders in the *up* position we have taken the first step in activating a two-bus effects subswitcher (*A* and *B* banks), which has its own control levers. It is with these two banks that transition effects such as *wipe* are accomplished. The specific effect is chosen by means of buttons or rotary selection controls, and then the transition is made by moving the effects levers from one bank to the other.

With the less-complex special effects generators, one specific bank is usually structured as the effects completion bank. For example, a top-left *corner wipe* would always start with the original picture on the *A* bank. The new *B*-bank picture would gradually fill the screen as the levers are moved down to the *B* bank. (Moving the levers *from* the *B* bank to the *A* bank would produce the exact reverse corner-wipe effect.)

Effects such as split screens or corner inserts are produced by stopping the lever movement at the desired point in the transition between the two pictures (see fig. 7-10). In order to accomplish a dissolve to any such preset effect, the preceding shot must be punched up on the home-base *C* bank. The mix levers must be *down* so that the *C*-bank shot is feeding the program line; then as the program mix faders are moved *up* (to the *A/B* banks) we dissolve into the preset split screen or corner insert.

Setting up and dissolving in and out of *key* and *matte* effects involve a slightly different set of operating techniques. Using these same three banks, and again applying the principle of designated function, we can set up a two-camera key effect—first in preview and then on the program line. In figure 7-9 we are back on the *C* bank, feeding the program line (since the mix faders are in the down position) with camera 1. On the upper two buses, one specific bank (either *A* or *B*) must be designated to handle the special electronic action necessary to achieve the white lettering *cutout* keying effect. On some switchers the assignment of this function could be optional among two or more banks. On simpler units it is usually built into one specific bank. For our example, we will make it the *B* bank; therefore we will punch up camera 2—which is on the title card to be keyed—on the *B* bus. Camera 3, on the *A* bank, is on a wide shot of the set, which is to be used as the background scene for the key.

The ability to preview **brightness** and color levels is essential if the key effect is to be used at all. The levels of the two signal sources involved (cameras 3 and 2 in our example) must be kept within a narrow tolerance to function. Therefore, there must be a control that adjusts the level at which the keying action occurs. This control is sometimes called the *clipper* because when properly used it takes out or *clips out* extraneous video **noise** and *bleedthrough* effects. Depending upon the type of key being produced, there may also be a brightness control that can vary the lettering from pure white to solid black. On switchers with a color-generating component, the white lettering on the studio key card can at this point be replaced electronically with a properly contrasting color. Adjustment of these levels is accomplished with the preview monitor. (The *A/B* effects faders are not used in this electronic effects process; when the two banks are in the key mode, the fader levers are temporarily inoperative while adjustments are made with the clipping and/or brightness controls.)

What we have set up in our example (fig. 7-9), then, is a studio picture (camera 1) on the program line—being fed through the *C* bus—and a second studio picture (camera 3) being previewed in composite with a title key (on camera 2) on the *A/B* effects banks. When ready, the dissolve to the keyed effect (camera 2 over camera 3) is accomplished simply by moving the program mix faders to their upper position.

Instead of dissolving to the desired key effect (from camera 1 to camera 2 over camera 3), we also could fade in the key over the existing line picture. In this case, let us assume

we wanted to gradually bring in the key camera (camera 2) over the shot we have on camera 1. Leaving camera 1 on the *C* bus (going out over the line), we would also punch up camera 1 on the *A* bank. We would then preview the effect and set the key levels—adjusting camera 2 (*B* bus) over camera 1 (*A* bus). Then, when ready for the effect, we would move the program mix faders to their upper position. As the fader arms were raised we would gradually bring in camera 2 keyed over the camera 1 picture; in essence, we would be dissolving from a solid picture on camera 1 (*C* bank) to a key of camera 2 over camera 1 (*A/B* banks).

7.4 Special Electronic and Digital Effects

In addition to basic switching functions and simple camera transitions, there is a variety of special electronic effects that more complicated switchers and SEG equipment can handle. New processes and effects are constantly being developed. It is sufficient at this stage that the production student simply be aware of some of the basic effects and how they can be used; skill and refinement in using these sophisticated techniques can come at a later period in a student's professional development.

Indeed, there is a very real danger in getting too involved with elaborate electronic effects at an early stage. Too often these effects are used solely for the sake of playing around with the equipment. The student should learn to master the basic pieces of standard equipment before jumping unprepared into the world of electronic wizardry. A person must master the disciplines of communicating effectively with the medium of television before trying to exploit its full electronic potential. For this reason, we will not be concerned with diagrams and illustrations of how these various effects can be applied.

Specialized Transitions

Of course, even the *dissolve* is a type of electronic transition—a means of blending two different video images. Its use, however, has become so standard—as a result of its long ancestry as the lap-dissolve in motion pictures—that its function has become routine.

Most other electronic transitions can come under the heading of the *wipe*. With a standard wipe, one image is pushed off the face of the program monitor in a straight line as another image replaces the first one. The most standard patterns are the vertical wipe (similar to pulling down—or pushing up—a window) and the horizontal wipe (similar to pulling a sliding door across the picture).

Wipes are manipulated on the switcher by a special effects bus and another pair of control levers or faders. The desired pattern (left to right, bottom to top) is selected on one set of push buttons; the two cameras are punched up on the special effects buses (on some switchers the mix buses also serve this function); and the special-effects fader arms are moved to produce the effect. In a typical setup, one fader arm would control the vertical movement and one would control the horizontal movement.

On most simple special effects switchers, it is possible to combine the horizontal and vertical movement to effect a *corner wipe* that will have both a horizontal and vertical line. Other switchers may include a diagonal wipe.

More complicated SEGs will be able to produce a wide variety of patterns for the transition. Boxes, circles, diamonds, and stripes are common patterns. Most of these can be modified by adding any degree of *wiggle* desired. Color changes in *hue* can be added to the effects. With a *wipe positioner,* or *joy stick,* these effects can be positioned to start anywhere on the screen.

Just as the superimposition is a dissolve that is held on the screen without effecting a transition, so can the electronics of the wipe be extended into a *split-screen* effect. The split screen is a means of combining two pictures with either a horizontal or vertical (and occasionally a diagonal) line separating the screen into two distinct areas, with a different picture (from separate cameras) in each part of the screen. By means of the special effects faders, relative sizes of the two pictures can be adjusted. By manipulating the horizontal and vertical special effects levers separately, it is also possible to achieve a **corner insert** (see fig. 7-10). This places one picture in any quadrant of the screen (say, in the lower left-hand corner), with the video from another camera filling the rest of the screen. Again, the exact size and proportion of the corner insert can be easily manipulated by the control levers.

More sophisticated switchers and special effects generators have been developed with even greater refinements on the basic wipe and split screen. The *soft wipe* blurs the distinct line between the two images so that, at the actual line where the two (or more) images meet, there is a narrow superimposition; the result is a softening of the wipe effect. Another technical advance is the *multiple-source split screen.* With this device, it is possible to split the screen into a number of individual sections, each with a separate picture. Again, these separate divisions can be positioned and shaped to meet a variety of artistic demands—even resembling bordered snapshots in a photo album. The most conventional multiple-source split screen is probably the four-camera *quad split.* Another useful special effect is the *spotlight,* which enables the operator to darken the entire screen except for one circle of light, which can be shaped, changed in size, and positioned anywhere on the screen with a joy stick.

Keying and Matting

Several different keying and matting processes enable the switcher to use the video information from one video source to cut a pattern into another picture electronically.

Figure 7-11 Two monitors illustrating the difference between a super and a key. The monitor on the left shows a black-and-white graphics card supered over the woman's face. The right-hand monitor shows the same card keyed over the woman's face.

There are three basic, closely related types of keying effects—the *insert key,* the *matte key,* and the *chroma key.*

Insert Key. The insert key is the most common and easy-to-use keying device. Often identified as the **internal key,** it is typically used for titling and written information. The key card is prepared the same as a super card (section 9.4)—white letters on a black card. Unlike a super, however, wherein the white letters are simply superimposed over another background picture, the key actually blocks out a portion of the picture from the background camera that corresponds to the white information on the key camera. The resulting composite picture is not a superimposition; the white lettering is solid and opaque, with no information from the background picture bleeding through. Figure 7-11 compares a super and a key.

Electronic keys—as well as wipes, split screens, and similar effects—all can be enhanced by the *border feature* found on many switchers. Bordering, or edging, can outline any key or insert to make its boundary distinct. The width, color, and softness of the border all can be altered electronically. The *edge key,* for example, will make keyed letters stand out in bold relief by edging each white letter with a thin black line. This makes them more legible against a busy background. The *shadow key* can add a heavy shadow around two sides of each letter to give a solid three-dimensional feeling as the letter apparently stands out in front of the background.

Matte Key. With an insert key, the electronic hole cut out by the keying camera is filled with the information supplied by that key camera—titles, graphic designs, or whatever. With a matte key, however, the electronic hole can be filled with information from any other video source—color, patterns, or picture information from another camera.

The **external key** uses the picture information from a third picture source to combine two other pictures. For instance, the key camera may be shooting a white circle on a black card; this determines the cutout pattern or shape the other cameras will use. When this is combined electronically with two other cameras, the picture from one camera is used wherever the key camera was shooting black (around the circle) and the picture information from the other camera is used wherever the key camera was shooting white (inside the circle).

The concept of keying is extended into *monochrome matte effects* whereby any black or very dark portions of a foreground picture are electronically cancelled when combined with some other background picture. The foreground image then appears to be a solid picture (not a superimposition) in front of the background scene.

Chroma Key. Now one of the most common of the electronic special effects, the **chroma key** is a matting process that has become a staple of much color production. This is a technique in which a specific color—rather than a graphic design or pattern—is used as the electronic key to cut out part of the picture. (Any color can be selected by the SEG as the key; however, blue or green is most often used because it is farthest from any skin tones.) Wherever the foreground or key camera detects the designated hue (or *chroma*) in its picture, that video information is discarded and background picture signals are supplied from a second—or background—camera (often from the film chain, although it can be from another studio camera, a videotape, or any other source).

Thus, if the talent is standing in front of an evenly lit blue background and not wearing any blue item of clothing, this picture can be combined with any other background picture and the background will appear only where there was blue in the foreground picture. The talent can hence be placed in front of any other

picture desired. This type of chroma key application is routinely used, for example, in newscasts where the picture information for a particular news story is keyed in behind the newscaster (fig. 7-12). This matting technique also has obvious applications for dramatic formats, instructional programs, variety shows, and virtually every other type of production.

Although the use of the chroma key is widespread, it is not without numerous potential difficulties. The electronic equipment has to be delicately adjusted; lighting of the color background of the key camera has to be perfectly even; considerable attention must be given to selection of costumes and scenery. Slight problems in any of these areas lead to conspicuous troubles such as tearing of the foreground image, an obvious border around the foreground figure, discoloration, or indistinct contours.

Single-Camera Effects

In addition to the electronic transitions and keying and matting effects, certain other single-camera electronic effects should be briefly mentioned here. These are devices for image manipulation that do not involve the use of a second camera.

The video engineer has the ability to effect several changes through manipulation of the camera control unit (CCU). **Sweep reversals** can electronically reverse the scanning process of the camera. *Horizontal sweep reversal* reverses the left and right directions of a picture, creating a mirror image. This can be useful when shooting through a mirror for special angles (for example, shooting up at an overhead mirror to get a view of a table top, and then reversing the horizontal sweep in order to counteract the mirror reversal). On the other hand, *vertical sweep reversal*—turning a picture upside down—is usually only for obvious spectacular or comedic effects.

Picture from "key" camera. Subject in front of solid blue background.

Background picture from telecine or other camera.

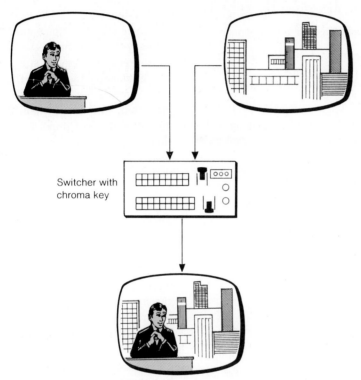

Switcher with chroma key

Composite picture. Foreground subject set against background image—wherever blue appeared on the key camera.

Figure 7-12   Chroma key.

On black-and-white cameras, a negative-like image can be created with **polarity reversal.** This changes all of the blacks to white and whites to black. This has some fascinating artistic possibilities as well as some practical uses (for example, projecting negative film from which no positive print has been made).

High-contrast images can be achieved a couple of different ways. One is through **debeaming.** The video engineer can turn down one of the CCU controls (the intensity of the scanning beam), which reduces the image to stark white and black contrasts. A similar effect can be achieved with the internal key on the switcher. By keying a picture over black and adjusting the *clipper,* a strong high-contrast image can be created with all of the grays removed.

Just as it is possible to get audio reverberation or an echo effect by recording and playing back almost simultaneously a given sound source (section 3.4), so is it possible to achieve a form of **video feedback.** By feeding a camera's signal into a floor monitor and then using the same camera to shoot the face of the monitor, a wide variety of bizarre video effects can be obtained. The picture in figure 1-6 was achieved by keying over black and then using video feedback.

(a) Representation of an analog signal.

1-0-0-1-1-0-1-1/1-0-0-1-1-0-1-0/1-0-0-1-1-0-0-1

(b) Representation of a digital signal.

Figure 7-13 Comparison of analog and digital encoding.

One area in which color television is especially exciting is the possibility of **colorization.** This process involves a special colorizing generator—also referred to as a *color video synthesizer*—that can add various colors to black-and-white pictures, create various abstract patterns, and even produce color images without the use of a camera at all. Such artistic applications move out of the realm of basic communication and into the arena of video art (section 1.3).

Digital Effects

One of the most exciting frontiers of video imagery is in the area of digital manipulation, or *digitalizing*. With digital technology it is possible to expand the creative and production capabilities of television far beyond what had been possible up to the mid-1970s.

The audio and video signals described in chapters 2 and 5 are *analog* systems; that is, systems in which variations in electrical current actually represent and define the sound and picture. The brighter the image hitting the lens, the greater the intensity of the electrical signal. With *digital* coding, on the other hand, the video information is transformed into a series of *binary* (base-two) numbers (fig. 7-13). Each of the 400 picture elements that are spread across a single scanning line, for example (see section 5.2), is reduced to a brightness level on a **luminance scale** from 1 to 256. The video signal can thus be translated into a series of binary numbers expressed as off/on blips. (A point registering at a brightness level

of 155 on the luminance scale, for instance, would be encoded as 1-0-0-1-1-0-1-1 in the binary system.)[4]

Once the television signal is encoded into a binary-digital format, the system has many advantages: memory or storage capacity can be significantly increased; the quality of the video information does not deteriorate as it is processed, amplified, channeled, and transmitted; and, most importantly, the signal information can now be manipulated, rearranged, enhanced, and augmented in ways that are impossible with analog information.

Digital Video Manipulator. Several marvelous television devices, introduced in section 5.1, have emerged from the digital age so far: the **time-base corrector,** so important in restoring sync in editing and switching operations (see section 8.2); the *framestore synchronizer,* used for synchronization of all major network feeds and remote pickups. None, however, offers as much excitement as the **digital video manipulator (DVM).**

The electronic wonders described at the beginning of this chapter are a result of the DVM. Other advances include *continuous image compression,* which enables the switcher operator to compress the full-frame picture down to the size of a tiny circle (at any rate, to any size) and—with a joy stick—to place the shrunken image anywhere on the screen. This is what makes the squeeze zoom possible as a transition.

Image expansion allows the director to take any segment of the video frame and enlarge it up to four times its original size (beyond which point it becomes unintelligible). A combined phenomenon is *image stretching.*

4. Binary encoding, of course, is what forms the basis for all digital computers and microprocessing equipment. It is built on the base-two counting system, which reduces all numerical information to a two-symbol number (using 0 and 1). Thus, all numerical data can be handled as a series of *off* (0) and *on* (1) electrical connections.

Any portion of the picture can be expanded or compressed in any direction; ratios can be altered; and graphics can be shaped to fit the picture. (See fig. 7-14.)

Other transitional devices—in addition to the fold-over and squeeze zoom—include the *video split,* which literally can take a picture and pull it apart in the middle to make room for a new frame, and the *push-off,* which simply shoves a whole frame off the tube sideways while replacing it with another image (as opposed to the wipe, which does not move the two stationary frames involved in the transition).

The impact of many of these advances is with postproduction editing (see chapter 12). Once the basic video images have been recorded, the director can sit down with an editor and decide how to time each transition, when to compress this image and bring in another, whether to electronically zoom in on a particular frame, how to shape graphics as they are added later, and so forth. The video editor now has at his or her command more sophisticated and less expensive creative opportunities than film editors have ever enjoyed.

The switcher, the SEG, and the DVM are a long way from the crude connection panel we described at the beginning of section 7.1.

7.5 Commands of Preparation and Execution

In discussing audio production techniques (section 3.5), we stressed the difference between commands of preparation and commands of execution. Nowhere is this distinction more important than in giving commands to the technical director. Because the switcher operator has two entirely different physical operations to perform—depending upon which command is given—the commands of preparation must allow for sufficient lead time. Such

Figure 7-14 Technical director working at Grass Valley 300 series Production System and using the DVM to develop new effects patterns. (Photo courtesy of the Grass Valley Group)

commands, given over the intercom system, also give a warning to the operator of the upcoming camera.

One helpful rule is that the command of preparation for any straight take is "ready." The preparation for any dissolve, super, fade, or special transition or effect that involves getting something set or prepared on another bus, uses the command "prepare." (A few directors prefer to use the command of "set up.") Although some directors use the command "stand by" as a preparation for both takes and dissolves, this can be confusing to the crew. The use of correct terminology immediately lets the technical director know whether he or she simply has to get ready to push a button on the same bus or whether it is necessary to prepare or set up another camera on another bus.

The command sequence for a direct take from camera 1 to camera 2 would be stated by the director as follows:

(Preparation): "Ready camera 2" (or simply) "Ready 2"
(Execution): "Take 2"

The word *ready* lets the technical director know that he or she only has to place a finger on the camera 2 button on the activated bus.

No matter how rushed the director may be or how fast-paced the program may be, the director should never skimp on the command of preparation. *Accuracy in getting the technical director properly prepared is the most important part of calling shots correctly.* If the director does not have time to give full commands, he or she should abbreviate the commands of *execution,* not of preparation.

(Preparation): "Ready 2"
(Execution): "Take it" (or simply) "Take"

If time is so short that even this much of a preparation command is impossible (for example, while shooting a game show, a fast-paced panel discussion, or a football game), the command of preparation still must be given priority.

(Preparation): "Two"
(Execution): "Take"

A dissolve requires a different-sounding command of preparation to allow the technical director time to prepare for a more complex series of actions. Considering that camera 1 is already on line, the correct commands for a dissolve would be

(Preparation): "Prepare a dissolve to 2" (or) "Prepare 2" (or) "Set up 2"
(Execution): "Dissolve to 2"

For a super, the actions are the same, so the commands are much the same.

(Preparation): "Prepare 2" (or) "Prepare to super 2 over 1" (or) "Set up 2" (or) "Set up a super of 2 with 1"
(Execution): "Super camera 2" (or) "Super 2 over 1"

The commands depart slightly from the basic pattern whenever two cameras are to be taken together in a super. Although this effect also involves a movement of the control levers, the movement is not one of program execution. In other words, the result of the lever movement is not seen, when it is being done, on the line monitor or on the air. As previously outlined, the command of execution is a "take"—calling only for the pressing of the *line mix* output button or *take bar.* For this reason, the voice procedure in this case should be as follows:

(Preparation): "Ready to take 2 and 3 in super"
(Execution): "Take 2 and 3 in super"

The "in super" at the end of the command is optional, but does reinforce the intent of the command.

When the director wants to preview a super of two cameras prior to their use, there is no necessary command of execution that follows the preparatory command. The preparatory command must be given far enough in advance so that the technical director has a chance to set up the preview at a time most convenient during the ongoing program. The director keeps an eye on the preview monitor to see when the preview is ready and gives the following command:

(Preparation): "Prepare a preview of cameras 2 and 3 in super"

Whenever there are two cameras supered together, there are two optional ways to remove one of those cameras from the picture. To gradually fade out the super, one of the following two command procedures can be used:

(Preparation): "Prepare to lose camera 2"
(Execution): "Lose 2" (or) "Fade out 2"

Or the more definite and safer way:

(Preparation): "Prepare to dissolve through to camera 3"
(Execution): "Dissolve through to camera 3" (or) "Go through to 3"

In this situation, the technical director is simply moving the fader arms as if completing a dissolve.

If the director wants instead to instantly remove part of a super—and there is a switcher with a program bus—then the technical director can go full to the intended remaining camera with a simple take to that camera on the program bank. The same sort of command and response structure works if a take-bar system is employed.

(Preparation): "Ready to take out camera 2"
(Execution): "Take out 2"

Or better yet:

(Preparation): "Ready to take to camera 3 full"
(Execution): "Take to camera 3 full"

Commands that call for special effects keys and wipes will generally follow this same pattern—with allowances for some of the more complicated displays and setups. Even with such simple effects as a key, the director should always emphasize important information such as the signal source (by number) that has the title graphic.

(Preparation): "Prepare a preview of a key of chain 6—with the graphics—over camera 2"
(Continued Preparation): "Prepare to dissolve to the key of 6 over 2"
(Execution): "Dissolve to 2 and 6" (or) "Dissolve to 6 over 2"

For a corner insert:

(Preparation): "Prepare to wipe in corner insert of camera 2 over camera 1"
(Execution): "Wipe in 2"

Finally, fades to and from black are handled in a manner very similar to the dissolve (as the fade to or from black is in essence a dissolve to or from black). At the beginning of a program, let's assume the director wants to fade in from black with a slide on film chain 2. The typical commands will be something like the following:

(Preparation): "Prepare film chain 2" (or) "Prepare to fade in film 2"
(Execution): "Fade in from chain 2" (or) "Fade up on film 2"

And the closing fade to black would be simply:

(Preparation): "Prepare black"
(Execution): "Fade to black" (or) "Fade sound and picture out"

These, then, are the basic elements of television's visual language: camera takes, dissolves, supers, cameras taken together in super, cameras undercut while in super, and fades to black. In the creative sense, the important consideration is that the transitions be appropriate to the context of the visual idea that the picture sequence is expressing. Technically, their use depends upon the operating capabilities of the technical director, which can come only from a certain amount of hands-on practice and discipline.

Crucial to the successful operation of the switcher is the use of the proper preparatory commands: "ready" for a take; "prepare" or "set up" for a dissolve, fade, or super. This terminology is fairly standard throughout the country, and its use is essential to any good control room operation. Just the use of the word *prepare*—even before the camera is mentioned by number—starts a response pattern in the thinking process. This is an integral part of the discipline of the technical director.

Summary

The switcher is the key *channeling* and *mixing* device in the video signal flow system. In conjunction with the special effects generator (SEG) and digital video manipulator (DVM), it is also involved in *shaping* the video signal.

The switcher can be thought of as a simple connection panel, with additional *buses* and *fader arms* added to increase the flexibility of the unit. The basic camera transitions and effects used on the switcher include the *take, dissolve, fade,* and *super.*

There are several variations of more complex switchers that, in conjunction with the various video *monitors,* enable the technical director to *preview* and *preset* certain effects. Special electronic effects include *wipes* and *split screens* and numerous *keying* and *matting* effects—including the insert (internal) key, the matte (external) key, and the chroma key. Single-camera effects include sweep reversals, polarity reversals, debeaming, video feedback, and colorization.

Effects available through the *digital video manipulator* encompass image compression and expansion and image stretching—as well as transitions such as the foldover, squeeze zoom, video split, push-off, and numerous others.

Vocal command procedures stress the importance of the correct preparatory commands: the use of "ready" before any cut or take; and of "prepare" or "set up" before any dissolve, fade, super, or special effect.

This chapter has been concerned with the operation of the TV switcher and the techniques of live studio editing. In chapter 8 we will look at videotape recording.

7.6 Training Exercise and Class Production Project

Class Exercise

The following written exercise is designed to help the student think about the actual operating process of the control room switcher in preparation for its use in later production exercises:

First draw a sketch of the switcher in your own control room, with the appropriate identifying terminology. Consider that only the black buttons on all buses have been pressed and that the control levers are in the *B*-bus position.

Then, following each command of preparation or execution, write in the necessary sequence of operation, the buttons to be pressed, and the levers to be moved in order to accomplish the command request. Keep in mind that this exercise represents an ongoing series of actions, as in a program sequence. Each movement is done only in the light of what has just been done previously. A technical director must constantly ask himself or herself, Which buttons are already pressed, and what is the position of the faders?

If possible, each student should have the opportunity to run through the exercise at the switcher, with another student giving commands as the director. For contrast, title cards, as well as wide, waist, and close-up shots, can be used. If done also as a studio exercise, the sequence of commands can be altered in order to give some variety of action.

Command Sequence

Prepare to fade up from black to camera 2

Fade up on camera 2

Ready camera 1

Take camera 1

Prepare a corner wipe from bottom left to camera 3

Wipe to camera 3

Prepare to super camera 1 over camera 3

Super camera 1

Prepare to dissolve through to camera 1

Dissolve through to camera 1

Preview a key of cameras 2 and 3; camera 3 has a title graphic

Prepare a dissolve from camera 1 to the key of cameras 2 and 3

Dissolve to key of cameras 2 and 3

Prepare to fade out camera 3

Prepare to fade to black

Fade to black

Class Production Project (Appendix D-2)

The first combined use of all production facilities is a rewarding but difficult step. For this reason, we have devised a picture-card production exercise that concentrates on the development of basic switcher and camera control techniques. Later exercises will expand upon this introductory work to include the lighting and audio techniques required for larger studio productions.

Seven photographs and one super title card are included in appendix D. At relatively small cost, these can be photographically enlarged to a width of at least 2 feet to provide for adequate camera use when mounted on a hard backing. Each photo offers both long-shot and close-up aspects of the subject material for the promotional sequence. Depending upon how one wishes to use the images, there are opportunities for pan, tilt, and zoom camera work.

There is no one correct way to do the exercise. Each person should study the photographs and decide upon a meaningful sequence of images. The production is designed to allow for a maximum of individual input in the selection of music as well as the direction of the pace and style of the announcer and related camera work. Promotional copy also is provided in appendix D. Students should be encouraged to rewrite the script with possible changes in the order of the pictures. The concluding section offers an opportunity to intercut a montage of several pictures used earlier or to undercut them with the title card. What students are working toward is a totality and unity of production in which the end result is more than equal to the sum of its parts.

Function and Operation of the Videotape Recorder

8

One of the last steps in the video signal flow is the recording (and playback) operation. This chapter deals specifically with the electronic and functional aspects of magnetic recording. We will examine the general concepts of electromagnetic videotape recording and playback, relating the various component functions to operational controls. The equipment involved in electronic editing will only be peripherally mentioned. Chapter 12 will extend the discussion of magnetic video recording with a careful analysis of editing equipment and procedures as we get into *postproduction editing*—especially as it relates to ENG/EFP single-camera production techniques.

In spite of the rapid development of the television industry during its first decade, there was no satisfactory way of recording the electronic camera picture until the mid-1950s. The *kinescope* process (developed in the 1940s) was a specialized technique that used motion picture film to photograph the moving image off a receiver (kinescope) tube; the result was a blurry, washed-out picture with degraded audio quality.

A way had to be found to record the electromagnetic signals that actually generated the television picture. The subsequent development of videotape technology not only changed the nature and scope of video production but shaped the whole modern telecommunications industry.

8.1 Principles of Videotape Recording

The idea of video recording is based upon several aspects of the electromagnetic phenomenon. We will be looking at two interrelated electromagnetic concepts—electronic and magnetic principles. In chapter 5 we presented a simplified model of how the three-tube camera creates an ongoing sequence of signals that are translated by the receiver tube into a color video picture. Although a brief recap of that material will be presented here, it is suggested that you go back and carefully review section 5.2 before proceeding.

The Electronic Basis of Videotape Recording

Both the camera tube **target** (see fig. 5-8) and the picture tube **raster** (display area) are organized into 525 horizontal scanning lines. Each of these lines is composed of somewhere around 400 separate illumination points or *picture elements*. Even though some of the top and bottom lines are used for synchronizing signals and information other than the video picture, this means that there are still over 200,000 separate picture elements whose collective illumination produces the mosaic-like picture.

In the camera tube, each of these *pixels* (to use the computer term) must be energized to produce the electric signal that is the electronic version of the optical image focused on the face of the tube. This is accomplished by an incredibly rapid scanning process. A stream of electrons (scanning beam) is made to contact the successive points on each of the horizontal lines by means of electromagnets located just forward of the electron "gun," which is the source of the electron beam.

The scanning process actually occurs in two phases. Starting at the top left of the picture, the odd-numbered lines are first scanned to produce a top-to-bottom picture field. Only one-half of the illumination points have been used to produce this picture. With this completed, the scanning beam then starts at the top left of the tube and scans all the even-numbered lines to produce another picture field. There are 60 of these one-half picture fields occurring every second, which are interlaced to produce the effect of 30 complete frames per second.

Horizontal and Vertical Sync. Examining this process in greater detail, we find that several additional factors are needed to ensure the stability of the picture. As the electromagnets in both the camera and picture tubes pull the stream of electrons left to right and top to bottom, it is imperative that the scanning process in both units be precisely synchronized. A series of specialized pulses, generated separately from the color and intensity portion of the video signal, are utilized for this purpose. There is a *horizontal sync pulse,* which activates the video system at the beginning of each scanning line and turns it off for a brief retrace period (blanking) as the beam returns to the beginning of a new line on the left side of the tube.

At the completion of each field there is a similar retrace period as the scanning beam returns to the top left of the picture. At this point a *vertical sync pulse* is used to coordinate the start of each new field. While there are only 2 vertical sync pulses for every 525 horizontal sync pulses, they must nevertheless be considered as an extremely important part of the video sequence. Because it denotes the beginning of a new picture field, the vertical sync pulse has an important application in videotape editing.

The Magnetic Basis of Videotape Recording

In earlier sections of the text, we saw how sound waves (section 2.2.1) and light waves (section 5.2)—through a series of transformations (transducing)—can be put into an electromagnetic form that is suitable for broadcast. By utilizing these and other qualities of magnetism and electrical energy, this complex broadcast signal can be permanently "memorized" for later use. As youngsters, many of us demonstrated how a magnet on the underside of a piece of paper can align iron

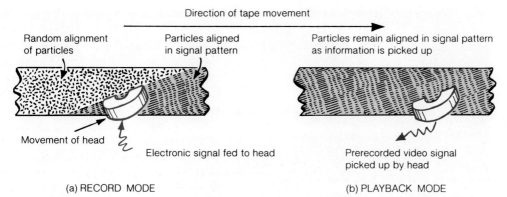

Direction of tape movement

Random alignment of particles

Particles aligned in signal pattern

Particles remain aligned in signal pattern as information is picked up

Movement of head

Electronic signal fed to head

Prerecorded video signal picked up by head

(a) RECORD MODE

(b) PLAYBACK MODE

(a) **Record Mode.** The electronic video signals sent to the record head activate the magnetized head to align the iron oxide particles on the tape to retain a permanent (until erased) pattern of the recorded electronic video signal.

(b) **Playback Mode.** The prerecorded video signals on the videotape generate a small amount of electrical current in the playback head that is an exact duplicate of the original video signal.

Figure 8-1 Video recording and playback heads.

filings into a magnetic pattern. The principle involved in this action provides the basis for all audio and videotape recording.

The record-playback **head** on any tape machine is actually a magnet, and the tape is a polyester strip coated on one side with iron oxide particles. If electrical energy—organized into a video signal—is fed into the head, the iron oxide particles on the tape passing in contact with the head will be aligned into a continuing series of magnetic patterns (fig. 8-1). Thus, in the *record mode* the resulting magnetic patterns are themselves a memory of the video signal. (The patterns are physically visible only if the oxide is treated with certain chemicals.)

In the *playback mode* no electrical energy is sent to the magnetic head. As the tape moves, however, the interaction of patterned iron oxide particles on the tape and the magnetic head produce an electronic signal in the playback head that is a duplicate of the original input.

Occasionally, even with the best of equipment, there can be some loss of quality. The tape itself may have imperfections that cause momentary *glitches*. The very process of

having the tape pass through the transport system makes it vulnerable to small but destructive changes in speed. If any one of a number of setup adjustments are done incorrectly, quality can be seriously impaired. But for the most part, state-of-the-art video recording equipment is very impressive. It is reliable, with a high degree of fidelity to the original signal. With equipment like a **frame synchronizer,** a recorded image can even have its quality enhanced. Such was not always the case. For those who were present for the beginnings of video recording, this ability to upgrade picture information has been a minor miracle.

Development of the Quadruplex Videotape Recorders

In the fall of 1956 CBS first used a videotape machine to delay the broadcast of its early evening newscast to the West Coast. It originated from an Ampex machine that utilized a **quadruplex** video head assembly. The *quad head* recorder was named for the four rotating video heads that vertically came into contact with a 2-inch videotape. (See fig. 8-2.)

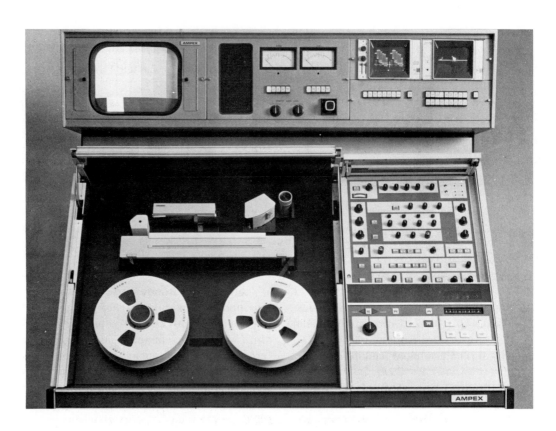

Figure 8-2 Quadruplex high-band videotape recorder. (Photo courtesy of Ampex Corporation)

Some very impressive control signals and editing equipment were developed for the quad machines, and these recorders became the industry standard for many years. They are still in use at many television stations.

It became apparent, however, that this format had some very definite limitations. Because of the basic elements of its design it could not produce a recognizable picture at tape speeds other than precisely 15 inches per second (ips) or, with modifications, 7½ ips. Slow motion as well as faster-than-normal search speeds were not possible. Also, the tape could not be stopped in order to produce a **freeze frame.** Not only did this make the editing process difficult, it also ruled out the production use of any stop-motion special effects.

Additionally, the quad-head recorders were very bulky and quite expensive—advanced models costing well in excess of

$100,000 by the mid-1970s. Finally, the machines were costly to maintain; they were delicate electronically and to keep the four heads aligned involved considerable engineering attention.

8.2 Helical-Scan Videotape Recorders

The answers to many of the problems of the quad-head recorder were to be found in the **helical-scan** (*slant-track*) videotape recorders (VTRs) developed in the late 1960s. Introduced originally as low-cost alternatives to the quadruplex machines, these helical-scan video recorders were rapidly adopted for nonbroadcast applications—school TV projects, hospitals, industrial training, and television production curriculums.

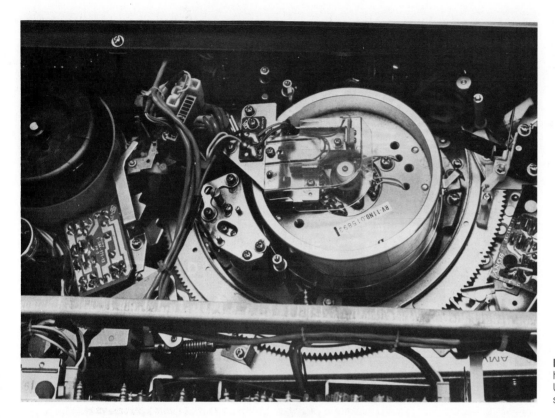

Figure 8-3 Helical-scan head assembly of a U-matic ¾-inch VTR as seen from above.

Evolution of the Slant-Track Machines

With the helical-scan recorders, equipment costs are much lower, videotape is cheaper, there is less machine setup time and maintenance "down time," operating costs are smaller, and there is less need for highly trained operators. Despite the fact that the technical quality of early helical-scan VTR machines did not generally match the broadcast quality of quad-head machines, many closed-circuit systems and educational institutions choose to rely upon the helical-scan formats for reasons of economy, reliability, and ease of operation.

During the late 1960s numerous manufacturers brought out competing formats and standards, utilizing tape widths from ¼ inch to 2 inches. Altogether there were close to forty different, noncompatible standards. Then, under the leadership of the SMPTE (Society of Motion Picture and Television Engineers), the industry adopted a ½-inch format that was picked up by most educational and training institutions.

In 1970 the ¾-inch U-matic videocassette system was introduced (fig. 8-3). Although there were earlier attempts to establish a standard cassette or cartridge system, the U-matic format was the first to become solidly accepted by educational and industrial users. With its many refinements and editing innovations, it became the workhorse of the closed-circuit television field. And it eventually became the ENG standard for broadcast stations.

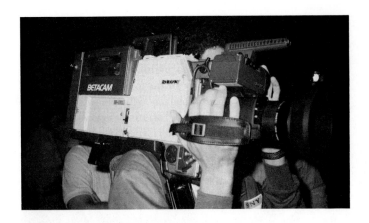

Figure 8-4 Sony Betacams: *top*, original BVW–3 broadcast camera and ½-inch videorecorder in one unit; *bottom*, the newer Betacam BVW–2 "Newsmaker" weighs in at just 9 pounds (photo courtesy of Sony).

After several abortive attempts to establish a consumer market with a home cartridge or cassette system, Sony finally succeeded with its Betamax format—followed closely by other manufacturers with the VHS system. Today, Beta and VHS dominate the growing home entertainment field.

The newer 8mm and ¼-inch formats are attempting to move into both the home and professional markets. Many practitioners are waiting until the various competing formats are winnowed out and one clear-cut superior format emerges as the standard.

In the meantime, the ½-inch Sony Betacam system (not the same format as Betamax) and the ½-inch RCA/Panasonic M-format have both impressed video professionals and have been adopted by hundreds of stations and network news operations. The two competing (and incompatible) ENG formats are both *camcorders*, containing the camera and recorder in a single unit; and both systems produce picture quality that far surpasses the much older ¾ U-matic format. (See fig. 8-4.)

Even though the video signal of the early helical-scan recorders was inherently less stable and less reliable than that of the quadruplex format, the slant-track picture and electronic information could be significantly enhanced. By using a *time-base corrector*, the electronic information from the helical-scan machine could be made virtually as stable as a quad-head signal. Time-base correction (in essence, upgrading the control track synchronizing information) could greatly reduce picture jitters and drifting; several machines could

Figure 8-5 Two 1-inch type-C videorecorders: *left,* RCA TH–900 videorecorder (photo courtesy of RCA); *right,* Sony BVH–2000 videorecorder.

be locked together for editing and dissolving between recorders without synchronization problems.

Through the use of the time-base corrector, the U-matic ¾-inch format VTR machines were soon upgraded to meet broadcast standards. Indeed, the dramatic changeover to ENG newsroom techniques was made possible in large part by the many advantages to be found in helical-scan recording. In addition to lower operating costs and simpler maintenance requirements, these machines offered important advantages in the process of electronic editing. They could produce still-frame, slow-motion, and faster-than-normal search-speed modes, which were not possible on the quadruplex recorders. By the early 1980s, the

reliable but aging "quads" were being replaced by the new industry standard—the 1-inch, helical-scan, type "C" format. (fig. 8-5).

These improvements in machine capacity were all made possible by the innovative design of the helical-scan video head assembly. Each of the angled parallel lines shown in figure 8-6 represents one continuous scanning of the tape by one of the several video heads mounted on the circular drum (as shown in fig. 8-7). Each single scan contains exactly the video information needed to record one complete 262.5-line picture field (section 8.1).

As the tape is pulled around the head drum, successive parallel angled (helical) tracks are scanned. In the *record* mode (as shown in fig. 8-1), the heads are leaving a magnetized memory of the picture signal from the camera.

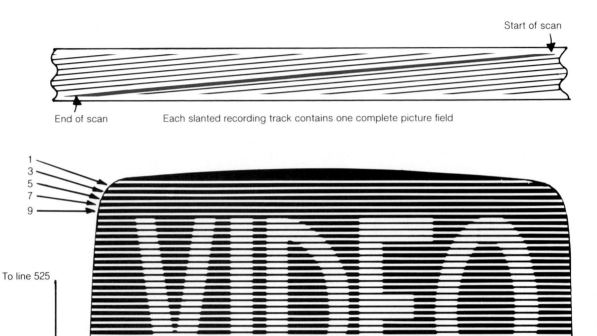

Start of scan

End of scan   Each slanted recording track contains one complete picture field

1
3
5
7
9

To line 525

The 262.5 odd-numbered scanning lines equal one picture field (½ frame).

Figure 8-6 Helical-scan slanted track.

The continuous video signal from one slanted video track contains enough information to record 262.5 odd-numbered scanning lines (one complete field) and to play back the field on the picture tube raster.

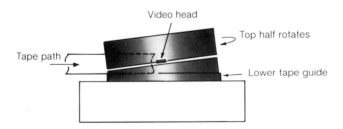

Video head

Top half rotates

Tape path

Lower tape guide

Figure 8-7 Helical-scan videocassette drum assembly.

The playback/record heads are attached to the rotating top half of the tilted head assembly.

In the *playback* mode, a still picture can be produced if the tape movement is stopped while the video heads are still revolving; the heads will scan and reproduce the same picture over and over again. If the tape is moved at a slower-than-normal speed then a slow-motion effect is achieved. As long as the revolving head speed remains constant, the video sync of the picture is maintained—no matter how quickly or slowly the tape is pulled around the head drum.[1]

It must be remembered that this 262.5-line picture *field* contains only one-half of the video information necessary to reproduce a full 525-line picture *frame*. This problem is solved on broadcast-quality 1-inch "C" type units by means of some electronic wizardry. One of the five video heads on this machine has a special function that allows the unit to "borrow" part of a stored video signal. This is used to fill out the rest of the 525-line picture.

The Helical-Scan Video Head Assembly

The slanted track on the tape is achieved by one of two slightly different methods—one for the 1-inch reel-to-reel "C" type machines and one for the enclosed cassette formats. On the reel-to-reel models, the tape is angled as it wraps around the circular video drum. With cassette formats, the tape cannot be angled (since it travels in the same plane from feed reel to take-up reel), so the drum itself is tilted (as shown in fig. 8-7) to achieve the angled, helical effect.

In either case, the video drum is made up of two separate segments. The bottom half is a part of the base on which it rests; this does not move. The top half, called the *head wheel*, has two or more very small video heads placed

at equidistant points around the drum—with the heads protruding just slightly from the lower circumference of the movable wheel.

With the head wheel rotating rapidly in one direction and the tape moving in the opposite direction, a ¾-inch U-matic cassette format will achieve a *writing speed* of 700 inches per second—even though the tape itself is moving through the unit at only 3¾ ips. (Note that there are many more scanning lines on the tape—roughly sixteen per inch—than could be indicated in fig. 8-6.)

Transport Mechanism. The various mechanisms that move the tape from the feed reel to the take-up reel are called the transport system (fig. 8-8). Note that the tape wraps almost completely around the drum in the "C" type format. This gives the picture more stability, better resolution, and more sophisticated special effects capabilities.

With sophisticated broadcast machines, extreme care is taken to protect the tape from stretching or scratching. Some of the round tape guides are actually lubricated by compressed air. The *servo capstan,* the main drive mechanism that pulls the tape through the unit, keeps its firm grip on the tape by means of a vacuum pressure rather than with the usual pinch roller, thus protecting the tape from any potential abuse at that point. The capstan function is extremely important in that it must maintain a constant tape speed. It does this by means of a feedback signal from the *control track* on the tape itself.

The video drum is but one of several magnetically activated heads within the transport section of a tape machine. In some of the new professional equipment there may be six or more heads that perform various video, audio, control, cueing, and erase functions. The configuration will vary with the complexity of the recorder. One can get an idea of this basic structure, however, from figure 8-9, which shows the arrangement of a VHS cassette unit.

---

1. In the quadruplex 2-inch machines, the tape speed must remain constant (slow motion is not feasible) because each of the 1½-inch vertical scans provides only enough information for *one-sixth* of a picture field. By contrast, the simplicity of the helical-scan recorder is that it is a *continuous field* format, with each scan providing one complete field.

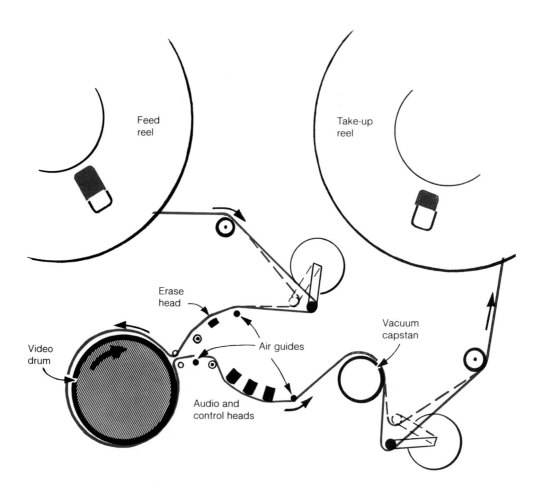

Figure 8-8 Transport mechanism of the RCA TH–900 Type-C videorecorder.

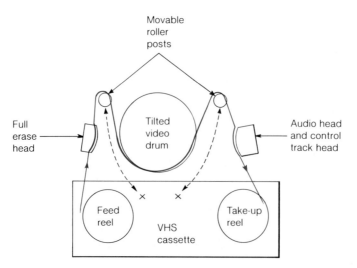

Figure 8-9 VHS cassette engaged by transport system for play/record mode.

Control track

Video tracks

Channel 2
audio or cue track

Channel 1
audio track

Figure 8-10
Configuration of ¾-inch
U-matic videotape format
(not to scale).

"Upstream" of the video drum (before the moving tape reaches the drum) there is a full erase head. "Downstream" there is a unit that contains two separate heads—one for the control track and one for audio. Figure 8-9 also shows the way in which the two movable rollers engage the tape and pull it out of the cassette into the play/record position. They move along two grooved metal tracks (dotted lines) to put the tape into contact with the heads. (There are several other guides and rollers not shown in this figure.) The ¾-inch U-matic cassette machines operate in a similar fashion, although they are much more complicated. A large loop of tape is pulled out of the cassette, wound around the drum, and put into contact with the other heads.[2]

8.3 Videotape Track Functions

As discussed earlier, the videotape contains more information than just picture signals. Figure 8-10, for example, is a representation of the four tracks that are used by the U-matic

2. As with self-contained audio sources, the term *cassette* refers to a two-reeled unit in a semi-closed case; the videotape is not exposed to human handling. Once the cassette is inserted into its loading deck, the player mechanism automatically engages the tape around the recording head assembly. A *cartridge,* on the other hand, refers to a single-reel container that is, in effect, a sealed supply reel; the take-up reel is enclosed in the player mechanism. When the cartridge is inserted into the player, it is automatically threaded; again, human hands do not become involved in the loading and threading operation.

format. Other VTR formats will use a slightly different configuration to achieve similar functions.

The Video Track. The portion of the videotape that carries the series of slanted video scanning lines is known as the *video track;* this occupies roughly 80 percent of the tape area in helical-scan formats. It is here that the information dealing with the picture signal, color, and brightness is carried. As mentioned before, with the ¾-inch U-matic format (fig. 8-10) the tape moves through the transport assembly at the rate of approximately 3¾ inches per second. During this time, sixty of the slanted tracks are scanned to produce sixty fields—resulting in the rate of thirty completely scanned picture frames every second.

The newer 1-inch (C-type) and ½-inch (Betamax and VHS) formats pack even more video information on the tape by means of the *Azimuth* system. With this process, the distance between the parallel lines is reduced even further by having alternate "A" and "B" video heads (two of each) touch the tape at slightly different angles.

Sony's Betacam recording system (fig. 8-4) uses the A/B concept in a slightly different way. One video track carries the *luminance* (brightness) signal and the next track carries the *chrominance* (color) signal. Each track has two designated video heads. And there are also two "flying" erase heads—one for each track—revolving around the drum head (as opposed to stationary erase heads) needed to erase specific fields prior to editing in new information. The concept of keeping

Audio 2 track
Audio 1 track
Luminance tracks
Chrominance tracks
Control track
Time code (cue track)

Figure 8-11
Configuration of ½-inch Betacam format (not to scale).

Note that alternate video tracks carry the luminance signals while every other video track carries the chrominance information.

color and brightness information separate has many advantages in terms of picture control. It is no surprise that the emerging ¼-inch and 8mm formats are also utilizing this system.

As shown in figure 8-11, in addition to the video tracks there are several tracks on the videotape for other information—on the Betacam format as well as in all other formats. There are two *audio* tracks, a *control* track, and a separate "address" or *cue* track at the bottom of the tape.

The Control Track.   Section 5.2 described how the continuous display of the picture on a monitor is synchronized with the original camera picture by means of vertical and horizontal *sync* pulses. For every 262.5 horizontal pulses there is 1 vertical pulse that initiates the scanning of either the odd- or even-lined picture field. When a broadcast picture is received, it is these sync pulses that "lock together" the TV set with the camera signal.

When the television picture information is recorded, these sync pulses—and some related information—are separated from the color and brightness signals and recorded on an individual band or **control track** of the tape. During the playback of recorded videotape programs, the sync pulse serves an additional important purpose. The playback machine reads the signals and uses them to regulate the speed at which the *capstan* pulls the tape through the transport system—as well as the

speed at which the video head wheel turns. This **servo control** system, in effect, tells the playback VTR exactly how fast the tape was moving when it was originally being recorded.

On some playback editing machines (such as the Sony 5850), the control track serves as the basis of a tape-location counter. Its readout displays elapsed tape time in minutes and seconds (forward or backward) from any designated zero point. This is a different operating principle from the system described in the following section.

The Cue Track (Optional Second Audio Track).   On older videorecorders, a second audio track or **cue track** can be used either for an auxilliary audio track (for stereo broadcasting or for a second language audio track) or as a *cueing* track—so named because it was originally used to record either verbal cues or high-frequency tones as cues for early editing systems.

This track is often used to lay down the signal for an editing location system called the **SMPTE time code.**[3] This location system produces a digital clocklike numerical read-out or *address* for each hour, minute, second, and frame recorded on the videotape. It can reflect the "real time" at which the tape was being

---

3. This editing system was so named because the technical standards were established by the Society of Motion Picture and Television Engineers (SMPTE).

Figure 8-12 Display of time-code information. The SMPTE time code (hours, minutes, seconds, and frames) is displayed at the touch of a button.

Figure 8-13 LED read-out of the time code on an ECCO TCR–65. In addition to the time code showing directly on the monitor, it also can be displayed on editing peripherals designed as rack-mounted components. (Photo courtesy of ECCO Incorporated)

recorded or it can be added later, showing time elapsed from the beginning of a production or from some other reference point on the tape. The read-out, as illustrated in figure 8-12, can be displayed on the picture monitor by a process similar to the way titles are matted over any picture source.

For some editing applications, the *window* display becomes a part of a "workprint" tape dub and is seen as a permanent part of the picture. Also, during the editing process the time code can be viewed by means of LED (light-emitting diode) read-outs located at the control panel and on the machines themselves (fig. 8-13).

In advanced editing systems (see section 12.3), a computer can "read" the unseen time code to locate predetermined edit points for the execution of cuts, dissolves, and special effects. The system is used on most productions at the network level—except for news. Time-code referencing is especially important for programs such as "Wide World of Sports"— or the Olympics—where tapes from a number of recorders in many different locations must later be edited together in precise chronological synchronization. Newer tape formats— such as the type-C standard—have two audio tracks *plus* the cue track, so that the time code can be utilized in conjunction with a stereo production or a dual-language sound track.

It should be noted that newer ¾-inch U-matic equipment has been developed that allows the time code to be incorporated in an unused portion of the video signal or placed on a separate horizontal address track that overlays the slant video track.

The Audio Track. The audio track hardly needs further explanation. The technology involved is exactly that of conventional sound recording. It must be noted, however, that the quality is somewhat less than that of professional audio equipment that is used in recording studios. The television industry is just beginning to take advantage of its capacity for stereo and high-fidelity sound—up to the 15,000 Hertz level now heard on FM radio. As more home receivers are sold with this capacity, stations and cable systems will begin to make the necessary modifications. Most VTR machines designed for educational and industrial use have a 5,000 Hertz limitation and cannot be easily upgraded.

8.4 Video Recorder Operations and Controls

The setup and operation of any VTR machine involves the use of components that generally fall under three headings: *connectors, control mechanisms,* and *visual indicators.* The arrangement, appearance, and even terminology may vary with the manufacturer, but once one knows what to look for, these basic components can be identified on any video recorder.

First, since videotape machines work in conjunction with other electronic units (cameras, switchers, microphones, other recorders, speakers, receivers, editing equipment, and so forth), we must be able to make such hookups as a primary step. Second, we must learn how to manipulate the collection of knobs, switches, levers, and push buttons that are used to start, stop, or change the basic audio and video functions of record, playback, and editing. Third, we must be able to use and understand the set of components that tells us whether or not the machine is operating the way we want it to—feedback provided by things such as indicator lights and meters.

Connections

Of these three concerns, it is the area of *connections* that demands most of our attention. In a studio situation where equipment and its related cables are permanently in place, the connection process takes place primarily at the patch bays where labeled receptacles indicate the sources and termination points of feeds.

However, much of the small-format video for educational and industrial purposes—and much of the semi-EFP production for training purposes—involves a temporary "lash-up" of video recorders, cameras, mikes, monitors, and associated gear. In either case—whether in the studio or not—the operational linking of components is most efficiently accomplished when the following three interacting factors are kept in mind:

1. The nature and purpose of all signal feeds
2. The direction and pathway of all signal flow
3. The structure of the connective hardware

If you know *what* your signal is supposed to do, it is easier to know *where* it should be going and *how* you are going to have to connect it to get it there.

Figure 8-14 is a composite drawing of the sort of receptacles that you would find on ½-inch home recorders and industrial-level VCR machines. This illustration indicates the variety of different connections that handle audio and video signals. This apparent duplication of inputs is due to the fact that the elements of picture and sound are processed in differing strengths and forms during various stages of both recording and playback. The machine is designed to accommodate a number of production and editing situations.

The principle involved here is a matter of working with varying amplification levels and with signals that are combined to become *composite* signals. This basic concept was introduced in discussing audio hook-ups—both amplification considerations (section 2.2.5) and impedance levels (section 3.1). Note the difference between a relatively weak voice signal generated by a microphone and the amplified signal that is the output of the audio console.

The same basic concept applies to the way in which the video recorder handles audio and video. The recorder has the provision for the input of an external microphone ("mike in"). This low-level signal is then automatically amplified to *line level* within the machine before being recorded on tape. However, previously amplified signals (an audio recorder, for example) are to be plugged into the "line" audio inputs. If these are plugged into a "mike" input, you will get a distortion from the double amplification.[4] Similarly, the separate video sync and picture signals generated by the camera must be combined and slightly amplified before they can be recorded or further processed for broadcast.

The broadcast composite audio/video signal that is transmitted to a house has been *modulated* into an **RF** (*radio frequency*) signal; that is, the audio and video information have been superimposed on a radio-frequency carrier wave in order to be broadcast through space as part of the electromagnetic spectrum

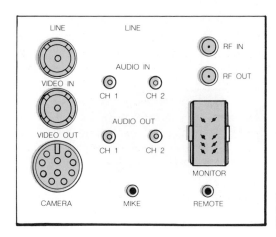

Figure 8-14 Video recorder connection area (composite illustration).

(section 2.2.1).[5] This signal picked up by the TV antenna is then carried on a twin-lead (two-wired) 300-ohm line to the set. If the signal is transformed to be carried on a 75-ohm coaxial shielded cable, it is then the same type of signal that comes from the local cable TV company. Most home and industrial VCRs have provisions for both input and output of the RF signal. All of them will be able to process pure unmodulated video and audio (line) signals also.

The multi-holed receptacle (from 10 holes up to 14) labeled "camera" and the 8-holed receptacle labeled "monitor" are the connection points for some multiple-line cables that carry a number of signals (including power for the camera) both to and from the recorder. We will examine their functions—and an additional remote-control line—in greater detail as we look into the sequence of signal flow in two typical small-format video operations.

4. Recall our discussion regarding impedance levels (section 3.1). In the studio, where the distance from the mike to the audio console may be up to 50 feet, a *low impedance* (low line resistance) cable and microphone are used. However, home VCRs and many industrial-level recorders are designed to work with less expensive *high impedance* (greater resistance) mikes and lines designed to carry not more than 6 to 8 feet. If you mismatch these two elements, you will cause intolerable audio distortion.

5. A pure unmodulated audio or video *line* signal can be distributed only over a cable or closed-circuit. Generally this video signal is of higher quality than an RF signal. However, in order to broadcast a signal, it must be encoded or modulated onto the carrier wave and then decoded (demodulated) by your home receiver.

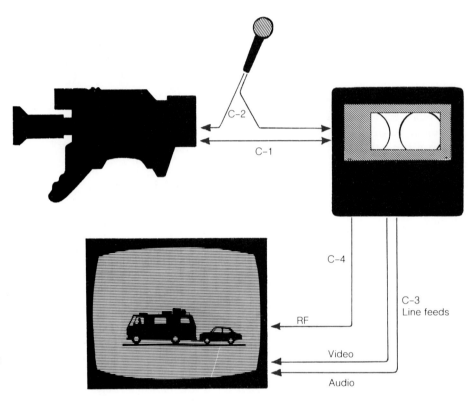

Figure 8-15 Signal flow in a camera-mike-VCR-monitor hookup.

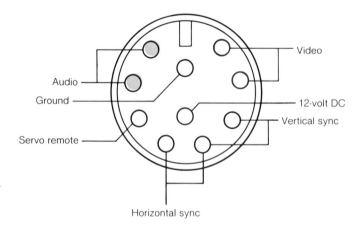

Figure 8-16
Configuration of signal flow in a 10-pin connector during record mode.

Examples of Signal Flow and Connecting Hardware. As one example of a typical simple setup, you may want to connect a camera to a ½-inch industrial portable video recorder. You will want to use a hand-held mike, and you will need an audio-video monitor so that you can periodically check the audio and color quality of individual *takes* (scenes). (Your camera viewfinder will play back only black and white.) Although each of the components may have arrived with some instructions relating to the connecting process, what you need is the total picture of your specific setup. It will help your visualization of the total system if you lay all the equipment on the floor and make a signal flow sketch similar to figure 8-15.

With single-feed wires such as "line video" you should think of each connection in terms of a component source *output* going through a cable to its *input* destination on another piece of equipment. This is a good working concept to keep in mind even though the precise nature of the signal flow is sometimes more complex. For example, a cable going from the camera to the portable recorder (fig. 8-15, C-1) can have ten or more separate lines and functions in both directions. In the *record* mode (fig. 8-16) it carries audio, video, sync, and a servo signal for the remote on-off control of the recorder. At the same time, DC power is flowing from the recorder *to* the camera. In the viewfinder *playback* mode, the audio and video flow is reversed.

If you choose not to rely on the built-in microphone in the camera, there are two connection options available when using an external hand mike (fig. 8-15, C-2). There is usually a mike input receptacle located on the camera itself. It will take the Sony-type *mini plug* usually associated with a high impedance line (see fig. 8-17). When this connection is made, the feed from the built-in mike is automatically cut off. However, sometimes better quality can be obtained by plugging the mike line directly into the mini-plug receptacle on the recorder itself (see fig. 8-14).

With quality industrial-level equipment, you have two options in the connection of the recorder to the picture monitor. The better picture would usually be obtained by taking the separate line audio and video feeds from the recorder (fig. 8-15, C-3). In this manner you are using the pure video signal rather than the modulated RF picture. Generally the receptacles for both audio and video at the recorder as well as at the monitor will take RCA-type plugs. Some of the Sony-related Beta formats will have line audio connections using the mini plug.

Your other option will be to use the RF connectors between the recorder and the monitor (fig. 8-15, C-4). This is a composite audio and video feed using an "F"-type connector and shielded cable (see fig. 8-17). The illustration is of a studio-type video/audio monitor primarily to show the variety of connections that could be made. For most EFP production uses, the viewfinder playback and an earphone connection to a mini-plug receptacle would probably suffice.

As a second example, look at a small-format production setup as illustrated in figure 8-18. This could be thought of as the sort of semipermanent installation found in many educational institutions. Because you will be sending your camera feed to an AC powered nonportable video recorder, you will have to include the use of a transformer/amplifier *power pack*. The 10-wire cable (fig. 8-18, C-1) takes low-level audio, video, sync, and servo signals to the power pack. Here video and sync are combined and modulated to line level. These three outputs are shown in figure 8-18, C-2.

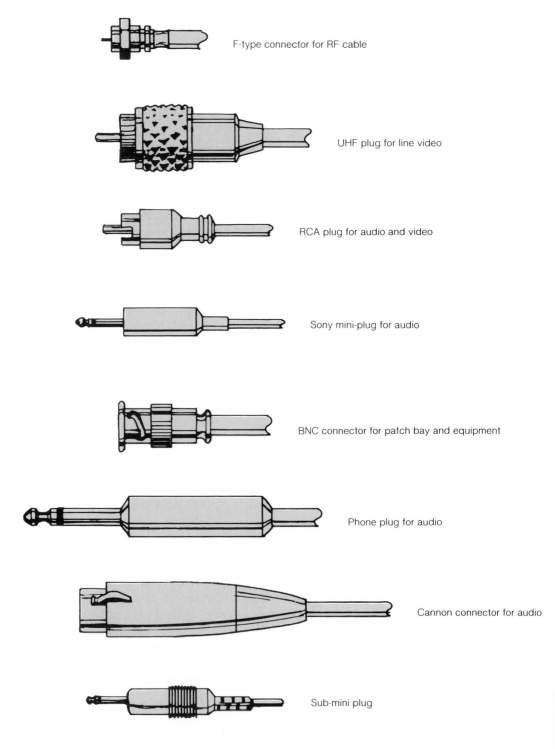

F-type connector for RF cable

UHF plug for line video

RCA plug for audio and video

Sony mini-plug for audio

BNC connector for patch bay and equipment

Phone plug for audio

Cannon connector for audio

Sub-mini plug

Figure 8-17 Commonly used audio and video plugs and connectors.

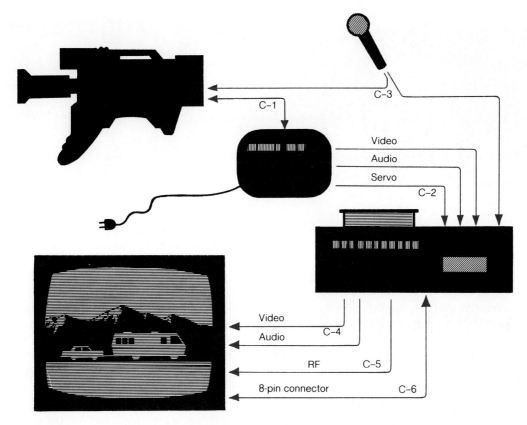

Figure 8-18 Signal flow with a nonportable VCR hookup.

The video output connection usually calls for a UHF-type plug with an RCA plug at the furthest end. The amplified audio line output generally uses a cable with an RCA plug at both ends. The third line from the power pack is for the on-off remote control of the recorder. It takes a smaller version of the mini plug, called a *sub-mini plug* (see fig. 8-17). As with our previous example, the hand mike can be plugged into the camera input or into the recorder (fig. 8-18, C-3) as long as the recorder is designed to accept the high-impedance-level line. On more sophisticated industrial-level recorders this will not be the case, and a low-impedance line must be used.

The connection from the video recorder to the monitor may offer as many as three options. In addition to the line feeds (fig. 8-18, C-4) and the RF composite feed (fig. 8-18, C-5), you may be able to use a two-way multiple-line connection if both components are equipped with the proper 8-holed receptacles (fig. 8-18, C-6). This specialized cable does more than just send audio and video to the monitor in the playback mode; if the monitor has a tuner, then audio and video can be sent from any selected channel to the recorder in the record mode. All such connections should be made with caution. Multiple-pin connections may look the same but are not necessarily all compatible—even when made by the same manufacturer. Any attempt to force mismatched connections together can cause serious damage.

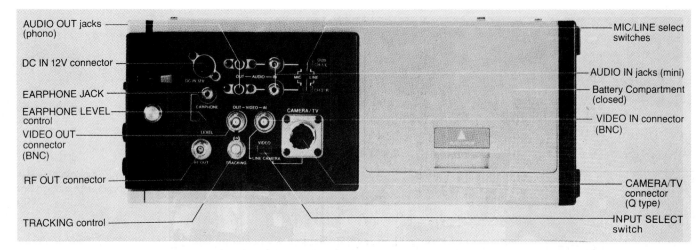

AUDIO OUT jacks (phono)

DC IN 12V connector

EARPHONE JACK

EARPHONE LEVEL control

VIDEO OUT connector (BNC)

RF OUT connector

TRACKING control

MIC/LINE select switches

AUDIO IN jacks (mini)

Battery Compartment (closed)

VIDEO IN connector (BNC)

CAMERA/TV connector (Q type)

INPUT SELECT switch

Figure 8-19 Sony VO 4800 rear panel connections. The input-output panel is designed to provide compatibility with equipment found in professional studios. (Photo courtesy of Sony Corporation)

Examples of Sophisticated Systems.

The so-called video revolution has produced a seemingly endless supply of new and constantly improving equipment. In many ways, the top-of-the-line industrial and educational units now available are operationally superior to broadcast-quality recorders of just a few years ago. Although the budgets of many educational institutions do not permit continuous updating of facilities in order to keep up with the state of the art, the student should nevertheless be generally familiar with some of the options and opportunities available with these more sophisticated machines.

One good example is the Sony VO 4800 portable video recorder (fig. 8-19). It has a much more complex input-output panel and more extensive controls than one finds on most home and industrial models. The connector receptacles reflect a necessary compatibility with the sort of jacks that are to be found in professional studios and editing facilities.

For example, the two *audio out* receptacles for channels 1 and 2 take a phone jack. Both of the *audio in* channels utilize mini plugs. (Note the switch to select "mike" or "line" input.) *Video in* and *video out* use a BNC connector. *RF out* takes the standard F-type connector. There is also an *earphone* jack which fits a mini plug. And the large 14-pin receptacle provides the two-way connection between the camera and the recorder—as well as additional monitor applications.

Adaptors, Splitters, and Terminators.

As observed, connective hardware for audio and video equipment involves a wide variety of plug types. *Line video* may utilize a BNC, UHF, or RCA phono plug. *Audio* is usually handled by a phone plug, Sony mini plug, or RCA plug. With low-impedance mike lines a 3-pin Cannon connector is quite common. (Review fig. 8-17.) Temporary setups for audio mixing, editing, and camera work often mean borrowing components from various sources and lashing together pieces of gear that were not originally designed for convenient connections. This connecting process is greatly aided if there is a good supply of **adaptor plugs** on hand (fig. 8-20). Essentially, any short cable that has different types of female and male connectors on the two ends can be used as an adaptor. With a sufficient variety of these, an RCA phono plug can be adapted to connect into a Sony mini plug or a BNC plug as necessary, and so forth.

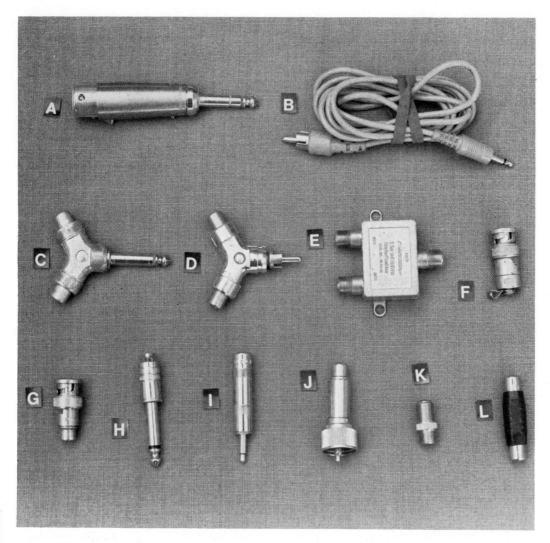

Figure 8-20 These are some of the more common adaptors, splitters, and terminators found in typical video and audio hook-ups: (*A*) convertor plug, female cannon to phone jack; (*B*) RCA to mini-plug converter line; (*C*) phone jack to female RCA splitter; (*D*) RCA male to RCA female splitter; (*E*) RF (75-ohm) splitter; (*F*) BNC terminator; (*G*) RCA female to BNC convertor; (*H*) mini-plug to phone jack convertor; (*I*) phone jack to mini-plug convertor; (*J*) RCA to UHF convertor; (*K*) RF barrel plug; (*L*) RCA barrel plug.

Attempting to connect two or more audio or video monitors to a single feed calls for the use of another type of specialized connector— a **splitter.** For instance, "Y" and "T" plugs allow us to tap into a line and send the signal to two different points—feeding one monitor while sending a signal on to another. The effect is much the same as using an *RF splitter* on a home system to send an incoming cable TV signal to more than one receiver. However, splitting a signal does weaken its strength, and

thus additional amplification may be needed. Most industrial video monitors can easily be set up in series so that the "video out" receptacle from one monitor can feed the same signal on to the next set. However, in this case, the final monitor in the chain must **terminate** the signal flow—either by means of a termination switch or with a video termination plug (see fig. 8-20).

Power Sources. Another type of connection to be considered is the AC power and/or battery source. The internal battery in the Sony VO 4800, for example, can power the recorder and camera for up to an hour of continuous use when fully charged. Over a period of time, however, batteries lose the ability to hold a charge, and battery time is always precious. For that reason, most portable recorders have an AC power adapter/charger for use wherever AC power is available. This unit is also used to recharge the battery as needed.

It is not uncommon to find an AC power outlet located alongside the input/output connections on the recorder. Most manuals will list a 500-watt limit when this outlet is to be used to power lighting equipment or some other component. It is important to note that the provision for the third rounded prong is an important grounding device. Do not try to defeat this safety feature. It also helps to ensure that the other two prongs go into the proper power outlets. If a two-prong adapter is used to go into a two-pronged wall receptacle, the ground wire on the adapter should be connected to the screw that fastens the wall socket plate to its wall box, or to some other suitable ground.

In thinking through the connections to be made with any system—regardless of how simple or how sophisticated the recorder and its components may be—the important thing is to think ahead and carefully plot out the types of connections to be made. Try to visualize all of the related signal flows—as emphasized at the beginning of section 2.3. *What* is the signal supposed to do? *Where* must it be directed? And *how* must it be properly connected?

Controls

Regardless of the age or simplicity of design, the transport (tape movement) functions on all video recorders will have eight to ten basic controls. Normal-speed playback is accomplished by activating the control (pressing a button on most models) labeled either *play* or *forward*. The recording mode is initiated by pressing *play/forward* simultaneously with the *record* button; this activates the record head while the tape is moving forward in the play mode. (Because there is the possiblity of accidentally pressing the record button at the wrong time and inadvertently erasing information on the tape, the record control is usually interlocked with the play button so that it can be activated only when they are both pressed at the same time.)

On most cassette machines, the *stop* control not only stops the tape movement, but it also causes the tape to unwind from the video drum and be retracted into the cassette. This allows the *eject* control to be used to remove the cassette from the machine. "Stop" should not be confused with the *pause* control that halts forward tape movement but leaves the tape in contact with the heads that are still revolving. In this pause mode, the heads continue to scan the same slant track over and over again. This produces, on some machines, the freeze-frame effect. However, the machine should not be left in this mode for more than a minute or so at one time as the heads are continually wearing away at the oxide on one specific track; tape damage and/or head clog can occur—especially when old or inexpensive tape is being used.[6]

To get the tape quickly from one point to another, *fast-forward* and *rewind* controls are used. On some units, these two modes will produce a somewhat recognizable picture for "search" purposes. Many VTRs—especially those designed for editing—also will have *variable-speed* controls that facilitate slow or speeded-up motion, either forward or backward.

---

6. On the newer professional editing machines, such as the Sony BVU 800 and 820, the *stop* button actually puts the machine into the "freeze-frame" *pause* mode. Head movement stops only when the *eject* button is pressed.

Figure 8-21 The Sony VO 5850, designed for studio-based recording and editing, has sophisticated transport controls such as *skew* to assure picture quality. (Photo courtesy of Sony Corporation)

The *audio dub* (audio edit) control puts the audio record head into the record mode without activating the video record heads. This enables the operator to make audio-only edits or to lay in a whole new audio track.

There is one other control that is important to accurate tape transport. The path of the tape around the video drum is crucial to the playback of a proper picture. Bands of picture distortion sometimes result when a tape recorded on one machine is played back on another VTR with a slightly different horizontal alignment. This problem can usually be corrected by an adjustment of the *tracking* control. The normal operating setting as determined by the factory is located at the top point (12 o'clock position) on the dial. The slight click one feels when passing this point is known as a "detent" position. After any tracking adjustment is made, the knob should be returned to this position for each new recording or playback.

On studio-based recorders designed for production playback and/or editing purposes, the controls (and their related meters and indicators) become more numerous and at first

seem quite complex to the uninitiated operator. It helps to keep in mind that each control has been created to help make the job easier or to maintain the best possible picture quality.

For example, on units such as the Sony VO 5850 (fig. 8-21) there is an additional control for the tape transport called *skew*. When the top third of the picture appears to bend to the left or the right, it is usually caused by an incorrect amount of tension on the tape as it passes around the video drum. This is adjusted by means of the skew-control knob. Keep in mind that this is a problem on the playback machine, not on the machine being used to edit or dub. As with the tracking control, the knob should always be returned to the detent position before that same machine can be used for a subsequent recording or playback.

Selector Switches. As discussed before, most video recorders are designed to function with a variety of different types of inputs such as a *camera*, the tuner in a *receiver/monitor,* or a studio *line* feed. There must therefore be an *input selector switch* that differentiates among the various levels and/or sync sources

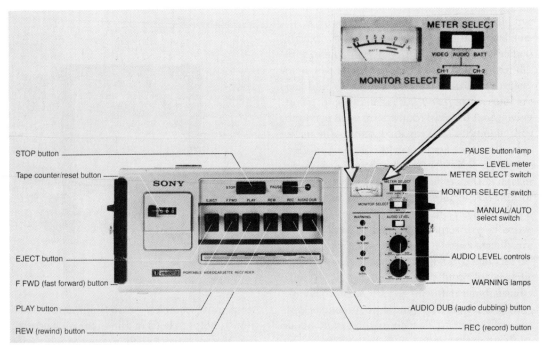

Figure 8-22 The control panel on the Sony VO 4800 shows how a single control system (VU meter) can be used for multiple functions (monitoring video level, battery condition, audio channel 1, and audio channel 2).

of these inputs. The advice of a studio technician may be needed to determine proper switch position. Whereas a camera signal from the studio switcher would feed through the line input, a single camera might utilize some other selector position.

On some machines there is another switch that separately controls the use of internal or external *sync sources*. (On several VTR makes the alternative to the external position is labeled "defeat.") This *internal sync* position allows the recorder to "strip off" any incoming sync signal and utilize the synchronization pulse from the machine itself during the recording process.

Visual Indicators and Meters

Our final area of concern is with visual monitoring and feedback indicators. Although these will vary from machine to machine, there are a number of controls that group together in operational units and directly relate to a vi-

sual read-out—starting with the *pilot light* that indicates when the *power on/off* switch is activated.

One important indicator on most VTR machines would be the *VU meter*. Some machines will have multiple meters—perhaps one for each audio channel and one for the level of the video signal. However, the number of meters does not necessarily correlate with the sophistication of the machine. As an example of effective economy of design, the Sony VO 4800 (fig. 8-22) has only one VU meter. By means of monitor and selector switches, this one meter can show the video level, either or both audio channels, or the battery strength. There is, of course, a separate *potentiometer* for each of the two audio channels. (Video gain is adjusted at the camera control.)

Most portable recorders now have an *automatic gain control* (AGC) option. When this is switched on, the AGC serves as a limiter (section 2.2.4) that keeps incoming feeds

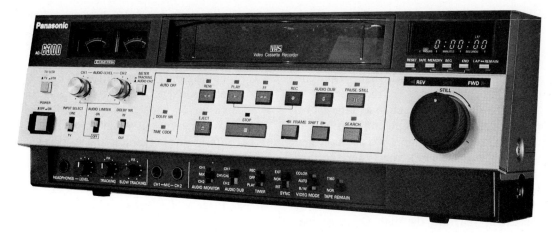

Figure 8-23 Panasonic videorecorder AG 6300. On this industrial-quality editing VCR, the conventional revolutions counter is replaced by a time-code display (right side of the control panel) in hours, minutes, and seconds. (Photo courtesy of Panasonic Industrial Company)

within a range that does not exceed the capabilities of the recorder. However, the AGC often will automatically boost the "noise" of the line signal when there is momentarily no other incoming signal (a pause in the voice or music source), thereby recording an unwanted hiss. The AGC selector switch allows you, therefore, to defeat this feature.

Many machines, such as the VO 5850 will reflect their recording and editing functions with additional video control switches and indicators (see fig. 8-21). There will be a *video control* knob, which adjusts the level of incoming video, as well as a related *AGC off-on* switch, which allows for automatic gain control of the video signal. These are usually grouped with the video VU meter.

An increasing number of portable recorders are including a number of warning lights and status indicators that provide several types of important feedback to the operator. On some machines there is a *pause mode* light, which serves as a reminder that the heads are continuing to scan the tape. There are also lights that indicate the condition of the *battery;* the presence of moisture, which is dangerous to the circuitry (*auto off*); a *tape supply* warning light; and a *servo* lamp, which warns of improper tape transport.

Counters and Location Indicators.
Virtually all recorders have some sort of *counter* or other component that allows an operator to locate predetermined points on a recorded tape. On portable machines and older studio models there is simply a three- or four-digit read-out that counts the revolutions of the take-up reel. Since the circumference of the tape on each reel will change as the reels unwind and wind, the operator must keep in mind that a given number of revolutions will indicate differing amounts of tape footage—depending upon how far into the program one is.

There is also a counter *reset* button that allows you, as the operator, to set the counter at zero at the beginning of the tape or to designate an arbitrary "zero point" anywhere on the reel. Advanced industrial models, such as the Panasonic AG 6300 (fig. 8-23) have an LED read-out in hours, minutes, and seconds. An important adjunct to these search controls is the *memory on* switch, which allows you to mark any new point on the tape as a new zero point. When put into rewind or fast-forward, the machine will return to this point and come to a stop.

Recorders that have the hours-minutes-seconds electronic read-out operate on the basis of signal information derived from the control track on the tape, as differentiated from the

SMPTE time code (used on much broadcast-quality editing equipment) that comes from the cue track (section 8.3). Both of these electronic digital read-outs are designed to work with *variable-speed* control dials. They are engineered to allow you, as the operator, to "feel" the speed and direction of tape movement. At the straight-up detent position, the tape is in "pause." The more you twist the dial to the right (clockwise), the faster the tape moves forward. As you turn the dial to the left (counterclockwise), the tape moves in reverse (rewind)—again with the speed determined by the extent you turn the dial. On most machines, speeds range from slow motion one-frame-at-a-time to five times normal speed.

Successful Performance and Maintenance.

The key to successful operation of the videotape recorder—whether a complex broadcast-quality machine or a simple **backpack** for basic location recordings—is *familiarity* and *practice*. Instructions and specific controls will, of course, vary significantly from machine to machine. Become familiar with the ones you have access to. Make certain you have taken full advantage of the instructions and directions for the particular models you will be working with. Especially, follow the recommended care and maintenance instructions; this is particularly important for routine cleaning of the video heads. And then practice. Become familiar with the recorder. Under the guidance of a trained technician or instructor, work with the machine; experiment with it. Find out what it will and will not do. Then you should have the confidence and discipline to handle any video recording and playback assignment given to you.

A major part of your professional discipline will be care and respect for all production equipment; and the video recorder is one of the most expensive and delicate machines you will handle. Everyone will benefit if you follow a few common rules of preventative maintenance.

1. Videotape recorders require a constantly renewed supply of clean, cool, dry air. Heat, moisture, and cigarette smoke are damaging to all electronic equipment—especially VTR machines. Never place books, cassette cases, or papers on top of the recorder; it seriously inhibits the flow of air. Liquid containers and ashtrays—anywhere adjacent to video recorders—are simply a disaster in the making.

2. Place a dust cover on the machine when it is not in use—but only after the unit has had time to cool off.

3. When a video recorder is moved, be extremely careful not to bump or jar the unit. Delicate components are easily damaged by slight shocks. Do not attempt to operate a recorder immediately after it has been moved from a cold to a warm environment.

4. Videotape should not be left in the recorder when the unit is not in use. Tapes should be rewound and properly stored in a cool, dry place.

5. Keep the recorder and tapes at a distance from other equipment that may be generating strong magnetic fields.

6. Do not tinker with various controls and functions without a clear purpose and idea of what you are doing. Do not fool around, for example, with the color lock control and other critical mechanisms. Maintenance personnel who are unaware of the misadjustments may spend hours trying to find and correct the resulting problems.

7. As the videotape operator, always allow yourself time to carefully think through all connecting and patching procedures as well as the basic disciplines of machine operation. The time spent always pays off later in time saved.

Summary

The video recording process involves an understanding of the entire electromagnetic concept. For our purposes, we have looked at two aspects of the electromagnetic phenomenon: *electronic principles* (such as the horizontal and vertical sync pulses) and *magnetic principles* (the electromagnetic properties of an electric current rearranging iron oxide particles) to record a video signal on videotape.

The first VTR machine, introduced in the late 1950s, was the *quadruplex videotape recorder,* which utilizes four revolving video heads to record video information transversely to the path of the 2-inch tape. The bulky and expensive quad-head machines have largely been supplanted by the *helical-scan video recorder,* which wraps its narrower tape around a cylindrical head drum in a slant-track pattern.

Both *reel-to-reel recorders* (such as the broadcast-quality 1-inch type "C" machines) and the *cassette recorders* (like the professional ¾-inch U-matic, the ½-inch Betamax and VHS home formats, and the combination camera-recorder such as the Sony Betacam) have videotape configurations that include space for picture information, control track, cue signals, and audio track(s).

Operational functions for VTR machines include three considerations: *connections* (with cameras, switcher, line feeds, microphones, other recorders, speakers, monitors, editing facilities, and so forth); *controls* (for all operating modes such as play, record, fast forward, rewind, stop, pause, variable speed, dubbing and editing, input and sync selection, tracking and skewing adjustments); and *indicators* (lights, VU meters, counter, and so forth).

In chapter 9, we will be concerned with important scenic and graphics elements that apply to both single-camera and multiple-camera studio production.

8.5 Training Exercise

Ideally, each student should be able to go through the following exercise individually. If time or facilities do not permit, then students may be assigned in pairs.

On the videotape recorder(s) available in your facility, go through every step mentioned in the chapter. Thread the VTR machine and work with it in every function: play, fast-forward, rewind. Record some sample programming from the studio. Use the pause-hold modes; experiment with any variable-speed controls. Carefully, with engineering supervision, familiarize yourself with other adjustments such as tracking and skewing.

Pictorial Elements: Sets and Graphics

9

In this chapter, we want to examine some of the actual scenic elements that make up the picture of the television production. What are the principles of design that should be applied to the use of sets and the construction of graphics? These graphic principles apply whether we are using physical graphic cards or computer-based electronic graphics.

Although the student of production is initially concerned with the technical aspects of reproducing sound and picture—the hardware of microphones, cameras, lights, switchers, and recorders—he or she must also concentrate on the pictorial elements of what the cameras are looking at. Without a decent setting and without intelligible graphics, the best mechanical reproduction of video components can result only in a technically sharp program with no meaningful content.

9.1 The Concept of Pictorial Design

There are several elements of pictorial design that apply both to sets and to graphics. Although these two topics will be discussed separately in the remainder of this chapter, it may be helpful to consider some of the common elements first.

Functions of Design Elements

In discussing audio production and lighting techniques, we mentioned that there were both *technical considerations* and *creative aspects* to the use of these elements. To some extent we have a parallel consideration in examining pictorial elements. Here, however, instead of thinking in terms of technical and creative criteria, it is more applicable to consider the differences between *informational* functions of design and *emotional* or *psychological* functions of design.

First, the *informational aspects of pictorial design* must be considered. They are concerned with conveying appropriate information cues to the audience as accurately and efficiently as possible. In the case of a dramatic setting, we ordinarily want to tell the audience as much as possible about the time and locale of the action. Where is the scene taking place? In what historical period? What time of day is it? We may also want to give other pictorial cues. What is the status of the main character? Where does he or she live? (Of course, there are many dramatic programs where this type of information is deliberately concealed from the audience for purposes of suspense or dramatic surprise.)

Nondramatic programs also need to convey this kind of information data. Is the setting a newsroom? Is it a stage in front of a live audience? Is it a pulpit? How much do we need to tell the viewers about where they are? What should they know about the program's surroundings? All television staging considerations should start out with these types of questions.

With graphics, the informational considerations are even more important. The overwhelming use of graphics—especially for simpler productions and basic formats—is to convey information. What is the name of the program (title card)? What is the name of the person talking (super card)? How much of our tax dollar goes to education (pie chart)? What does the race course look like (diagram)? How does the piston work (animated graphic)? How bad was the accident (photo)? In designing graphics, the need for clarity is paramount. The director must always be asking, How can I get this information across as clearly and efficiently as possible? Most of the discussion in sections 9.4 and 9.5 is concerned with this question.

Second, the *emotional* or *psychological functions of pictorial design* must be considered. There are many subtle messages that the total production design can convey. All of the scenic elements—sets, props, graphics, furniture—combine to give a "feel" or "image" to the program. In a news program, do we want the image of an advanced technological communications center, of an abstract setting (fig. 9-1), or of a working newsroom (fig. 9-2)? In an instructional TV program, do we want the image of a typical classroom setting or of a research lab? In a religious program, do we want the image of a traditional church service or of an avant-garde contemporary movement? In a variety program, do we want the image of a conventional stage presentation or of the electronic collage of a music video? Again, it is important that the director and designer begin with these types of questions before any decisions are made regarding the design or assembling of set pieces or graphics.

In dramatic programs, of course, the overall *atmosphere* or *mood* is very important. Staging elements—combined with lighting—will tell us much about the mystery of an event, the state of mind of the hero, the lurking tragedy, the atmosphere of a family gathering, the majesty of an accomplishment, the power behind a particular move, the potential danger behind a closed door, the emptiness of a certain thought. The designer should always be concerned with maintaining or building the mood or feeling of every particular scene.

The emotional function of design would also include creating a given *style* or *continuity* to a program—helping to maintain a unity throughout the entire production. In the use of graphics, for instance, it would be jarring to establish a pattern of cartoons to illustrate a certain process and then suddenly switch to a series of detailed photographs.

Figure 9-1 Abstract news set for local news program. (Photo courtesy of KABC-TV, Los Angeles)

Figure 9-2 Two views of a working newsroom used as actual on-the-air background for news set. (Photos courtesy of KCBS-TV, Los Angeles)

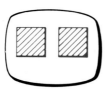

(a) Symmetrical balance results in a rigidity and precision that is usually not desired—except for certain formal settings.

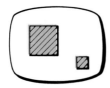
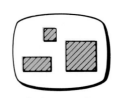

(b) Asymmetrical balance usually is more interesting and dynamic—resulting in a more fluid and creative mood—and just as well balanced aesthetically.

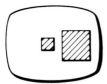
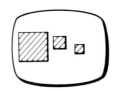

(c) An unbalanced picture can result, however, if care is not taken to position the asymmetrical elements with respect to their weight and mass. Temporarily, this may be desired.

Figure 9-3 Symmetrical and asymmetrical balance.

Several years ago, a church group produced a syndicated variety program dealing with the broad theme of the family. It was a composite of serious vignettes, vocal numbers, comedy sketches, talks, and dances, and featured many different performers and guest stars.[1] The production very easily could have fallen apart into many mini-programs; however, the entire production was held together by its scenic design. Every segment of the program was staged on

1. "The Family and Other Living Things," produced by the Church of the Latter Day Saints, 1976.

and around one scenic unit—a large, white, abstract, open set combining several different levels, platforms, and stairs. Because it had a scenic unity, the production had a continuity that it otherwise could have lost.

Thus, every pictorial design should serve both an *informational* function and an *emotional* function. The set should not only tell us what time of day it is but also give us a hint as to what is going to happen that day. The chart should not only tell us the information but emphasize how important the information is.

Elements of Pictorial Design

Artists and critics discourse long and eloquently about the many different factors that constitute aesthetic criteria—unity, harmony, texture, color, rhythm, proportion, and so forth. It is beyond the scope of this book to get into any detailed treatise on aesthetics of the still and moving picture.[2] The beginning production student should be aware, however, of at least three fundamental elements of pictorial design: (1) balance and mass; (2) lines and angles; and (3) tone and color.

Balance and Mass. The concept of balance was introduced in section 6.3 in connection with camera work. Asymmetrical balance is generally preferred over formal symmetrical balance. The larger a mass, the nearer it must be to the center of the scene in order to preserve a sense of balance with a smaller mass (fig. 9-3). In addition, the placement of mass within a scenic element will tend to affect the stability of the picture. A heavy mass in the

2. For a good discussion, see Gerald Millerson, *The Technique of Television Production* (New York: Hastings House Publishers, 1972), chapter 15. See also Herbert Zettl, *Sight, Sound, Motion: Applied Media Aesthetics* (Belmont, Calif.: Wadsworth Publishing Co., 1973), especially chapters 4–6.

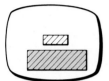
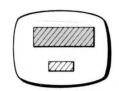

(a) Heavy weight in the bottom of the frame tends to give an impression of stability and security.

(b) If the top of the picture contains more mass than the bottom, the result is a feeling of uneasiness and suspense.

Figure 9-4 Location of mass in the picture.

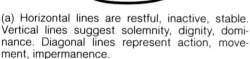

(a) Horizontal lines are restful, inactive, stable. Vertical lines suggest solemnity, dignity, dominance. Diagonal lines represent action, movement, impermanence.

(b) Curved lines generally imply change, beauty, grace, flowing movement. With an upward open curve there is a feeling of freedom and openness. A downward open curve has more of a feeling of pressure and restriction.

bottom part of the picture implies firmness, solidarity, support, importance. A heavier mass in the top part of the picture projects more instability, suspense, impermanence (fig. 9-4). These considerations of balance and placement have strong implications for the design of sets and graphics as well as for camera composition. A title card with lettering in the bottom of the frame projects a solid, strong opening. A scenic unit with heavy ornamentation near the top implies a feeling of uneasiness, suspense.

Lines and Angles. The use of dominant lines is one of the strongest elements available to the scenic designer. Straight lines suggest firmness, rigidity, directness, strength; curved or rounded lines imply softness, elegance, movement. The direction of the dominant lines in a picture will carry strong connotations. Horizontal lines represent serenity, inactivity, openness. Vertical lines are dignified, important, strong. Diagonals imply action, imbalance, instability, insecurity (fig. 9-5).

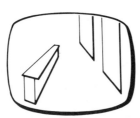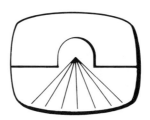

Figure 9-6 Lines and perspective.

A forced perspective can be created by careful use of scenic elements and even by painting false perspective lines directly on the studio floor.

Figure 9-7 Tone and balance.

(a) A darker tone tends to imply more mass; thus the darker tone will overbalance the lighter mass (*left*). A smaller dark mass can be used to balance a lighter mass that is larger (*right*).

(b) A darker tone or darker color at the top of the picture or scenic element will tend to imply a top-heavy feeling of depression (*left*). The lighter tone or brighter color at the top gives a feeling of more solidity and normalcy (*right*).

Lines and angles can also be used to reinforce or exaggerate perspective, giving more of an illusion of depth. Painted on the studio floor, *forced perspective* lines can reinforce a great feeling of depth. *False perspective* lines can also be worked into other scenic elements. This kind of false perspective is limiting, however, in that the illusion works from only one specific camera location. (See fig. 9-6.)

Tone and Color. The predominant tones determine, to a great extent, the overall emotional image of a production. Light tones result in a delicate, cheerful, happy, trivial feeling, whereas dark tones result in a feeling that is heavy, somber, serious, forceful. Tone also affects balance. A dark tone carries more mass, weighs more, and can be used to balance a larger mass that is light in color or tone. The position of various tones or blocks of dark and light mass in a picture also affect its stability

and emotional quality. A dark mass at the top of a picture tends to induce a heavy, unnatural feeling of entrapment and depression; heavier tones in the bottom of a picture give it more of a stable base. (See fig. 9-7.)

Color is usually discussed in terms of three characteristics. **Hue** is the actual color base itself (red, green, purple, orange, and so forth). **Saturation** refers to the strength or intensity of a color, how far removed it is from a neutral or gray shade. **Brightness** (or *lightness*) indicates where the color would fall on a scale from light (white) to dark (black). The considerations mentioned for tone apply to color; for example, a highly saturated color (a vivid red) appears heavier—for purposes of balance—than an unsaturated color (a grayish red).

Various hues are also subjectively classified as *warm* (yellows and reds) or *cool* (blues and greens). Warm colors appear to be "heavier" than cool colors. Much of the secret

Figure 9-8 Example of decorative or abstract setting.

of achieving good color balance is the art of mixing various hues that are compatible, balancing highly saturated colors with grayer shades and selecting the right brightness of a particular hue (for example, baby blue rather than navy blue).

All of these elements of design—balance, line, tone—must be kept in mind as we look specifically at the elements of set design and graphics construction.

9.2 The Staging Design

As we begin to plan for scenery and staging, there are several different aspects we need to consider: staging styles, scenery elements, and staging requirements and considerations.

Staging Styles

One of the first decisions to be made by the director and the designer concerns the style of staging that will be right for a particular program. Neutral, decorative, and realistic settings are three options.

Neutral Setting. One basic approach, which is appropriate for many different production purposes, is the **neutral** or *nonrepresentational* style. This is a **nonassociative** approach in which there is no identifiable setting at all. All of the action takes place in **limbo** and there is no attempt to establish any locale. *Cameo* staging (section 4.3) would be an example of a neutral setting, as would some types of *silhouette* staging (although the latter usually is used only for a fragment of a larger scene). Most limbo settings, however, will be staged simply in front of a gray cyclorama or other neutral-colored plain background. In terms of overall production effect, the neutral staging might be used with the reportorial camera perspective (section 6.2) for segments of a variety show, newscast, instructional TV lesson, and so forth.

Decorative Setting. If some elements are added to the neutral setting—purely for the sake of artistic gratification—then it slips into a **decorative** (or even a *fantasy*) style. Although some elements may be added in an *abstract* setting, there still is no attempt to suggest any kind of realistic location or identifiable elements (fig. 9-8). Lighting effects and

Figure 9-9 Typical realistic setting with flats, set pieces, and furniture all contributing to a generalized atmospheric realism.

colors may be used; different scenic elements—platforms, steps, a podium—may be incorporated; but there still is no endeavor to represent anything recognizable. The various shapes, textures, colors, levels, and other scenic elements are used purely for their own artistic impact.

Again, this abstract kind of decorative setting would be appropriate for many reportorial uses of television such as newscasts, talk shows, educational programs, and so forth. The biggest programming format to use this kind of staging, however, would be music videos and variety shows—dance numbers, musical performances, concerts, stand-up comedians, singers, magicians, and others.

Realistic Settings. In dramatic programs, almost all staging is realistic to one extent or another. There are several levels of realism in stage and television setting. *Replicated realism* refers to replication of an actual

locale—the Oval Office of the White House or the interior of Grand Central Station—in a set accurate down to tiny details. This style corresponds to the *naturalism* of the stage. For the most part, the approach is too detailed and cluttered for successful television production.

Much more common is *atmospheric realism*, where the set conveys a certain type of place—a Western saloon, an elegant drawing room, a busy office. (See fig. 9-9.) With this modified form of realism, we can use selected details and highlight certain elements that help to strengthen the drama. It is certainly realistic enough for virtually all dramatic purposes.

Another type of realism that is often employed is *symbolic realism*. In this staging style an open set is used. Rather than have a solid-walled closed set, the background is discontinuous—relying upon the viewer to fill in the missing pieces with *psychological closure*. In this staging style, selected symbols and props are used to represent the idea of the real thing—a table and two chairs suggest a kitchen, a tree trunk and tent imply a campsite, a desk and a filing cabinet symbolize an office. There is no attempt to create an illusion of reality—just to suggest it.

Symbolic realism is often employed for brief comedy skits and slapstick sketches that are incorporated into a larger variety program, for example. Some abstract dramas may be staged entirely in symbolic realism. Nondramatic formats also make use of symbolic realism—the talk show with its desk and sofa, the homemaker program with a few kitchen appliances, and the illustrated lecture in front of a freestanding bookcase.

The open set gives the director much more freedom and flexibility in staging and shooting patterns. Blocking, camera movement, lighting, and microphone placement are all much easier to handle in the open set.

Scenery Elements

Regardless of the staging style, the director and the crew will probably find it convenient—for purposes of ordering different items, constructing needed units, and considering storage and construction—to think in terms of the following three broad categories of scenery and staging elements.

Settings. The term **setting** is usually used to refer to all of the major scenic pieces that make up the background and surrounding environment of the scene. This category would, in turn, include about three different kinds of scenic elements: **standard set units** such as flats, two-folds, and other standing background pieces; **hanging units,** including various cloth drops, hanging drapes, and the cyclorama (or cyc), that might cover two or three walls with a flat, neutral surface; and **set pieces,** which include pillars, steps and stairways, arches, platforms, wagons (platforms on casters), fences, lamp posts, and so forth. Many of the set pieces can be incorporated into realistic settings; others can be used in various artistic configurations in decorative or fantasy settings. The construction and use of some of the setting components are discussed below.

Set Dressings and Furniture. The terms *set dressings* and *furniture,* along with the label *stage props,* are used by different practitioners to mean slightly different things. Basically this category includes all of those major items that are involved in *dressing* a set, filling out the naked setting represented by the flats and major set pieces. This would include all of the major items of *furniture* (desk, lectern, chairs, tables, appliances, and so forth) and large exterior stage props (bicycles, cannons, trees, and other natural or manufactured objects). The term **set dressing** is often used to refer even more specifically to those smaller items that are used to make the set look lived in—lamps, ashtrays, pictures, books and magazines, household plants, vases, and other paraphernalia. Set dressings and stage props come from different sources, depending upon one's ingenuity and budget: a station's prop storage, the Drama department, secondhand stores, or one's own living room.

Hand Props. A specialized, but extremely important, category is that of **hand properties**—those items that are actually handled and manipulated as part of the television production. They include all those props needed for a dramatic production (telephones, bottles, kitchen tools, food, books, glasses, weapons), or for a commercial in a talk show (the box of cereal or the can of dog food), or for an instructional program (globes, models, chemistry apparatus). Obviously some of these items overlap with other set dressings, the distinction being that hand props are actually *used* in the program, rather than being planted as *decoration.*

Staging Requirements and Considerations

At this point, before the director proceeds any further, there are several other considerations that must be given some thought. All of the staging and scenery elements will have to fit in with a total production design. Staging concerns have to meet other criteria also.

Camera Movement. No matter what staging style is used, there must be provision for adequate camera movement. Several cameras will have to be free to have access from different angles in the setting. This usually poses no problems with neutral or limbo sets; it generally is no major problem with decorative settings or open sets; but it could be a problem with some elaborate realistic settings. For this reason, sets are usually constructed as just two-walled or three-walled sets. The open wall (the missing side of the set) is used for camera access. In three-walled sets, the walls do not have to be set at exactly 90 degrees; they can be left open at oblique angles so that the camera can have even more access. In some sets (occasionally a four-walled set may have to be used), it is possible to position cameras behind the flats or other scenic elements and shoot through a window, doorway, hole in the bookcase or fireplace, and other camouflaged openings.

Microphone Placement. The setting also has to have provision for adequate microphone placement and (if on a boom) movement. Although the wireless microphone (section 3.2) is increasingly used in studio dramas—soap operas and situation comedies—the beginning audio operator must learn how to cope with staging concerns involved with wired microphones. For most *dramatic* productions (since lavaliers usually are not worn, hanging mikes result in bad audio, and hidden microphones are not encouraged) some sort of boom or giraffe or fishpole is used. This can lead to two kinds of problems.

First, if the set is small and the boom is large, there will be real movement and coordination troubles. Cameras also will have to maneuver around the boom and microphone cables. Adequate room has to be left open. Second, the mike boom can cause bad boom shadows. If the lighting has not been carefully worked out with the precise boom placement in mind, there will be a strong possibility of unwanted shadows from the horizontal boom or fishpole. Ironically, this could be more of a problem in a neutral setting, with its plain background, than in a busy realistic set that may make a shadow less noticeable. In most cases, however, either the mike boom or the lighting instrument will have to be repositioned somewhat or the light will have to be *barn doored* off so the light will not hit the boom (section 4.6).

Lighting Instruments. Other lighting problems can be caused by certain kinds of setting arrangements. Occasionally, pillars or other foreground set pieces may block crucial front lighting from a certain angle. Sometimes a strong key light may throw a very distracting shadow on a close-up shot of some small object; or if the talent is lighted too close to the set (flat or cyc), the key light may throw too much illumination on the set. One of the most common problems, however, is the blocking of the backlight by a flat. If the flat is too high for the studio (a 10-foot flat may be high if the studio has a low ceiling), or if the flat is out too far into the studio from the backlight, or if the talent is standing too close to the flat, then it is going to be difficult to hit the talent with the backlight. (See fig. 9-10.) In this case, something—the backlight or the flat or the talent—will have to be moved.

Talent Movement. Finally, the setting has to take into consideration all anticipated movement by the talent. How much action is required? Will several people be moving in the same direction simultaneously? How much space is needed for certain movements (dance steps or tumbling demonstrations)? Is there plenty of room for all entrances and exits? Will the talent be forced to maneuver so close to the set walls that part of their lighting will be cut off? Or, if the performers work too close to the set, will they cast unwanted shadows on the flat or cyc? Once the director is satisfied that there is enough room for talent movement, lighting instruments, microphone placement, and camera movement, he or she is ready to look at the functional aspect of using scenery.

9.3   Using Sets and Scenic Elements

Having considered several of the principles of staging design, we turn now to some of the practical factors connected with handling scenic elements and specific studio production techniques.

Handling Scenery

The physical manipulation and handling of all scenery units—construction, assemblage, and storage—is a major study by itself. Television scenery is closely related to stage and film scenery; anyone who has ever worked in technical theater or visited the back lot of a major motion picture studio has a feel for the scope of the scenery and props department. All we can do in this text is touch upon some of the basic elements involved in making scenery units, assembling them for studio use, and storing them for repeated use.[3]

3. For a full discussion of scenery construction and use, consult any good theater stagecraft text or manual, such as W. Oren Parker and Harvey K. Smith, *Scene Design and Stage Lighting,* 2d ed. (New York: Holt, Rinehart & Winston, 1968), or Willard F. Bellman, *Scenography and Stage Technology: An Introduction* (New York: Thomas Y. Crowell Co., 1977).

In this kind of situation, either the back light will have to be mounted higher, the light will have to be repositioned closer to the flat, the flat will have to be moved back (closer to the back light), or the talent will have to move forward, farther away from the flat.

Figure 9-10   Back-lighting problems with scenic flat.

Construction.   The basic scenic unit for television, like that for the stage, is the **flat**—a cross-braced wooden frame faced with either canvas (which is lightweight, but too flimsy for repeated heavy use) or thin pressed board or plywood (which will take more abuse, although it is heavier to work with). Studios are increasingly turning to other rigid but lightweight materials such as foamboard and corrugated feather board for making flats and other scenic elements.

Typical construction for a flat is shown in figure 9-11. Flats can be made in any size, but common heights are 10 feet for larger studios and 8 feet for studios with lower ceilings.

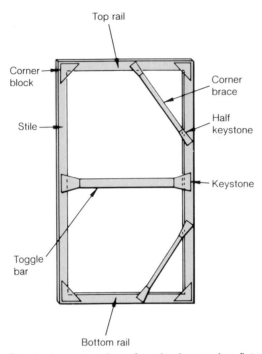

Top rail

Corner
block

Corner
brace

Stile

Half
keystone

Keystone

Toggle
bar

Bottom rail

Standard construction of a simple wooden flat consists of a frame made of 1″ × 3″ pine with ¼″ plywood for the corner blocks and keystones. The front of the frame is typically covered with canvas or with plywood (or pressed hardboard). If a solid wooden front covering is used, then the corner braces will not be needed.

Figure 9-11   Construction of an ordinary flat.

Widths also will vary, although they are seldom broader than 5 feet (the width that one person can comfortably handle with arms outstretched).

Whenever wider widths are needed, flats can be hinged together semipermanently. Two flats hinged together is known as a **two-fold.** Three flats similarly connected (seldom will you see more than three) is known as a **three-fold.** When a wider span needs to be covered, the flat units are temporarily lashed or connected together. (See fig. 9-12.)

Construction of other set pieces (stairways, platforms, and so forth) is more complicated, requiring heavy bracing and sturdy framing for the amount of abuse and wear they will be subjected to.

Cycs can be either a permanent solid cyc (faced with plywood or some other hard surface, which may tend to give audio problems) or a *cyc cloth* (canvas, duck, or gauze, depending upon the desired texture and reflectance quality desired). Cycs as a rule are designed to be used while stretched taut, giving a smooth limbo background, although they may be hung loosely in pleats to give the appearance of opened drapes. Drapes, which are usually of a heavier material and often darker than a cyc cloth, can be either pulled taut or pleated, depending upon the desired effect. Darker, low reflectance drapes are effective backing for cameo lighting. Drapes usually are used in smaller widths than a cyc and can ordinarily be easily rigged or hung for specific applications. A cyc, on the other hand, usually is permanently mounted, covering two or even three walls of a studio.

Assembling.   Most flats are built with special hardware that facilitates easy temporary joining of two or more units. The stiles of the flats can be fitted with cleats so that a line can be used to lash two flats together quickly. (See fig. 9-12.)

Other methods of joining flats include the use of various metal fasteners (such as *L-plates,* which have drop-in fasteners and loose-pin hinges) and the use of large *quick-fix* clamps, which can be used to clamp together the stiles of two adjoining flats.

Most flats also have some sort of bracing or supporting unit so that they can be completely freestanding as a self-supporting unit. Several different types of stage braces are used. One of the most common is the **jack,** or hinged wooden brace. (See fig. 9-12.) When the flat is in place, the jack is swung out behind the flat at right angles to the front of the flat and held in place with stage weights or sandbags.

Most set pieces are solid and freestanding units that need no special bracing when assembled for use in the studio. However, many

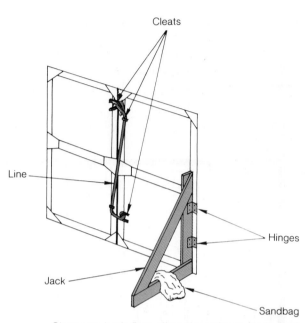

Cleats

Line

Jack

Hinges

Sandbag

Cleats on both flats allow the units to be lashed together by means of the line, which is permanently tied onto one of the flats. The jack is a hinged stage brace that, when weighted, forms a good self-supporting unit.

Figure 9-12 Connecting and bracing flats.

of them—such as stairway units—do need to be fastened to other units or flats to make them as secure and immobile as possible. Door flats also need to be securely fastened to other set units to guarantee that the doorway will function properly without sticking or falling down when used. Some set pieces such as *parallels* (collapsible platforms) can be partially disassembled and folded for storage. They must be carefully put together and securely set up before being used.

Storage. In many small stations and educational institutions, scenery storage can be a serious problem. There is never enough room to house everything that is needed, and scenery storage always seems to be one area that suffers the most. This can be a particularly critical problem because so many of the flats and

special set pieces can be reused over and over in a variety of ways—with different set dressings—in a number of configurations. Yet, they have to be stored somewhere and catalogued for easy retrieval.

Flats and other narrow units usually are stored in racks, which are simple frames designed to hold a number of flats in an upright position. Each rack can be designed and labeled to hold similarly matched scenic units (for example, living room flats, office flats, green-speckled flats, log cabin flats, and so forth).

Props and other small items can be stored on deep shelves in the storage area. Again, it is important that each shelf and/or cubicle be clearly labeled: "telephones," "dishes," "bottles," and so on. Even furniture and other large stage props can be stored in multitiered shelves.

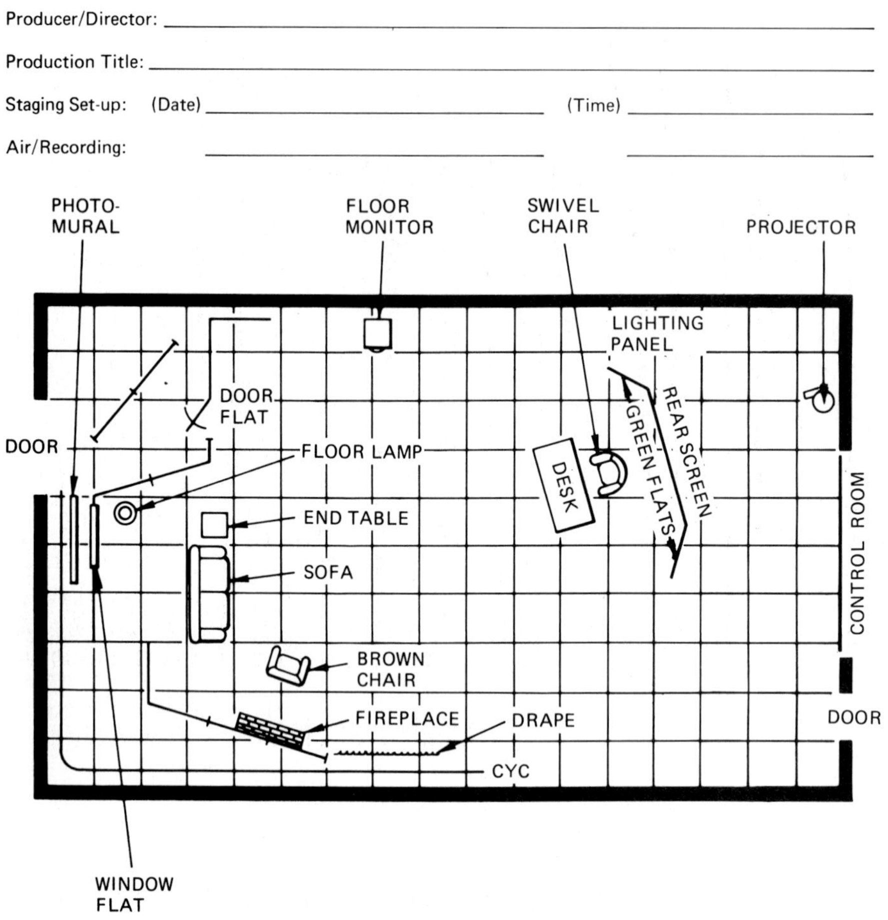

Producer/Director: _____

Production Title: _____

Staging Set-up: (Date) _____   (Time) _____

Air/Recording: _____   _____

PHOTO-MURAL   FLOOR MONITOR   SWIVEL CHAIR   PROJECTOR

LIGHTING PANEL

DOOR FLAT

DOOR

REAR SCREEN

GREEN FLATS

DESK

FLOOR LAMP

END TABLE

SOFA

CONTROL ROOM

BROWN CHAIR

FIREPLACE   DRAPE

DOOR

CYC

WINDOW FLAT

In this particular floor plan, the squares on the floor correspond to 3-foot tiles actually laid on the studio floor. In other floor plans, a lighting grid or pipe battens might be superimposed over the studio layout.

Figure 9-13 Sample staging floor plan.

Large overstuffed chairs, sofas, and heavy tables can be stored on the floor level; medium-sized chairs and tables can be stored on another level (4 to 5 feet off the floor); and lightweight chairs and stools and small appliances can be stored on a third level (perhaps 7 to 8 feet above the floor).

Studio Techniques

In moving into actual studio usage, there are several other factors that the director and staging director need to be aware of.

Floor Plan. First of all, as we have stressed throughout this text, the success of any television production is dependent to a great extent upon the discipline exercised in preproduction planning. As with the considerations of the lighting director, much valuable studio time and frustration can be saved by careful planning and plotting (section 4.6).

A good floor plan allows the director to make the most economical use of all studio and staging space. Sets can be planned efficiently; equipment can be placed with precision. The

Figure 9-14 Use of a cucalorus pattern to project a shadow on the back wall of a set.

director can plan how best to take advantage, for example, of the *corner set*—a two-walled setting positioned in a corner of the studio—that provides good set backing for many types of productions (better than a flat backdrop), while allowing great depth and freedom of camera movement (more so than with a three-walled set).

A typical studio staging floor plan will include the placement of all flats and other set pieces and the exact location of all stage props and furniture. Other prominent studio facilities should also be included, as they are important to the production setting. It is important that all flats and furniture be drawn to exact scale; otherwise the director's shooting angles, the talent's movement, and the lighting design will all be off. Figure 9-13 shows a typical plot plan, drawn to the scale of ⅛-inch to 1 foot. Once the accurate floor plan is drawn, it will be used by the director, staging director, staging assistants, floor manager, audio engineer, talent, and even the lighting director (to

confirm and complement the lighting plot). It is therefore essential that the plan be prepared with as much detail and precision as possible.

Lighting Effects. In addition to the regular lighting required for illumination of the production area, there are other special lighting effects that should be considered as part of the overall staging design. We have already mentioned the use of the cucalorus, or cookie, pattern (section 4.4) to cast various shadow patterns (venetian blinds, prison bars, Moorish lattice-work, and so forth) on the set wall. (See fig. 9-14.) Colored gels can be used to throw colored lights on a plain cyc or other surface. Subtle lighting changes (with the dimmer) can be employed to change color or shadowing as dramatic action unfolds. Other creative lighting effects (determining shape and texture, modifying reality, and establishing mood) were discussed in section 4.3. Staging and lighting must be considered as one integral production element; they cannot be looked at as isolated independent components.

Special Staging Effects. There are several different kinds of mechanical and optical **staging effects** that can be used. Although some of the effects depend upon expensive equipment and elaborate arrangements, others can be adapted to most studio situations.

Large electric fans can create *wind* effects. Dry ice plunged into a tub of hot water creates *fog*. (Both of these effects cause studio noise that can be compensated for in a number of ways, including sound effects records.) *Lightning* and *explosions* are best suggested by lighting effects (off set) coupled with sound effects.

A *fire* effect is produced by shaking silk strips on a stick in front of a spotlight to create flickering shadows, or by supering film footage of a flame over the set (since flame is translucent the super effect works well). Again, sound effects are used to present a total contextual effect. *Smoke* can be added by carefully pouring mineral oil on a hot plate.

Rain can be simulated by preparing a rain **drum** graphic—a continuous loop of black paper with white streaks splashed on it that is attached to a studio crawl (section 9.5)—rotating the drum, and by superimposing a slightly defocused shot of the drum over the scene (with the actors in wet clothing). Again, sound is added for a total effect.

There are several different kinds of optical effects that also can be incorporated into many kinds of productions. **Rear screen projection** can be used in many dramatic and reportorial settings. Ranging in size from about 4 or 5 feet wide up to 12 feet across, rear screens can be used with regular slide projectors or, preferably, with special high-powered 4″ × 5″ projectors. They can be placed behind talent for newscasts or ITV lessons or they can be incorporated into a dramatic setting for outdoor locations or window backing. Special lighting and studio problems can occur, however. The use of the rear screen takes up quite a bit of floor space behind the set. Lighting is critical because no spill light (from the front or rear) can be allowed to fall upon the screen; lighting has to be from the sides or from very high steep angles.

Mirrors can be used in a variety of ways. For example, a large mirror suspended from a lighting grid can be used to get a shot looking straight down onto a demonstration table or into a cooking pot. Mirrors can also be used in musical productions. High and low shots—for example, dancers' feet on a bandstand program—can be obtained by using a double-mirrored periscope.

Gobos are another handy staging device that enable a camera to frame a shot through some special foreground design. The gobo is a cutout (for instance, a simulated gunsight or keyhole) that is positioned several feet in front of the camera; it is an obvious stylistic effect that can be used judiciously to good advantage. Other optical devices using special filters and prisms also can be utilized in more sophisticated situations.

Production Problems. Finally, mention should be made of several common troubles that periodically plague even the best-planned staging plan. One is the difficulty of obtaining a consistent background from all angles. Whether a person is using a lighted cyc or a realistic set of flats, care must be taken to make certain that the set is evenly lit so that each camera, shooting from its particular angle, will be getting the same background shot. Also, care must be taken to ensure that the sets are wide enough—that there is enough cover at each end of the set—so that camera shooting from outside angles will not be shooting off the set.

Troubles frequently occur with functional furniture. Chairs, stools, and sofas must be appropriately matched with talent. There are some common furniture problems: the *swinging swivel chair,* in which a guest vents nervous energy by rotating back and forth; the *precarious perch,* which involves sitting uncomfortably on top of a high, hard stool; and the *talent swallower,* an overstuffed chair or sofa that is so plush and soft that the person sinks down so far that the director is left with nothing but a shot of knees. Solid furniture should be comfortable but firm.

One last production problem that has ruined many a final take is the forgotten prop. In any kind of production that relies on hand props (dramas, variety acts, demonstration shows, instructional TV), there is always the danger of failing to return a given prop to its starting point. The gun must be returned to the bedside table; the magician's paraphernalia must be repacked and checked; a new set of vegetables must be prepared for the cooking demonstration; the toys must be put back in the clown's sack; and so forth. Both the talent and the stage manager should double check, after the dress rehearsal, to determine that everything is in place for the final production.

9.4 Principles of Graphics Design

In this section we turn from the large picture of the entire setting to the area of television **graphics**—those two-dimensional visuals specifically prepared for television presentation. This definition includes items such as title cards, charts, drawings, cartoons, diagrams, photographs, maps, super (key) cards, slides, and the chalkboard. Further, in today's well-equipped production centers, we must become increasingly involved with electronic graphics and computer-generated visuals. In many professional studios, the computer graphic has virtually totally replaced the physical card.

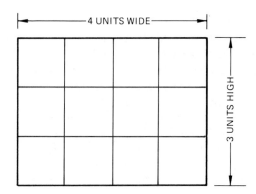

Figure 9-15 Regardless of the size of the television graphic—whether it is 4 centimeters wide or 8 feet wide—it must always be in the 3 to 4 aspect ratio if it is designed to be used full frame.

Aspect Ratio

The first rule of graphics preparation is that all visual material must be prepared with a *3-to-4* **aspect ratio**—the television screen is three units high and four units wide. Nothing can be done to change that ratio: regardless of the size of a graphic, it still has to fit into that three-to-four ratio. (See fig. 9-15.) This is approximately the same ratio as a horizontal 35mm (2″ × 2″) slide. Most slides, therefore, can be used *horizontally* in the television format.

Vertical slides, of course, cannot as a rule be used successfully on the television screen. There are some exceptions when a graphic that is not in the three-to-four ratio can be used. A long horizontal card can be used as a **pan card**—that is, the camera can pan across the card, revealing part of the information at a time. Similarly, a tall narrow graphic can be used as a **tilt card**—the camera tilts down (or up) the card, revealing only a portion of it at a time. Also, it is possible to use a tall card as part of a split screen (section 7.4), with the remainder of the screen filled by the talent or some other subject. Similarly, it is possible to use a vertical slide if it is projected on a rear screen, and the rest of the television picture is filled with something else (like the talent

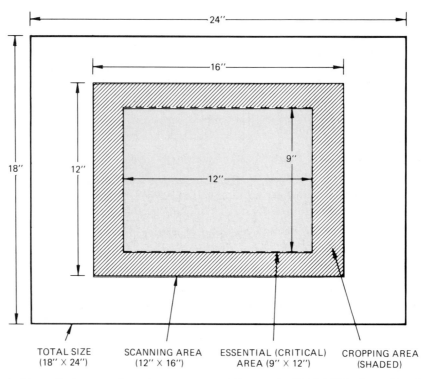

TOTAL SIZE   SCANNING AREA   ESSENTIAL (CRITICAL)   CROPPING AREA
(18″ X 24″)   (12″ X 16″)   AREA (9″ X 12″)   (SHADED)

In this particular example, suppose you are working with a card that is actually 18″ X 24″. The scanning area is two-thirds of the total card size, or 12″ X 16″ (which includes the shaded area). The essential (or critical) area is three-fourths of the scanning area (or half of the total card size); that is, 9″ X 12″ (indicated by the area in color). The cropping area (shaded) is the portion of the scanning area that may be seen by the television camera, but that may or may not be seen on the home television receiver.

Figure 9-16 Relationship of scanning area to essential area.

standing next to the screen). In general, however, all television material must be prepared with that 3-to-4 aspect ratio to fit on the television screen.

Scanning and Essential Areas

All material that is prepared on a graphic card will not be seen on the home receiver. There has to be some room around the border of the card for the numbering and the identification of the graphic, handling, smudge prints, and so forth. Let us call this the *border area* and assume that it will not be used for any information at all. The camera will never intend to shoot this area. To give ourselves plenty of room, let us assume that this margin should be about one-sixth of the total card: that is, if the card is 24 inches wide, we will take off one-sixth, or 4 inches, from each edge. This leaves us with a total usable width of 16 inches. (See fig. 9-16.)

The remaining area that we have left is called the **scanning area.** This is the area actually to be scanned by the television camera. If we started out with a card that measured 18″ X 24″ and reduced that with a border ⅙ the dimension of the card on all sides, we would now have a scanning area of 12″ X 16″—still in the 3 to 4 ratio. (See fig. 9-16.)

Still, not everything in the scanning area will be transmitted through the entire system to reach the home TV set. The scanning system of the camera monitor may be slightly misaligned, so the camera operator will inadvertently cut off part of the graphic. The home receiver also will clip off, or crop, some of the picture. To be safe, we should decrease the total width of the useable scanning area by taking off about one-eighth on all sides. Starting with our 24-inch-wide original card, we now have a remaining width of about 12 inches. (See fig. 9-16.)

The remaining area is known as the **essential area,** or the **critical area.** All of the essential information that we want to transmit through the system must be placed in this critical zone. This amounts to about one-half of the original card size. It is still a three-to-four ratio.

The information that is outside of the essential area but still within the scanning area (the shaded area in fig. 9-16) may or may not be seen on the home receiver. Depending upon the various components in the total transmission system, some of this information may reach the home set; some of it will be cropped. This information, therefore, must be part of the total graphic design, but it cannot be essential. Anything outside of the scanning area—on the border of the card—is technically known as *garbage,* and it is assumed that the camera will not try to transmit any of it.

Graphic Mask.   To assist you in the preparation of graphics, it may be helpful to make a template or mask as a guide in laying out standard graphic cards. One convenient size for graphics is 11″ × 14″ (this is not only a convenient size to work with, it is also one-quarter of a standard sheet of 22″ × 28″ railroad or poster board). Take a piece of poster board 11″ × 14″ and cut out a 6″ × 8″ rectangular hole in the exact center. This will give you a good approximation of the essential area

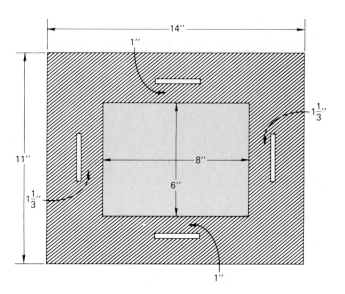

Start with an 11″ × 14″ piece of poster board, cut out a 6″ × 8″ hole in the center, and you will have a convenient guide or template for the preparation of 11″ × 14″ graphics. All information placed in the center cut-out area will be in the essential area. By making a slit 1″ above and below the central area, and 1⅓″ to the sides of the essential area, you will also define the scanning area.

Figure 9-17 Graphic mask.

for your graphic. The border is actually a little less than that recommended, but it is close enough to be functional. Also cut some slits in your mask 1 inch above and below the essential area, and 1⅓-inch to each side of the cutout. These mark the edges of your scanning area. Your mask should resemble the illustration in figure 9-17.

Quantity of Information

The amount of information that can be communicated on television is obviously limited. The quantity of data that can be successfully included in one TV picture is determined basically by three factors: the size of the symbols (lettering); the style of printing; and color and tonal contrast. Each of the three factors is discussed in the next three sections.

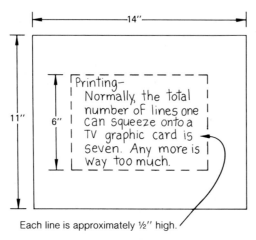

On a typical 11″ × 14″ graphic card, the essential area will be about 6″ high. This means that each individual letter will be about ½″ tall. The information on the card above represents the maximum amount that should be put on one card.

Figure 9-18 Quantity of information on a graphic card.

Symbol Size

As a rule of thumb, lettering on television should be *no smaller than one-fifteenth of the screen height*. If the critical area is 15 inches high, the lettering can be no smaller than 1 inch. If the critical area is 2 inches high, individual letters will have to be a little over ⅛ inch high. In the example of the mask constructed in figure 9-17, with a scanning area 6 inches high, the minimum height for each letter must be at least ⅜ of an inch. (Actually, it should be just about 1 centimeter.) Figure 9-18 indicates the amount of material that should be considered maximum for a typical TV graphic. If no line is less than one-fifteenth of the height of the critical area (and assuming some space is left between each line of letters), this would mean that normally *no more than 7 lines of information* should be included on a TV graphic card. Of course, artistic considerations—balance and arrangement of mass—might dictate that much less material be used. And it is recognized, of course, that there are specialized exceptions to this rule; print information stored on videodiscs, teletext printing, computer displays, and other high-resolution formats may include more than 20 lines on the screen. But 7 lines should be considered generally the maximum number of lines for a normal TV graphic.

Simplicity and Style

If there is one primary rule about the preparation of TV graphics, it is simply this: *Keep it simple*. All lettering. All design elements. All artwork. The screen is too small and the scanning lines are too blurry to permit any fine detail work.

This is particularly true with lettering styles. Letters should be bold, thick, well-defined, with sharp, firm contour. Elegant lettering with fancy serifs and swirls must be avoided (except possibly for large, stylized, two- or three-word titles). Letters should be of even thickness throughout—both horizontal and vertical lines should be the same. (Thin horizontal lines, for example, can be obliterated in the scanning lines.)

Any other art work on a graphic card with lettering should also be kept simple. If it is too detailed, the audience will not get a chance to comprehend it; if it is too confusing and domineering, the audience will be distracted from the lettering.

All nonverbal graphics—pictures, cartoons, drawings, slides—must also be kept as simple as possible. Drawings or photographs showing a certain component or step in a process must show only what is absolutely necessary. One of the main troubles in trying to use visuals prepared for other media (for example, charts from a book or photographs from a magazine) is that they invariably contain too much detail. They are designed for a medium without the pressing temporal limitations of television. Usually they are visuals designed to convey as much information as possible in a single picture; they are designed for detailed study and comparison. Television, by contrast, may have to use three or four graphics sequentially to get the same information across.

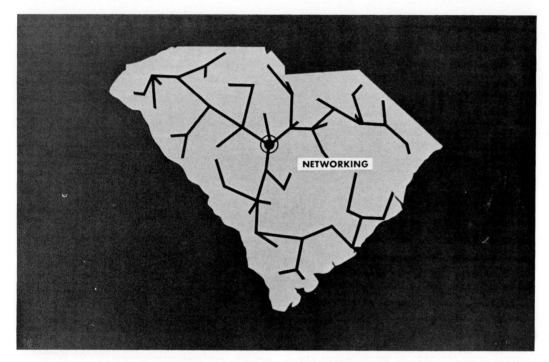

Figure 9-19 Example of a simplified map appropriate for a television graphic.

This admonition is particularly true with *maps*. It is safe to say that no prepared maps (designed for nontelevision application) can be safely used on television. Any television graphic that tries to squeeze in more than twenty-five words is really too cramped and the information is too small (See fig. 9-18.) How many words are there on a typical map section that you might want to use? Maps have to be redone for TV. (See fig. 9-19.) Use only outlines of countries or natural geographical bodies and a few key labels or key locations. Use a series of maps if movement or detail is needed.

Color Contrast

A third factor that can help determine the readability of a graphic and the quantity of information it can contain is color contrast. Working with color graphics, it is important to use hues that contrast and complement each other without actually clashing. Artistic judgment and experience will help to determine which hues go well together. It is often very effective to combine different saturation levels of the same or closely related hues. Contrast in brightness levels also is effective in making certain segments of a graphic stand out.

Video engineers like to have just a little white and a little black in a picture for reference points. Thus, a good graphic would be one that has two or three shades of brightness plus a little white and black for sparkle and interest. Avoid graphics that are all black and white (except for super and key cards, which have to be white letters on a black card).

One problem to be avoided is the use of colors of the same brightness or saturation in preparing graphics. Two different hues (say, red and blue) will contrast best if you also consider differing levels of saturation and brightness. A dark brownish red will contrast better against a brilliant royal blue than against a dark navy blue.

In fact, contrasting saturations of the same hue (for example, a vivid chartreuse and a grayish olive green) provide considerable contrast. Even contrasting brightness or lightness of the same hue and saturation (for example, a light pink and a dark rose) provide essential contrast and legibility.

Having considered these basic principles of designing television graphics, and keeping in mind some of the basic concepts of balance and line discussed in section 9.1, let us now look at some of the functional aspects of how TV graphics can be used in the studio—either working with physical cards or computer graphics.

9.5 Construction and Use of Graphics

In the actual preparation and use of graphics, several questions need to be answered about the way in which they are to be displayed, the ideal size for graphics, how they are to be constructed, and specific production applications. Most of these considerations have evolved with the use of physical graphic cards—still used predominantly in small-format productions and many training situations. However, many of these considerations apply equally to computer-generated graphics.

Location and Display

Perhaps the first question to be asked about the use of a particular graphic is where and how it is to be displayed. There is one basic distinction that must be made. Is the graphic to be used on the set? Or is it to be an off-set graphic?

On-set graphics are meant to be displayed in front of the audience. Usually, a shooting pattern will be worked out that includes some shots of the talent and graphic(s) in the same shot. On-set graphics can be placed on a floor easel or on a desk easel. They can be hanging as a decoration in the middle of the studio; they may be attached to freestanding poles. They may be mounted on a wall of the set. They can be used on a rear projection screen with the talent in front of the screen. One of the most common examples is the news scene electronically matted behind the reporter in a typical news set (section 7.4). In one way or another, however, they are designed to be used as an integral part of the set. The audience sees where and how they are used.

Off-set graphics, on the other hand, are never seen as an integrated part of the set. They appear out of nowhere. The audience has no reference point for them; for example, the audience would never know the actual size of the graphic. Off-set graphics can be employed in a variety of ways, but most often they are used on a graphics stand or floor easel. They also might be mounted on a drum, or **crawl**—a large revolving drum that can be turned at varying speeds (either by hand or by an electric motor) with a long flexible graphic card attached to it.

Computer-generated visuals, of course, are also considered off-set graphics—unless they are projected behind the talent. Off-set graphics may also be used as slides from telecine or the master control room film chain. This is often much easier and more convenient in that (1) the graphics are already framed and readily accessible without the chance of a slip-up on the floor, and (2) a camera can be freed for other studio work.

One reason that the distinction between on-set and off-set graphics is important is that you may design a graphic differently if it is to be an on-set graphic. For instance, conceivably you could use a vertical ratio if you know that the talent will always be standing in the same shot with the graphic. Or you may be able to design a graphic with more information than is otherwise recommended if the talent will be talking at considerable length (perhaps with the aid of a pointer) about different parts of the graphic. In addition, color coordination and the use of mass and balance may be different if it is an on-set graphic, designed to be seen in the same shot with something else.

Whether a graphic is to be used on set or off set, if it is not firmly attached or stapled to some other scenic unit (such as a wall or a studio crawl), it must be firmly mounted. All graphics for easel stands must be either constructed directly on heavy poster board or firmly attached (glued) to heavy board.

Size of Graphics

To the viewer at home, it does not matter what size the graphic actually is as long as it is attractive and legible. For production purposes, however, size makes a difference.

On-set graphics have to be a reasonable size that balances with the talent and/or with other set elements. Size depends upon the purpose and the setting. A good average on-set size will probably be the full 22″ × 28″ poster board size. For simpler desk-top graphics, an 11″ × 14″ size is probably adequate. Seldom will on-set graphics be any smaller than that. At the other extreme, on-set graphics can be quite large—covering an entire wall or, as has been done, covering half the studio floor (a painted map).

Off-set graphics can vary considerably in size, again depending upon the exact use to which they are put. For most purposes, the ubiquitous 11″ × 14″ would be a good size. It is convenient, readily available, and easy to handle. When necessary, much smaller sizes can be used. Many cameras can focus in on a 3″ × 4″ card without too much trouble. The smaller a graphic is, however, the more time and difficulty it takes for the camera operator to adjust focus. It is possible, with many camera and tube complements, to get tight enough on a small area to use typewritten material on camera.

One general consideration to keep in mind is that the smaller a graphic is, the more every little camera movement is going to be magnified on the screen. With a 3″ × 4″ card, the slightest camera jiggle will turn out to be a major movement on a 21-inch screen. Also, every little blemish on the graphic itself and every minor letter imperfection will be magnified. For these reasons, directors usually like to stay away from undersized graphics. In addition, if a camera is going to have to execute any movement on a graphic—panning or tilting, moving around on a map—then the bigger the graphic is, the smoother the movement will appear. For these purposes, the 22″ × 28″ size is often utilized.

Graphics Preparation

There are quite a few methods for lettering on graphics. Depending upon one's artistic abilities, budget, and access to equipment, any one of the following might be appropriate. *Hand lettering* can be done with quite a variety of media and tools: pen, pencil, paint (poster paints, tempera), charcoal, chalk; felt-tip marking pens may be one of the fastest and easiest means (for rough lettering). There are a number of ready-made, *ready-to-apply letters* that can be purchased: wax rub-on letters come in a variety of styles; large cutout, paste-on letters in various formats are available. Different types of *mechanical lettering aids,* stencils, and lettering sets can be effectively used in some applications. Specific *printing machines,* such as the hot press and other mechanical cold-press machines that use ribbon or tape acetate, can be very useful, if available.

The *typewriter,* as mentioned, can be considered for some jobs—under some conditions. In particular, if large primary type is available, plus a good sharp carbon ribbon, the typewriter can prepare simple textual material. But as a rule, an ordinary typescript magnified by the camera does not look very

SPACING SPACING

(METHODICAL)   (OPTICAL)

Left, in methodical spacing, each letter is spaced exactly the same distance from the one on either side of it. This results in an uneven appearance because letters with vertical lines (such as the ''I'' and the ''N'') appear very close together, while those with open spaces at the top or bottom (such as the ''P'' and the ''A'') appear too far apart when next to each other. *Right,* with optical spacing, variations can be taken into consideration as each letter is spaced visually according to its shape.

Figure 9-20 Methodical and optical spacing of letters.

satisfactory. Also, the camera runs into extensive production problems when trying to work with something as small as ordinary type. Many newer lenses, however, have a close-up **macro lens** setting designed to make it easier to get tight shots of small objects.

In working with these various media and materials, care should be taken to avoid—or to work very carefully with—any highly reflective matter. Some of the cold-press acetate tape, for instance, makes letters that are very shiny. Matte finishes are to be preferred, if there is a choice, to glossy photographs. Otherwise, lighting is critical in order to avoid reflected glare.

One advantage to hand lettering and some of the ready-to-apply rub-on and paste-on letters is that the letters can be optically spaced. With most of the machine-generated letters, such as the typewriter and some character generators, each letter is mechanically spaced from the ones next to it—with a rigidity that is more convenient than artistic (see fig. 9-20).

One other hint to successful graphics preparation is to assemble your graphics in segments. Prepare your lettering—by whatever method—on appropriate shades of colored paper and then cut the segments out in blocks and glue them onto the different colored basic board for your graphic. This accomplishes two things for you. First, it allows you to work more easily with blocks and masses; you can better control the balance and layout of each graphic. Second, the approach gives you more of an opportunity to work with varying textures and shades on one graphic. If you print black letters on a light gray paper and then cut out the blocks of paper and paste them onto darker gray poster board, you have introduced another tone in a rather pleasing and easy-to-handle manner.

Finally, before moving into the fantasy world of the computer, it should be noted that the **character generator** (fig. 9-21) is a very handy, always available source for the quickest jobs of all. The character generator allows the operator to electronically type right on the screen. Most models allow for quick retrieval of previously prepared material and flexible positioning and movement on the screen. The character generator, of course, cannot produce an artistic graphic card, but for many kinds of verbal displays its speed and efficiency make up for aesthetic drawbacks.

Computer-Generated Graphics

Most major production studios, networks, and an increasing number of stations have added the computer to their art departments. Furthermore, as the costs of microcomputers and simple software programs have come down, many schools and audiovisual operations have also been able to utilize the computer for graphics work. It is possible to get into basic computer-generated graphics production with equipment costing as little as $500.

Computer graphics are used for a variety of training programs, titles and credits, illustrated lectures, weather charts, news graphics, cartoons and animation, commercials, and numerous other applications. It is essential that tomorrow's video professionals become as familiar and comfortable with the computer as they are with the TV camera and switcher.

There are several essential pieces of hardware that are common to all computer-graphics operations. First, there is the **central**

Figure 9-21 Chyron RGU character generator.

processing unit (CPU). This is the microprocessing heart of the computer that does all of the actual "computing." For most small-scale graphics operations, the familiar personal computers or PCs are used (Apples, IBM PCs, Ataris, Radio Shack TRS models, Commodores, and so forth). Second, there is the **keyboard,** an integral part of any simple computer. This is used both for typing instructions to the CPU and for typing text directly onto the screen—as with the character generator. As we stressed in section 1.5, the typewriter is the first and most basic tool used in any TV production. As keyboarding/typing skills are transferred to the computer keyboard, it must be stressed that any student who is not familiar and comfortable with a computer keyboard—who is, in effect, not computer-literate—is seriously handicapped in the professional world.

A third component would have to be **input memory devices**—like the **disk drives, cassettes,** or **cartridges.** Most "professional" computers use disk drives (either the familiar 5¼-inch, the newer 3½-inch, or 8-inch floppy disks or—for higher priced systems with large memories—the hard disk drives). However, many of the family-oriented low-priced computers using cartridges or cassettes also can be adapted for simple graphics purposes.

A fourth component of the computer graphics system—the first item that relates directly to graphics generation—is the **graphics tablet,** also called a "data tablet" or "bit pad." This tablet is used with a special electronic pen to enter digitalized coordinates. In essence, it converts the pen's touch on the pad or tablet to a precise position (defined by X and Y coordinates) on the computer monitor. Therefore, it allows direct artist input to

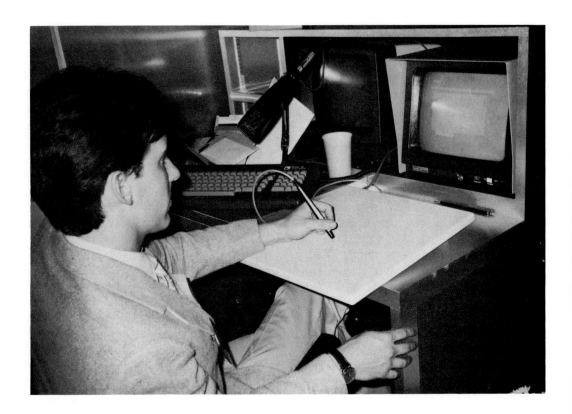

Figure 9-22 The 3M Model BFA Paint System. Artist using the digitizing graphics pad to create computer-generated graphics.

the computer by using the electronic pen. It takes but a few hours for the graphics artist to get used to creating art work by looking at the TV screen while "drawing" on a tablet located below the screen (see fig. 9-22). Other similar types of input devices include game paddles, joysticks, light pens (that write directly on the screen), hand-held cursors, and the fanciful "mouse" made popular by Apple.

A fifth component obviously is the **computer monitor.** Higher quality systems usually will feature an RGB ("red-green-blue") monitor. Because this high-quality monitor does not break the picture information down into the chrominance and luminance channels used for broadcast signals, the resulting "noncomposite" picture is not an NTSC (National Television System Committee) broadcast signal. However, both the color rendition and resolution are sharper than in a broadcast

monitor or TV set. Often, a computer-graphics work station will also include a black-and-white monitor for text information.

In more sophisticated computer systems, another component would be a **digitalizing camera**—one that picks up picture information, either graphics materials or a live scene, and immediately converts it to a digitalized format. Then the image can be manipulated by computer instructions—rotating images, squeezing and elongating the picture, changing colors, and so forth (see section 7.4).

Computer Graphics Software. It takes more than just the hardware, of course, to use a computer system. The programming instructions or software package comprise the other half of the operation. Graphics software—often referred to generically as "paint box" programs—can be considered in roughly three levels of sophistication (and corresponding price categories).[4]

The simplest level typically will cost from $20 to $80. Sample programs include *Higher Graphics II* (Synergistic Software), *Special Effects* (Penguin Software), *Graph It* (designed for Atari), *Apple World* (United Software of America), and *The Art Gallery* and *Micro Painter* (both from Radio Shack). Generally these simple programs will allow you to create a variety of shapes and enable you to draw basic original designs. They also give you most of the text-creation features of a much more expensive character generator. They will provide fairly good resolution—the best going up to about 256 by 192 **pixels.** A pixel (a computer term derived from "picture element") roughly corresponds to one dot on a scanning line on a TV set (section 5.3). It is the smallest definable unit or dot that one can manipulate and work with. So a resolution of 256 (horizontal) by 192 (vertical) pixels is considerably less than the capacity of a typical TV set— however, it is quite good for defining a bar graph or pie chart or lettering for a super card.

Once you add a graphics tablet to the system and incorporate a slightly more sophisticated "painting box" program, you are talking about the middle-priced systems— about $150 to $500: *Super Chartman II* (Graphics Software, Inc.), *Creative Graphics* (Accupipe Corporation), *Graphwriter* (Graphic Communications, Inc.), and *Bizgraph* (Micro-Labs), among many others. These systems, often designed to be used in conjunction with spreadsheet computer programs, offer considerable flexibility and detail. They are designed to be used with computers of the IBM PC level.

Moving up to the professional level, prices may range from a couple thousand dollars to

4. The term *paint box* actually is taken from a registered trademark of Quantel, referring to its specific advanced computer-graphics system Paint Box®.

more than $100,000. These systems incorporate features that were undreamed of just a few years ago. The *Auroa/100 Digital Video-graphics System,* developed in 1973, was the first to be used by network television; it includes three different levels of animation. *IMAGES,* developed by the New York Institute of Technology, is a high-level animation system that features one of the most advanced **key-framing** programs available, "Tween"; this enables the artist to draw one pattern, give the computer a second drawing, and then instruct the computer to fill in all of the intermediate frames to metamorphose (or "interpolate") from one image to the other (at any desired speed or number of frames).

The 3M Model *BFA Paint System,* like several others, offers the artist a theoretical total of 16.8 million colors to choose from; the working palette can display 256 colors at any one time. The Dubner *CBG-2 Video Graphics Generator* combines the features of a character generator, background generator, animation system, electronic paint box, and 3-D solid modeling system; its very high resolution of 1,024 by 525 pixels is illustrative of the most sophisticated systems. The Quantel *Paint Box®* probably does the best job of emulating fine-art characteristics—allowing the artist to simulate oil paints, watercolors, chalk, crayon, and other media—with colors actually "mixed" on the artist's electronic palette. Many other high-priced systems offer similar features and flexibilities.

Regardless of the sophistication of the system, there are a number of standard procedures and capabilities that are common to most computer graphics arrangements. With most graphics-tablet setups, for example, the following operations are possible:

1. Using the electronic pen to select from a **menu** (an on-screen display of various options available) the type of drawing medium to be used—brush, pen, airbrush, and so forth.

2. Selecting a color by touching the desired color on a menu display. Sophisticated systems allow you to mix colors (hues), and to change saturation and brightness.
3. Drawing on the graphic tablet while watching the monitor.
4. Giving directions for specific lines and geometric shapes. Plot two points and the computer will draw in the line connecting them. Specify centers and radii for circles and ellipses, coordinates for rectangles and cubes; the computer will draw them in.
5. Typing text directly onto the screen. Select from any number of type fonts, styles, sizes, or make up your own. Add shadows and dimension to the lettering.
6. Using special effects. Create mirror images, rotate designs, enlarge and shrink art work, tilt, skew, warp, change widths and shapes. Replicate small images all over the screen. Execute any kind of "cut and paste" job.
7. Filling in all areas (drawings and text) with colors and textures.

The flexibility and sophistication of these systems continue to increase at an astounding rate. And it is entirely likely that some of these $100,000 systems will someday be mass-produced for costs that the average small station or basic studio will be able to afford.

Production Uses of Graphics

Finally, we want to mention different ways that graphics can actually be incorporated into a production. The innovative director will do much more with graphics than simply parade a number of similar static graphics before the camera.

There are many times, of course, when a *sequence* of graphics will have to be used. As mentioned above, because TV graphics have to be simple, it often takes a number of them to get across the same information that could be incorporated into one detailed visual in a print medium.

There are two different ways of sequencing a series of graphics. The smoother method is usually the *alternate camera* technique. Every other graphic is placed on each of two camera easel stands (all the odd-numbered graphics for one camera and the even-numbered graphics for the other camera). Then the director can simply take, dissolve, or wipe from one graphic to the next. *Single-camera sequencing* can also be used, although sometimes with less-than-satisfactory results. All graphics are set up for one camera, and while that camera remains on the air, the graphics are either flipped forward or pulled sideways. (Masking tape tabs on the sides of the cards can facilitate smoother pulls.) With practice—and a steady hand of the grip or floor assistant—this method can sometimes be effective.

An even smoother, more secure way of handling a sequence of graphics is to put them on *slides*. Then, by simply alternating between two different slide drums, the director and technical director have accurate control of the sequencing with fewer chances for a mishap—once the slides are set up properly.

In working with a graphics stand or camera easel, make certain that the camera is exactly perpendicular to the easel; otherwise the lettering will appear to be running uphill in one direction or the other, getting smaller as it goes. This effect is known as *keystoning*. To correct it, rotate the easel and bring the uphill (or smaller) side of the easel closer to the camera.

Many production uses of graphics will involve *panning* and *tilting* large graphic cards. Ideally, if such moves are to be effective, the cards should be large enough so that the camera can get some distance back and still use a wide-angle lens for smooth movement.

If the graphic is so small that the camera has to be too close, it will be hard to keep all areas of the card in focus as the camera lens moves closer and then farther away from the card during a pan. On the other hand, if the camera operator has to use a narrow-angle long lens on a small card, it is difficult to execute a smooth move without the magnification of every little shaky camera movement. With a good pedestal mount, *trucking* and/or *pedestaling* moves can be smoother and remain in sharper focus than with panning and tilting.

In many situations, *animated graphics* can get a particular message across best. Although special effects and film animation can often do the job much better, there are still opportunities for actual live-studio card animation. Different kinds of animation are possible. In some constructions, parts of the card can be made to move by means of wires or tabs manipulated from the side. In other versions, pull-off strips can be removed from the rear or pull-out inserts can be removed from the top or side (for example, to add color to a bar graph as each new figure is introduced). The ingenious designer will find other ways to make information appear or disappear while a card is on the air. Supers, of course, can be combined with other graphics cards.

Related to the animated graphic is what might be termed the *build-up* sequence. This is a production technique whereby additional information is sequentially added to a basic graphic. For example, a map with only one city indicated on it is shown first; then a second city is added without any change in the basic map; then a third city is added; then dotted lines are added to show relationships; then a county outline is added; and so on. Although this kind of build-up can be achieved live in the studio with clear acetate cells of transparent overlays, the execution of such an operation can be rather tricky and uncertain. A much more secure method of handling such a build-up is to shoot the successive graphics with a still

camera on a good copy stand and then use the slides on the air, alternating between two slide drums as for the slide sequence described previously.

Many other uses of graphics will be explored by the inventive director. Generally, basic productions do not take full advantage of the potential of good graphics. There are limitless possibilities in the use of graphics to reinforce and augment both verbal and nonverbal messages.[5]

Summary

Good pictorial design—for sets and graphics—starts with consideration of both *informational* functions and *emotional* functions of the picture. Emotional aspects include establishing an *image* for a program, creating *atmosphere,* and sustaining a *continuity* throughout the production. Basic elements of design that should be considered in every production include *balance and mass, dominant lines,* and *tone and color.* Color components include *hue, saturation,* and *brightness.*

In working on staging design, there are three basic staging styles that can be used— *neutral* setting, *decorative* or fantasy setting, and variations of a *realistic* setting. Scenery elements that we have to work with include *settings* (standard set units, hanging units, and set pieces), *set dressings and furniture,* and *hand props.* In designing a studio setting, we must also consider *camera movement, microphone placement, lighting instruments,* and *talent movement.*

5. For a fuller discussion of the possibilities of graphics in educational programs, see Beverley Clarke, *Graphic Design in Educational Television* (London: Lund Humphries, 1974). Many popular and professional computing magazines contain frequent articles on the evolving technology of computer graphics.

In handling pieces in the studio, we should know the basic *construction of a flat,* how flats can be *joined,* and the best way of *storing* flats, set pieces, and properties. Some other studio techniques involve the preparation of a staging *floor plan,* use of *lighting effects,* other special *staging effects,* and dealing with *basic problems* of backgrounds, furniture, and props.

Some of the important principles of graphics design are the *three-to-four aspect ratio,* the relationship of the *scanning area* and *essential area,* how much *information* can be included on a card, the *simplicity* needed and the basic *style of lettering,* plus the correct use of *color* and *tonal contrast.*

In constructing graphics, the first distinction to be made is whether the graphic is to be used *on set* or *off set.* The application will help to determine the best *size* for the graphic. Graphics preparation, *lettering,* can be handled with a wide variety of tools and techniques, including hand lettering, ready-to-apply letters, lettering aids, printing machines, the typewriter, and the character generator. Computer-generated graphics are increasingly used by major production centers; sophisticated systems utilizing a *graphics tablet* and a *digitalizing camera* offer a bewildering assortment of drawing, text, and animation possibilities. There are several different production uses of graphics, including alternate and single-camera *sequencing,* the use of *pan* and *tilt cards, animated graphics,* and *build-up graphics.*

This chapter has been concerned with the nonhuman aspects of the television picture. Chapter 10 discusses the human element of the picture—the actors and the performers.

9.6 Training Exercises

Both of the following two exercises should be carried out individually by each student in the class:

1. Using the dimensions and layout of your studio, design a basic staging plot for a standard dramatic scene. Be as realistic as you can in terms of the set elements, furniture, and set dressings that are available to you. Make sure that everything is accurately done to scale, and include as much detail as you can.

2. Make yourself an 11″ × 14″ graphics mask, following the dimensions in figure 9-17. Using this mask, prepare two sample graphics. The first should be just lettering—a credit card (for the credits at the end of a mock TV production), using five or six lines of information. The second card should combine art work and lettering—some sort of diagram or chart with a written explanation or heading. On both of these cards, make sure you carefully follow the principles spelled out in section 9.4.

On-Camera Talent: The Performer and Actor

10

In television, anyone who appears in front of a camera is referred to as *talent.* This is a traditional use of the term whether the person is giving a cooking demonstration, reciting Tennyson, interviewing the mayor, running for mayor, singing a ballad, acting in *Hamlet,* teaching long division, or giving a weather report. In this chapter we are concerned about working with talent from several different points of view.

10.1 Working with Talent

What does the director have to know in order to direct actors? How do you control a rambling interviewer? How should the crew react to a nervous guest? How do you instruct talent to use notes or cue cards? How can you get the talent to relate to the audience? These are the questions that you, as a crew member and budding director, have to answer one way or another.

In this text *we are not concerned with training television performers and actors.* We cannot attempt to teach students how to become accomplished announcers, stand-up comedians, singers and dancers, dynamic interviewers, controversial reporters, or award-winning actors. What we *are* concerned with is how to work with these people.

One effective way to train people how to *work with talent* is to look at the topic from the perspective *of the talent.* This chapter, therefore, will be examining various performance and acting requirements that the talent must face. By gaining some insight into the talent's position, the director and crew members should better be able to cope with the talent's problems in various production situations.

At the same time, however, we are aware of the fact that many production personnel and station executives do have their turn in front of the camera. Numerous professional positions—especially in smaller stations—combine off-camera work (writing, producing, selling, managing) with some on-camera work (reporting, hosting, selling, interviewing). Therefore, it is helpful at this stage to have some insight into the world of on-camera talent.

Also, realistically, in many types of production classes, the students will be performing the various on-camera roles. Production classes revolve around lab exercises in which all of the class members take their turns as newscasters, interviewers, TV lecturers, and actors. This chapter should be of direct assistance in helping you cope with these assignments.

In discussing on-camera activities, the distinction is often made between two groups: (1) those presentational or reportorial roles where the talent is serving essentially as a communicator, serving no role except that of host or reporter; and (2) dramatic roles where the talent is portraying some theatrical character. Those in the first category are referred to as *performers* while those in the second group are referred to as *actors*. Although the two groups share many characteristics and concerns, it may be helpful to look at them separately.

10.2   The Television Performer

The category of *performer* includes announcers, emcees, hosts, narrators, reporters, interviewers, demonstrators, TV lecturers, panel participants, and the like—talent who are communicating personally with the audience, usually addressing them directly. In examining the performer, it may be helpful to look at his or her role as it relates to others. Specifically, let us look at performers as they relate to the *audience,* to the *production crew,* and to *other performers.*

Audience Relationships

The primary responsibility of the performer is, of course, to the audience. In addition, the performer-audience relationship is crucial to the success of any television program.

Audience Concept.   Television is an intimate medium. It usually is received on a small screen, in the privacy of the home, and as a rule by just a few people. The television performer is most successful when he or she conceives of the audience in that manner—three or four people sitting just a few feet away. The TV director must help the performer to think of the television camera as one close acquaintance. In the mind of the individual TV viewer watching a TV performer, the aggregate audience of thousands or millions of people does not exist. It is basically a one-to-one relationship.

There are occasions, of course, when the TV camera is recording a performer who is playing to a large audience—the singer before a theater audience, the politican addressing his or her supporters, the minister preaching to a church congregation. In these situations, however, television is just an *objective* eavesdropper, covering an actual event. If the singer, politician, or minister is using television as a *reportorial* medium, addressing the audience directly and personally, then the director must help the performer adapt his or her style to a different audience relationship—the style must become more intimate, subdued, using direct eye contact, and a conversational tone of voice.

Speaking Voice.   The natural, conversational, speaking voice is one of the most elusive qualities the performer has to try to attain. The performer who can project the feeling of spontaneity and intimacy in his or her speaking style is on the way to capturing one of the most sought-after qualities of any television performer—*sincerity.*

This is not to argue that the performer should not exhibit enthusiasm or animation or exuberance (if that is the person's natural style). It is only to point out that the speaker's *desire* to communicate with three or four people on the other side of the camera is, perhaps, the single most important ingredient in successful performing. If the host-announcer-reporter-teacher *sincerely* and earnestly *wants* to communicate (without an obvious artificial eagerness), then he or she should succeed in that communication process. The director must also help the talent learn how to concentrate while on camera.

Eye Contact.   Just as important as vocal directness is the intimacy of specific visual directness—eye contact with the TV camera. In reportorial program formats when the performer (newscaster, TV lecturer, host, commentator) is speaking directly to the audience, the talent must attempt to maintain a direct and personal eye contact with the camera lens at all times, looking straight into the heart of the lens. In the case of a camera with a lens turret, the performer must know which of the four or five lenses facing him or her is the *taking lens.*

This direct eye contact is the secret of maintaining the illusion of a one-to-one relationship with each individual member of the audience. By looking directly into the lens, the performer is directly and personally addressing everyone who is in contact with the television receiver. A third-grade pupil was once asked why she was so enthusiastic about her television teacher, and the child replied, "Why, because he is always talking directly *to me.*" The child's own live classroom teacher, of course, had to share her attention with thirty students at one time, but the TV teacher was talking directly to that one child—and to every individual viewer.

In maintaining the illusion of direct eye contact, the performer must be skilled, of course, in some of the artifice and techniques of the medium. The director must help in teaching some of these skills to the performer. In many productions the director will cut from one camera shot of the performer to another. The performer will have to reestablish eye contact with the new camera immediately. Whenever possible, the performer should be aided by the floor director's waving the talent to look at the new camera a split second before the camera cut is made. In some situations, the performer can make the transition look as natural as possible by momentarily glancing downward (or upward)—as if glancing at some notes or trying to collect his or her thoughts—and then immediately establishing eye contact with the new camera.

With the help of the director and the stage manager, the performer should also be aware of what camera might be used exclusively for close-ups of some object he or she is demonstrating or discussing. If it is clearly explained to you (as talent) that camera 3, for example, will always be getting just a close-up of the globe, then you need not worry about looking at camera 3 every time the tally lights change on the cameras. You can maintain continual eye contact with the camera that has the medium shot of you. (See fig. 10-1.)

Distracting Mannerisms.   Because television is such an intimate, close-up medium, the talent should also be aware that any visually or vocally distracting mannerism will certainly be captured with full impact. Some nervous mannerisms, such as a facial twitch or the unconscious habit of licking lips, may be hard to control. On the other hand, some fidgety distractions—such as playing with a pencil or pulling an ear lobe—can be corrected if the director or the floor manager discreetly calls it to the performer's attention.

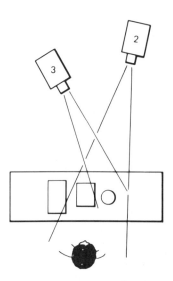

Figure 10-1 Camera pattern for shooting a close-up.

If the talent knows that camera 3 will be used only for close-ups of the objects on the table—and that camera 2 will always be getting the basic shot of the talent—then he or she will not have to worry about establishing eye contact with camera 3 every time the tally lights change. The talent can keep solid eye contact with camera 2.

Many an audio engineer has had a few hairs turn gray because a performer thumped his or her fingers on the table next to the desk mike or idly tapped his or her lavaliere while pondering a weighty question.

Vocal habits and mannerisms also can be distracting. The use of vocalized pauses (saying "um" or "ah") every time there is a second of dead air is a problem many of us share. The ubiquitous "I see" somehow always becomes part of the interviewer's basic vocabulary. (Why is it that in day-to-day conversation we seldom feel the need to say "I see" every time somebody makes a point to us, but as soon as we get on the air "I see" becomes part of our interview response pattern?) The talent also should be made aware of the tendency to state the obvious for the audience. While commenting on a series of slides with voice-over narration, there is no need to repeat, "Here we are looking at . . ." and "Here we see . . ." Just explain simply, "This castle is one of . . ."

Handling Scripted Material. Depending upon the specific function of the performer, he or she may be working from a _full script,_ speaking extemporaneously from a _semiscript_ or full outline, or speaking spontaneously or _ad lib_ with no preparation at all. Actually, aside from dramatic programs, there are only about three types of productions that call for working from a full script: (1) _political talks_ and other critical presentations or speeches (such as editorials), when it is extremely important to get every fact completely accurate and to phrase every comment on controversial issues precisely; (2) _commercials,_ when the time element is so crucial that every second must be carefully accounted for with exact scripting; and (3) _news and sports reporting_ (as opposed to ad lib, on-the-spot news coverage, or play-by-play announcing), when—again—accuracy demands that every fact reported be carefully checked and worded and all elements be delivered in a precise sequence.

When working with a fully scripted program, you have a choice of several different means of handling the material. _Memorization_ usually is required only for dramatic works and is best left to the professionals. Seldom can typical television talent—unless they are exceptionally talented—deliver memorized copy without sounding too artificial and stiff. You are better off reading your copy from a physical _script_ in your hands, from **cue cards** held next to the camera, or from a prompting device such as the **teleprompter.**[1]

Reading directly from a script is satisfactory if you are somewhat familiar with the material and do not have to keep your eyes

1. TelePrompTer® is a registered trademark of the Teleprompter Corporation. It is a mechanical prompting device that attaches to the front of a camera. The prepared copy, on a long sheet of continuous paper, is projected into a glass plate directly in front of the camera lens. Thus, the performer can read the copy while staring directly at the lens; and the lettering is too close to the lens to come into focus from the camera's perspective.

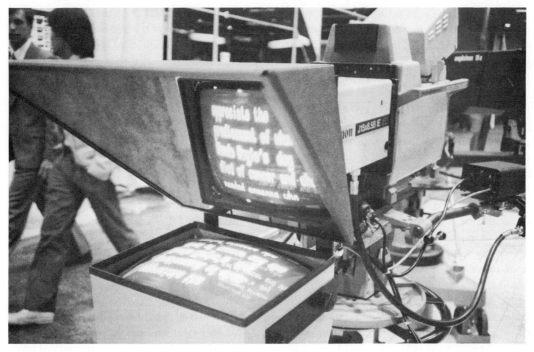

Figure 10-2 Listec A-2000 prompting system. Like many other prompting systems, this on-camera display unit reflects copy from a 15-inch monitor (bottom of picture) on to a mirror positioned in front of the camera lens. The camera simultaneously shoots through the mirror to pick up the talent's image.

glued to the script. Some people can handle a script very well, glancing down only occasionally. Others, because of insecurity or nervousness, get completely buried in the script and never establish eye contact. If the talent has a tendency to fall into the latter category and read too much word-for-word, then the director would be better off using cue cards or, if it is available, a prompting device. (See fig. 10-2.) If a script is used, make sure that you, as director, have the talent unstaple the script before going on the air and see that all of the pages are in order before starting the actual take.

If you decide to avoid the problems of working with a script, it will take some amount of extra coordination to use cue cards properly. Either the performer or some crew member will have to transfer the entire script onto large cue sheets (heavy oak tag paper or similar stiff stock). The cue-card holder also has to be trained to do a good job—holding the cards right next to the lens, reading along with the talent and raising each card to keep the exact line being read next to the lens, dropping each card silently, and positioning the next one. With a hefty stack of cue cards, holding them can become a very wearying and demanding assignment.

If you enjoy the luxury of using a teleprompter, these tasks are taken care of with a minimum amount of trouble, and the exact spot on the script is always positioned directly in front of the lens (by means of mirrors) so that the reader's eyes cannot wander away from the lens. (The astute viewer will probably catch the eyes scanning back and forth, however, if you are using either cue cards or a teleprompter.)

Many performers think they have to work from a full script when they probably would be better off working from an outline or a semiscripted format. This enables the talent to have enough of a solid outline to speak with confidence; yet, by composing the exact words on the spot—*extemporaneously*—one can add vitality and sincerity that is difficult to achieve with a prepared text. When speaking extemporaneously it is easier to use cue cards, because only one or two cards might be needed for the program outline. Many experienced performers prefer, however, to work from small note cards that they carry with them. It is a convenient and relatively unobtrusive way to handle material with confidence and ease. The talent can glance down at his or her notes when necessary but does not try to hide them from the audience. The talent can speak primarily and sincerely directly to the camera lens.

Many times the performer will be called upon to serve in specialized roles such as that of announcer, game show host, voice-over narrator, and so forth. Some of the functions of these roles come close to needing the dramatic talent of an actor—interpreting lines and/or assuming a certain part. We would just reinforce the general advice that talent should try to handle any such role with as much naturalness as possible and avoid the temptation to try to sound like what one thinks an announcer or narrator should sound like. For more detailed assistance, there are several handbooks available.[2]

Crew Relationships

After examining the primary relationship the performer has with the audience, you should think about the relationship of the performer and the production crew. As talent, you will be working closely with many people who directly can affect your performance—helping you to look good and to do your best job. If you inadvertently cause them trouble, however, they will not be able to do their best job; consequently, you will wind up walking out of

2. See, for example, Stuart W. Hyde, *Television and Radio Announcing,* 2d ed. (Boston: Houghton Mifflin Co., 1971).

camera range, speaking off mike, missing important cues, or finding yourself with nothing left to say and 2 minutes to fill. You should be thinking specifically about what you—as a performer—need to do in conjunction with the director and the associate director, the camera operators, the audio engineer, and the stage manager.

The Director and the A.D. Up to the beginning of the actual on-the-air production, your closest relationship will be with the director and the **associate director (A.D.).** In virtually every kind of performance assignment, the director and the talent must work closely on the preparation of the program—arranging segments, developing material, finding resources, designing graphics, working out cues, and so forth.

As a performer, you will find that the A.D. is probably your best friend as far as timing is concerned. In many formats—variety shows, interview programs, newscasts, ITV lessons—the program will be broken down into a number of timed segments. During the actual production, you will be receiving cues relayed from the A.D. to let you know how the timing on each segment is working out—when you need to speed up, and when you should slow down.

During the program, you will find that there are many times when you can help the director with some indirect signals. This is especially important on rather standardized nonscripted shows when you have not had an opportunity for a full rehearsal. You can aid the director with such cues as, "Now if we look at this through the microscope. . ." (setting up the first slide), or "Three elements are necessary for this demonstration. . ." (getting ready to walk to another area). The performer should avoid giving direct instructions to the crew, however: "Now, if I could just get a shot of this wristwatch!"

Figure 10-3 Talent signaling his intention to rise by "leaning into" the move.

Camera Operators. As a polished performer, you will eventually find that you can put yourself in the place of the camera operator—perceiving yourself from the camera's perspective. You develop a "feel" for how you should move, for instance. You know that you cannot make any big or sweeping gestures; the chances are that the camera has you on a fairly tight medium shot. You must be careful with facial grimaces; there is a likelihood that the camera has a close-up of you.

When you are ready to make a big move, you lean into it gradually, because you want to give the camera operator ample warning. For example, you may be sitting in an easy chair and are ready to stand, turn, and walk over to the demonstration area. There are several tell-tale cues that you give to the camera operator. For example, you place both feet firmly on the floor, you lean forward, you put your hands on the sides of the chair, you now *slowly* lift yourself out of the chair. (See fig. 10-3.) The camera is able to follow you smoothly since you prepare the operator for your moves. The warnings are also of value to other members of the production crew—the boom operator, for one, who must follow the move with you. You also develop a habit of moving slowly as you go from one area of the set to another. Again, this gives the camera operator a good chance of moving with you gracefully. (And it always looks fast enough to the viewer.)

It does not take long before you also begin to get a feel for holding up objects to the correct camera for a close-up. In figure 10-1, the cameras are positioned correctly for a right-handed person to demonstrate something in a close-up shot. As you pick up or point to the

Figure 10-4 Talent holding an object close to her face for a close-up (when no second close-up camera is available).

object, it is automatically angled for a good close-up on camera 3. You intuitively position any object or graphic on your right side, aimed off to your left (camera right) for the close-up shot.

Most of the time, in the situation in figure 10-1, you would not pick the object up off the table. You would be certain the camera had a clear, unobstructed shot of the object on the table top; it is much steadier and more stable to leave it on the solid table. If you must pick up the object, you move it slowly; you move it as little as possible; you rest your elbow on the table or steady the object with your other hand. You do not ask the close-up camera to hold a shot of the object while you are gesturing with it.

Intuitively, if you see that the director does not have a second camera free for close-ups and you want to get a good tight shot of the object, you pick it up and hold it next to your face, pointing it straight at your camera, holding your arm tightly against your body to steady the hand, as shown in figure 10-4. Now the director can get a good tight shot of your face and the object, using the single camera available.

Audio Engineer. You also develop a feel for the positions and problems of other members of the crew. We mentioned consideration for the boom operator. You also help the audio engineer by making certain you do not abuse any of the mikes. Do not handle any of the microphones except hand or stand mikes. Avoid playing with the mike cords. Know the position of all microphones and avoid any sudden or explosive noises in their vicinity.

In addition, be sure you are consistent in giving the audio engineer your audio level when he or she is setting up the mikes and establishing proper mike levels. The audio person will ask you for a **level;** you are to speak into the mike so that the fader-pot levels can be determined. Some performers will mumble a relatively weak audio check and then boom out on the air with their best basso profundo. A few will do just the opposite—give a good strong audio test to set the level and then start out rather weakly on the air.

Stage Manager.   Finally, you will come to know your floor manager, or stage manager, rather well. Once the studio doors are closed and the production is underway, the floor manager is the one person assigned to be of general assistance. One of the stage manager's prime jobs is to give you different cues (to speed up, slow down, move in this direction, speak up, and so forth). Generally, you do not have to acknowledge the cues that call for some sort of immediate action on your part; you just do as instructed. The floor manager, however, will also be giving you time-remaining cues (time left in this segment, minutes remaining until the end of the program). Occasionally you will want to acknowledge these cues to reassure the floor manager that you have received the message. One covert way of doing this (a nod of the head is too obvious for the audience) is with a prolonged blink. The audience will scarcely notice the blink, but it will be picked up by the floor director. (See appendix C for illustrations of the various cues and floor manager's hand signals.)

As talent you will not have to worry about where the floor director is. If you do not see him or her, it is because you do not *have* to see the floor manager at that moment. It is the job of the floor manager to be where you will definitely see him or her when you need to.

In some productions, however, the floor manager may get positioned so that he or she is always fully visible to the talent. For many performers, it is helpful to have the floor manager standing right next to the camera on the air, eagerly hanging on every word of the speaker—nodding encouragement, responding (silently) and reacting to the performer. This provides a sense of feedback and stimulation that many performers need. On the other hand, feedback can be distracting to some performers. One of the authors of this text recalls one production where the talent was so desperate for any live appreciation that every floor crew member had either to hide behind set pieces and cameras or, in the case of the floor manager, turn his back on the talent—in order to get the talent to look at the camera. If the performer could find one pair of eyes in the studio, he would address that single individual rather than the camera lens.

Relationships will vary tremendously among performers and persons in crew positions. Both the performer and the crew should try to be as sensitive as possible to the feelings and working patterns of others. This is all part of the *discipline* of the production crew.

Relationships with Other Talent

Finally, some mention must be made about the relationship that you—as talent—will have with other performers in the studio. As host, panel moderator, or interviewer, you may often find yourself in a position of organizing and controlling others. As a host-moderator-interviewer, one of your concerns will have to be with the comfort and emotional security of others, particularly guests at the television studio and inexperienced performers who may not feel at ease. One tangible aspect of this concern will be professional courtesy while you are off-camera. For the sake of the talent in front of the lens, you will be quiet, attentive, and as unobtrusive as possible.

You will get used to the idea of close physical proximity to other talent. For the sake of good camera shots, performers have to work very close together, especially in two-person interviews. You may feel uncomfortably intimate (and you may want to keep a good supply of breath fresheners handy), but to the audience the staging looks natural. One old television adage is, "If you ain't touching, you ain't close enough."

Interviewing Techniques. One prominent situation in which you, as the performer, will frequently find yourself is the basic interview format. This may take many forms: the celebrity interview, the unprepared person-in-the-street interview, the factual interview (basically trying to present information to the audience), the controversial interview (with some outspoken public figure), and so forth. There are a few basic points to be aware of in preparing for a studio interview.

1. *Preparation.* Find out as much as you can about the guest. Research the background of the subject you will be discussing. Be familiar with what the guest has written, produced, or said about the topic. Go to other sources for outside opinions.
2. *Hospitality.* Be on hand to welcome the guest to the studio well before air time. Make the guest comfortable. Explain all of the studio procedures, the nature of the program, and the intended audience.
3. *Organization.* Determine with the guest what main points the interview will cover. Arrange the points in a well-organized pattern, keeping some material for the middle and end of the interview.
4. *Focus.* Remember that the spotlight should be on the guest. He or she is the one that the audience wants to learn more about—not you. Avoid the temptation to dominate the session by explaining all of your viewpoints and ideas on the topic.

5. *Questioning.* Ask questions requiring some solid comments and explanation (avoid *yes* or *no* answers). Ask only one question at a time (avoid double-barreled questions). With a controversial guest, do not compromise the integrity of the interview by avoiding awkward topics or hard issues; press on, courteously but tenaciously, for honest answers to honest questions.
6. *Transitions.* Keep the interview moving. Follow up on interesting answers, but do not get bogged down. Use answers as a transition to the next point. Summarize and clarify if necessary, but keep transitions short.
7. *Control.* Remember that, as host, you are in control. Do not allow yourself to be overwhelmed in the presence of a powerful personality. Be ready to take over entirely for the last 30 seconds or so—to summarize, thank the guest, and bring the interview to a smooth close, right on time.

These are a few guidelines for the interviewer. As director you will be helping the talent to establish similar hints for other on-camera assignments—as lecturer, newscaster, demonstrator, and so forth.

10.3 The Television Actor

Although we cannot begin to present a separate treatise on television acting, there are a few points that should be made. Assuming that you, as a director, will be working with skilled or trained actors, we do not need to get into the basics of acting methodology in this book. Anyone seriously interested in television drama will, of course, be pursuing additional class work in acting and dramatic directing. Many actors who have been trained on the stage and may have some film experience, however, are not prepared for the adaptations they will have to make to the television studio.

Many of the observations made under "The Television Performer" apply equally to the television actor. Actors, too, must be concerned with their relationship with the *audience* (television is an intimate medium compared to the stage, or even to film); with the *production crew* (where everyone is immediately involved in the execution of the dramatic scene); and with *other talent* (all dramatic blocking is more compact and precise in the TV studio).

Television acting invariably is compared with acting in other media, and actors must make adaptions as they move from one medium to another. The theater, film, and television stages all have their unique requirements and frustrations.

Theatrical acting is, of course, the ancestor of all other acting. Furthermore, the stage is where most actors begin. Early television resembled the theatrical stage in that a continuous performance was presented. Actors would have to create and sustain a characterization for a full 60 or 90 minutes—but the similarity to the theatre stage stopped there.

Film acting, like television acting, is subject to the medium of the recording camera, and as in television, there is no proscenium arch. But there also are many differences.

In discussing television acting, one must keep in mind the wide variety of TV formats, recording techniques, and editing considerations used in different situations. Of course, "live" television acting (where the action is broadcast at the very moment it is being performed) has virtually completely disappeared. For the most part, we are discussing acting recorded either by the electronic camera (on videotape) or by the film camera.

Today, most television acting consists of recording short scenes, seldom running more than 5 minutes in length. Some situation comedies use a multiple-camera technique (pioneered by *I Love Lucy* and continuing through *Happy Days* and many contemporary sitcoms), which uses three or four cameras (either electronic or film), then recording the output of each camera separately, and splicing together the best shots in postproduction editing. Some sitcoms, on the other hand (*All in the Family* was one of the first), will use a "live-on-tape" format. The production will run straight through a 3-to-5-minute segment, with the director making live editing decisions and switching during the final "take" (with the knowledge that postproduction editing—for example, splicing in shots from a recorded dress rehearsal—can tidy up a final tape). Both of these formats are suited to shooting in front of a live audience. Daytime serials (*soap operas*), using electronic cameras, run scenes straight through but shoot the scenes out of order and edit the show together in postproduction.

However, most television dramas, nighttime *soaps,* "TV movies," mini-series, and many other sitcoms are usually recorded on film in single shots, using variations of the basic single-camera filmic technique that has dominated the motion picture industry since the turn of the century.

Nevertheless, in discussing the requirements for television acting, there are several broad observations that can be made. Some of the following points apply only to certain categories of TV acting as outlined earlier, but the director must be ready to work with actors in making all of these adaptations.

1. The Missing Proscenium. There is *no proscenium arch;* there is no firm boundary separating the audience from the actors. The audience's perspective is switched every time the camera is changed. The director can move the audience 90 degrees with the push of a button. Even in a theatre-in-the-round, or arena theatre, each individual viewer is in one spot for the entire production; the viewer's

Figure 10-5 Differences in the scope of gesturing. *Left,* a large sweeping gesture appropriate for the theatre; *right,* a more subdued, intimate version of the same gesture appropriate for television.

perspective cannot be changed. In television, the viewer can be transported sideways, closer or farther from the action, or (with the use of the subjective camera) into the mind of the actor. (Even when a live audience is in the TV studio watching the taping of a situation comedy, the action is staged for the cameras and the television audience; the live audience is just watching the production of a program.) Actors must learn to adjust to this concept of moving audience perspective.

2. Limited Projection. Actors must adjust to a *smaller scope of projection.* Instead of the exaggerated movements and sweeping gestures that must be seen in the back row of the theatre, the TV actor has to restrict all actions and movement to the camera only 10 feet away. (See fig. 10-5.) Instead of projecting his or her voice so that every line is heard clearly 60 or 70 feet from the stage, the actor must restrict voice volume level—without losing emotion or intensity—for a pickup point only 3 or 4 feet away. Television is a close-up medium, and actors must adjust to this intimacy.

3. Blocking Precision. Actors must learn to work with a *physical precision* in television. Compared to the stage, television blocking is very precise; every move and tiny gesture has to be carefully planned and controlled. On the stage, each movement may be accurate to within a few feet. In television, the action must be measured by inches. If the actor's head is tilted at the wrong angle, the framing for a given shot may be off. This is a discipline that many actors find difficult to adapt to.

4. Pacing Precision. Television exists generally in a demanding and *nonflexible time frame.* Except for some programming on public television, all dramatic programs have to be squeezed (or stretched) into given time slots—multiples of a half-hour, minus requisite time for commercials. This means that an actor may have to adjust pacing, speeding up or slowing down delivery of lines or action. This is especially a major concern with soap operas and situation comedies where there can be little flexibility in timing. It is less of a concern for filmed dramas, however, where the exact timing can be worked out in the editing process (either on the film editor's bench or by electronic editing) by cutting or augmenting silent footage, action shots, panoramic long shots, and chase sequences.

5. Out-of-Sequence Shooting. Filmed or single-camera videotaped dramas are almost always shot *out of sequence*. There is no continuity of drama from the actor's standpoint. All of the scenes in a given location are shot during the same setup. For example, once the camera, audio, and lights are set up for the drugstore exterior, every bit of action that takes place in the locale will be filmed—from the opening boy-meets-girl shot to the final boy-dies-in-gutter shot. This demands a great deal of concentration and training on the part of the actor.

6. A Quick Study. Compared to the stage and to theatrical motion pictures, television drama (both filmed and "live-on-tape") is a *quick study* medium. Whether working with single-camera or multiple-camera techniques, regular actors in a continuing series must learn up to an hour-long script every week—the equivalent of two feature-length motion pictures every month. For the actor in the hour-long daytime soap opera, the pace is even more demanding—up to a half-hour of dialogue every day!

Thus, from a variety of viewpoints, the task of the television actor is quite demanding and complicated. Your job, as a television director, is to make the transition as easy as possible for the inexperienced TV actor. The stage actor and motion picture actor will need some amount of guidance in adapting to the television medium.

10.4 Clothing and Costumes

Some attention also must be given to what the performers and the actors will wear. There are a few general observations that are appropriate for a book of this scope.

Design Considerations

Many of the design criteria discussed in chapter 9 apply here also. In any color production, for example, the clothing and costumes of the performers have to be considered in conjunction with the color scheme of the entire setting. All designers certainly would consider costuming an integral part of the overall production design. Even in small station and educational closed-circuit operations, color has to be a major consideration. The hostess for a local talk show normally would not wear a red ensemble on her predominantly green set (unless it was for her Christmas program).

The same color factors that were discussed in section 9.1 (*hue, saturation,* and *brightness*) apply to clothing and costume design. Unless a spectacular, deliberately colorful, dazzling effect is advised, performers generally should be encouraged to stick to clothing of a dull saturation—to choose muted aqua rather than chartreuse, tan rather than brilliant yellow. Brightness and tonal balance also should be considered in terms of the overall emotional effect that is desired. Would dark, somber grays and browns be more or less appropriate than lighter shades and pastels?

Line also is an important design consideration. Vertical lines tend to emphasize tall and slender proportions; horizontal stripes tend to exaggerate weight and mass. Performers who are concerned about appearing too heavy (and television has a tendency to make people appear a little heavier) should stick to vertical lines.

Figure 10-6 The fine design on a blouse such as this would be substantially lost once it is translated into scanning lines.

One other word of advice to the performer in street clothing: be natural. Do not try to emulate the latest fashions in order to make a striking television appearance. Avoid fads, extreme styles, and flashy finery, unless that is your natural inclination. If you step out of character for the sake of making a striking appearance, the chances are that you will wind up looking more foolish than fashionable.

Production Considerations

In addition to color, line, and style, there are some other practical considerations and potential problems that you should be aware of. Try to avoid high contrast and extremes in color brightness. Remember that the television camera has a relatively limited contrast ratio (section 4.2), which makes it difficult to handle white shirts against a dark suit. Try also to avoid high contrasts with skin tones. Dark clothes will make a pale person look even more pale; light-colored clothes next to a tanned complexion will make the skin appear darker. Blacks and other dark-skinned performers, on the other hand, should be careful of light-colored clothing that would tend to heighten the tonal contrast and wash out facial details in the dark areas.

Generally, finely detailed patterns should be avoided. Whereas clothing with a rich thick texture will photograph well on television, clothing with a fine pattern usually will not (fig. 10-6). The pattern that is too busy and distracting fights with other picture elements, including the talent, for the viewer's attention. Thin stripes, herringbones, and small checks also can create the **moiré effect**—a distracting visual vibration caused by the interference of the clothing pattern and the TV scanning lines.

Highly reflective jewelry can also cause trouble. Too much flashy jewelry—even if it does not cause glare problems as a result of its high reflectance qualities—still can be distracting and needlessly gaudy.

There is one other minor production consideration with color TV. Be careful of wearing the *key* color (usually blue or green)—even a tie—if any chroma key effects are to be used in the production (section 7.4). Any blue or green shade worn by the performer (depending upon the chroma key setting) will form part of the keying pattern and the background picture will appear wherever the chroma-key color clothing is otherwise visible to the camera.

Dramatic Costumes

Again, all the points made for performer clothing (color harmony, line, tonal contrast, details, and jewelry) apply to theatrical costuming as well. In many respects, the use of color and style in a dramatic production is even more important.

Virtually all costuming considerations that apply to theatrical costumes apply equally to television: authenticity, historical accuracy, color, durability, and so forth. One aspect that needs to be emphasized more strongly for television than for the stage is *detail*. Although you may be able to get away with a few loose threads and a modern patch on the stage—where the nearest spectator is 15 feet away—you cannot afford to try to fool the television camera, which brings the viewer only a few inches away. This is especially critical in costuming around the neck, shoulders, and chest areas, where the close-up picks up costume details with microscopic clarity.

10.5 Television Makeup

The field of television makeup is a specialized area that most production personnel seldom get into. The student should be aware, however, of some of the basic principles and major considerations. All television makeup is used for one of three functions: (1) to *enhance* appearance (improving the performer's basic physiognomy with color correction or emphasis on highlights); (2) to *correct* appearance (creating the effect of pulling back protruding ears or straightening a broken nose); or (3) to *create* appearance (building a new character such as Frankenstein's monster or Mr. Hyde). Ordinary television production situations rarely go beyond the first function; the last two areas are left for the specialist.

Principles of Basic Makeup

The object of television makeup is to have the performer or actor look as natural as possible. A good, basic, unobtrusive makeup job should help to enhance normal colors (evening up flesh tones), minimize any blemishes or distortions (covering up birthmarks, bags under the eyes), compensate for flat television lighting (which may tend to wash out facial characteristics), and emphasize good points. However, with the close-up lens any exaggerated makeup certainly would be perceived as unnatural. This is opposed to theatre use, where exaggerated makeup is necessary in order to highlight facial features for the last row of the audience.

In many kinds of situations, a minimum amount of makeup will be necessary. If a performer looks basically good *on camera,* there is no reason to consider any heavy makeup job. For many female performers, ordinary street makeup *may* be all that is needed. However, television lighting and color technology often will distort street makeup; so its use should be carefully checked out on camera before deciding to go with it. For many male performers, a little powder to control perspiration or to reduce the shine on a bald head may be all that is necessary. Even in dramatic situations, little makeup may be called for. However, it must be recognized that in many situations—especially in educational or industrial applications (where the performers are nonprofessionals and the equipment may not give the best color rendition)—makeup may definitely be called for.

For minor skin problems or blotchiness, a base or foundation may be all that is needed. It should cover uneven skin coloring, surface blemishes, beard shadow, and so forth. The foundation can be further used, if needed, to cover lip lines, eyebrows, and other features before a new formation is drawn in.

Appearance often can be improved or enhanced by careful use of highlighting and darkening. Within prudent limits, localized highlighting will tend to enlarge the evident size and prominence of a facial feature. Darkening a feature with shadows will tend to de-emphasize its size for the camera. Thus, it is possible to strengthen cheekbones, the forehead, or the jaw with highlights. Shadows are often used to emphasize facial hollows—under the cheekbones or behind the temple. Features can be subtly altered; highlight a thin nose to make it look broader; use shadow on either side of a broad nose to make it look thinner.

Color Correction. Some improvement in appearance often can be achieved by color correction. Depending upon lighting conditions, facial colors may need to be touched up in order to give a truer color rendition. Generally, cooler colors (those hues with a slight bluish tint) tend to emphasize facial shadows and dark areas. For this reason warmer colors (those with a reddish tendency) generally are preferred for the basic foundation.

Care must be taken, however, that the Caucasian or Oriental skin tone is not tinted too pink and that the Black or Latin skin color is not turned too reddish. Although makeup companies will furnish detailed instructions and charts with their products (suggesting proper colors to use for different races and skin types), every individual skin tone will react differently under various lighting conditions and with diverse camera adjustments. Only by experimenting with each individual under actual lighting and camera conditions can the best color combination be determined.

Be especially careful in selecting colors for lipstick, rouge, and eye shadow. Color TV equipment may tend to distort colors that are in the blue-green range. Reds that are rich in blue or orange also may tend to be exaggerated.

Makeup personnel should also work closely with the lighting director for any production. The lighting director may be using colored gels, for instance, that could tremendously distort the effect desired by the makeup person. A green gel on a dark or black skin, for example, will completely wash out any color distinctions on the face. Generally—since most foundation color is in the reddish range—backgrounds should tend more toward blues and greens. But these subtleties must be coordinated with the lighting director.

Basic Makeup Procedures and Materials

Regardless of the extent of the makeup job to be performed, basic procedures should follow a fairly well-established pattern.

1. *Preparation.* All makeup materials should be collected and organized in one specific area of the studio complex. Ideally, there should be plenty of working space, a well-lighted mirror, and a chair of adequate (preferably adjustable) height.

   A basic makeup complement should include foundation or base colors, translucent and tinted powders, creme or powder rouges, a variety of lipsticks, eye shadows, eyeliners, mascara, and eyebrow pencils. Other materials should include a variety of natural and rubber sponges, various small brushes, powder puffs, tissue, towels, cleansing cream, and soap.[3]

Before applying any makeup, the face should be cleaned and either a moisturizer, for dry skin, or an astringent (such as alcohol or witch hazel), for oily skin, may be applied.

2. *Foundation or Base.* The primary makeup element is the base, or **foundation.** This is the initial covering that usually is applied to the entire face or the exposed area being treated (arms and hands and other parts of the body often need makeup treatment). This base is to provide the color foundation upon which all the rest of the makeup will be built. The foundation comes in several different media. *Pancake* is a water-based covering that is applied with a moist sponge; it is convenient to use and is preferred by many stations as the basic makeup treatment. *Cream-base* foundation usually is dabbed onto small areas and spread by the fingers; left unpowdered, it results in a noticeable sheen. *Greasepaint,* an oil-based theatrical standard for many years, is easily worked and occasionally used for major jobs. *Panstick* is a combination of pancake and grease paint that, like

the other bases, comes in a wide variety of colors. *Powder bases,* supplied in compacts, provide fair covering power for small areas and touch-up jobs.

3. *Powder.* Powder is usually applied next in order to set the base, dull any sheen or gloss, and help to keep the base from smearing. Generally, more powder is needed with a cream- or oil-based foundation than with pancake (which goes on with more of a matte finish). More powder may also be used on oily skin. Powder is usually applied that is a little lighter than the base color.

4. *Highlights, Shadows, and Rouge.* Highlights and shadows are used to emphasize or minimize facial features. The forehead, nose, cheekbones, and jaw all can be highlighted with lighter shades or de-emphasized with darker tones. Normally, rouge is next applied to the cheeks, nose, forehead, and chin as needed to give a healthy complexion and to counteract the flatness of both the foundation color and the evenness of the lighting.

5. *Eyes and Lips.* Finally, special attention is given to those most expressive features of the face—the eyes and the lips. (See fig. 10-7.) Accessory makeup items are applied as necessary: lipstick (avoiding colors with blues or oranges), eye shadow (preferably the dry or cake type), eyeliner (to give needed accent), eyebrow pencil, mascara, and possibly false eyelashes. The extent of the use of these accent items depends upon the need for remodeling and the individual taste of the performer.

3. Four of the major makeup companies that offer a wide range of supplies and more detailed instructions include the following: Max Factor & Co. (1655 North McCadden Place, Hollywood, CA 90028); Bob Kelly Cosmetics (152 West 46th Street, New York, NY 10036); Syd Simon Studios (2 East Oak Street, Chicago, IL 60611); and Ben Nye, Inc. (11571 Santa Monica Blvd., Los Angeles, CA 90025).

Figure 10-7 Makeup artist applying final touches with a fine brush. (Photo courtesy of KABC-TV, Los Angeles)

Final Considerations

In addition to the basic makeup job, the styling and treatment of hair need to be considered. Hairstyles with a definite shape or firm silhouette usually compliment the performer more than wispy, fluffy hairdos. Hair should be carefully combed because back lighting will tend to make loose strands stand out.

The performer should strive for as natural an appearance as possible. For this reason, fancy hair treatments and fresh permanents should be avoided. The performer should wear glasses if he or she ordinarily wears them; they should not be removed simply for cosmetic reasons.

For dramatic purposes, of course, much more makeup treatment is needed, which gets into the third function of *creating* an appearance for certain characterizations. This includes hair pieces and wigs, *collodion* scars, nose putty, surface molding by plasticine and special waxes, and larger rebuilding jobs using latex prostheses and face masks.

Aside from these extreme theatrical applications, the aim of good television makeup, like that of good costuming, is simply one of accentuating the natural appearance of the performer for purposes of more accurate rendering by the electronic camera. For this reason, no makeup job can be considered complete until it has been checked out on camera under the studio lighting conditions. The television monitor, not the naked eye, must be the final judge in determining whether or not the makeup has succeeded in merely making the talent appear natural looking.

Summary

Although the production student may not aspire to be a great television performer, he or she should nevertheless be familiar with the problems of on-camera performers and actors. Otherwise, it will be difficult to work with *talent* with any real understanding. Some on-camera experience and training is important for everyone connected with the production of programs. Generally, television talent is divided into two categories—*performers* (reportorial communicators such as lecturers, newscasters, hosts, announcers, interviewers) and *actors.*

The performer must be concerned with three kinds of relationships. The first is an *audience relationship,* which includes a sense of intimacy with the audience and an ability to project sincerity that is expressed by the *speaking voice* and *eye contact.* The performer also must be aware of the need to control certain distracting mannerisms. Problems in handling *scripted material* and *extemporaneous material* can be worked out for individual performers depending upon their own delivery styles and the requirements of particular production formats. The second is *crew relationships,* which include the *director* and *A.D.* (preparation of the program and on-the-air timing), the *camera operators* (how to move on camera, how to handle a close-up of an object), the *audio engineer* (treatment of equipment, establishing audio levels), and the *floor manager* (accepting directions and cues). The third is *relationships with other talent,* which include playing host to other performers, moderating panel discussions, and handling interview situations. Conducting an *interview* involves several basic factors—preparation, hospitality, organization, focus, questioning, transitions, and control.

The *television actor* usually has been trained for other media—the theatrical stage and/or film. There are quite a few differences between acting for television and other media. The TV actor must be helped to adapt to the following differences: lack of the proscenium arch; a smaller scope of projection (both in gestures and vocal level); physical precision in blocking; nonflexible time frames; shooting out of sequence (in filmed TV drama); and quick-study methods of preparation.

Clothing and makeup considerations are primarily to help present as natural an appearance as possible without creating any production problems. Clothing should adhere to the fundamental design considerations of *color* and *line.* High *contrasts* should be avoided and *small patterns* should not be worn. Other problems can be caused by jewelry and by *blue or green clothing* (because of chroma keying). Dramatic costumes must pay special attention to *detail* for the close-up medium of television.

For most television applications, makeup consists of a few basic steps for the purpose of *enhancing natural appearance*—including covering skin blemishes and color correction. Fundamental procedures include proper *skin preparation;* applying a *foundation* or *base;* a *powder* set; using *highlights, shadows,* and *rouge;* and accenting *eyes* and *lips.* Theatrical uses of makeup for *corrective purposes* and for *creating characterizations* are seldom employed in most station operations.

This chapter has been concerned with the people in front of the cameras. Chapter 11 explores in more detail the responsibilities and attitudes of those behind the cameras.

10.6 Training Exercises

The first exercise should be conducted for the entire class. The other two exercises may be considered optional, depending upon how much emphasis the class wants to put on costuming and makeup.

1. Set up three role-playing interview situations. For each one, assign one student to play the role of the interviewer; he or she is to do as good a job as possible. For each interview, another student is assigned

as the guest; unknown to the interviewer each guest is instructed to manifest some particular negative trait that should give the interviewer considerable trouble in handling the situation. Each 5-minute interview is conducted in front of the class. After each interview, the class should critique the situation and discuss what could have been done to handle that particular troublesome guest.

2. Select four or five class members and set up a camera demonstration to see how their street clothes look on television. Select those who are wearing clothing and accessories that may present specific problems—wide stripes, small patterns, high contrast, jewelry, and so forth.

3. Select one female student as a model. Have her remove all makeup. On camera, using a close-up, have her apply ordinary street makeup in sequence. Have her continue to apply what would be considered more than the usual amounts of accent items (lipstick, eye shadow, and so forth). Critique the results. If theatrical makeup supplies are available to the class, select a male model—one with a heavy five o'clock shadow—and go through the same process on camera, emphasizing a good foundation base.

The Production Crew

11

Throughout this text we have touched on some of the duties and *techniques* of specific crew members as well as the development of a professional *discipline* among all members of the production team. At this point we want to look a little more carefully at some considerations and task responsibilities of various crew positions. We will be concerned with the lighting and staging personnel, audio engineer, camera operators, technical director, recording engineer, projectionists, and grips and floor assistants. We will also be introducing the position of the unit manager. And we want to look at the titles of "production assistant" and "script assistant."

In particular, however, we will be discussing the jobs of the two key crew members that we have not had an opportunity to cover previously—the associate director (A.D.) and the stage manager (or "floor manager" or "floor director"). We have saved these positions for discussion at this point because their jobs are primarily people-oriented, and we have been looking, up to this point, at the various crew positions that are equipment-oriented.

11.1 The Associate Director

If one were to think of the television director as the captain of the production team (with the producer, executive producer, sponsors, and network executives as the higher officers), then the two lieutenants would be the assistant director or *associate director* (A.D.) and the *stage manager.* The latter is in charge of virtually everything that takes place on the studio floor while the A.D. is the director's right-hand person and surrogate in all other matters.

General Duties of the A.D.

In almost all respects, the A.D. is considered the director's top assistant—ready to handle virtually any task that the director may request. Depending on the actual production setup and the traditional organization of the studio/station, the A.D. may be labeled either the "assistant director" or the "associate director."[1] The position often will carry quite a bit of responsibility for the production, independent of the director's orders. In some network situations, the A.D. will be responsible for setting up all of the camera shots on the air.

In virtually every kind of studio operation, however, the A.D.'s primary job will be that of timing the production. The A.D. will time individual segments during rehearsals; get an overall timing of the program, if possible; and then be in charge of the pacing of the program—speeding up or stretching as required—during the actual recording.

In any extensive production that involves postproduction editing, the A.D. will also be intimately involved at that stage. The A.D. will be making editing notes before and during the production and then, with or without the director's direct supervision, will be in charge of much of the later editing process. Other duties of the A.D. can be outlined in terms of time periods before the studio rehearsal, during the rehearsal period, during the actual program, and after the production.

Before the Studio Rehearsal. In any major production undertaking, the A.D. will work with the director well in advance of the actual production period—attending production conferences, working during **pre-studio rehearsals** with talent, and assembling props and other materials. During this pre-studio period, the A.D. may also be able to start figuring some rough timings of the program.

Additionally, the A.D. will begin to assemble notes on what postproduction editing may have to be done. Some editing can be anticipated—especially in dramas and in some

---

1. The Directors' Guild of America officially refers to the position as *associate director,* because the *assistant director* title is traditionally used in the film industry.

public affairs formats (reaction shots in interviews, for example). In other types of productions (game shows, sports documentaries), the A.D. cannot anticipate what editing may have to be done later.

Once the production moves into the studio, the A.D. often has several tasks before the rehearsals actually start. The A.D. may be in charge of the rest of the crew—checking to make certain that everyone is present and reporting this to the director. This is especially true on small-format productions and in training situations. The A.D. may well be in charge of arranging substitute assignments, thus ensuring that every position is covered.

The A.D. will obtain all copies of the scripts and other production instructions from the producer and/or the director and distribute them to members of the crew. He or she may also be in charge of distributing slides to the projectionist in telecine, graphics and props to the floor manager, and other materials to the proper crew positions.

If timing arrangements have not yet been worked out with the talent, the A.D. will at this point determine exactly what kind of time cues the talent would prefer (in other words, how many minutes warning the talent would want before the end of the program or before the end of each segment of the program). If there is nothing else to be done, the A.D. will remain at the director's side, ready for any requests the director may have.

During the Rehearsal Period. The A.D. will time as much of the program as possible during the various rehearsals (technical rehearsal, walk-through rehearsal, dress rehearsal, and so forth), including individual segments, film inserts, and opening and closing elements.

During the rehearsals, the director will mention various production items that need attention before the actual take: the back lighting is weak in area 2; the talent doesn't know the roll cue to the third film segment; the graphics are out of order during the map sequence; the guest's hair needs to be combed; and similar items to be cleaned up after the rehearsals. The A.D. will be jotting down the production notes, or "critique notes" as the director spots them. Additionally, the A.D. should be making notes of similar items that might have escaped the attention of the director. If the A.D. notices a major item, it should be called to the attention of the director before the rehearsal proceeds. Minor items are simply written down to be cleaned up later (note that it is the A.D. who has to make the distinction between minor items and those that are important enough to warrant interrupting the rehearsal). The A.D. will be especially concerned with noting all of the script changes that are made.

Depending upon the production techniques of the individual director, the A.D. may or may not get involved with actually making production decisions. In some situations, the A.D. will be helping to compose shots for the director by giving direct orders to the camera operators. The A.D. also may be making other suggestions regarding talent moves, graphics, revision, lighting problems, or whatever else needs attention. In other situations, the A.D. traditionally stays out of these kinds of directorial/aesthetic decisions and sticks pretty closely to the note-keeping and timing functions.

After the rehearsal and before the actual take, the A.D. will want to do several things. First, he or she must make certain that the director follows through on all production notes that were jotted down (fixing the back light, taking care of the talent's hair, and so forth). For minor corrections, the A.D. may take care of them without even bothering the director. Next, the A.D. must make sure that everybody involved has all of the script changes marked down; as certainly as one person did not get a crucial script change, that omission

will lead to an on-the-air mistake. Finally, the A.D. must remind the director of how much time is remaining before the program must get started on the air.

During the Program. Just prior to production, the A.D. will read down the clock, letting the director know how many seconds until air. Once on the air, the A.D. should remain alert to any and all potential problems—ready to take any action needed or to call major troubles to the attention of the director. The A.D. must show initiative in this regard.

The A.D. should be following the director's marked script at all times, ready to give any assistance necessary. The A.D. will be alerting camera operators, audio personnel, projectionists, and other crew positions to any special cues coming up in the script. Depending, again, upon the production complexity and studio philosophy, the A.D. may help to get the camera shots lined up. In some network and station production situations, the A.D. will be giving the crew—including the camera operators—virtually all their instructions, based upon the director's script and rehearsals. The A.D. may even be giving "readies" and "prepares" to the technical director. This gives the director freedom to handle last-minute adjustments, make final artistic decisions, and call the actual takes on the air.

In many instances, the A.D. will at least be calling out shot numbers to the cameras. (In a thoroughly rehearsed production, the director will have every shot numbered in his or her script, and the camera operators will have a list of their shots by number. As the A.D. calls out the shot number on the air, all camera operators know exactly where they are in relation to the actual on-the-air shot.)

The primary job of the A.D., of course, is giving all time signals to the talent. The A.D. will have his or her script marked with all of the time cues and, either directly or through

Figure 11-1 A.D. checking script timing with a stop clock.

the director, tell the floor manager when to give each time signal to the talent. (See fig. 11-1.) Sometimes individual program segments will be timed. At the very minimum, time signals indicating the amount of time remaining in the program must be relayed to the talent. The A.D. will also be determining when the talent needs to be signaled to speed up or slow down (stretch).

Also, the A.D. will be taking down notes for postproduction editing—both those items that the director points out, which need to be taken care of in the later editing session (a missed shot, timing that was a little off, an opportunity to insert a reaction shot), and the items that the A.D. himself or herself notices need to be corrected.

Finally, the associate director will be ready to take over at any time. The A.D. is literally the standby director. Should the director be unable to complete the program, the A.D. will assume responsibility for the calling of shots and the production will continue. (Once on a network program, the director had a heart attack at the beginning of a production and the A.D. continued to direct the program on the air. The ambulance arrived before the program was finished. The director lived.)

After the Production. Once the production is completed, the A.D. still has a couple of obligations—especially in a training situation. The student A.D. should remind the director to thank the cast and crew; help to clean up the control room of extra scripts, notes, and other materials; and debrief the director on any errors that occurred during the program, looking forward to the next day's program.

A crucial postproduction job of the A.D. in many situations is the final editing session. The associate director may need to set up a schedule with the director for any planned editing (especially on dramatic programs—daytime serials and situation comedies); for **sweetening** of the program (adding audience reactions and recorded laugh tracks), or for correcting unanticipated production problems. The A.D. may simply continue as the director's right-hand assistant in these assignments or, depending upon the nature of the

SEGMENT (Description)	IDEAL (Unit) Cum.	REHEARSAL (Unit) Cum.	DRESS (Unit) Cum.	AIR (Unit) Cum.
1. TEASER	(:20) 0:20	:25	:25	:25
2. OPENING TITLES	(:30) 0:50	:40	1:05	1:10
3. INTRO	(1:05) 1:55	1:30	2:15	2:20
4. CHART	(2:00) 3:55	1:50	4:00	4:10
5. DEMO.	(4:00) 7:55	4:45	(4:15) 8:15	(4:20) 8:30
6. INTERVIEW	(5:30) 13:25	6:00	13:45	(5:00) 13:30
7. WRAP-UP	(:30) 13:55	:20	14:05	13:55
8. CLOSE	(:35) 14:30	:45	14:50	14:30
		16:15		
		(+1:45 over)		

Figure 11-2 Sample segment-timing sheet.

In this particular example, we have a demonstration/interview program with several segments, which include a teaser, the opening titles, an introduction by the host, a 2-minute chart talk, a demonstration, an interview, the host's summary, and the closing credits. The ideal times are entered in the first column. During the stop-and-go rehearsal, various unit or segment times are obtained. By totaling up these times in the "Rehearsal" column, we can see that the program is likely to run 1:45 (1 minute and 45 seconds) long. Adjustments are made—the interview segment is cut short—and the actual cumulative times are entered during the "dress" rehearsal and the actual "air" recording.

production arrangements, the A.D. may be substantially in charge of the postproduction editing session—following the director's instructions, of course.

Timing the Program

As previously outlined, the A.D.'s primary job is timing the program—ensuring that the entire production ends on time. Timing all of the segments to be electronically glued together in the editing session is also an important consideration here. In carrying out this function, there are specific hints that the beginning A.D. may want to use.

Segment Timing Sheets. The fundamental tool of the A.D. is, of course, the stopwatch. The A.D. also needs some way, however, of keeping track of the various timing notes and reminders. The stop watch is not of much use if the A.D. does not have some organized way of writing down the timing information. One way is the use of a **segment timing sheet.** It may take several forms and be used in different ways. One sample format is shown in figure 11-2. In this particular example, there are five columns for the A.D. to use. The first column is for a brief description of each segment in the program. The next four columns are for timing notations of one kind or another. "Unit" means the actual *length of the individual segment or unit.* "Cum" stands for the *cumulative time* of the program up to that point; it marks the time in the program that each particular segment should (or did) end.

The "Ideal" column is the estimated time that each segment *should* run; both the ideal unit-segment times and the ideal cumulative time should be figured out in advance of setting foot in the studio. The "Rehearsal" column is for jotting down the unit times as various segments are worked through in a technical or stop-and-go rehearsal. It is difficult to get an accurate picture of the actual cumulative times at this point, but the total of the unit times should give the A.D. a rough picture of how long or how short the program is likely to be. The "Dress" rehearsal column should give the A.D. a clear picture of how the actual cumulative times compare to the ideal times. The "Air" column is filled in as the program progresses. It lets the A.D. know how much to tell the talent to *stretch* or—in this case—to *cut* in order to come out on time. In this program, for example, we can see that several segments ran long, so the interview segment had to be cut short (from an ideal of 5½ minutes to an actual 5 minutes).

There are many variations of timing sheets. Some will include "Time in" and "Time out" cumulative columns. Some will work with only one or two columns. This sample, however, should give the beginning A.D. an idea of what is needed to get the program times accurately on the air.

Program Time and Body Time. Time signals are given to the talent in terms of *time remaining.* Thus, as the end of a program approaches, the A.D. will have the stage manager signal the performer that there are "5 minutes remaining," "3 minutes remaining," "1 minute to go," "30 seconds left," and so

forth (depending upon exactly what time cues the talent and A.D. had previously agreed would be used).

In many programs, such as the one illustrated in figure 11-2, the talent will need time-remaining cues in specific segments. Thus—working from the *ideal* times—the host will get, for example, a "30-seconds remaining" cue at 3:25 into the program (as a reminder that there are 30 seconds left in the chart-talk) and at 7:25 (30 seconds left in the demonstration). The talent might want time cues to get out of the interview segment on time (that is, a 30-second cue at 12:55) or simply time cues to get through with the wrap-up summary on time (that is, a 30-second cue at 13:25). Care must be taken that the talent clearly understands what these intermediate segment cues are so that they will not be confused with time remaining in the body of the program.

This brings up one other point of potential confusion. The A.D. must be concerned both with getting the talent wrapped up on time and with getting the program off the air on time. In figure 11-2 the talent needs a 30-second cue at 13:25 because he or she has to be completely wrapped up and finished by 13:55 (leaving the director 35 seconds for the closing credits). Also, the director has to have a 30-second cue at 14:00 in order to get the program off the air and into black at precisely 14:30. Thus, the A.D. has to work with both **body time,** the actual *length-of-the-program content,* including the host's closing summary but not the show's closing credits, and with **program time,** the *total length of the show* from fade-in to fade-out. Figure 11-3 illustrates this. Throughout the production, the A.D. has to be very careful to distinguish between *body-time cues to the talent* and *program-time cues to the director.* As can be imagined—solely from the standpoint of giving time cues—the A.D. has a very confusing and crucial role to play in any production.

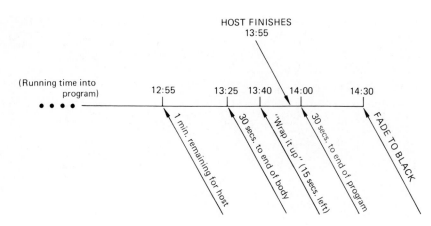

If the host is to be completely finished by 13:55, the "time remaining" *body time* cues to the host are "1 minute" (at 12:55), "30 seconds" (at 13:25), and "wrap it up" (at 13:40). The *program-time* cue to the director would be "30 seconds" (at 14:00).

Figure 11-3 Body time and program time.

11.2 The Stage Manager

The other right hand of the director is the stage manager (floor manager or floor director).[2] The stage manager is the director's surrogate to handle everything that happens on the studio floor. Actually, the stage manager's duties can be broken down into two very distinct areas: *handling the talent* and *managing all production activities* in the studio.

Working with Talent

On most major professional productions, the floor manager's primary job will probably be that of talent liaison. The floor manager will have to be a combination counselor, PR person, sympathizer, interpreter, and pillar of strength.

Ideally, the floor director will have taken part in production conferences preceding the date of studio production. He or she has probably already met the principal talent and can

---

2. The official Directors' Guild of America designation is *stage manager*, but all three terms are used in various stations and studio operations.

anticipate the kind of problems that may exist. Once the production moves into the studio, the floor director is the primary contact the talent has with the rest of the world—the studio door is shut; the director is huddled with producers and technicians; all lights are focused upon the talent, who is left isolated, facing the cameras alone, except for the support of the floor director.

There are two different kinds of talent needs that the floor director should be aware of and ready to minister to. First, there are *emotional-physical needs* that the talent may have. With inexperienced or exceptionally nervous talent, the floor director has to be especially sensitive in this area. Is the talent physically comfortable? Can you offer him or her a glass of water? Can you get the talent out of the lights for a few minutes? Does the talent need to talk to someone? Would he or she be better off left alone for a few moments of quiet reflection? What production mysteries should be explained to the talent?

This last point is important. Because the talent is not tied into the P.L. intercom, he or she is not aware of what is going on most of

Figure 11-4 Stage manager using hand cards to relay time signals to the talent. (Photo courtesy of KABC-TV, Los Angeles)

the time. Explain to the talent why there is a delay (a result of the audio recorder malfunction); explain why all the crew is laughing (at the A.D.'s story—not at the talent's clothing). Try to put yourself in the position of the talent—isolated, in the spotlight, being stared at by the crew, and receiving no feedback as to what is going on.

With more experienced talent, this function becomes less of a priority. The routine production—with the continuing host/actor/teacher/newscaster—can be done fairly smoothly for the skilled performer without having to cater to emotional needs. A few wisecracks, a slap on the back, and the experienced talent is ready to proceed.

The other kind of talent needs are more tangible *technical-production* requirements. The floor director must work these out with the talent on a program-by-program basis.

What props must be available and where? How will this movement be handled? Where is the talent to stand for this demonstration? What kinds of special cues might be needed? The details of each production must be worked out so that the talent is always sure of exactly what to do and the floor director is always sure of what specific tasks and cues he or she need execute to get the talent's job done. These types of production details are unique to each program; it is imperative that both the talent and floor manager are completely aware of what the other is doing.

One inevitable production requirement, common to every program, is the communication of information to the talent through various hand signals and/or flip cards (see fig. 11-4). The floor director—usually upon instructions from the director or A.D.—has to be concerned with relaying quite a bit of material to the talent: stand by to start, begin talking, talk to this camera, get closer to the mike, speed up, slow down (stretch), get closer together, get further apart, move in this direction, everything is O.K., such and such number of minutes remain, 30 seconds to go, wrap it up (about 15 seconds), cut, and so forth. (See appendix C for examples of the various hand signals.)

Production Management

In addition to handling talent, the other main job of the stage manager is that of handling all production details on the studio floor or stage. This may become the most important responsibility of the stage manager in small-format and training situations. In such low-budget operations, you, as stage manager, are less likely to have electronic graphics and sophisticated lighting setups. Therefore, the stage manager is going to have to handle more physical paraphernalia. (Also, there will be fewer assistants or specialized union positions to take of specific lighting, staging, graphics, and camera details.)

Production management includes a variety of concerns: broadly supervising staging and lighting setups and handling all staging and lighting changes during the program; coordinating all audio, camera, and other facilities; directing all studio traffic; taking care of all graphics changes and movement ·(where electronic graphics are not used); managing all talent movement; executing special effects; and every other production detail that may possibly occur.

The stage manager is ultimately in charge of virtually everything that happens on the studio floor, exercising dominion over all things technical—except the actual selection of shots for each camera. (In union situations, however, the stage manager may be restrained from crossing jurisdictional lines, such as giving orders to the lighting crew.) He or she must have a great deal of authority because virtually every other floor position is concerned with the production from only one specific viewpoint; for example, the camera operator, the audio engineer, and the lighting director all have their particular perspectives to take care of. Perhaps each of these three will have selected the same spot on the floor to position a camera, a mike boom, and a light stand. It is up to the stage manager to coordinate these needs and decide what goes where.

The stage manager does not work alone, of course. He or she will have a crew of floor assistants or grips, graphics flippers, cable pullers, rear-screen projectionists, special effects operators, stagehands, lighting assistants, camera assistants, and so on. In a small-scale production, all of these positions and assistants may be combined in just one or two persons. In elaborate dramatic productions, the stage manager may have an assistant stage manager to coordinate the production activities of a floor crew of a dozen or so while the stage manager is occupied primarily with the job of talent managing.

As with the A.D., it may be convenient to think of the stage manager's responsibilities in terms of specific production periods: before the rehearsal period, during the rehearsals, and during the actual production.

Before the Studio Rehearsal.   Ideally, the floor manager will have been working with the director ahead of the production date, attending production conferences and contributing ideas to the production process. On the day of production, before the actual rehearsals start, the floor manager has several immediate tasks. Again, the smaller the scope of the production (small-format and training situations), the more crucial the stage manager's job will be.

He or she should obtain copies of the script and other specific instructions for various crew members and distribute them to everyone involved. The floor manager will assist the staging and lighting personnel however possible—assigning other floor people to help in the initial stages, coordinating set and light placements with the technical requirements for cameras, microphones, and so forth. The floor manager will obtain all physical (nonelectronic) graphics and props to be used in the production, making certain they are set up and arranged according to the script and the director's instructions. The floor manager, of course, will meet with the talent, cater to their comfort, and discuss any special requests.

Just as the primary tool of the A.D. is the stopwatch, the main tool of the floor manager is the clipboard. At this point in the production, the floor manager will have a pretty good idea of all that must be done before and during the program. He or she will have started to organize lists of key tasks and requirements—people to contact, props to secure, specific instructions to pass out, special effects to develop, talent needs, specialized crew problems, staging considerations, and so forth. The clipboard will have the master checklist that the floor manager will be working from during the rehearsal and the production. This checklist will include all of the various action items that he or she must check on, supervise, or initiate during the production—arranging props, checking the sequence of all floor-card graphics, securing water for the talent, checking the slides for the rear screen, closing the studio door, supervising the tricky camera move, setting up the lighting effect, ringing the buzzer, cueing the talent, changing the set piece, and on and on.

During the Rehearsal Period. The floor manager must remain alert to the entire production process. He or she must try to anticipate problems before they escalate into crises, and constantly ask, What can I do to help the

production? In addition, the floor manager must be especially sensitive to coordination problems among lighting, audio, special effects, staging, graphics, cameras, and other elements.

The floor manager will plan and coordinate all movement. What set elements have to be moved during the production? What props are to be placed where? What special effects will have to be cued? All graphics activity—moves, flips, pulls—will have to be planned and executed. Grips and floor assistants should be assigned to these various tasks so that each will know his or her cues and what to move when.

Working with cameras and audio on any special problems—camera and boom movements, for example—is also the responsibility of the floor manager. Does the camera operator need an assistant for one particular trucking shot? Will the placement of camera and microphone cables affect other moving elements? The floor manager should always be looking ahead 2 minutes to see what problems might be averted by action *now*.

In addition, the floor manager gives the talent his or her undivided attention—always being in a position to be spotted easily by the performers. The talent should never have to turn his or her head to find the floor manager. All verbal instructions that come over the P.L. intercom from the director to the talent should be relayed clearly and tactfully, and all hand signal cues given promptly and forcefully. The floor manager will coordinate cue cards to ensure that they are handled properly.

After the rehearsals and before the final take, there are several things the floor manager needs to check. All sets, props, and physical graphics (and anything that is used during the body of the program) should be in place, ready for the beginning of the production; all consumables that need to be replenished—water glasses, special effects, canisters—should be at hand. The chalkboard should be erased, and so forth. The stage manager should generally console and reassure the talent that everything is fine and that they are doing well, assemble the crew, and make certain that everyone is ready and standing by for the beginning of the program.

During the Production. The stage manager must remain extra alert for any problems and double-check to ensure that all crew and talent are in their places, handling their moves, executing their cues. The stage manager will supervise all of the rehearsed moves and effects and make certain that all cues are clear and unambiguous. In general, he or she must guarantee that everything that was worked out during the rehearsal period is executed.

After the production, the stage manager supervises the strike, helps collect the graphics and props, assists the staging and lighting crew in getting their elements properly stored and taken care of, and generally polices the studio to see that everything is returned to where it belongs, ready for the next production.

In summary, the floor manager must think of himself or herself as *the* pivotal person in charge of the studio. The floor manager is in complete control of all production elements. He or she must take the initiative in getting things done. *The floor manager gives orders; the floor manager does not stand around waiting for someone else to tell him or her what to do.*

11.3   Other Crew Positions

Throughout the text, we have had occasion to mention various duties of several crew members as we discussed equipment items. It may be helpful at this point to summarize some of these tasks and procedures of the key crew members. There are also a couple other non-equipment-oriented positions that need to be introduced.

The Unit Manager

Every television production involves not only the creative talents of numerous people but also demands the disciplines and techniques of persons who can handle the budgets for the program. Controlling the costs of a TV production is a crucial and demanding position. In most professional situations, this becomes the job of the *unit manager.*

Most major commercial television production work is handled under contracts. The typical pattern is that the *producing agency* (say, an independent producer, a program packager, or an advertising agency) will contract with a *production facility* (network studio, station, or independent production house) to do the actual production.

In these contractual arrangements, a detailed budget is drawn up, based upon the **rate card** of the production facility. This rate card usually consists of three components: the technical personnel chart, the facilities rates chart, and the personnel hourly rate chart. (See appendix E for a detailed illustration of the rate-card structure and sample budget forms.) In essence, the rate card includes all of the below-the-line costs for the equipment and personnel furnished by the production facility (see section 1.6).

In some instances, of course, a network or production house serves both as the producing agency and as the production facility. Such "in-house" productions do not necessitate outside contracts. Strict budgets, however, must still be established and tight cost-control procedures must be followed.

It is the unit manager (sometimes referred to as the "production manager") who has primary responsibility for seeing that the production costs do not go over the contracted budget figures. Usually the unit manager is a staff member of the production facility (network, production house) and it is his or her

Figure 11-5 Unit manager discussing budget concerns with director on the studio floor.

main job to protect the production facility by ensuring that below-the-line production costs (equipment used, graphics supplies, studio rehearsal time, and so forth) do not exceed the contracted amount. The unit manager serves as the crucial liaison between the production facility and the producing agency.

As the A.D. lives by the stopwatch and the floor director the clipboard, so the unit manager's main tool is the rate card. In many cases, the unit manager has been an integral party in the contractual negotiations from the start; in all cases, the unit manager is intimately involved with every detail of the complex budget process. (See fig. 11-5.)

It is also essential that the unit manager be thoroughly schooled and experienced in all aspects of the production process. Although he or she may never touch a camera or adjust a microphone, the unit manager must be knowledgable about everything going on in the studio process. As the chief fiscal overseer of all matters dealing with the production, the unit

manager must be able to make intelligent decisions about the equipment needed, the utilization of personnel, the rehearsal procedures, the telecine problems, and anything else that might come up in the studio or control room.

Lighting and Staging

Depending on the scope of a production, all lighting and staging activity may be handled by one lighting and staging supervisor, or there may be a lighting director and also a staging director. In any case, they will work closely together. (See fig. 11-6.)

Lighting and staging personnel are usually the first to tackle their assignments in the studio. Copies of the lighting and staging plots should be given to key crew members. Tools—hammers and screwdrivers, asbestos gloves and wrenches—should be distributed as needed. All major scenic units should be erected first—hanging units, flats, large set pieces. Then furniture and set dressings can be positioned as the lighting is being set up.

All lighting patches should be made with the current turned *off*. Instruments should be patched into the dimmer or nondim circuits as called for on the lighting plot and detailed lighting worksheet. Lights should be trimmed—aimed and focused—using the talent or stand-ins of the same size and complexion. The finished lighting effect must be checked with both light meters and the control room monitors. A note of any malfunctioning equipment must be made and reported to the technical director, instructor, or supervising engineer.

After the lights are set and all ladders are put away, the set dressing and positioning of hand props should be completed. Someone should be assigned to work with the stage manager to execute any staging changes or lighting effects that are to take place during the program. After the production, lighting and staging personnel strike all set elements, return all furniture and props to their proper storage areas, unpatch all lighting instruments, and return the studio and control areas to their original condition.

Audio

The audio engineer (and any assistant) should select the proper microphones, plug them into the studio inputs, position them on stands or booms as required, and handle all patching in the audio control booth. All other sound sources (records, audio tapes, 16mm film soundtracks, VTR audio, cartridges) should be properly patched and threaded and checked out. Any equipment malfunction should be reported to the proper person. (See fig. 11-7.)

The audio operator will then obtain a level from the various talents, testing each one and setting a correct balance. If a musical production is involved, determining the best audio balance can demand quite a bit of time. All special cues are checked out with the director or A.D. During the production, the audio director must watch the VU meter, ride levels

Figure 11-6 Lighting director giving instructions to lighting crew during production setup. (Photo courtesy of KCET and Hollywood Television Theater)

carefully, and listen closely for all audio cues from the director. Generally, microphones should be turned off except when they are actually in use. The audio director must also anticipate cues for film and VTR inserts.

After the production, the patch bay should be cleared, all switches and pot/faders returned to off or neutral positions, and all microphones, stands, and cables returned to their proper storage areas.

Cameras

The camera operator should attach a shot sheet (if they are being used) to the camera. After staging and lighting have generally cleared the area, the camera operator can pull the camera into its approximate position, making certain to uncoil enough cable for estimated moves. He or she should then go through the uncapping and unlocking safety procedures, as outlined in section 6.4, and report any apparent

Figure 11-7 Audio engineer during complex television drama. (Photo courtesy of KABC-TV, Los Angeles)

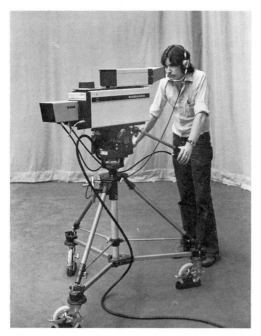

Figure 11-8 Camera operator working with studio camera.

camera malfunction to the proper person. The pan and tilt drag should be loose enough for smooth camera movement, but not so loose that the operator's arm carries all the weight. (See fig. 11-8.)

The camera person should be attentive to all directions from the control room while working through the shot sheet. The zoom lens should be preset so that it maintains focus on major zooms. An operator should not leave a camera without permission and should lock the pan and tilt head whenever letting go of the pan handle.

Composition is part of the camera operator's responsibility. If the picture has odd amputations, incongruous juxtapositions, confusing information, poor framing, and so forth, the operator is responsible. These things should be corrected before going on the air. If the shot is put on the air with bad composition, the operator may *cheat* (make slow minor adjustments that the audience will not perceive). The camera operator must always notice from the tally lights when the camera is on the air and not move unless ordered to do so by the director.

It is the camera person's responsibility after the production to cap up and lock up the camera, returning it to its studio storage area, and to wind the cable in a figure-eight pattern.

Technical Director

In an actual professional situation, the technical director is just what the name implies—the chief technical person on the production team. He or she usually will be initially involved in physically checking out all of the crew positions working with electronic facilities—cameras, audio, videorecorders, and so forth. Prior to the beginning of the technical rehearsal, then, the T.D. will assume his or her position at the SEG/switcher.

In a training situation, however, the title of "technical director" is often used to refer solely to the switcher operator. Unless given some other specific assignment, the student T.D. should report early to the switcher and put on the P.L. headset. While all other personnel are working around the studio in other capacities—setting up equipment, working with talent, and so forth—the T.D. is the one person who can be anchored in one spot in intercom communication with anyone else. The audio engineer, master control room, telecine, camera operators, and even the director can reach the T.D. from any other point to ask a question or to relay a message (simply by putting on a headset). Thus, until other positions are settled and the director gets into the control room, the T.D. can function as the director of all production operations.

In a major studio or network production, separate P.L. hookups will be used by the production and engineering staffs (section 3.5).

Figure 11-9 Technical director operating a complicated production switcher. (Photo courtesy of KABC-TV, Los Angeles)

Thus, the T.D. will be in intercom contact only with all of the union engineering positions.

If the program is complicated or tricky from the switching standpoint, the director may want to have the T.D. go over the script and rehearse any complex transitions. (See fig. 11-9.) Otherwise, the T.D. should need no special rehearsal. The T.D. should make certain, however, to check with the director about the speed of dissolves, fades, wipes, and so forth. During the production, the T.D. may have to ask for clarification of the director's commands of preparation ("ready's" and "prepare's"). The T.D. should respond as accurately and as quickly as possible to the director's commands but not anticipate the director's orders and not try to direct from the T.D.'s chair.

Another function of the T.D. is to participate in any remote survey for any on-location shooting session (see also section 12.4). Prior to any out-of-studio production, the T.D. must accompany the producer and the director and other key personnel to survey the site of the

Figure 11-10 Videotape operator, or recording engineer, supervising the taping of a studio drama. (Photo courtesy of KCET, Los Angeles)

proposed program origination—especially for multi-camera productions. It is the T.D.'s job to scout camera positions, check for adequate power supply, anticipate lighting problems, look for potential audio interference sources, set up studio microwave links or recording facilities, decide what backup equipment should be taken, and so forth.

Recording Engineer

As with other positions, procedures will vary tremendously from one production center to another, but there are several steps that recording engineers (also referred to as "videotape operators") generally will have to follow. The recording engineer must determine that the correct recording tape and correct machine are being used. (If the facility has more than one of the same model, the instructor or supervising engineer may have some reason why a particular video recorder should or

should not be used.) The recording engineer sets up all master control room patching and checks out all lines to verify that both the audio and video signals are getting into the recording machine properly. The audio engineer should send to telecine an audio tone or some other signal at 100 percent of the audio board output so that the recording engineer can set the VU meter on the recording machine. (See fig. 11-10.)

If the program also has a video insert—to be played back on some other VTR machine—the videotape operator must make sure that it is patched up properly for a transfer. He or she should play back a segment to the studio control room to verify that it is patched correctly and clarify the exact cue points with the director so that the insert can roll properly. At the onset of the production recording, the recording engineer should make sure he or she *pushes the record button.* Many a student program has been lost because one button was

Figure 11-11
Projectionist checking a slide in the telecine area of the master control room.

not pushed! After the production, the recording engineer is responsible for turning off all equipment, removing all the patches, labeling the videotape, and returning it to its assigned spot.

Projectionists

The job of the projectionist is to handle any film (8mm and 16mm) or slides that may be used in a small-format or student production. Most major productions today will transfer film to videotape prior to the production; and most material for still projection will be computer-generated and stored electronically. However, the projectionists will still be in evidence in many corporate, medical, and training productions.

The projectors usually will be clustered in a film island, with two or more projectors feeding into a single camera through a system of mirrors and prisms. One or more of the film chains will be found either in the telecine area or in the master control room. The projectionist must be completely familiar with threading and loading procedures for all film and slide projectors. The instructions for different machines can sometimes be complicated.

Once the film and slides are loaded, the projectionist should check them out and then double-check to make certain that everything is set up right—that the film has the correct-sized loops and the right tension and that all of the slides are loaded right-side up in the correct order. The projectionist must make sure that all projection bulbs and exciter lamps are working and that all switches are turned on and that prisms are set for the first projection. During the production—if the projectors are not controlled remotely from the studio control room—he or she must listen carefully for cues. (See fig. 11-11.)

Projectionists may also be involved in rear screen (and occasionally front screen) projection in the studio. In this situation, standard film or slide projectors are likely to be used, with a live studio camera shooting the image off the screen. It may take some time to get the projector(s) and screen properly set up and aligned. Location of the screen and projector has to be carefully coordinated with the floor manager and camera operators. This can be a very critical setup from the standpoint of staging and lighting, especially with rear screen projection. Any light falling on the face of the screen can easily wash out most of the image. Once the screen and projector are set up satisfactorily, operation of the equipment should be no problem. In many studio slide applications, the talent—using a long remote-control cord—will be the one to advance the slides on the air.

Grips and Floor Assistants

Stagehands, floor assistants, grips, cable pullers, graphics flippers, and camera assistants are the people who actually get the work done. Although often relegated to the lowest position in the production pecking order, these people are crucial because they actually *do things* on the air. If their jobs are not handled well, the whole production looks and sounds bad. In fact, on the professional level, if you do not do well in these beginning positions, you are not likely to have an opportunity to show how well you can do at the higher echelons.

As the descriptive labels suggest, there are many different functions to be performed, under the supervision of the stage manager, by the grips or floor assistants. In some studios, depending upon union jurisdictions, some of these tasks may be engineering assignments, some may be labeled staging, and some may come under the jurisdiction of the Directors' Guild.

Cable pullers and camera assistants are concerned with helping camera operators make their moves as smoothly and effortlessly as possible. This includes manipulating camera booms and dollies; occasionally assisting in pulling the pedestal camera sideways for a trucking shot; or simply pulling cable so that the camera operator does not have to worry about running out of cable on a long dolly-in, or stumbling over his or her own cable during a dolly-back.

Graphics handlers are needed for simple off-air flips of graphics, for delicate on-air pulls and flips, and for some complicated animation effects. During a fast graphics sequence, the coordination between two cameras and their respective graphics flippers can be quite close. It is very easy to get out of sequence and throw a whole graphics segment out of order. Graphics handlers need to be sure-fingered and confident. After a rehearsal, the graphics handlers should check to ensure that the graphics on their particular stands or easels are all set up and in order for the beginning of the program. (See fig. 11-12.)

Other assignments for the floor assistants may include changing staging elements during a scene; handling special effects such as fog, wind, or shaking a fire-shadow stick; assisting talent in fast costume changes; any other special assignments; and the traditional **gopher** assignments (go-for a cup of coffee, go-for some paper towels).

In addition to being quick of foot, nimble of hand, and humble of heart, grips must possess two qualities of anonymity—they are not to be seen on camera or heard on microphone. To meet the first requirement they must always be careful never to cross in front of any camera or get their hands in a graphics shot. To meet the requirement of silence, grips must remember that almost anything can be done loudly if done carelessly. In addition to the obvious, such as talking on the air and knocking

Figure 11-12 Floor assistant, or grip, handling graphics on a camera easel. (Photo courtesy of KABC-TV, Los Angeles)

over set pieces, they must control the slightest noise associated with a particular assignment—even pulling cable or flipping graphics can be done noisily. One final hint: grips should wear sneakers or work in socks. The studio floor is no place for hard-heeled shoes.

Regardless of the assignment, if a grip is really concerned about the success of the communication act and serious about his or her intentions in the field, he or she will carry out the assignment efficiently and conscientiously.

Production Assistants

One other classification of special people must be included in any major television production. The label of "production assistant" is used to cover a multitude of varying tasks. The easiest way to categorize the position is to think

of it as an adjunct to the A.D. on any large complicated production (just as the floor assistant may be considered an adjunct to the stage manager).

Like the A.D., the production assistant is concerned not with hardware but with organizational details, script changes, critique notes, administrative messages, front-office liaison, urgent communications, talent arrangements, and anything else that a junior-level administrative assistant may be called upon to handle. Some studios see the production assistant basically as a nontechnical gopher.

In many situations, the terms **script assistant** or **production secretary** may be used to describe essentially the same position—especially if the assignment is concerned primarily with keeping track of scripting details and changes. Sometimes the production or script assistant will be assigned to the director and the job may even be a DGA (Directors' Guild) position. In other cases, the production assistant may be assigned directly to the producer and serve in a variety of secretarial tasks.

In many smaller-scale productions, there would be no need for a script assistant. However, on large studio or network programs, a variety of production assistants and secretaries may be involved. (Often the label, "Assistant to Mr./Mrs. _____" is used.) In these major production centers, the job of production/script assistant is often an entry-level position that can lead to more responsible production assignments. Any aspiring professional who has typing skills, enthusiasm, a quick mind, and a grasp of production disciplines will find the lowly production assistant job a valuable stepping stone.

Summary

The *associate director* (A.D.) is one of the director's chief lieutenants and may get involved in almost every aspect of program design and execution from program planning to helping set up shots on the air. The major responsibility of the A.D., however, is that of *timing* the entire program—getting the director started on time, giving time signals to the talent throughout the program, and getting the director off on time.

The *stage manager* (*floor manager, floor director*) is the other chief lieutenant of the director. The stage/floor manager is directly in charge of everything on the studio floor. The duties generally can be divided into two areas: *working with talent* (attending to emotional-physical needs and to technical-production needs) and *production management* (supervising all audio, camera, staging, lighting, graphics, special effects, props, and projection elements).

The *unit manager* has a crucial position in most contract production situations—handling all cost-control responsibilities and overseeing all production budget matters.

In addition to these key positions, every other assignment of the production crew has its own set of *techniques* and *disciplines* to master: those of the lighting and staging personnel, audio engineers, camera operators, technical director, recording engineer, projectionists, grips and floor assistants, and production/script assistants and secretaries.

In the final three chapters we will look at the one position that pulls it all together—the director's job.

11.4 Training Exercises

1. Using a stopwatch, time every segment of some talk show that you can watch at home. Start with a timing sheet similar to the one in figure 11-2. You will use three columns—"Segment," "Unit Time," and "Cumulative Time." You will need quite a few blank lines, however, as there will be a large number of individual segments. As the show progresses, write down every separate segment of the program—every commercial, every monologue, every demonstration, every station break, every musical number or variety act, every interview or discussion segment, and the like. Time each segment with a stopwatch, returning the

watch to zero between every program unit; enter these times in the "Unit Time" column. Using your wristwatch or a clock with a second hand, keep track of the cumulative time in the third column. When you are through, you should be able to total up the unit times and arrive at the total elapsed time as indicated in your "Cumulative Time" column.

2. If you have the opportunity, visit a recording session of some studio television program. Pay particular attention to the job of the stage manager. Before, during, and after the production, notice every task and responsibility of the floor manager. Keep a list of every specific job that he or she had to perform. What additional production and talent-liaison items might the stage manager have gotten involved with if the need had arisen?

Producing, Directing, and Editing for Single-Camera Video

12

In previous chapters we have been dealing primarily with video production that is for the most part accomplished by means of **real-time editing.** The multiple-camera technique requires considerable preproduction planning and rehearsal of camera shot assignments. Program elements must be carefully timed and organized into their projected sequence. During a live broadcast, the task of the director is largely that of making a series of precise editing decisions. The technical director uses the switcher to connect the succeeding elements of the program by means of takes, dissolves, and special effects such as wipes and mattes. Pre-recorded segments on disc, tape, and film are combined with the live camera inputs—all within the time disciplines of the continuous production operation. The spontaneous aspect of real-time production gives sports, news, and even game shows an important sense of immediacy and realism.

These benefits notwithstanding, there are also some serious difficulties that arise from working within the time constraints of the live or live-on-tape technique. The director, working in a moment-by-moment decision process, must also be constantly alert for unforeseen production difficulties. When the director is forced to solve production problems while on the air there is a good chance that the overall quality of the production will suffer. Some types of programs simply do not fit well into this studio concept of television production. In this chapter we will study the production options that have been made possible by a new generation of video equipment.

12.1 Postproduction and Preproduction Editing

Those persons who worked to develop the early TV equipment and production methods were quick to realize that a whole new range of production techniques were possible with the development of the videotape-based recording

Figure 12-1 A modern postproduction editing studio. Notice that the facility has been designed with "human engineering" factors in mind. Easy access to equipment, soft lighting, and comfortable working stations are important when editing sessions may last 12 hours or longer. (Photo courtesy of Pacific Video)

and editing capability. The term *postproduction editing* refers to a number of techniques that in many ways resemble the way film-makers have worked for years. The various program elements—whether a continuous 5-minute dramatic scene or any of the smaller bits and pieces of an opening or closing format—are shot out of sequence in a stop-and-go process. High standards can be maintained because retakes are possible. The work is done on a production schedule that is convenient according to the availability of facilities and talent as well as other budget considerations. Once the main production work

has been completed, the postproduction unit takes over and puts the show together. On many programs there may be a separate company that is hired on a subcontract basis to do this final assembly. (See fig. 12-1.)

This method of operation has had an impact on almost every type of video production. The nationally syndicated celebrity talk shows now use editing to "sweeten" a program. Minor errors and slow-moving segments can be taken out to improve the pacing of the show. Prime-time situation comedies—which are often shot in continuous 3-to-5-minute segments with multiple cameras—do later retakes of close-ups and other inserts that have not played correctly on the main run-through. These—along with sections available from the taped dress rehearsal—are combined with titles, credits, and other elements in the postproduction assembly.

Some situation comedies and dramatic programs utilize a different technique. Each of the four cameras takes an assigned series of shots as the scene is run straight through. However, instead of making "on-the-air" switching/editing decisions in real-time, each camera's picture is fed to its own separate videotape recorder. Then all of the editing is done later by means of a multiple-screen viewing technique.

This **isolated-camera** (**iso**) technique got its start as directors discovered the postproduction editing benefits of having one totally separate camera in operation during a traditional three-camera live-on-tape production. The director can concentrate on "cutting" the program through the switcher while the associate director (section 11.1) keeps an eye on the prearranged shots on the iso camera. Figure 12-2 shows the signal feed configuration of a commonly used technique combining several of these production methods.

The daytime soap operas are one major type of program to utilize editing as a basic part of the production operation. For many years these shows all ran one-half hour in length and were shot with a continuous live-on-tape multiple-camera technique. Usually two different directors would split up the five shows in the week. When the first "soaps" expanded to a one-hour time period, however, the whole approach to production had to change. Many of the segments are now shot out of their eventual program order. Sometimes two different directors will work on various elements of the story during the same shooting day. Postproduction assembly is typically done a little over one week prior to air date.

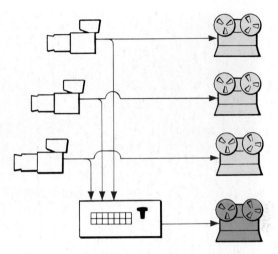

While the switcher is used to feed the "live" edited program to a master VTR, each camera is also feeding its individual signal directly to its own VTR for later postproduction editing and fine cutting.

Figure 12-2 Studio cameras feeding signals to individual "isolated" tape recorders.

Preproduction Editing

The ability to record and edit videotape has had a similarly important effect upon those programs that air live—especially news. (See fig. 12-3 and fig. 12-4.) Prior to the late 1970s, television news relied heavily upon film segments that had been edited prior to air. Lead time in terms of film developing and transportation had always been a problem. In 1975 CBS News decided to do a trial run of an electronic newsgathering (ENG) system at KMOX TV—its owned and operated station in St. Louis. There were no film cameras. A whole new staff structure was designed around the use of the electronic camera and videotape editing equipment. The **preproduction editing** techniques that they pioneered are now commonplace at most stations around the country.

One to two hours of preproduction time on the out-of-studio elements of a major news story can be saved when videotape is used instead of film. There is no delay while the film

Figure 12-3 Network news crew covering a still very active forest fire. Based at stations owned by the network, these units must be ready to go anywhere in the world with very little notice. (Photo courtesy of ABC News)

Figure 12-4 Temporary network editing and operations control center. Hastily constructed in a hotel room, such temporary hookups are often the basis for covering fast-breaking stories in foreign countries. Note clocks and monitors for incoming feeds. (Photo courtesy of ABC News)

is being developed. Segments can be immediately microwaved back to the station for editing—or the news team can go on the air live from the field as the story unfolds. The transition from the film-based news unit to ENG—also called EJ (electronic journalism) and EFP (electronic field production) in various professional circles—has been a gradual one at most stations.

Two different approaches to postproduction editing have evolved. The term **on-line editing** is usually applied when, as with television news programs, the original videotape footage is transferred directly to the edited air tape. The term **off-line editing** refers to a more elaborate procedure involving an intermediate stage wherein a *work print* copy is edited together first, allowing for more precise control and detailed planning of the final edited master tape.

Those working in related fields of corporate training and information processing have been equally quick to grasp the industrial and educational applications of this new technology. More and more industries now have their own video production units. A visit to any of the major equipment exhibitions such as those at the NAB (National Association of Broadcasters) convention will attest to the scope of professional nonbroadcast video. One of the more interesting aspects of this so-called video explosion has been the private use of video not only by individuals in the home but also by groups of people who are exploring the possibilities of communication and artistic expression through the access channels of local cable systems (section 1.3).

12.2 The Electronic Transfer Edit Concept

As the first videotape editors tried to emulate their film counterparts at the editing bench, they found some substantial problems that complicated the process. When the videotape was physically cut and spliced together, extreme care had to be taken in order to maintain the synchronization of the picture (using elaborate magnification and chemical procedures to make sure that the physical cut was precisely between the picture frames). On a bad day, half of the splices would cause picture breakup and have to be redone. The concept of editing as a production technique was a process that directors tried to avoid rather than utilize.

Recognizing the need for an entirely new system, leaders in the engineering field developed the present technology whereby segments taken from one (or more) original recorded videotapes are electronically transferred to a second tape machine, where they are re-recorded in the desired edited sequence. The two factors that are crucial to the process are *picture stability* and the *precision of operator control* over the edit points. The improvements of the past decade concerning both of these factors have produced a truly impressive technology.

Assemble Editing

As you would imagine, an editor usually constructs a short news *piece* or an entire program by transferring the individual segments in consecutive order from beginning to end. This procedure is known as **assemble editing.**

A somewhat different process—called **insert editing**—is involved when the editor simply wants to "drop in" or replace any segment in the middle of a program. This may be to insert a single piece of video and/or audio in a previously recorded (*live-on-tape*) program or it may be to exchange a segment in a completed assemble-edited program. The technique of insert editing—and some related information dealing with control track sync pulses—will be covered further in section 12.3.

In presenting the basic procedures and terminology of on-line assemble editing, we will utilize a simple editing situation such as

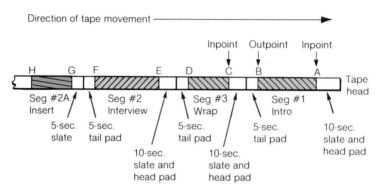

Direction of tape movement

Inpoint   Outpoint   Inpoint

H   G   F   E   D   C   B   A   Tape head

Seg #2A Insert   Seg #2 Interview   Seg #3 Wrap   Seg #1 Intro

5-sec. slate   5-sec. tail pad   5-sec. tail pad   5-sec. tail pad   10-sec. slate and head pad

10-sec. slate and head pad   10-sec. slate and head pad

Figure 12-5 Recorded segments on the original master.

In this example, there are three segments of program material plus one insert segment to be edited in later. These are to be "assembled" in the order of the segment numbers, that is, *A-B* first, followed by *E-F*, then *C-D*. The editing task is to remove the unwanted pads and slates between the segments and to rearrange the segments as indicated.

one would find in field production or news work. Figure 12-5 indicates how four separate camera segments might be recorded in the field on the *original master reel*. (In studying these illustrations, keep in mind that the direction of the videotape is left to right; therefore it is necessary that you follow the action from the head of the tape, on the *right*, to the end of the tape, on the *left*.)

Like single-camera film production, the individual shots would not necessarily be recorded in the order in which they will be edited together. In figure 12-5, the segment numbers (1, 3, 2, and 2A) refer to the eventual editing sequence—not to the shooting order. Segment #1 is the host introducing the program. Segment #3 is the solo host conclusion or wrap-up; this would actually be videotaped as the second shot (while the host is still in position and before the guest has arrived). Program segment #2 is the host interviewing a guest (actually shot as the third recorded segment). Segment #2A (the fourth segment to be shot) is some picture information that will be used later as a *video-only insert* over some of the interview audio. Its utilization will be covered in section 12.3.

Ahead of each segment you would have at least 5 seconds of picture and sound identification of the upcoming segment. Known as the **slate,** this material would consist of the camera pointed at a chalkboard or card with printed words such as "Segment 2, Take 1, Interview." The words should also be read aloud to confirm the audio level. With the tape still rolling, the slate would be pulled away to reveal the host and subject for a period of about 5 more seconds prior to their cue to begin. This short sequence and a similar continuation of picture at the conclusion of the interview are known as **head pad** and **tail pad.** The function of these pads is to provide an adequate margin of picture signal, which, as we shall see, is necessary to the editing process.

Figure 12-6 indicates how the segments from the original master, located on the *playback* VTR machine, would be transferred so as to be edited in program sequence onto the *edited master reel* located on the *record* VTR machine. It should be noted that in our example, the numbers given the various segments do not reflect the sequence in which the segments were recorded in the field, but rather, the numbers indicate their eventual program sequence. In many circumstances, the slate reflects the structure of the script—with prenumbered segments. (This underscores the importance of thorough preplanning before ever packing production gear in a box and heading for the field.)

Prior to the actual assembly process, there is usually a viewing session involving the director, the editor, and others responsible for the creative aspects of the program. This is called the **pre-edit session.** Its purpose is to carefully check the tape in order to determine not only what material will be selected for final editing, but also to designate the precise **inpoint** and **outpoint** of those segments that are to be used.

In our example (fig. 12-5 and fig. 12-6), let us say that segment #1 consists of the host/interviewer talking directly to the camera. Outpoint *B* is roughly the end of a sentence introducing a second person who will appear with the interviewer at the beginning of segment #2. Our edit must allow for a normal time lapse between the end of this final sentence and the beginning audio of the next (interview) segment. A pause that is too long or too short would be unnatural and would distract the viewer. Our **edit decision** (sometimes called the *edit event*) in this case is relatively simple. Outpoint *B* will be established at a point that will allow for one more second of picture to follow the final word spoken. Inpoint *E* of the segment #2 interview will be set to allow one additional second of establishing video ahead of the first audio.

The tape editor must look carefully for small but important visual elements that may have gone unnoticed at the time of the recording. For example, if the host was making a small hand gesture at the end of segment #1, then that gesture should be seen being completed before the edit is made. Similarly, if there was any movement at the beginning of segment #2, then that movement should be seen from its beginning or entirely eliminated.

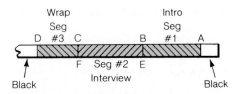

As the program segments (from fig. 12-5) are assembled, the outpoint of segment #1 (*B*) is butted against the inpoint of segment #2 (*E*); the outpoint of segment #2 (*F*) is butted against the inpoint of segment #3 (*C*); and the outpoint of segment #3 (*D*) is edited to the final segment of black.

Figure 12-6 Program segments transferred to the edited master.

To edit from or to a movement that is in progress produces a distracting edit, similar to the jolting effect of a jump cut or position jump (see section 13.1). Instead, the edit can be made by adding a little of the nonaudio tail pad at the end of segment #1 and *trimming* a bit of what was to have been 1 second of head pad at the beginning of segment #2. The idea is to have enough flexibility to achieve a perfectly matched picture before and after the edit decision. This situation illustrates how head pad and tail pad can give the editor a margin to play with when determining the precise edit point.

As each edit point is determined, its position on the reel must be noted in terms of some sort of numerical location or *address* system. Whereas off-line editing is usually done on VTR machines equipped for SMPTE time code (section 8.3), much on-line editing is done on equipment that utilizes a control-track-based counter unit. Some of these systems provide minute, second, and frame number read-outs, while others may only provide a minute and second read-out. (See fig. 8-13.) In either case, pre-edit notes are of limited value if they are not expressed in terms of specific numerical addresses, or locations, of edit points.

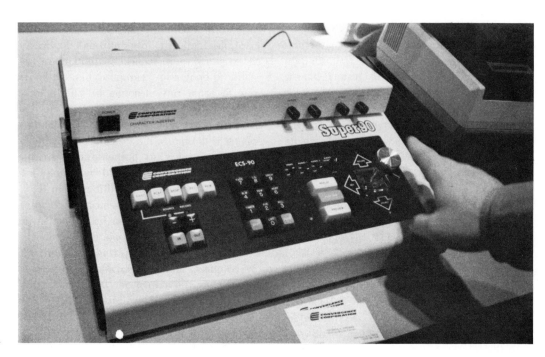

Figure 12-7 The ECS Super 90 Editing Controller.

12.3 The Inter-Machine Edit Control Unit

The process described, whereby exact edit points can be precisely adjusted, is relatively simple for the operator/editor as long as he or she is working with equipment that has the capacity to centrally control the movement of the playback and record machines. This intermediate unit, or *editing system,* is designed to perform several important functions. First, there must be a component such as a dial or **joystick** that allows the operator to move the tape on either machine at varying fast and slow search speeds (fig. 12-7). This same control must also be able to put the machines into the *pause* (freeze-frame) mode.

Second, the editing system must have the capacity to "remember" designated inpoints and outpoints on both the playback and record tape machines. Also, in the final stage the editing system must be able to provide a **preview** of the edit, showing exactly what the moving edit will look like but without executing any actual signal transfer. Then, on command, the editing unit is capable of progressing through the programmed series of mechanical and electromagnetic operations that accomplish the transfer edit.

Because of the constant upgrading of editing technology, state-of-the-art equipment will vary widely. A complete understanding of operating techniques must ultimately revolve around a detailed study of the operator's manual of each individual editing system. There are, however, a number of general operational concepts that can be applied to all such equipment. It is hoped that the following general operational examples will provide students with a basic approach to the facilities in their own studio.

In our initial discussion of *assemble editing* it was mentioned that the status of the signal on the control track had a relationship to the assembly technique. The likelihood of maintaining a stable picture through each edit is greatly enhanced if a continuous sync pulse pattern has been pre-recorded on the tape prior to the edit session. This is accomplished by your having the machine record a continuous black signal with **color burst** on it for as much of the tape as is needed for the edited master sequence.

With this prepared videotape in the record machine, you can proceed with the first step in the editing session—the transfer of segment #1. Referring again to figure 12-5, you will see that you must set up the tape so that the transfer begins at approximately 1 second before the host's first word. This strips away the slate and most of the *head pad*. You will, however, want to record 3 to 4 seconds of *tail pad* after the host's last audio. This provides you with plenty of sync picture for the editing manipulations.

Using the variable speed control knob (or joystick) and keeping your eye on the *playback* machine monitor, move the playback tape, 1 second ahead of the host's first word, to inpoint *A* of segment #1. Using the designated control, you enter this as the first inpoint into the editing system's memory. On equipment designed for simple assemble editing, the operator will designate the *temporary* end of the edit (or transfer) by waiting for the host's last word, and *punching out* of the edit mode. (On much of the newer equipment, this outpoint of the edit sequence can be programmed just like the inpoint.)

Whatever the sophistication of your equipment, the control unit will have a provision for returning both the playback and record tapes to a point 5 seconds ahead of where the edit/transfer is eventually to take place. This sets up the *preroll* period, which is designed to make certain that the video heads and tape transport are up to speed at the time that the edit occurs.

Your next step is to transfer segment #1. Roll the two machines and execute the edit at your predetermined point. Make sure that you have recorded 4 to 5 seconds of tail pad. After making the edit/transfer, check the entire segment on the record machine, verifying that there is a stable picture throughout. Now put the *record machine* into the *stop mode* (to save head and tape wear) and turn your attention to the *playback machine*. You are now approaching your first complete *edit event* (fig. 12-6).[1]

During the pre-edit session, you noticed that the outpoint of segment #1 should occur at the conclusion of a slight hand movement by the host roughly 1½ seconds after his last word. Considering that an audio pause of more than 2 seconds between the end of the introduction (segment #1) and the beginning of the interview (segment #2) would be too long, you decide to make the inpoint *E* of segment #2 just a ½-second before the host's first word in the interview segment. Maneuvering the search control to locate this point can be relatively simple if you are working with a counter system that provides a read-out that includes individual frames. On less sophisticated systems, a bit of guesswork may be involved.

With inpoint *E* located on the playback machine (and the machine left in *pause*), you turn your attention to locating a precise outpoint *B* of segment #1 on the record machine.

1. In some circumstances you may be able to leave the record machine in the *pause mode*, providing for a quicker relocation of the outpoint. Much of the newer equipment has a feature that, while the machine is in *pause*, will automatically advance the tape 1 frame every 60 seconds. This permits you to have a monitor picture of the tape location at all times. Check with your operator's manual, instructor, and/or supervising engineer to determine the best operating procedure for your equipment.

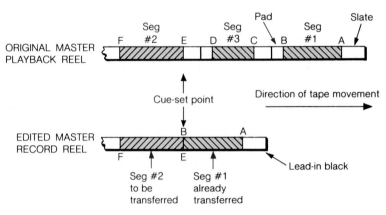

Figure 12-8 Playback and record tapes as they would be positioned relative to the cue-set point.

With segment #1 (*A-B*) already transferred from the original master (playback reel) to the edited master (record reel), the cue-set point is selected to determine the precise spot for the next edit (assembling segment #2).

(This machine is also left in *pause* once the endpoint is found.) You now have the two tapes whose position relative to each other is shown in figure 12-8. It may help to visualize the status of the tapes at this point, and during subsequent procedural descriptions, if you think of the video heads as being at a constant point in both time and space relative to tape movement. This is reinforced by the fact that freeze-frame pictures are available on both the playback and record monitors, as pictured in figure 12-9.

If the edit/transition point is satisfactory, then your next step is to activate some sort of **cue-set** control (the terminology and exact functioning of this component will vary with the editing system). This process programs the memory part of the editing unit, telling it that the positions now in *pause* on both machines are the locations for the next *edit event*. With many control units, the act of entering the cue-set command also activates both machines to

roll the tape in reverse and come to a stop at a point that sets up the 5-second pre-roll period necessary for proper tape speed. This new position of the tapes relative to the video heads is shown in figure 12-10.

The machines are now set up to perform an edit. At this point, however, most editors prefer to *preview* the point at which the sound and picture transition between the two segments will take place. This can be done without any actual transfer of the signal to the record tape. On command, both machines are put in motion. As the tapes reach the edit points *B* and *E,* the record monitor (showing the tail of segment #1) automatically switches over and shows segment #2 from point *E* on. On some editing systems, this preview period may run only 5 seconds; at this point the unit automatically stops both machines and reverses them to the preroll set-up points. On other systems, the operator has manual control and can terminate the preview at his or her discretion.

Playback   Record

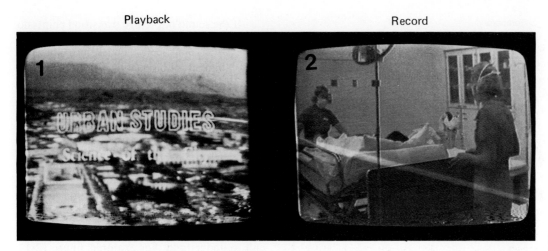

The operator watches the picture on the playback machine (*left*) while searching for the starting point of the next segment to be recorded. When located, the machine is put into the pause mode as

seen here. During this search, the last frame of the previously recorded segment can be viewed on the monitor (*right*). The operator can easily compare these two pictures while making the edit decision.

Figure 12-9
Simultaneous display of picture information from both the playback (original source) and record (edited master) machines.

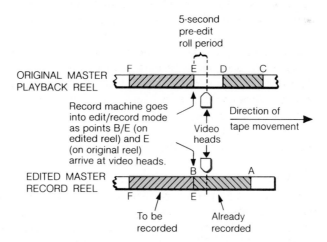

In this example, segment #1 (*A-B*) has already been transferred to the "edited master record reel" on the record machine; the next step is to transfer segment #2 (*E-F*) from the original master on the playback machine to the record machine at point *B*. Thus, the edit point (the cue-set point) will be *B/E* on the record machine. Therefore, both recorders are rolled back exactly 5 seconds before

point *E* (on the playback machine) and point *B* (on the record machine). Both recorders are started simultaneously, and precisely 5 seconds later (when the playback machine reaches point *E* and the record machine reaches point *B/E*) the record machine is automatically switched into the "edit" mode. The butt edit of segments #1 and #2 is accomplished at point *B/E*.

Figure 12-10 Tapes on the playback and record machines in position for the pre-edit roll period.

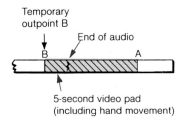

Figure 12-11 Segment as transferred from playback to record machine.

In this example, segment #1 has been transferred with a 5-second video pad, which includes the completion of a hand movement by the host.

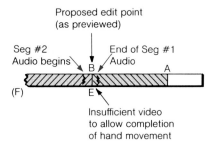

Figure 12-12 Preview of tight edit with insufficient video.

A preview of the proposed edit shows that the edit point cut off too much of the video pad; the edit was placed in the middle of the hand movement.

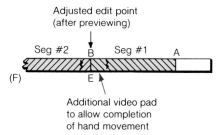

Figure 12-13 Adjusted edit point with sufficient video.

The completed edit has added 2 seconds more to the video pad at the end of segment #1 in order to allow for completion of the hand movement.

If the sound or picture transition points do not seem quite right, you can repeat the preview process as necessary and make **trimming** adjustments in the relative position of either of the tapes. On equipment that has the *trim* control for a frame-by-frame adjustment, you can easily add or subtract individual frames to or from either segment. On less sophisticated systems, adjustments made with the control knob or joystick are done with somewhat less certainty.

Whatever the complexity of the editing system, the process of adjusting the edit point between segments is important but not difficult to understand. For example, figure 12-11 shows segment #1 as transferred along with its 5-second tail pad. Had the edit shown in figure 12-12 been made without preview, it would have been discovered that there was not sufficient separation to allow for the completion of the hand movement. But by previewing the edit, the operator can see the need for added video pad at the end of the segment and adjust accordingly (fig. 12-13).

Once you are confident that the edit point has been properly established, the actual edit itself becomes a rather routine matter of telling the machine to go ahead and execute the programmed transfer. What takes your time is the decision-making and preparation process leading up to the edit event.

Immediately after the completion of the edit, the entire transfer must be carefully reviewed for both technical and operator errors. You must rewind back to a point at least 10 seconds ahead of the just-completed edit and roll through the whole segment—checking not only the edit point itself, but also the remainder of the segment for any deviation of picture quality. To shortcut this process is to invite trouble. Immediately redoing an assemble edit is much simpler than trying to fix it once the subsequent segments have been added on.

Insert Editing

With segment #2 transferred, you now have two options as to what your next step should be. You can either continue with the assemble editing of segment #3, or you can put in the video insert (segment #2A) that is to be included within segment #2. In the simplified example, it really would not make much difference which you do next. In a more complex editing situation the decision would be based upon time and efficiency factors as well as upon creative considerations. In one situation, the editor might decide to work in terms of whatever segment materials happened to be placed most conveniently on the playback reel. In another situation, the editor might wish to assemble edit all of the dialogue segments first—getting them in proper sequence with ideal timing—and then review them before doing any of the video-only insert work.

Whenever you decide to do the insert editing, the process must be based upon decisions made only after the segment has been carefully screened. You must determine the most logical times for the inpoint and outpoint of the inserted video information. In our interview example, for instance, you must listen for audio cues—specific oral references to some visual information—that signal the spot where the video insert should be placed.

For purposes of our illustration, the interview segment #2 runs a total of 30 seconds—this is the previously transferred segment from inpoint *E* to outpoint *F*. During this segment the host and guest are discussing a large piece of equipment that has thus far been seen only in the background of the two-shot (segment #2). During the original location *shoot,* at the end of the reel the director has taken an *anticipated insert shot* of the equipment (segment #2A) for later editing purposes. At 8 seconds into segment #2 the guest says the words, ". . . this machine." This provides you with the obvious cue for the picture transition point.

Choosing a suitable outpoint may be a somewhat more subtle matter. What you are looking and listening for is the point at which the insert picture has already provided the viewer with the maximum amount of information and is about to become redundant or distractingly boring. In this case, let us assume that the shot to be inserted has an "information life" of 10 seconds. Exact timing might depend upon the location of the end of a sentence or a phrase so as to provide a neat cue for the outpoint.

Figure 12-14 shows, with these considerations in mind, how the tapes would be set up in relationship to each other. Note that we have allowed for at least 5 seconds of picture head pad on the playback machine. This is necessary in order to assure proper picture sync at the time of the inpoint edit. As stated before, the insert will begin 8 seconds past the previously transferred edit point *B/E* and run for 10 seconds.

The operational techniques used in setting up and completing the insert edit will, of course, vary with the type of editing system used. On older equipment the operator must listen for word cues and manually *punch out* of the edit. On more sophisticated units the out-cue can be programmed just like the in-cue.

Insert editing is by no means limited to just video. The insert can obviously be video and audio combined. Most equipment is designed so that either one or both audio tracks can be edited or re-recorded while the original video remains untouched.

The Dissolve in Editing

Machine-to-machine edits as described to this point can be used only when the desired effect is that of an instantaneous *take* between pictures. Obviously for any kind of a dissolve transition between pictures, the levers and mix banks of a switcher must be utilized. As in any

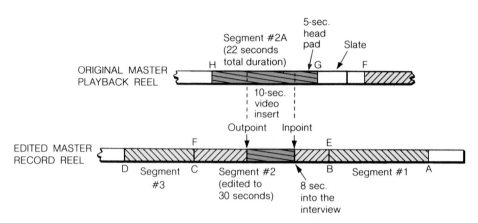

Figure 12-14 Playback and record machines set up for an insert edit.

The shot to be inserted (10 seconds taken from segment #2A) is to be edited into segment #2 (E-F) 8 seconds after point B/E (the beginning of segment #2). The two VTR machines are rolled simultaneously from points at least 5 seconds ahead of the anticipated edit, and the "edit" (insert in) and "edit out" (insert out) commands are executed either manually (on older editors) or by the pre-programmed microprocessor (on newer models).

dissolve, this means that there must be two simultaneous sources of video signal. Also, when mixing various video sources, the time-base corrector (section 8.2) is used to guarantee that all video signals will lock up with no picture breakup.

If we wanted to dissolve between segment #1 and segment #2 of our editing sample as shown in figure 12-5, we would need to set up separate tape feeds on *A* and *B* machines for playback. The technique is somewhat the same as in traditional *A* and *B* roll editing for film, where a final composite film is automatically printed from two specially edited film rolls. In television this system can either be set up for automatic computer control or be done manually at the switcher during the edit session. The basic principles involved in setting up the tapes are roughly the same in either situation.

When a dissolve between segments is planned, it is imperative to allow sufficient extra video pad following the outpoint of the first segment and the inpoint of the second. If in our example we establish edit point *B/C* as

the midpoint of a 2-second dissolve, then both playback machines must feed a video signal to the record machine throughout the duration of the dissolve. Although only 2 seconds of pad from each segment would actually be needed for the 2-second dissolve overlap, it is always advisable to have extra-protection source video available. Most professional directors and technical directors would not feel comfortable without a working margin of at least an additional 3 seconds added to each segment. Figure 12-15 shows how the video pad should be utilized in the setup of *A* and *B* roll tapes for dissolve edits.

A sequence in which all of the segments are to be connected by dissolves must be planned in order to be recorded from beginning to end. For all practical purposes there is no way in which the record machine can be stopped to set up the next dissolve without doing a butt edit. (Such an emergency matched-edit technique is difficult to achieve and need not be discussed here.) Our three-segment sequence would call for two dissolves.

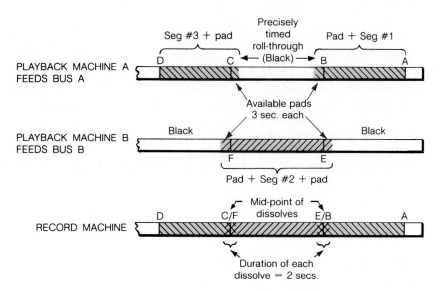

Figure 12-15 Three VTR machines set up for a dissolve edit.

In preparing the *A* and *B* playback videotapes, care must be taken to ensure that every segment and each "roll-through" (black space between segments) is precisely timed—including the exact pads that are wanted. As the two playback tapes are fed into the switcher, the actual dissolve edits (on non-preprogrammed editing units) are accomplished simply by using the fader arms.

Setting up the pre-edit roll periods on the *A* and *B* playback machines for a *B/C* dissolve edit poses no real problem. Note, however, that segment #2 is of such short duration that there is not enough time for the operator to stop and re-cue the *A* roll to get segment #3 in position. The solution to the problem is to have pre-recorded segment #3 on the *A* roll in a precisely timed position so that it will be available just prior to the end of segment #2. After the dissolve to segment #2 then, the *A* tape continues to roll and segment #3 is available for the next dissolve.

If our segments had been at least 2 minutes in length, then there would be time for the operator to locate each upcoming segment and set up the pre-edit roll period. In this situation, markings on the tape or beep tones on the cue track are important to the operator. In any case, the use of *A* and *B* rolls for dissolve edits must of necessity involve a carefully planned pre-edit transfer session just for the preparation of the playback tapes.

12.4 Preproduction Planning

You may ask why material on editing has been presented prior to the sections dealing with single-camera production as a whole. Obviously a project must be planned and shot before it can be edited. For an answer to this question, let us take a brief look at the planning and production sequence itself. In a live or live-on-tape multiple-camera program, the on-the-air editing done by the director provides a time-oriented structure for production operations. This is made possible by an earlier planning stage when camera shots and other insert materials are blocked out in their intended sequence. The editing plan develops as the program comes together.

With single-camera operations a similar process takes place—but in a slightly different sequence. When assembly occurs at a separate and final stage of the production, both planning and camera work must be done with the eventual editing process constantly in mind.

As each separate scene is shot the director must be aware of those shots that will precede and follow it. With the single-camera technique the director has the luxury of shooting several alternatives for a later edit decision. It follows, therefore, that an awareness of the basic concepts of editing is necessary to any understanding of the planning and camera phases of production.

The concepts of pictorial continuity and shot transitions discussed in sections 13.1 and 13.2 also apply to single-camera production.

Crew Structure

There is no longer any doubt about the predominance of the electronic camera in television *news, public affairs,* and *documentary work.* Most of the newer *industrial* and *educational* production houses are totally committed to the all-electronic system. The day when video completely replaces film as the medium for full-length *dramatic* productions lies somewhere in the future. Budgetary considerations have made the all-electronic system attractive to more and more producers of television *commercials.* Therefore, it is imperative that today's television student be familiar with the structure of crew assignments for ENG and EFP production.

The crew structure for this single-camera production work can range anywhere from two to ten or more people—depending upon the budget, union restrictions, and the scope of the assignment. There may be considerable variation in what is actually expected of a person who is functioning within a given job title. Most production groups divide their areas of responsibility into the following job descriptions: (See also chapter 11.)

1. *Producer:* Overall financial and creative responsibility. Makes it possible for everyone else to do their jobs at the highest level of efficiency

2. *Writer/Researcher:* Basic source of background information for graphics and final script
3. *Director:* In charge of studio and/or field production from a creative standpoint. Usually responsible for edited version of project
4. *Production Assistant:* Works directly with either director or producer or both. Keeps production notes, shot log, and other administrative papers. Handles many important details
5. *Camera Operator:* Chief technical person. Usually involved in all technical decisions. Supervises lighting
6. *Sound Operator:* Audio recorder. Technical backup. May do lighting
7. *Editor:* Responsible for final assembly, including a strong creative input

With larger budgets the crew structure will increase. Assistants are added to some of the described positions. Lighting will often require a separate person in any of the more complicated types of production. On the other hand, when the organization is small each person may wear several hats. A small-format or student production group (fig. 12-16) might have the following configuration:

1. *Producer* (also writer/researcher)
2. *Director* (also editor)
3. *Camera Operator* (also editor assistant, maybe lighting)
4. *Production Assistant* (also sound operator, maybe lighting)

As with most task-oriented working groups, an efficient operation must have a clearly established plan for areas of responsibility and authority.

Figure 12-16 This small-format student production crew worked out its own configuration of assignments under the leadership of the producer.

Script Preparation

Principle camera work on a project should only be started after completion of a script or at least a detailed outline of shot continuity. More than one student production team has found that all of those great ideas just seem to disappear into thin air upon arrival at the shooting location. The very act of putting things down on paper is an important test of the feasibility of the operational plan.

Fundamental Elements of the Audio/ Visual Vocabulary. The 3-to-5 minute minidocumentary is a staple of both local and network newscasts. It differs in many ways from the format of the breaking news story and its necessary deadline. With the *minidocs* the production disciplines are more those of background research, balanced presentations, and thorough preproduction planning. Even with a scheduled air date there is lead time to put together all of the essential ingredients. This format borrows much from educational and industrial films and tapes as well as from the traditional film documentaries of the past sixty years. In rather general terms, these are the main production elements that they all share.

1. *Host/Reporter/Narrator.* There is usually a central figure who is used both on- and off-camera to accomplish several important things. This person sets up the basic background information. The audience must initially be made aware of what the presentation is all about and what they

can expect to learn. When the information is complex or has negative connotations, the host/reporter/narrator must be viewed by the audience in an authoritative yet neutral perspective. He or she introduces new segments of information and gives them meaning in terms of what is to come. Ultimately there must be a summary of material presented and a conclusion as to its overall meaning to the audience. This is usually done in the form of a verbal and visual recapitulation of the highlights of material presented. Used properly, the host/reporter/narrator figure lends an important personal element that can give both credibility and continuity to the content.

2. *The Actuality.* News people refer to material that comes directly from an event or situation as an *actuality.* No news story is complete without at least one of two essential ingredients of the actuality: the *scene* itself (the fire in progress, the site of a plane crash, or even the lobby of the bank long after the robbers have fled) or the *interview* (with the citizen eyewitness or some authority figure such as a fire chief or corporate officer). As the very name implies, a documentary—whether for industrial training or for classroom instruction—needs the same sort of device to establish the credibility of the information. Productions designed for instructional purposes often will have the authority figure assume a dominant role. The actuality may be the operator of a certain piece of equipment on location in the factory itself. In medical production, the doctors and nurses may provide the bulk of the information presented.

3. *Titles and Graphics.* It is essential that a production and its subsequent segments be carefully titled. A few well-chosen words that can be quickly read by the audience can be very efficient in establishing the main concept of the production, its location and position in time, and its basic subdivisions. Name and title identifications by supers or keys are crucial. A good deal of other key information can be presented by means of graphic displays—either full frame or keyed over portions of the video. Numerical relationships are very difficult to grasp if they are only heard. They can have a very strong impact when presented on a bar graph or pie chart in which the drawings become a visual analog of the relative value of the numbers. Special effects animation and computer-generated graphics have reduced the time/cost factor that previously limited the use of artwork visuals.

4. *Stock Footage.* When there is no cost-effective way of shooting footage that is essential to a presentation, most professional producers turn to commercial sources. The price is high (a minimum fee of $300 is not uncommon), but those companies that supply stock footage have a large supply of videotape and film to cover a wide variety of situations. News departments that used to discard their old news stories now carefully index and file everything they shoot for possible later use. Students who cannot afford professional help should first examine the resources of their own university. Large companies that turn out numerous public relations films will often allow use of portions of

footage if credits are given. The copyright laws that govern the use of all stock footage are rather strict and should always be observed.

5. *Musical Score.* Music, carefully used, can add an important dimension to almost every kind of visual presentation. Here also there are commercial libraries where one can pay for the use of copyrighted material. The scoring of most professional films and tapes is usually done by production houses that specialize in the selection and editing of a complete musical background for a project. Students, however, can take advantage of the fact that after a specified period, musical recordings and compositions become part of the *public domain* and can be used without charge in most cases. Another interesting possibility stems from the fact that Russia and the United States do not have any reciprocal copyright treaty. Though limited in availability and scope, Russian records can be used freely with legal impunity.

Final Scripting. Taking all of the main production elements into consideration—the host, the actuality scene and interview(s), needed graphics, availability of stock footage, music, and so forth—the producer/director/writer must think in terms of the entire scripting process. Depending upon the complexity and sophistication of the production, several steps may be followed in preparing the final shooting script. A rough draft or outline of the content should certainly be drawn up at the outset. This should include a detailed statement of general and specific objectives for the program. Try to answer the questions: What do I really want to accomplish in this production? What content elements have to be included to meet those objectives?

A series of rough sketches, plotting every camera shot, will serve as a guide both for recording and for editing.

Figure 12-17 Sample of simple storyboard.

Perhaps a storyboard may be essential to your production. Lay out in cartoon or visual outline form what every shot should look like. This will force you to think pictorially and establish visual **continuity** for the entire shoot. These rough sketches, no matter how crude your artistic ability, will help immeasurably in setting up your shots once you are out in the field. It also facilitates determination of precise in-and-out points for your later editing. (See fig. 12-17.)

A final shooting script should indicate all of the important audio elements as well as each camera shot. Every word of an interview segment obviously cannot be written out in advance, but it should be outlined. Important introductions and transitions should be scripted before arriving to set up equipment. Like the major multiple-camera studio production, every hour spent in preproduction planning and scripting will save countless hours of valuable crew time on the shoot. (See chapters 13 and 14.) Careful script preparation and preproduction planning are perhaps the most crucial *disciplines* involved in single-camera production.

Preproduction Location Survey

If at all possible the shooting-day production schedule should be drawn up only after you, as the producer (preferably accompanied by the director and the camera operator), have made a personal inspection of all shooting sites. Draw up a floor plan of the location. Use Polaroid shots of the scene. This is the point at which any difficulties should be worked out— not on the day of production. If A.C. power is to be used, its location must be determined. Are extension cables needed? Is there available access to all locations? If not, who has the keys? What about transportation and parking?

Do scheduled events at the location conflict with the shoot? If the crew is shooting on campus, for example, will the end of a class send large numbers of people walking through the shot? Are there telephones in an office that will ring and interrupt the shot? What about those campus chimes?

Make a comprehensive checklist of everything to be taken care of on the shoot day: an inventory of all equipment (what backup gear should be taken?); all necessary permissions and clearances; and so forth. Do you need to arrange for field maintenance?

Once this information has been added to the planning process, an efficient schedule can be put together. Certain priorities begin to emerge. Since you are shooting out of the eventual program sequence, some of the more flexible shot requirements can be rearranged to fit into an optimum sequence of operations. The wise producer will still build in a few alternatives for the inevitable changes that do occur. If rain is a possibility on the day of an outdoor shoot, then optional locations or alternate shooting days must be available.

12.5 Production and Postproduction Planning

Many of the important elements to be considered in the preplanning and in the location survey also have to be treated in terms of production and postproduction concerns; for example, lighting, camera, and audio problems.

Lighting.   Attention should be given to any potential lighting problems during the advance survey. If available light is to be used then it must be checked with the shooting time of day in mind. A perfect setup for a morning shoot can mean shooting into an impossible glare in later afternoon. Available artificial light can be used as an effective source of fill if it is of the right type and strength. (Fluorescent lighting should be avoided if possible. It casts an unflattering blue tinge to faces and may create a hum or buzz on the sound track.) Enough lighting equipment should be brought to the location to ensure that a basic key light source can be established at the 3200-degree Kelvin minimum. Below this point the picture begins to take on an orange tinge (section 4.2). No amount of later adjustment can restore the proper flesh tones. When the light levels are considerably below minimum base-light standards, the darker areas of the background will produce a dark green effect full of video noise.

Camera.   Most of the newer industrial-type cameras are equipped with a *white balance* control unit that adjusts the strength of the basic video level to suit the light that is available for an individual shot. When this is properly set (with the color control knobs in their respective *fix* positions), the operator can have some confidence in getting a proper color balance. (See fig. 12-18.)

The *f*-stop setting has an important relationship to the balance of the various colors in any picture. A shot with perfectly adjusted colors can be considerably distorted by the

Figure 12-18 A professional camera designed for educational and industrial applications. Note that the white balance and lens controls are all placed for convenient operator access.

change of one or two *f*-stops. This can become a problem when the script calls for the camera to zoom in or out. When the lens zooms in, the focal length of the lens is continually changing. As it becomes a high-magnification lens it allows considerably less light to get to the tube than when it was a wide-angle lens; thus, what had been a proper *f*-stop setting can become an insufficient one. On most of the newer cameras this problem has been solved by an automatic iris control that continually adjusts to the amount of light hitting the tube. If this feature is not available, the operator should rehearse the zoom—checking the resulting picture in order to make a manual *f*-stop adjustment.

The high level of activity and unanticipated problems on any location production occasionally mean that some of the usual equipment precautions may be temporarily forgotten. Cameras, recorders, and tapes are very vulnerable to the careless treatment they may be given on location. The camera operator must take special pains that no one points an open lens toward the sun or other hot light source, for example. The lens should be capped or closed between shots. Shock, moisture, dust, and heat and cold extremes can cause considerable damage to all equipment.

Many types of professional location productions pose enormous engineering challenges for the optimum functioning and protection of cameras and other equipment. Special housings and mountings have to be used for many adverse situations: dust protection in arid country, heaters for Arctic conditions, shock-resistant mountings for rough

Figure 12-19 Underwater camera housing. Special equipment for underwater television coverage, such as this housing for Olympics diving events, represents an extreme in protection against environmental elements. (Photo courtesy of ABC Sports)

terrain chase sequences, gyroscopic mountings for helicopter shots, and underwater housings for perhaps the most adverse environment of all. (See fig. 12-19.)

Audio. The sound operator must be alert to a number of special location problems. For example, background noise—which to the human ear might seem to be at the proper level—can be exaggerated by the mike and interfere with spoken dialogue. A good set of earphones and careful attention to the quality of sound being recorded can do much to prevent any such problem. The operator must also be careful to keep the sound levels of all recorded materials within a consistent range so that they will match when edited. Use of the automatic gain control (AGC) is not always the solution to this problem. Actually, AGC can be the cause of another serious audio problem encountered with outdoor audio.

When no one is speaking, the sound level of the background is automatically amplified producing a hissing or roaring effect. Because there is a built-in delay factor of 1 second or so, the effect is most noticeable at the beginning of segments or during long pauses. Attempts to erase this unwanted sound involve risk of upcutting program audio. One solution may be to have the announcer say a few words up until 2 seconds prior to program sound.

During camera production, the director should be thinking of the audio as well as the video aspects of the editing job to come. Will there be a need for a *wildtrack* (separately recorded sound from any of the location shots)? For example, a narrator may be standing next to a machine that is important to the story line and that has a distinctive sound. In the final program, shots that include the machine are to have a voice-over narration, which is to be recorded later in the studio. If the director

PRODUCTION Campus Parking
SHOOTING DATE 8 Nov

PAGE 2
PRODUCER Evans

Slate	Count In	Count Out
Univ. Sec. Off. Seg 3 Shot 4 Take 3	Lt. Jones. 253 "My Job	270... this problem."
Sec. Off. Intro. Meyer Seg 3 Shot 1 Tk 1	275 "Lt. Jones ...	287... no parking."
———————— Cassette #2 ————————		
Parking Lot student #1 Seg 4 Shot 1 Tk 1	025 "Well everyday....	037... no spaces."
Parking lot student #1 Seg 4 Shot 1 Tk 2	045 "Everday....	051... really mad."
Parking lot student #2 Seg 4 Shot 2 Tk 1	059 "I don't see	071 ... parking ticket."

Figure 12-20 Excerpt from sample production log.

wants to have the sound of the machine as a part of the background under the narration, then it must be recorded for a later audio mix. Good sound operators will make a practice of recording numerous pieces of wildtrack sound as protection against unforeseen editing problems.

The Production Log

The importance of keeping an accurate record of production activities cannot be overemphasized. Important details that seem unforgettable at the moment somehow fade from memory at the end of a long, hard day. The log is also an important way of keeping the production day organized. It should be used for essential information in brief form. (See fig. 12-20.) Additional notes should be written on the shooting script or attached to it. All of this information together becomes the script for the editing process.

It should be kept in mind that footage or revolution counter numbers derived from the portable camera equipment may not be compatible with the counting system found on the studio editing equipment. An important part of the pre-edit session may have to be devoted to translating the one set of numbers to the format that is usable during the editing sessions.

The Postproduction Editing Process

To most people, the term *postproduction* is used to define all of those production efforts that take place after the field or studio camera work has been completed. It is important to note, however, that in many situations postproduction ("post") work can efficiently dovetail with the final phase of camera work. It makes a lot of sense, for example, to at least start working on such things as setting up titles and credits on the character generator. Other graphics, along with stock (file) footage, can be set up and prepared for more efficient utilization. Much important audio editing can be profitably accomplished before postproduction is totally underway.

As all professional producers know, this process of "getting into" the final phase of postproduction is a crucial time. Much of the strength—and discipline—of a good producer is an ability to generate the sense of momentum and enthusiasm that is needed to complete a production. In live television, the relentless clock focuses our attention. In single-camera postproduction, the constant pressure of a knowledgeable guiding hand is needed.

It may be difficult to understand the time frame that is necessary for the editing process; an inexperienced crew may initially waste a considerable amount of energy and effort. Usually, this phase passes as crew members become more efficient at their assigned responsibilities and the leadership and organization become more evident—just as they did during the shooting process.

Although many professional editing sessions involve only the producer or the director working in conjunction with the editor (or even the editor working alone with only a detailed set of notes), student postproduction sessions should, as much as possible, become a learning process for the entire team. Without proper organization, however, this process can drift into noisy chaos. The important thing is that there has to be someone who is acknowledged as being definitely "in charge." This may be the producer, the director, or the editor; but it should be the same person who has initiated the pre-edit session and established the basic structure of the project.

Editing sessions, which can last for hours, should be set up so that while the person operating the edit control unit is executing each transfer/edit, a second person or team is finalizing the next edit decision—locating the precise reel number, footage/revolution counter number, and exact word cue for the inpoint and outpoint. (See fig. 12-21.) Of course, much of the efficiency of the editing session will depend upon how much preparation—viewing and planning—has gone into the pre-editing process.

As stressed in the opening chapter (section 1.2), in all types of team-oriented video production it is the "people" part of the work that is at once the most rewarding and at the same time the most difficult aspect of putting a program together. As with professional situations, each new project with each new crew means a whole new process of each member fitting into the team. This personal interaction is never easy because personal needs and ego seem to keep getting in the way of the larger group project. But the discipline required and the ability to cope with these difficulties are the signs of the true professional.

Audio Editing. High-quality audio work in a video production all too often goes unappreciated. We are diverted by the flow of the picture images. But poor audio can quickly destroy the impact of a well-executed visual sequence. A good sound track is the result of the all-important *mixing* process (section 2.2.3). The average TV commercial, documentary, or top-flight industrial production has a final sound track that is the result of the skilled mixing together of anywhere from sixteen to thirty-two separate sound tracks onto the final **mix track**.[2]

Audio training facilities for most colleges and universities do not approach this level of sophistication. Additionally, many TV production students have not had the opportunity for a substantial course in audio production. Therefore, it is all the more important that the planning for the sound track must start with the very first planning of the shape of the project. The director and the producer should question each other continually as to the exact

2. Some professional music recording sessions will use in excess of 100 different tracks. Quincy Jones, for example, has used over 200 in some sessions! This involves several *slave* tapes (up to 24 tracks each) that are premixed before the final mixing session. Some audio consoles, however, can handle more than 50 inputs for a single mixing session.

Figure 12-21 For students, a two-person editing team can be a very efficient way to work. Many professionals, however, prefer to work alone whenever possible.

details of how each sound or combination of sounds (announcer, on-camera narrator, voice-over studio narrator, background noise, music, special sound effects, and so forth) is to be achieved. One often hears the phrase, "We'll fix it in post . . ." This is an invitation to audio disaster. If you have not thoroughly thought out the procedure during preproduction planning, it is often too late to fix it in postproduction.

In order to facilitate careful preproduction planning, the following cautionary suggestions are offered:

1. Avoid a production concept that calls for the mixing of music and/or sound effects with the words of an *on-camera* announcer. Once the voice track has been recorded in sync with the picture, it is difficult to mix it with additional sound unless some specialized equipment can be utilized. Instead, the benefits of music and sound effects can be mixed with *off-camera* narrative sequences, which can be more easily handled.

2. Avoid staging an on-camera announcer segment when background sound (traffic, equipment, music) will also be picked up on the sound track. As the various segments are edited into the program sequence, the disruption of the original continuity of the sound produces a "choppy" interrupted effect. If background sound is unavoidable (and, indeed, may even

be desirable for authenticity), one solution—if you have the audio equipment—is to utilize a **wildtrack** mixing procedure. Have the announcer work as closely to the microphone as practical (thus cutting out as much background sound as possible); then record a long sequence of the background sound or music on a separate track. In postproduction, you can then mix this continuous sound from the *wildtrack* with the announcer's voice at a level that will pretty well mask the discontinuous background audio picked by the announcer's mike. (This process works best when mixing machine or traffic noise, rather than music.)

3. Avoid the "two-track" solution in solving the problems of achieving a final audio mix. More than one student production has ended up with all spoken dialogue on one audio track and all music and sound effects on the second track. The plan usually calls for one more **dubbing** (duplicating) session during which the two tracks will be mixed into one final master track. Unfortunately, this means an additional generation loss of the video information. *If* all segments in the first edited master are of high quality, and *if* the dubbing facilities are all of top-of-the-line quality, then this two-track solution may be a suitable technique—but it should be approached with extreme caution.

There are situations, however, in which the two audio tracks of the videotape can be utilized without going through an additional video generation. Let's use the example of the wildtrack sound of a piece of machinery that is to be combined with the studio-recorded voice of the off-camera narrator. Using the studio facilities, these two sources are put together in

an audio *mix track* on a separate videotape work cassette. Now the editor has two working options. He or she can first assemble-edit the video for the sequence and then later do an audio-only dub to match it; or the mixed audio track can be transferred to the master tape as an audio-only track with the video added afterwards and edited to match the finished audio track.

Laying down an audio track and then editing video to it (the second approach) is often used when a picture montage is being matched to a particular piece of music. With this method, video shots can be edited to cut precisely with the rhythm of the music.

Once these and similar techniques have been worked out, the editing can proceed with maximum efficiency. Even after sufficient testing to check machine operation, the first few edits should be carefully checked. Audio, video, and control track levels should be continually monitored in order to provide consistent levels throughout the editing process. This is of special importance when editing takes place over a period of several days.

Summary

During the last few years the development of smaller, high-quality cameras and portable VTR recorders—and the evolution of sophisticated computer-based editing equipment—has resulted in a new era of *single-camera* or EFP (electronic field production) techniques.

Postproduction electronic editing processes allow TV producers to use videotape the same way that filmmakers have been using celluloid film for decades—shooting single-camera scenes out of sequence, setting up for each separate shot, and shooting retakes as needed. Another technique that has evolved is the *multiple-camera/recorder* method in which each of three or four cameras covering a continuous peformance is recorded as an *isolated camera* on its individual VTR for later editing decisions.

Preproduction editing of material to be inserted into live (or live-on-tape) programs evolved from ENG (electronic news gathering) techniques pioneered in the mid-1970s. Prevalent throughout commercial broadcasting, these methods also permeate educational and corporate video technologies today.

Electronic editing is based upon the *electronic transfer* of audio and video information from the original master to a second, edited videotape. *Assemble editing* consists of adding desired shots in the proper sequence on the edited tape—joining the head of one segment to the tail of the preceding segment. *Insert editing* involves dropping in a video segment to replace previously recorded material.

With newer *electronic editors*—using microprocessors, the SMPTE time code, joystick or search-dial frame locators, and precise synchronization—it is possible to set up an edit decision, preview the moving edit, and then execute the edit with single-field ($\frac{1}{60}$-second) accuracy. *Dissolves* and other *special effects* in editing can be accomplished by tying in the editor with a switcher or SEG.

Preproduction planning for single-camera location shooting, which involves crews of anywhere from two to ten persons, is as crucial as planning for multiple-camera studio productions. Script preparation must include consideration of elements such as the *host/reporter/narrator*, *actuality* scenes and interviews, *graphics, stock footage,* and *music.* Scripting stages encompass setting forth precise *objectives,* drawing up a *storyboard,* and compiling a *final shooting script.*

Production and postproduction considerations include special problems concerned with *lighting, cameras,* and *audio.* The *production log* is a crucial record of all production-day activities—especially the length and location of all actual recorded segments. The *postproduction edit sequence* requires considerable preplanning and coordination—especially with any special *audio dubbing and mixing.*

In chapter 13, we will look more particularly at the specific principles of editing continuity, camera patterns, and scripting that the director must be concerned with—both for multiple-camera studio work and for single-camera productions.

12.6 Training Exercises

The first exercise is an individual assignment that should be carried out by each member of the class. The second exercise is a class project that should involve everyone in the decision-making steps required.

1. Plan a simple, single-camera location production. Start with a precise statement of objectives, draw a simple storyboard, and write a final shooting script. Prepare a checklist of the items that you would want to include on your preproduction location survey.

2. As a class, record the segments necessary for editing a simple, single-camera location actuality. In the chapter (starting with fig. 12-5), we pointed out that EFP productions are seldom shot in the order in which they will eventually be edited. Most remote productions follow established filmic tradition in that all shots in a particular setting, using the same talent, are recorded at one time—almost always out of

sequence with respect to the final edited program. In this exercise let us assume that we want to shoot the interview segment first; then the opening and closing statements by the host/narrator are to be recorded (once we know what the interview consists of); and finally the silent insert segment of the item being discussed will be shot. Thus, the four segments should be shot in the following order:

a. A field interview with a simulated expert on any subject chosen—furniture making, automotive repair, pottery, or any other topic (segment #2)

b. An opening statement or introduction by a host/narrator (segment #1)

c. A summary by the host/narrator (segment #3)

d. An *insert shot* (silent) of the item being discussed in the interview—table, carburetor, or vase (segment #2A)

Assemble edit the first three segments together, in the proper sequence, following all due considerations of visual and audio continuity. *Insert edit* the insert shot into the appropriate spot in the interview.

Directing Your First Studio Production

13

This chapter and chapter 14 are designed to introduce you to some of the concepts and techniques that are needed in directing your first television production—principles of picture continuity, use of camera transitions, simple camera patterns, scripting formats, preproduction planning, rehearsal techniques, and control room disciplines. This is not designed as a complete text on television directing. It would take a much more voluminous work to present you with an understanding of the many facets of directing different kinds of television productions. It is recognized, however, that many introductory production courses will involve you, as a student, in directing some basic programs. These two chapters, therefore, present several production exercises and examples of different kinds of production formats.

Although written from the perspective of studio production, most of the pictorial and editing concepts discussed in this chapter apply both to multi-camera studio programs and to single-camera productions, as introduced in chapter 12. Whether one is cutting between multiple cameras "live" (editing on the switcher in real-time) or shooting with a single camera in the field (planning on editing during the postproduction process), the principles of picture continuity (section 13.1) and transitions (section 13.2) are virtually the same.

13.1 Principles of Picture Continuity

Early filmmakers quickly came to the conclusion that when one picture is immediately replaced by another, an interaction occurs in the mind of the viewer that communicates something more than if each picture were viewed separately. This intriguing concept obviously can have direct bearing on the process of shot

Figure 13-1 Comparison of wide shot and close-up. Whether in a drama, variety show, or panel discussion, the same need exists to balance wide shots (*left*) with close-ups (*right*).

selection for any television program. Each shot must be thought of as being part of a flow of images, each with a relationship to the one that precedes it and the one that follows it.

Wide Shots and Close-Ups

The succession of pictures should be motivated by the basic tenet, "Give the viewers what they need to see when they need to see it." To a great extent this is determined by a juxtaposition of **collective** shots establishing the whole picture—showing the relationship of all elements in the scene—and of intimate **particularized** shots—giving the viewers the closer details they want. The generalities of a scene or program situation are established by the *wide shot* or collective *cover shot*. Then the director cuts or dissolves to a series of medium or particularized *close-up shots* to examine the specific facets of that situation. (See fig. 13-1.) As the events of the program progress, the director again establishes the broader aspects of the program (with wide shots), and then provides another series of detailed particulars (with close-ups).

Even with the opportunity to preplan or *block out* the camera work, television's ongoing production technique forces the director to make some rather quick, on-the-air editing decisions. A basic challenge is to always have

the proper camera ready for a shot at the exact moment the situation calls for it. On the part of the director, this requires an ability to be able to think simultaneously on at least two levels—what is on the air and what is going to be on the air.

With a three-camera structure, the thinking process might work something like this: Camera 1 is on the air. You, as director, have the choice of using camera 2 or 3 for the next shot. Camera 3, however, has just been used on the previous shot. Camera 2, therefore, has more time to make a framing adjustment or even a change of position. (See fig. 13-2.)

By using the commands of preparation and execution properly (section 7.5), you can select the next camera to be used, allowing sufficient lead time to set the next shot.

It is accepted studio procedure in a three-camera setup to place camera 1 on the left, camera 2 in the middle, and camera 3 on the right. This setup allows you to keep track easily of the relative positions of cameras on the floor and the angle of shots available to them.

Obviously, cameras usually are not employed in a repeated 1-2-3-1-2-3 rotation. In order to observe the wide-shot and close-up shot requirements of any program, at least one of the three cameras at any given time will usually be designated as a wide-angle *cover shot* camera. This is especially important in

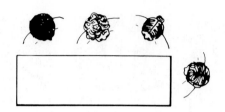

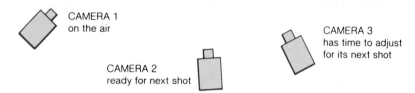

CAMERA 1
on the air

CAMERA 2
ready for next shot

CAMERA 3
has time to adjust
for its next shot

In this illustration, the director has just used camera 3 (before taking camera 1); therefore, camera 2 will probably have more time to get the next shot lined up.

Figure 13-2 Sequence of camera shots.

shooting unrehearsed programs such as panel discussions when there are sudden changes of the individuals talking. The technique on such a program is to cut to a wide shot on the change of voice if a close-up of the new person is not immediately available. You then have a chance to ascertain who is talking and call for the close-up. The most glaring error on any kind of television is for an unprepared director to be caught with a speaker or performer still on camera when that person is no longer speaking or performing.

In a rehearsed program, when the camera blocking has been worked out in advance, you can temporarily commit all cameras to close-up shots, having planned to return to a cover shot at a later specific time. Generally, however, the wide-angle and close-up shot balance requirements are such that at least one camera is always kept on a cover shot.

Shot Relationships

When changing from one shot to another the two pictures should relate to each other in both an informational and aesthetic setting. For example, the subject in two successive shots should be readily recognizable. As director, you would not want to cut to such a different angle that the viewer would not immediately recognize the subject from the previous shot.

Jump Cuts. On the one hand, for aesthetic reasons, you should avoid taking or dissolving between cameras that have almost exactly the same or matching shots. The result will be that the scene remains essentially the same, but the picture jumps slightly within the frame. On unrehearsed shows, the camera operators may inadvertently come up with almost identical shots, so that it is up to the director to watch carefully for this **jump-cutting** on the control room monitors.

Top: In this example, the cut from the long shot to the tight close-up is jarring to the viewer. For a normal transition, the director should cut to a shot that is no more than three times the size (larger or smaller) of the preceding shot.

Bottom: In this instance, the director has cut to an intermediate medium shot before going in for the close-up. The transition is much easier for the viewer to accept.

Figure 13-3 Three-to-one cutting ratio.

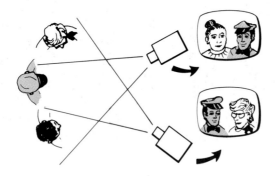

With both cameras shooting a standard two-shot, the central talent (Mr. "B") appears to jump from one side of the screen to the other as we take between the two shots.

Figure 13-4 Subject jumping positions.

Cutting Ratio.   On the other hand, you should avoid going from one shot to another if there is too much difference in size between views of the same subject. Taking from a long shot to a tight close-up can be quite jarring to the viewer. (See fig. 13-3.) One good rule to follow is that you should always keep your camera cuts within a 3-to-1 **cutting ratio.** That is, do not take to a shot that is three times larger or three times smaller than the preceding shot.

Position Jumps.   Another problem to avoid is that of having a primary subject jump from one spot on the screen to another position in the next shot. This can occur, for example, if three people are lined up facing two cameras and each camera is getting a two-shot of two adjacent persons. The center person will be on the left of one picture and on the right side of the other camera's picture. (See fig. 13-4.) This position jump can be avoided by having one camera go to a three-shot before cutting or, conversely, by cutting to a close-up single shot.

These related principles of shot relationships apply to single-camera productions as well as to studio productions. Of course, the principles are much easier to apply and control in the studio than in the field. When you are looking at three camera monitors side by side in the control room, it should be a simple matter to make sure that successive shots will not result in a jump cut, exaggerated cutting ratio, or position jump. In the field, however, with a single camera, you do not have the luxury of comparing shots side by side; you must shoot your pictures one at a time—recalling what the previous shot looked like. Then it is much easier to make a mistake and shoot several successive shots that, when edited to-

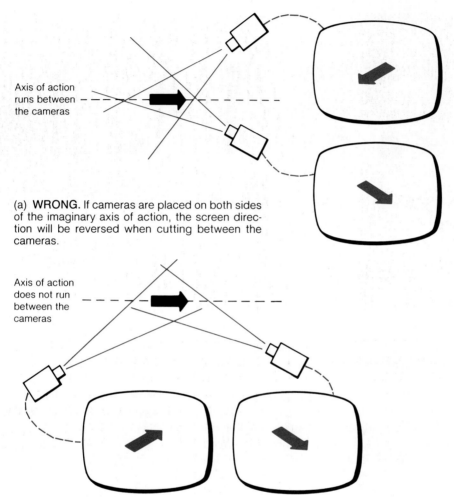

(a) **WRONG.** If cameras are placed on both sides of the imaginary axis of action, the screen direction will be reversed when cutting between the cameras.

Axis of action runs between the cameras

Axis of action does not run between the cameras

(b) **CORRECT.** When both cameras are on the same side of the axis of action, they will both perceive the action moving in the same direction.

Figure 13-5 Axis of action.

gether later, will violate these principles. This underscores the importance of very careful preplanning (section 12.4) for all single-camera productions.

Axis of Action/Conversation

Another basic principle of continuity involves *screen direction*. In successive shots you will want to make certain that all action is flowing in the same direction and that each screen character is facing in one consistent direction. The **axis of action** is an imaginary line extending the path in which a character is moving. As long as all cameras are placed on the same side of this axis, the action will continue to flow in the same direction. If cameras are placed on both sides of this axis of action, however, the apparent screen direction will be reversed when cutting between the cameras. (See fig. 13-5.) Directors, therefore, always try

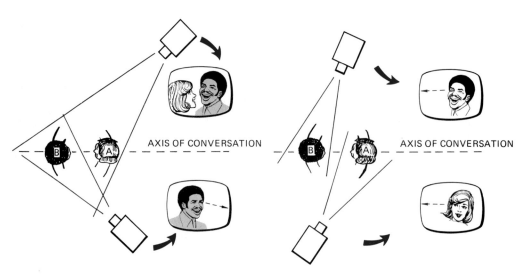

AXIS OF CONVERSATION

AXIS OF CONVERSATION

Figure 13-6 Axis of conversation.

In the left illustration, Actor B changes screen direction as we cut from one camera to the other. In the right illustration, both actors appear to be looking in the same direction, making it difficult for the viewer to establish the relationship between the two.

to avoid having cameras cross the line. It is for this reason that all cameras covering a football game or a basketball game must be placed on the same side of the field of action.

Closely related to the axis of action is the **axis of conversation.** If the imaginary axis is drawn through two persons facing each other, all cameras should be kept on the same side of this line. Otherwise the screen direction (the direction in which a person is looking) will be reversed when you cut to the other side of the line. This imaginary line—the axis of conversation—will shift, of course, as performers move. Figure 13-6 shows two common errors in crossing the axis of conversation.

As with the discussion of shot relationships, these principles of "not crossing the axis" apply to single-camera productions as well as to studio productions. Again, in a multiple-camera studio production it is a fairly routine job to make sure that all action is flowing in the same direction or that two persons in a

conversation are looking at each other. You physically keep all cameras on the same side of the axis. When shooting on location, it is much easier to inadvertently "cross the axis" when you have just one camera operator moving around and setting up for each individual shot. Again, this emphasizes the necessity of thorough preproduction planning.

Other Principles of Continuity

All of these generalizations and principles have to be interpreted with flexibility. There are occasions when the experienced director will deliberately break some of the principles in order to create a certain effect—to disorient the audience intentionally, for aesthetic shock value, or for exceptional dramatic impact. Keep in mind, however, that before departing from any such guidelines you should have first gained a good understanding of the reasons for the rules.

The same can be said for the following four additional principles in planning picture continuity. (And, again, keep in mind that these rules apply to single-camera productions as well as to multiple-camera programs.)

1. *Plan the camera sequence as a whole.* Every program or sequence within a program has a beginning, a middle, and an end. Design the image flow to capture the structural form of the performance or event, utilizing the collective and particularized perspectives.
2. *Follow the action.* Be sure that a motivating action or a movement is picked up by the camera as it occurs. Nothing destroys the flow of ideas and images more than late camera work. The thought process of the entire crew must be such that it anticipates the progression of events in the program.
3. *Choose camera work appropriate to the program situation.* Match the shot to the performance or action. A close-up shot denotes intimacy and personal expression. Extreme wide shots express a quality of "bigness" or importance. A superimposition serves to intensify further whatever is being expressed by the component images.
4. *Observe a consistency of style and pace.* Different types of programs require different types of camera work, ranging from the subjective artistic to the reportorial pragmatic. Similarly, there is often a pattern to the frequency of camera changes that stems from the program sequence itself. An effective series of fast camera cuts can lose its intensity if, for no motivated reason, a dissolve is suddenly used.

The essence of all television is movement, either physical or psychological or both. Pictorial composition and sequence flow must be designed to interact in such a way that they not only capture accurately, but also enhance further, the events of the production sequence. The skill necessary for effective camera work requires both study and practice as well as a great amount of judgment on the part of both the camera operator and the director.

13.2 Continuity and Transitions

Picture continuity refers to the sequential relationship of successive screen images. The mechanics of continuity are carried out by the actual camera transitions—the manner in which you change from one picture to another. This can be effected in several different ways. You need to be aware of the how, when, and why of camera transitions.

Types of Camera Transitions

Without getting into computer-based SEG devices, there are essentially five different transitional methods for going from one camera to another. You must be aware of the psychological and grammatical impact of each and when to use one and when to use another. These transitions can be accomplished in postproduction editing as well as with the switcher during a multiple-camera studio production.

The Take. The instantaneous *cut* or straight take replaces one picture immediately with another. It implies that there is no change in time or locale. It happens right then. The audience is not moved anywhere, except to a different perspective of the same scene. The shots relate directly to each other as far as time and space are concerned. It is the basic transition device, which audiences have accepted since the beginning of the motion picture film, for changing a point of view without making any major dramatic change. In terms of grammar, the take is the end of one sentence and the beginning of a new sentence.

The Dissolve. The dissolve, the simultaneous fading out of one picture and the fading in of another picture, creates a temporary overlapping of images. Dramatically, this implies a change of *place* or a change in *time* (usually a lapse of time). It shows a relationship with the previous shot, but there has been a change; the audience has been moved somewhere else or somewhere later in time. Grammatically, the dissolve corresponds to the end of a paragraph or possibly even to the end of a major section of a chapter. In nondramatic television, the dissolve often is used purely for aesthetic reasons—a slow dissolve of a singer from a medium to a tight close-up profile, or a close-up of the dancer's feet dissolving to a long shot of the dancer. No change in time or locale is implied in this case—the dissolve is just a pleasant visual effect. In musical productions, the dissolve can be used as an artistic connecting or relating transition, whereas it has the opposite effect in dramas.

The Fade. A fade from a camera to black or a fade up from black implies a very strong separation. It is used in going from one segment of a program to another—from the juggling act to the used-car commercial. Dramatically, the fade is the curtain falling—the end of a scene or an act. Grammatically, it would be the visual counterpart of the end of a chapter or of the story.

The Defocus. One specialized transition that can be used with no fancy electronic effects is the **defocus;** the camera on the air defocuses and dissolves to a similarly defocused

shot on another camera, which then comes back into focus. This is a specialized form of dissolve that has very strong overtones. It usually implies either a deranged state of mind or a transition *backward* in time. It tends, as do other specialized transitions, to call attention to itself and must be used very sparingly.

The Wipe. Wiping one picture off the face of the screen and replacing it with another is a highly stylized method of going from one camera to another. As with other electronic transitions—the circle wipe, the starbursts—the straight-edged wipe has to be used very cautiously. It has no special grammatical significance except, perhaps, as an exclamation—"Isn't this a fancy transition!"

Timing of the Transition

Describing the different types of transitions helps to explain the *how* and the *why* of changing cameras, but a word needs to be said about the *when*. Generally, camera changes must be adequately motivated; there has to be some reason for cutting at a particular point. The audience should want to see something else. ("Give the viewers what they need to see when they need to see it.") Unless the viewer feels the need for a change of camera, there probably is no reason to cut. Without proper motivation, you should avoid the temptation to change the picture just for the sake of change.

All of the following discussion on the timing of camera transitions applies equally to the timing of editing shots in the postproduction process for single-camera production.

Cutting on Action. One of the strongest motivations for cutting is to capture action. When the action starts, you need a wider view. When the talent walks to a new area, you need an establishing shot. When cutting on action, you should always try to cut *just prior to the* *action*—not too long before it and not immediately after it. Ideally, as soon as the action starts, the audience needs to see the wider shot.

Cutting on Dialogue.

During an interview or panel program, the strongest motivation for cutting is when a speaker *starts to talk*. The audience wants to see who is talking. The ideal timing of the take is precisely between one speaker and the next speaker—not 3 seconds after the next speaker has started. As a practical matter, cutting during an ad-lib discussion program will usually involve a delay of 1 second or so. To counteract this, you have to be sensitive to the body language and facial expressions of all the participants (watching his or her off-the-air camera monitors). Who has his mouth open? Who has her eyebrows raised? Who just leaned forward? Who just took a deep breath? Anticipate who the next speaker is going to be.

Cutting on Reaction.

Include appropriate—judiciously spaced—reaction shots. How are the listeners reacting? Which listener is especially animated? In timing reaction shots, *do not* cut at the end of an obvious statement or during a break in the speaking; it will look too much like a cut to the wrong participant. Reaction shots are most effective in the middle of a speech.

Cutting on the Beat.

During musical numbers, time your cuts to fit the music. The cuts should be crisp and clean, following a regular rhythmical pattern—cutting every four bars or eight bars—as the music dictates. (In slower tempos, purely for an aesthetic "feel," dissolves may be effective transitions.) See section 14.2 for an extended demonstration of camera usage during a musical number.

Cutting with Movement.

Generally, do not cut from a moving camera to a stationary camera. If the camera is panning a shot or zooming in or out, wait until it stops to take

to another stationary camera; and vice versa, do not cut from a static shot to a moving camera. The effect is somewhat jolting to the viewer. It can be effective, however, to take or dissolve from a moving camera to another camera panning or zooming in the same direction—assuming there is a continuity in subject and tempo.

As with the rules given under "Principles of Picture Continuity," these guidelines can be interpreted in a flexible manner if you know what effect you are after. Exceptions can be made to the basic rules once the rules are mastered.

13.3 Basic Camera Patterns

In setting up the **camera pattern** for a studio production or blocking (positioning) the cameras for a scene, there are several principles to keep in mind. As contrasted with the several considerations discussed so far in this chapter, these following principles apply only to multiple-camera productions—situations in which you have to be concerned with the placement and movement of several cameras simultaneously.

1. *Cross the camera angles.* In most staging setups, the natural pattern will have two people facing each other or a person facing a graphic or demonstrating an object. Shooting this situation with two cameras you can get the best head-on shots by having the cameras shoot across each other's angles; that is, each camera should be shooting the person or object farthest away from that camera. The camera on the right should be getting the shot of the person on the camera left and vice versa. (See figs. 10-1 and 13-7.)
2. *Start blocking in the center of the program.* Pick the most crucial or difficult part of the production and figure out your camera pattern for that segment first. Once you know how that

Easel (TC)

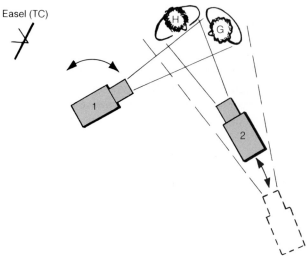

Camera 1: Title card (TC).
Camera 2: Single-shot (MS or CU) of host. Dolly back or zoom back to two-shot as guest is mentioned.
Camera 1: CU of guest (for the introduction) and CU of guest and two-shots favoring guest (during interview).
Camera 2: CU of host and two-shots favoring host (during interview). Dolly in or zoom in to single of host at end of interview.
Camera 1: Closing credits and title card.

Figure 13-7 Camera pattern for simple interview.

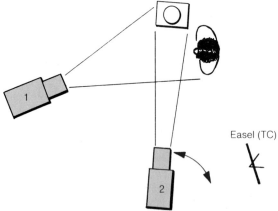

Easel (TC)

Camera 2: Title card (TC).
Camera 1: Single-shot (MS or CU) of talent. Dolly back or zoom back to include object to be demonstrated.
Camera 2: CU of object.
Camera 1: Two-shot of talent and object. Optional dolly in or zoom in to single of talent.
Camera 2: Closing credits and title card (TC).

Figure 13-8 Camera pattern for simple demonstration.

segment has to be blocked, you can figure backward to see how you will want to work your way up to that position. Continuing to work backward, you will be able to determine how you want to set up your cameras for the beginning of the program.

3. *Select the easel positions last.* As a corollary to principle 2, you should not figure out where you will place your graphics stands until all of the crucial camera blocking has been taken care of. Once you know how the whole production is set up, you can best figure out the most convenient spot to place the easels. Too many beginning directors start by positioning the opening title card first, and then work their way into a bind from there.

Starting with these simple principles, let us see how some simple camera patterns could be worked out for a few basic formats.

Simple Interview

Following the principles outlined before, a two-person interview can be staged as indicated in figure 13-7. With the host seated on the left and the guest on the right, cameras 1 and 2 will cross angles so that camera 2 will get the basic shot of the host (and an over-the-shoulder two-shot favoring the host) and camera 1 will get the basic shots favoring the guest. Assuming that camera 2, on the host, will be the first camera shot in the body of the program, this means that camera 1 is free to get the opening title card (before breaking to the basic shot of the guest). Until you decide on the camera pattern in the body of the show, however, you will not know which camera will be free to get the title card.

Simple Demonstration

The same basic pattern holds true for a simple demonstration program. Figure 13-8 indicates how a demonstration sequence may be set up.

In this case, working from the body of the program you may determine that the host, being right-handed, would like to work with the object to be demonstrated on his right side so that he can hold the object in his right hand. Crossing angles, camera 1 will therefore get the basic head-on shot of the talent (and a two-shot of the host and object) while camera 2 will get the close-ups of the object. (Note the similarity to fig. 10-1.) This means that camera 2 will be the one that will be free for the opening title card.

Note that the camera pattern illustrated in figure 13-8 can be used for a graphics sequence in which the talent is working with an on-set graphic. In this case, the pattern is set up for a left-handed host; the easel is positioned on his right side in order to enable him to turn in towards the graphic and work with his left hand to gesture, point, or write on the graphic. It is most comfortable for a right-handed talent to work with the graphic positioned on his or her left.

Demonstration-Lecture with Graphics

Following the same basic principles, let us see how a slightly more complicated camera pattern may be worked out. The talent is going to start by talking directly to camera with nothing else in the shot (position *A*). She will then walk over to her right to demonstrate an object (position *B*). Then she will cross back to a graphics stand to go through some on-set graphics (position *C*); she is right-handed so you will want the graphics stand to be on her left side. The basic title cards are on slides to be projected from telecine (camera 4), but there are super cards to be used at both the open and the close.

Where do you begin to block out the camera pattern? (See fig. 13-9.) The most crucial position will probably be at the graphics stand (position *C*); begin there. You will want camera 2 to get the cover shot of the talent, with camera 1 crossing angles to get the close-up of the graphics. This means that camera 2 will probably be the best camera to pan across with the talent on her move from position *B* to *C*. Working backward at position *B*, you therefore want camera 1 on the basic head-on shot of the talent at position *B;* this means that camera 2, which is in the best location for the close-ups of the object, will have time to zoom wide for the walk-over shot from position *B* to *C*. (Camera 2 is the best camera for the walking shot because it is a stronger move to have the talent walking toward the camera; she is walking away from camera 1.)

Camera 1 will be the best camera for the walk-over shot from position *A* to *B*. (First, this will give camera 2 time to get prepared on the close-up of the object, and second—as mentioned before—it is a stronger move to have the talent walking toward the camera.) Working your way backward to the opening shots, you therefore see that camera 2 is the best camera for the opening shot of the talent at position *A* (you want to be able to take to camera 1 on the beginning of the action/walk-over shot to position *B*). Thus, camera 1 will get the opening super cards on an off-set easel placed to the camera left of the set (the easel stand is placed last). Camera 1 will also be free to get the closing super cards; since camera 1 will be positioned on easel #2 (for the on-set graphics sequence in position *C*), camera 1 can get the closing super cards on easel #2.

Although the explanation may seem complicated at first, if you read through it carefully, checking the illustration in figure 13-9, you should be able to see how all of the principles mentioned at the beginning of this section apply.

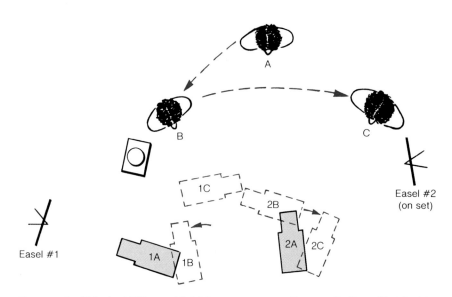

Camera 4: (Telecine) Title card (slide).
Camera 1: Super cards, easel #1, position A.
Camera 2: Single of talent, position A.
Camera 1: Pan with talent to position B. Cover shot, position B.
Camera 2: CU object, position B.
Camera 1: Two-shot, talent and object, position B.

Camera 2: Pan with talent to position C. Two-shot (cover shot), talent and easel #2.
Camera 1: CU graphics (easel #2), position C.
Camera 2: Closing shot, talent, position C.
Camera 4: Title card (slide).
Camera 1: Super cards, easel #2.

Figure 13-9 Camera pattern for demonstration-lecture with graphics.

13.4 The Television Script

The television script is the basic working document of the TV director. Everything starts with the script, and the beginning director must learn how to interpret it, break it down, and how to mark it for use during the actual production.

Scripting Formats

Basically, there are three different script forms that the director might have to work with: the *fully scripted program;* the *outline,* or *semi-scripted program;* and the *show format,* or *rundown sheet.*

The Fully Scripted Program. Programs that are likely to be fully scripted include dramatic programs, newscasts, documentaries, commercials, station breaks, editorials, some talk programs such as political broadcasts, and similar productions where it is important that every single word and picture element be precisely controlled. Section 14.3 is an example of one kind of dramatic script format (appendix D-4). Section 14.4 is an example of the fully scripted station break and promotional copy (appendix D-5).

Although there are exceptions, scripts generally are constructed in vertical columns, with one column (usually the right-hand side) for audio and another column for video. On some scripts, the video column will be written in (section 13.5), and in other formats the video column will be left blank for the director to fill in. Some formats (see figs. 13-10 and 13-12) will have both the audio and video integrated into one column, with the other column left open for the director to use for markings.

(This column is left blank for the director's notes.)

GRAPHIC: STREET SCENE

<u>MUSIC</u>: THEME, ESTABLISH, AND UNDER

<u>ANNC</u> (OFF CAMERA): Good morning, and welcome to . . .

SUPER CARD (OVER "STREET SCENE"): "LIVE"

<u>ANNC</u>: "Live," . . . a penetrating look at some

   of the issues and controversies surrounding the

   American scene. This fast-paced discussion

   is brought to you, live, . . .

DISCUSSION SET, IN SILHOUETTE

<u>ANNC</u>: . . . from the studios at KCSN-TV.

   Today's topic is "The Tax Squeeze on Middle

   America."   Your host is . . .

   _____.

HOST: Welcome, etc.   Introduces each guest.

    BODY OF DISCUSSION

    (Points to be covered:

      Federal income tax

      State income and sales taxes

      Local property taxes)

HOST: Summarizes.   Thanks guests.

DISCUSSION SET IN SILHOUETTE

<u>MUSIC</u>: THEME, SNEAK IN, ESTABLISH, AND UNDER

<u>ANNC</u>: For the past fifteen minutes, you have

  been watching another stimulating program

  in the series, . . .

SUPER CARD (OVER SET): "LIVE"

<u>ANNC</u>: . . . "Live," from KCSN-TV.

<u>MUSIC</u>: OUT

BLACK

Figure 13-10 Sample semiscripted outline.

```
                    VIDEO                              AUDIO
      ─────────────────────────────────────────────────────────────
                                      Concept of green leaves as food

                                      factories:

            CHART: DIAGRAM OF             1.  Oxygen-CO₂ cycle

                    CYCLE                 2.  Water and Nourishment up from

                                              roots

            SLIDE #1                      3.  Manufacture of chlorophyll

                                      Role of chlorophyll in growth of

                                      vegetation

            FILM:  1'20"           FILM ROLL CUE:  Now suppose we take a

                                      look at the inside of a green leaf

                                      and see for ourselves.
```

Figure 13-11 Sample semiscripted ITV lesson: two columns.

```
                              AUDIO/VIDEO
      ─────────────────────────────────────────────────────────────

                       Concept of green leaves as food factories:

                           1. Oxygen-CO₂ cycle

                                CHART:  DIAGRAM OF CYCLE

                           2. Water and Nourishment up from roots

                           3. Manufacture of chlorophyll

                                SLIDE #1

                       Role of chlorophyll in growth of vegetation

                       FILM ROLL CUE:  Now suppose we take a look at

                           the inside of a green leaf and see for

                           ourselves . . .

                                FILM:  1'20"

                       FILM ENDS WITH SHOT OF PULSING DOTS SLOWING

                       DOWN TO A DEAD STOP
```

Figure 13-12 Sample semiscripted ITV lesson: single column.

The Outline, or Semiscripted Program.

Many kinds of programs do not have every word written out in advance. Among them are variety shows, educational/lecture programs, interview programs, and other formats where there is a good deal of ad-libbing and extemporaneous discussion.

Section 13.5 (appendix D-3) is an example of a semiscripted outline for a discussion program in which both columns are written out. Figure 13-10 is an example of an abbreviated script outline for a discussion program in which the audio and video elements have all been integrated into the right-hand column so that the left-hand (blank) column can be used for more extensive director's notes.

In figures 13-11 and 13-12 we have two different versions of the same program content. In figure 13-11, the ITV script outline utilizes both columns. In figure 13-12, exactly the same content is incorporated into the outline, but all the material is included in the right-hand column.

One technique that is used in some scripts, as in the previous examples, is to use upper- and lowercase letters for everything that is actually to be heard on the air. Note that all of the announcer copy in figure 13-10 is written out, which is done in many semiscripted formats, and the summary of the host's remarks are also in upper- and lowercase. All other material (video instructions, audio cues) is put in uppercase letters only. This makes it easy to identify which is which.

In addition to writing out the announcer copy in full, most outline scripts will also write out exact roll cues to be used in facilitating correct timing into film and videotape inserts. The semiscripted format will also include a somewhat detailed outline of the content, together with fairly complete video information.

The Show Format, or Rundown Sheet.

Many routine programs that are produced on a daily or weekly basis by a station will not even work from a complete semiscripted outline. The daily homemaker show, ITV lectures, regular interview programs, game shows, weekly panel discussions, and other programs—where the same talent uses the same format continually—may use only a **show format,** or **rundown sheet.** This would list just the order of the basic segments. Perhaps exact **roll cues** for film and VTR inserts might be included—along with times for inserted elements. Figure 13-13 illustrates a typical rundown sheet for a local variety show.

Once you, as director, have the script in hand, your job is ready to begin. Your task now is to break down the script, decide how each element is to be handled, block camera movement, mark the script for your own directing use, and prepare instructions for the key crew members and engineering staff.

Marking the Script

Almost all script formats are at least double-spaced. This not only makes it easier for the talent and others to read, but also allows room for the numerous notes and markings that the director will have to make on the script. It is your task to decide what cameras will have to be used where, what instructions the technical director and engineers must have, where the audio cues will have to be, what cues the talent will need, and so forth. Preparing and marking the script is one of the most critical tasks the director has. On a major studio drama, it can involve numerous detailed drawings and hundreds of abbreviated cues and instructions and notes; with a fairly routine ongoing program (such as "Mollie's Morning"), script preparation may mean no more than a few penciled reminders of unusual cues.

```
                    "MOLLIE'S MORNING" (NO: 87-0314    )

                                  FAX:

                                  VTR:
    _____

              VIDEO                        AUDIO

        1.  TEASER:  MOLLY AND DOG     STUDIO:  MOLLIE LIVE              ( :30)

        2.  OPENING FILM               THEME MUSIC UP: S.O.F. MAG TRACK  ( :45)

        3.  MOLLIE:  MONOLOGUE         STUDIO:  MOLLIE LIVE              (2:00)

        4.  INTERVIEW SET              INTERVIEW: JOHN LOOMIS            (5:00)

              LOOMIS SLIDES (6 OR 7)     VOICE-OVER NARRATION

        5.  MOLLIE, TO CAMERA          (ROLL CUE):  One of the most enchanting

                                         things about interior decoration is

                                         the impact that simple ideas can have

                                         when done creatively.            ( :10)

        6.  FILM: THE WORLD OF         FILM: S.O.F. OPTICAL             (2:25)
              JEAN JAMESON

        7.  MOLLIE, TO CAMERA          BOOM #2:  INTRO TO NELSON         ( :30)

              WALK TO LIVING ROOM SET

        8.  LIVING ROOM SET:           INTERVIEW: HEATHER NELSON        (7:00)

              DEMO:  FABRICS

              7 OR 8 GRAPHICS

        9.  MOLLIE, TO CAMERA          SUMMARY AND CLOSE                 ( :40)

       10.  CLOSING FILM               THEME MUSIC: S.O.F. MAG TRACK     ( :30)
```

Figure 13-13 Sample show format.

Standard Symbols. In preparing their scripts for production, most directors will use a system of shorthand symbols. Experienced directors have worked out their own set of symbols; each set is a very personalized system and does not have to make sense to anyone but the director. Your symbols will work if they are clear, easy to read, unambiguous, and do not take up much space.

There are some standardized symbols, however, that form the basis for most of the personalized systems the directors adopt. Some of these universal markings are indicated in figure 13-14. In using the symbols to mark your script, you generally should use pencil. Once you get into rehearsal, there are script changes, camera positions that do not work, graphics that did not turn out, and many other production modifications—some major and many minor—that will necessitate your changing your script markings. Therefore, it is always safer to start with pencil.

Generally, the script markings should remind you of every preplanned command you will have to give—to cameras, T.D., talent, audio, projectionists, floor crew, lighting, and everyone else. The marked script may indicate not only the necessary commands of execution but also the important commands of preparation ("ready's" and "prepare's") and other off-air directions. Figure 13-15 illustrates what a thoroughly marked script looks like. As you become more experienced and comfortable with the medium, your scripts will not be marked this heavily. For the purposes of illustration, figure 13-15 shows virtually every command and preparation for the open and close of a discussion program.

Experienced directors will work with a less detailed marked script in order to concentrate on the camera monitors. You must be able to watch everything that is going on; you cannot be content just to keep your eyes glued on the prepared script, reading off all instructions in order.

Shot Sheets.   Once you have the script completely marked, you can prepare detailed instructions for other crew members—for the floor director, audio, the technical director, the recording engineer, the projectionist, lighting and staging, and anyone else who might be handling a complex assignment. Some of these forms have already been discussed (lighting and staging plot plans). The prepared written instructions can save considerable studio time once you are ready to set up and start rehearsals.

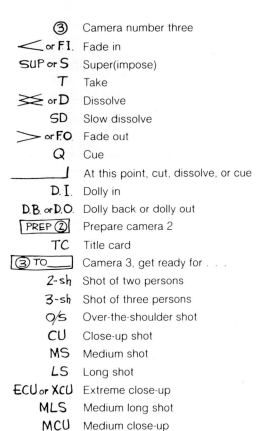

Figure 13-14 lists the following standard script-marking symbols:

③	Camera number three
< or F.I.	Fade in
SUP or S	Super(impose)
T	Take
≫ or D	Dissolve
SD	Slow dissolve
> or F.O.	Fade out
Q	Cue
_____⌋	At this point, cut, dissolve, or cue
D.I.	Dolly in
D.B. or D.O.	Dolly back or dolly out
PREP ②	Prepare camera 2
TC	Title card
③ TO____	Camera 3, get ready for . . .
2-sh	Shot of two persons
3-sh	Shot of three persons
O/S	Over-the-shoulder shot
CU	Close-up shot
MS	Medium shot
LS	Long shot
ECU or XCU	Extreme close-up
MLS	Medium long shot
MCU	Medium close-up

Figure 13-14 Standard script-marking symbols.

The most common form of these specialized instructions is the *shot sheet* for the camera operators—an abbreviated description of every shot that a particular camera has to get. It is compact enough to be attached to the rear of the camera where the operator can quickly refer to it. Shot sheets are particularly valuable for complex, fully scripted programs such as dramas, where every shot has been carefully worked out by the director and where the cameras will have to be moving quite a bit to get various shots as requested. In preparing the marked script for a drama, for example, once the blocking is firmed up and you have every shot planned, each shot should be numbered; the shot sheets then list each camera's

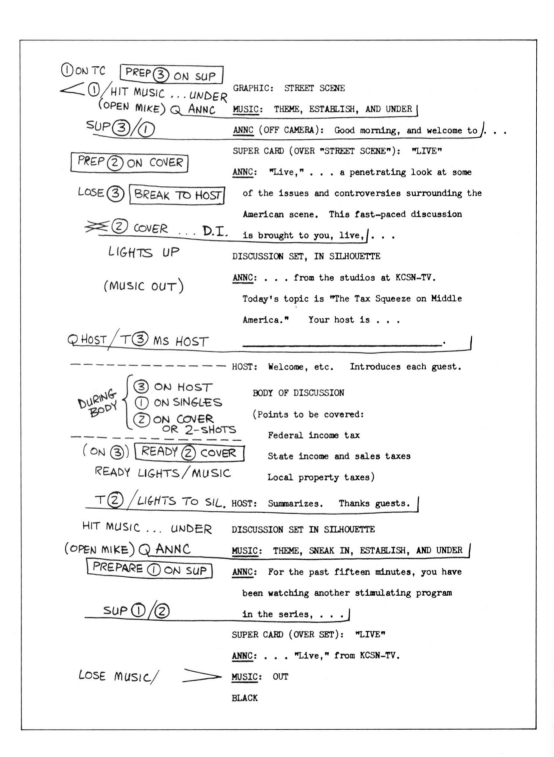

Figure 13-15 Sample marked script.

```
|                             |                               |                               |
|         CAMERA 1            |          CAMERA 2             |          CAMERA 3             |
|                             |                               |                               |
|  2. GR #2                   |  4. Wide Sh., Kitchen, hi-angle|  1. TC (GR #1)                |
|  6. LS, Mary in doorway     |       boom down.              |  3. Sup cards (A, B, C, D)     |
|  8. LS, David in doorway    |  7. MS Mary.  Follow her      |  5. CU coffee cup, pan to      |
| 10. MS David (he walks into O/S)| 15. 2-sh., Pan L as David  |       ash tray                 |
| 12. O/S David               |       crosses behind Mary     |  9. MS Mary (she rises)        |
| 14. CU David                | 18. MS David. D.B. as he comes| 11. O/S Mary                   |
| 17. MS Mary (she sits)      |       to her.  Open to 2-sh.  | 13. CU Mary                    |
| 23. Loose 2-sh. (Mary rises)| 20. CU Mary                   | 16. MS David                   |
| 25. O/S Mary (in doorway). She| 22. 2-sh. (tight)           | 19. MCU David (bust-shot)      |
|       walks toward David.   | 24. (Crane up) Hi angle 2-sh. | 21. CU David                   |
|       David turns to camera.|       D.I. & crane down to    | 26. 2-sh. as Mary turns        |
| 27. CU David                |       single of David         | 29. (Hook wheels) 2-sh. D.I. to|
| 31. 2-sh. Mary walks past   | 28. Single David (wide).      |       ECU Mary                 |
|       camera.  Hold on David|       D.B., follow as he walks| 32. MS Mary                    |
| 33. MS David.  Pan to door as|      to Mary.  Open to 2-sh.  | 35. Loose 2-sh. (Mary, David)  |
|       Alice enters          | 30. CU Mary's hands           | 38. Loose CU, Mary             |
| 36. 3-sh., favoring Alice   | 34. MS Alice                  | 41. ECU Mary                   |
| 39. CU Alice                | 37. MS David (he sits)        | 44. ECU Mary                   |
| 42. CU Alice                | 40. ECU David                 | 46. CU of knife                |
| 45. Wide 3-sh., follow action| 43. (Crane down) Loose MS Alice.|                             |
|                             |       Follow her to table.    |                               |
|                             |       Follow action w/cup.    |                               |
|                             |       Crane up & D.I.         |                               |
|                             |                               |                               |
```

Figure 13-16
Representative shot sheets.

shot by number. Figure 13-16 shows the three shot sheets for a three-camera drama. In the illustration all three camera shot sheets are indicated on one page. In practice these three sheets would be cut out separately, and each camera operator would have his or her own shot sheet taped or clipped by the viewfinder.

Summary

The successful television director must keep in mind the principles of picture continuity: the balance of *wide shots* and *close-ups,* correct use of *shot relationships* (avoiding jump cuts, extreme cutting ratios, and position jumps), observing the *axis of action* (and *conversation*), and other principles of continuity. He or she must also use different *types of transitions* knowledgeably and be careful with the *timing of transitions.* These principles apply both to multiple-camera studio productions and to single-camera field shooting.

In blocking cameras for a multiple-camera production, the director should *cross the camera angles,* start blocking in the *center of the program,* and position *graphics easels last.* The director must be familiar with *three types of scripting formats*—the full script; the outline or semiscripted program; and the show format or rundown sheet. In preparing for the production, there are standard symbols that most directors use in *marking the script.* Directors should also prepare other production instructions such as *camera shot sheets.*

In chapter 14, we will summarize the scope of the director's job and look at the production requirements for a couple of specialized formats.

Figure 13-17 Typical setup for an *L*-shaped staging arrangement for a discussion program.

13.5 Production Project: The Discussion Program

Although no single phase of production can be considered as the sine qua non of any successful television program, the process whereby the director plans the staging and camera blocking of a show is, for most programs, one of critical importance. Most directors refer to it as their "homework," but in actuality this process of making interrelated staging and blocking decisions usually continues right through the final rehearsal.

In some programs—such as drama—this effort may entail plotting every performer movement and camera shot. For programs of a more spontaneous nature, the director usually sets up a flexible shooting plan designed to cover all the various program contingencies.

Planning the Discussion Program

That sometimes maligned but nevertheless ubiquitous stalwart of television programming, the *talk show,* provides an excellent format for understanding the fundamental principles involved in staging and camera blocking. The absence of performer movement on such programs allows for concentration upon picture composition and clarity.

Staging. The majority of talk shows utilize some variation of two basic staging configurations: an L-*shaped grouping* that places the host on the end facing down a row of other participants (fig. 13-17); or a *semicircle,* in which the

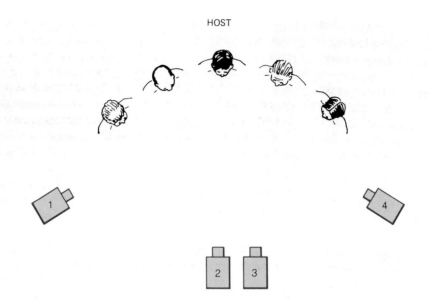

HOST

In this typical "talk show" camera pattern, one center camera (either 2 or 3) remains on a cover shot of the entire group while the other center camera (3 or 2) holds a close-up of the host.

Figure 13-18 Camera pattern for semicircular staging.

host is generally placed in the center. This conformity of staging is not due as much to a lack of originality on the part of the directors as it is to their recognition that these seating plans provide arrangements whereby the guests can best relate to each other and the host, and at the same time, provide the director with the best camera angles of the participants.

Figure 13-18 shows a very open semicircular seating arrangement similar to that used on several syndicated talk shows.

On these programs, four cameras are utilized. One of the center cameras holds a wide shot of the entire group at all times. The other center camera holds a shot of the host for use at all

times in the program. On a three-camera show, one center camera will have to alternate between these two shots. Note the extreme angle of the set of the two outside cameras. Although both can provide shots of the entire group from these positions, their primary assignment is that of providing close-up shots of those persons facing their direction by crossing their angles (section 13.3).

On a musical or comedy-variety type of production, the performers generally face toward a stage-front camera and the audience area as they would in a conventional stage show. In a discussion program, the participants relate not to the audience but to one another, and as a result face not to the front but in the direction of the persons to their right and left. Depending upon the role of the host-moderator, the other participants will tend to face in his or her direction during much of the program.

Lighting. Two suggested lighting plans for an L-*shaped* seating configuration were presented as sample lighting plots in figures 4-21 and 4-22 (section 4.5). A review of that section of material will be of value in the preparation of lighting plots for any of the several main seating configurations. On a discussion program, care must be taken to ensure that the face, especially the eyes, is properly lit from all potential camera angles. The locations of the cameras provide a good guide to the location of the main lights in relation to the subjects. The amount of light reflected back from each subject to the camera must be individually balanced occasionally for equal intensity. Differences in hair, clothing, and complexion can produce unsuitably dark and light close-up shots. When taken in succession, such shots are noticeably objectionable.

Shot Continuity. In section 13.1, reference was made to *wide-angle* and *close-up* shots in terms of their respective abilities to communicate collective or particularized program information. Wide-angle *cover* shots are used within a program sequence to re-establish the

relationship of program participants to each other and to the elements of the set. It is the *collectivizing* view of all those production values that contributes to the program as a whole.

By contrast, the close-up shot is a *particularized* view of a person or an object at a precisely appropriate point in the program sequence. As such, the information it conveys is selective and personal, even to the point of being intimate. The eyes and facial muscles add important dimensions to the total meaning of what a person is expressing in words. This is especially true of actors or other personalities who often speak in public or on television. For this reason, the most effective close-up shots are those in which the camera angle is not more than 45 degrees from a head-on position. (See fig. 13-19.) Close-up shots from profile angles, while extremely valuable on many types of productions, should be used with caution on discussion programs.

Transitions. The most important production value on a discussion program is the precision with which the camera shots follow the spontaneous flow of the conversation. Each time a new person begins to speak, the camera on the air—whether on a cover shot or a close-up—should include that person. To linger for more than a second or two on someone who has just stopped talking or to cut to the wrong person is very distracting to the audience.

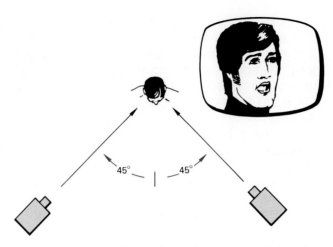

Any camera getting a close-up shot should be as perpendicular to the talent as possible. The camera should not be more than 45 degrees from a head-on shot for a good close-up.

Figure 13-19 Optimum angles for close-ups.

Ideally, each change of voice will be accompanied by a change of cameras to a close-up shot or one that predominately features the person talking. On a three-camera show that features four guests and a moderator, this is not always possible. By carefully watching the panel for clues as to who may be speaking next (section 13.2), the director may somewhat improve the chances of having the shot ready.

Most directors solve the problem by having a cover shot of the entire group available for use at all times. When a close-up shot of a new speaker is not readily available, a take to the cover shot performs several important functions. Primarily, it gives the director a chance to be certain of who is speaking before assigning a camera to the shot. In a fast-paced discussion, this alternative is the only way the director can stay with the quickly changing flow of the conversation. Once the cover shot has been taken, the close-up need not be used immediately. The director can let the wide shot re-establish the collective aspect of the group while waiting for the end of a sentence as a convenient point to cut to the close-up.

During a discussion program, the situation often calls for shots other than a close-up of one participant in the total group. Shots including two or three persons not only add pictorial variety but are quite useful when several people begin a rapid interchange of short statements or questions and answers. Smaller group shots have an added dimension, showing the silent but often revealing expressions on the faces of persons other than the speaker. A brief close-up shot of someone moving his or her head in agreement or disagreement—a reaction shot—is especially useful when one person has been speaking for an extended period of time.

On the other hand, the director must be alert to avoid group shots in which those persons who are not talking are looking away from the speaker. Whether or not intended, the visual effect is one of boredom and, as such, has a negative impact on the program as a whole.

Camera Blocking. The range of shots available to each camera in a program situation is dependent upon the two interrelated variables of camera and subject position. These factors must be considered together when plans for shot coverage are made. On a discussion program, where the staging options are somewhat limited, the director generally uses the seating arrangement as a starting point in the camera blocking process. Primary camera positions can then be selected on the basis of the best angles for the close-up shots and the important requirement of wide-angle cover shots. All of the shot possibilities for each camera should be plotted so that each camera operator can work within the parameters of established shot assignments. Graphic stands, the drum or crawl, and other off-camera visuals should be positioned for easy accessibility to

camera positions after the basic camera pattern has been established (section 13.3).

The use of a definite shooting plan aids in having critical shots available when they are needed and at the same time helps in holding down the talk on the P.L. intercommunication system.

The direction of conversational flow may vary at different times during a program. For this reason, directors usually develop several shooting plans to cover all contingencies. Figure 13-20 shows two such plans that would be used in the coverage of an L-shaped arrangement. Plan *A* is designed to provide maximum close-up coverage of the three panel members, with the moderator being seen only on the wide shot on camera 1. Plan *B* is set up for situations in which the moderator takes a very active role in the program and, as a result, needs a close-up shot ready at all times, or for a period during which conversations develop between two guests.

Plan *A* has obvious limitations but has a basic utility in predictable situations such as a period in the program during which the host is bringing out individual responses from each participant. The beginning and ending of discussion programs usually assume this structure.

A director would probably quickly shift over to Plan *B* during the more active phases of the conversation. By holding camera 3 on a cover shot, camera 1 is able to get a close-up shot of the

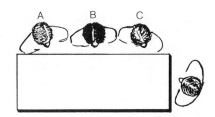

Plan A: *Camera 1* remains on a wide-angle cover shot. *Camera 2* gets close-ups of panelists as they face camera right and two-shots or three-shots of panelists. *Camera 3* gets singles of panelists as they face camera right and over-the-shoulder shots (with host in foreground).

Plan B: *Camera 1* gets close-ups of moderator/host, two-shots of host and panelist C, and singles and two-shots as panelists turn to camera left. *Camera 2* gets close-ups of panelists as they face camera right and two-shots or three-shots of panelists. *Camera 3* remains on a wide-angle cover shot.

Figure 13-20 Camera patterns for *L*-shaped staging.

moderator. Camera 1 also has the option of getting close-up shots of those who turn camera left for a two-person conversation. In this situation, camera 2 then has the option of a close-up of the other person or a two-shot of both speakers. The reverse structure is also possible with camera 1 on the two-shot and camera 2 on the single of the person facing camera right.

Even taken together, these two shooting plans by no means exhaust the possibilities available within an L-shaped seating configuration. The use of camera 2 as a cover camera from either a left-side or right-side studio position opens up another series of coverage patterns. The suggestion of cameras 1 or 3 for cover shots stems from the fact that their angle to the set allows for a more interesting grouping of all participants in the frame. Each person's face occupies a larger proportion of the frame than in a wide shot from the center (which also results in empty space at the top and bottom of the frame).

In the press of a fast-moving program, the director often is tempted to give up the cover shot and use that camera temporarily for smaller group shots and close-ups. It is an option that even the most experienced directors use with considerable care. Invariably, when all cameras are committed to the three people who are dominating the conversation, the fourth (off-camera) voice suddenly starts speaking. It takes quick thinking to avoid 5 or more seconds of nontalking faces being aired or, worse, a wrong shot taken in haste.

Shooting in the Round. Many directors of discussion programs have had considerable success in staging program participants in a full circle and shooting from all points outside that circle. There are several benefits to be derived from this camera arrangement and a goodly number of problems as well. Because of the varying angles involved, it is difficult to get ''clean'' close-ups or two-shots. Heads, hands, and whole bodies seem always to be in the way of the shot that is needed. It also is very difficult to position cameras to avoid seeing other cameras in the shot, unless the set is specially designed.

Depending upon the intended nature of the program, it is sometimes possible deliberately to use these crowded, poorly framed shots, taken from unusual angles, in an effective manner. The very roughness of the shooting technique is visually compatible with the sense of conflict created by varying points of view. The resulting *cinema verité* quality would be suitable for a program

confrontation between activist and establishment representatives. Even the presence of cameras in some of the shots would communicate something of the reality of the total program situation.

Calling Shots. In a discussion program, it is essential that preparatory commands always be used in conjunction with the commands of execution (section 7.5). An inexperienced director might be tempted to think that a needed shot could be put on the air instantaneously if only the command of execution were given. To do so, however, would be to increase appreciably the possibilities for error. The spontaneous nature of talk programs makes the command of preparation doubly important. The technical director needs this lead time to be certain of the switcher operation. Of equal importance is the possibility that the camera operators need this time for final adjustment of the framing or as a warning to hold a shot they might otherwise be in the process of changing.

A good procedure for the director on a fast-moving talk show is to give a ''ready'' for a probable next shot as soon as possible after the previous shot is on the line. This does not remove any option for a subsequent change in the upcoming shot; it simply aids the director in staying ahead of the action. An example of how the director can inform the crew of several probable courses of action would be as follows (referring to the pattern in figure 13-20):

"Ready camera 3 . . . take 3" (cover shot). "Ready camera 2 on a close-up of guest C . . . camera 1, hold the moderator close-up, but be ready to move over to guest B."

In this situation, guest C has just interrupted the moderator. The director can afford to wait on the cover shot to see whether guest C will continue talking or whether the moderator will start talking again. At the same time, the director has noticed that guest B also is trying to break into the conversation.

Discussion Program Production Project (Appendix D-3)

The somewhat simplified opening and closing format in appendix D-3 is presented as an aid to an all-class production exercise. This discussion format can be used for a repeated number of production exercises within the class. Practical experience in the utilization of cameras in a spontaneous program situation is valuable not only in itself but also serves as an important

background to camera blocking procedures in more complex productions such as music and drama (see chapter 14).

A minimum running time of 5 minutes for each exercise is suggested so that each director has an opportunity to become familiar with the pattern of the conversational flow and the related continuity of camera shots. A realistic element can be added by having the A.D. and the stage manager feed the moderator countdown cues for time remaining in the exercise. Directors should be prepared for the fact that the transition from the body of a program to the closing segment can be difficult unless cues and other instructions are given well in advance.

Discussion topics should be carefully selected so that the conversation does not lag. One way to ensure an active interchange of comments is to have the panel members role play assigned roles such as judge, police officer, and taxpayer. It often is easier to verbalize the supposed opinions of generalized cultural types than to express one's own point of view.

Directing Techniques for Various Formats

14

In this final chapter, we want to summarize some of the elements that the beginning director should keep uppermost in his or her mind. We also want to present some specific considerations for directing particular formats—a musical production and a dramatic sequence. Finally, we will introduce a concluding production project—in the form of an extended station break—that involves the beginning director in integrating a number of production elements (slide, film, studio, and videotape) in one short production segment. The scripted production model appears in appendix D-5.

14.1 From Planning to Postproduction

At this stage, it may be helpful for you, as the student director, to take a *chronological* look at the entire operation of putting a program together. Throughout the text, we have touched on many individual elements in the production process. In this section, we want to pull the ingredients together and add a few other considerations in creating a total perspective on the directing process.

Preproduction Planning

The discipline of thorough preproduction planning cannot be overemphasized. The success of every production is determined—to a very great extent—by the quality of the preproduction planning that the director has undertaken. For the purposes of organizing your thinking, it may be helpful to consider preproduction planning in five areas: *script familiarization, facilities and equipment, cast and crew, production requirements,* and *script preparation.*

1. Script Familiarization. In many academic and closed-circuit settings, the director will also function as the producer-writer and thus will have shaped the script from the beginning. In many other situations you, as director, will have the script handed to you and will take the production from there.

Your first concern should be to determine the *specific purpose* of the script. What is the objective of the program? What should happen as a result of this production? How do you want the audience to be different when this program is over? Then you can begin to think in terms of the overall "feel" and image of the program. What kinds of settings, lighting, graphics would be most effective in this particular *communication* process?

Next, there may be several immediate steps that need to be taken. Check the script for rough timing; read through it and get an idea of how long it might run. Is the length all right? Does it need to be cut? Does it need to be lengthened? The script should be put in its final television production format and duplicated for all personnel involved. Is any rewriting necessary? How many copies are needed? The script must be checked for any necessary copyright clearances. Can it be used as it stands? In a professional situation, this is the point at which you must be working out a specific budget. How much money do you have for the production?

2. Facilities and Equipment. Once you are completely comfortable with the script, you should be able to start specific *facilities planning*. In the case of a remote coverage of some event, you have to scout the location, of course. You must make arrangements for mobile equipment. In other professional situations, you may have to make arrangements for the rental of actual studio facilities. How large a studio do you need? What size sets will you be using? How long will you need the studio? This, obviously, is one of the largest items in your budget.

In most academic and training situations, the studio will be assigned to you for a definite period of time. In many institutions—even for training purposes—you still will have to fill out a Facilities Request Form, reserving a specific studio and control room(s), cameras, microphones, video recorders, lights, sets, graphics, and other requirements. The items are requested for a particular production date and time. Failure to attend to such paperwork carefully at this stage can result in costly problems and misunderstandings later.

3. Cast and Crew. Again, in most academic situations, you may not have to be concerned with securing personnel. The technical crew may be assigned from your class or from some other cooperating class. There still may be some occasions, however, when you will be involved in selecting specific individuals for particular crew assignments. You should be familiar with the process of making out crew sheets to get the positions filled that you need for your production.

Casting for actors or other performers also may be done on an informal basis in the academic setting. You may work through the Drama or the Theatre Arts departments, or you may prevail upon your personal friends. In securing such volunteer help, make certain that you have a firm commitment; many a student production has been ruined because some friend or casual acquaintance backed out of a production at the last moment. In professional situations, of course, casting is quite an involved process. The producer will probably line up the major talent and the rest of the casting will be handled by a specialized casting director.

4. Production Requirements. Production requirements are what the bulk of this text has been concerned with. Now comes the job of pulling it all together. In any kind of major production, you should plan on holding one or

Figure 14-1 Production conference with director, A.D., stage manager, T.D., and staging and lighting director.

more production conferences involving the chief production heads—set designer, art director, lighting chief, engineering supervisor, other key production persons, and, of course, the A.D. and floor manager. (See fig. 14-1.) Depending upon the nature and complexity of the program, there may be several different kinds of conferences: *script conferences* (involving writers and the producer), *art conferences, engineering conferences,* and so forth.

You must now make sure that all of the necessary preproduction elements are properly requested and constructed. The *lighting and staging plans* are developed at this stage. If any special *costumes* or *props* have to be rented or fabricated, orders are initiated now. All *graphics* have to be ordered and produced; if you have access to an art department, graphics request forms have to be turned in. What computer graphics can be prepared in advance? Any *film* or *still photography* has to be planned well in advance. Are station photographers available? How much will you do

yourself? Will you have slides made of some of your graphics? Equipment for any *special effects* will have to be arranged for. *Music* and *other special audio* selections must be chosen and/or ordered.

During all of this preproduction process, you have to work within a very tight interlocking schedule of *checkpoints* and *deadlines.* You cannot wait until the last minute to get things started. Many production elements cannot proceed until other items are taken care of first. Everything, therefore, must be scheduled days and weeks in advance. The exterior tape cannot be shot until the costumes arrive. Costumes cannot be designed until the overall color scheme of the setting is determined. Slides cannot be shot until the graphics are made. Set pieces cannot be constructed until the setting design is completed. And the graphics cannot be made until the talent decides what he or she wants to do.

To protect yourself, put into your schedule *pads* or *cushions*—a few extra days of leeway throughout the schedule. In major productions the intertwining complexities of the production schedule can become pretty awesome.

5. Script Preparation.   During all of this activity you also must be concerned with your script breakdown and specific preparations for the day of production. Start with the basics—reminding yourself that your primary job is that of delivering a clear communicative *message* in an effective, interesting, and artistically pleasing manner. How are you going to use your cameras? What balance of wide *collective* shots and close-up *particularized* shots will you strive for (section 13.1)? What kinds of transitions will best move the program forward without ambiguity? What is the pacing you want to achieve? In short, what images and sounds do you want to create to achieve your purpose?

This process, of course, takes into consideration all of the elements of picture continuity and transitions and camera patterns discussed in chapter 13. You prepare your script with specific markings and instructions, and you prepare other written instructions for key positions on the production crew—camera shot sheets, audio instructions, and so forth.

Rehearsals

By now, you should have moved into rehearsals in one form or another. You should think in terms of several different kinds of rehearsals: pre-studio rehearsals, floor rehearsals, and control room rehearsals.

Pre-Studio Rehearsals.   For many extensive productions—especially dramas—you will want to have some rehearsals prior to coming into the studio. Studio time is too precious to start from scratch with basic blocking. Using a rehearsal hall, an empty studio, a warehouse, or a living room, you can begin working with actors. Specific areas can be measured off and marked with masking tape or furniture to represent major staging areas, and much of your blocking of action can take place in such surroundings as well as quite a bit of the dramatic interpretation and reading of lines.

For nondramatic productions there are also many good reasons for pre-studio rehearsals. Documentaries, educational programs, political broadcasts, and the like, can benefit from early **dry-run** sessions in which the director and talent work together.

Studio Floor Rehearsals.   When you and the production crew start to work in the studio, you usually will spend some amount of time on the studio floor before assuming the director's chair in the control room. There are a couple of different ways in which you may profitably spend this rehearsal period (fig. 14-2). Depending on the type of production, either the talent or the technical crew may benefit most from your presence on the studio floor. If the talent is particularly insecure or if the technical coordination of a production is really complicated, you might spend quite a bit of your time on the studio floor. On the other hand, if the talent is in control of the situation and the technical elements are no special problem, you probably will benefit from getting into the control room as early as you can.

One of the first rehearsal techniques you conduct from the studio floor will be a *walk-through rehearsal*. This may be either a *talent* walk-through (if they are not really sure of their positions and movements) or a *technical* walk-through (to explain major camera moves, audio placement, scene changes, and special effects). In many instances, the walk-through is a combination, taking both the talent and crew through an abbreviated version of the production.

Figure 14-2 Director (facing camera) working out production problems with stage manager during a walk-through rehearsal on the studio floor.

Control Room Rehearsals. The full rehearsals are usually conducted with you, as the director, calling shots from the control room. If time is critical or if technical problems exist, however, you may elect to work longer on the studio floor. The initial type of full-facilities rehearsal is called a *camera* rehearsal. For the first time the camera operators are behind the cameras and all other technical personnel are at their positions.

This first camera rehearsal usually is a *start-and-stop,* or *stop-start,* rehearsal. In this approach, you interrupt the rehearsal every time there is a major problem. You correct the trouble and then continue the rehearsal. This type of rehearsal procedure *may* be conducted from the floor if you feel that the potential problems need your immediate and direct supervision. It is quite a time-consuming process but effective if you have the luxury of enough studio time. Another approach to the first

camera rehearsal is the *uninterrupted run-through.* This should almost always be conducted from the control room. In this approach, you attempt to get through the entire production with a minimum of interruptions. If time is short—and if problems are minor—you keep on plowing through the rehearsal regardless of what happens (assuming that your A.D. is keeping thorough production notes about what needs to be corrected after you are through the rehearsal).

Finally, there is the *dress rehearsal.* Theoretically, this is the final rehearsal—a complete, uninterrupted, full-scale rehearsal after all of the problems have been straightened out. In practice, this stage is rarely reached. Realities of the medium are such that there simply is never enough studio time to do as polished a job as you want. In many instances, you will wind up with a combination start-and-stop and dress rehearsal, stumbling through as fast as possible to try to complete at least one full camera rehearsal of some description before air time.

When time is short, you must economize and try to make the most efficient use of the time available. Do not stand around waiting for others to finish their jobs before starting your rehearsal; you can rehearse even while the lighting crew is still trimming the lights and while the audio engineer is establishing levels. In an abbreviated walk-through rehearsal, at least make certain you get through all of the rough spots in the production; *rehearse the open and the close* and *the crucial transitions* that call for coordination of several kinds of movement. Pick your priorities; do not get hung up on small details (such as worrying about the possibility of a boom shadow) when you have only a few minutes to work out major problems (the talent doesn't know where he or she should move next). Before you know it, the A.D. will be telling you, "45 seconds to air."

Production and Postproduction

Finally, you are ready to start calling shots on your first production. As we pointed out in section 1.6, you, as the director, have three main functions—as *planner, artist,* and *executor.* You have done all you can in the first two areas—as planner and as creative artist—and you now are ready to execute the program.

First, try to control your physical anxieties. Regardless of what may be churning inside, try not to let it show. Force yourself to sit down and present a calm facade. During the final minute before you go on the air, make a point of quietly and calmly assuring everybody that all will go well. Force yourself to sit back and take a deep breath; let it out slowly; and now coolly and confidently tell all of the crew and the talent that everything shall proceed without problems. Remember that the composure or the anxiety you communicate to the crew will surely be returned to you in the same, or even in an exaggerated, manner.

Give all of your commands and directions as clearly as you can. Refer to talent (when talking to the floor director) by name—"Cue Dr. Morgan," not "Cue him"—to avoid misunderstandings. Refer to camera operators, on the other hand, by numbers; you are less likely to slip up and get confused. Make sure you use correct and precise commands of preparation to the technical director (section 7.5) and to all other production positions; the commands of preparation are at least as important as the commands of execution.

Keeping the lag time of various equipment and personnel in mind, give your cues in a sequence designed to get things happening when you want them to. In opening your program say, "Hit music" and then "Fade in camera 2." It always takes a second or so before the music will be heard (if it is properly cued up), but the camera is there with the push of a lever. Similarly, always cue talent before putting his or her camera on the air. "Open-mike-cue-talent-dissolve-to-2" is often given as one command of execution. By the time the stage manager reacts and throws the cue and the talent takes a breath and starts to talk, the camera will be on the air.

Watch and listen to your monitors. Always be aware of exactly what is going on over the air as far as picture and sound are concerned. If a picture is not what you want ("what the viewer needs"), then change it. The viewer watching his or her home receiver could care less about your sinus headache or your incompetent T.D. or your fight with the talent or the camera cable with the bad connection; all he or she knows is what comes over the receiver, and if it is bad, it is bad. Also, always check your camera monitors before calling a shot to be put on the air. You cannot afford to get buried in your beautifully marked script while ignoring the realities of the picture and sound you are sending out. (See fig. 14-3.)

Figure 14-3 Director calling shots during a production, checking the camera monitors while following his script.

During the course of your program, always be looking ahead 2 or 3 minutes. What possible problems lie ahead? What about the close-up we didn't get a chance to rehearse? Did the mike boom get repositioned all right? If something should go drastically wrong, tell yourself you are going to remain in control and salvage what you can. Camera 2 just went dead? Get a wide shot on camera 1 and keep going. The graphics easel fell over and mixed up all the graphics? The talent will have to explain the best he or she can. Whatever happens, it is your job to keep going. Do not give up until the producer or instructor tells you to throw in the towel.

Finally, no matter what else happens, television is a time-bound medium. Everything has to fit into scheduled slots. If you are directing a program that is supposed to be exactly 7:30 long, that means exactly 7 minutes and 30 seconds—not 1 second more or less.

Listen to your A.D., and when you are told you have 5 seconds to black, that means you fade it out and sneak out the music; you have no choice, unless, of course, you know that you are working with a flexible time slot.

Once the program is off the air, use the studio address (talk-back) to thank the crew and talent. Assure them that everything went well. Keep your composure until you have a chance to collapse in private. Supervise the strike and make certain you clear the control room of all scripts, graphics, props, and everything else.

If there is any postproduction editing to be accomplished, your job is far from done (chapter 12). If it is a simple matter of inserting a clean shot to cover the one bad blunder on the air, you may be able to get it done right away. If it is a major postproduction editing job of assembling video pieces from several different sources, it will take quite a bit of scheduling and lonely master control room sessions.

In the next two sections, we want to look at two specialized production formats—the musical and the drama—and examine camera blocking and other considerations for these production types. You should read through and study the sections carefully—whether or not they are used as class production projects—to become familiar with these specialized situations.

14.2 Production of the Musical Number

The techniques used for shooting instrumental groups are, for the most part, based upon the same collective and particularized considerations previously outlined. Musical productions, especially jazz and rock, offer the director an opportunity to explore the use of extreme wide and close-up shots. Shots that include portions of an audience can be used very effectively. At the other extreme, tight close-up shots of the face of a performer can be used to a degree that would be unsuitable in another program context.

Camera Blocking. The primary consideration in any musical production is that of consistently matching the visual aspect of the performance to the sound being heard. A "big" sound with the entire group playing and/or singing calls for an equally "big" look from a visual standpoint. The director seeks to achieve visual contrast and a sense of movement by tight and loosely framed group shots from various angles. Vocal and instrumental solos require a more intimate use of the camera. The director explores the more particularized elements of the performance by means of close-up shots of the face, hands, and the instrument itself. The close-ups will be interspersed with re-establishing full and waist shots to capture performer movement and to show the relation of the performer to his or her instrument.

The director must at all times seek to capture visually the intensity and mood of the performance. If, for example, the entire group is playing at a low sound level, the intent may be a mood of sadness or alienation. To produce a matching visual effect, the group can be shot in such a way as to produce a sense of isolation. This can be achieved by shooting the group in tight profile or extremely low-angle shots.

At the other extreme, there are those numbers that create a certain degree of excitement with high sound levels and a great deal of performer movement. The director can capture and even enhance the action by dolly and trucking movements of the cameras themselves. Two camera shots can be superimposed to further enhance the intensity of a performance. A close-up shot of the lead singer supered over a wide shot of the group may capture both the particularized and collective aspects of the "high point" of a big production number.

The musical structure of the number serves as the basis for the sequence of camera shots. In an ad-lib concert performance, the director is forced to attempt to predict the sequence of the action. In a rehearsed studio production, the director will have the leader provide a breakdown of each number. This usually is given in terms of the number of measures (bars) within 4-, 8-, or 16-measure phrases. If the number is prerecorded and the musicians are going to mime and lip sync their performance, then the phrase groupings can be expressed in seconds. The exact timing of camera cuts or other transitions should always be on the beat (section 13.2).

Production Example

An illustration of both of these methods is given in the production script example (fig. 14-4) showing the camera blocking for the first 3 minutes of "Beginnings" as recorded by the

Musical Production Script Example

"Beginnings" Chicago Transit Authority Approx. First Three Minutes

Time	Bars	Camera	Shot
00:00	6	1	XCU Guitar/hand zoom out to tight waist
06	2	2	Drummer solo
09	4		Zoom out to include Guitarist
13	4		Pan to include Bass
17	7	1	Group profile Brass foreground
24	1	2	Drummer
26	8		Zoom out to Group wide
34	8	3	CU Singer low 45° angle
43	6	1	Bust Singer zoom in CU profile
49	4	2	Group high angle 45° from left
54	8		Arm across to right dropping
1:02	8		to low 45° from right
1:11	4	3	CU Singer profile from right
1:15	4	1	Tight 45° Group
1:19	4	2	CU Singer 45° angle
1:24	4	1	Tight 45° Group
1:28	4	2	Waist Singer and arc across
1:37	8		to left
1:45	8	1	Profile Group
1:54	6	3	Low 45° Singer Drums Bass
2:00	4	2	MCU head on high angle zoom out wide
2:05	8	2 slow diss.	High wide
2:13	8	3	Super CU low 45° singles
2:22	4		Dissolve thru and zoom in
2:26	4	1	Group profile
2:30	4	3	MCU
2:34	4	1	Group profile
2:39	16	2	Low angle—bust
2:55	8	1,2, and 3 ad lib takes	Drum solo
3:05	8	1	Vocal to conclusion Etc.

Figure 14-4 Sample musical production script. Columns provide time at beginning of each shot segment, the number of musical bars for each segment, the camera use, and shot description for each segment.

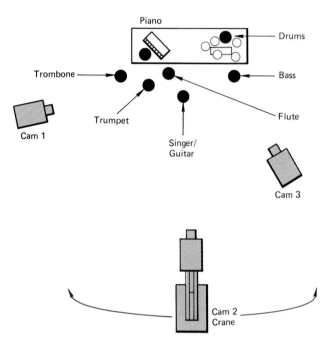

This represents typical camera blocking with cameras 1 and 3 fairly stationary and camera 2, on a crane, available for major moves.

Figure 14-5 Camera pattern for musical number.

group Chicago.[1] The sequence of camera shots for the production model is based on the staging configuration and camera positions as shown in figure 14-5. The camera work has been planned to include a crane mount for camera 2. Cameras 1 and 3 have been kept in relatively static positions to be ready for a quick succession of shots.

This scripted production model was designed to be used in two ways. By playing the record and envisioning the sequence of shots, the student is provided an opportunity to understand how the individual shots are made to fit together into a production whole. The script can also be used as the basis for a full class exercise. Class members can be placed in the

1. Columbia Records XSM-139684-CS 9809, side 1, cut 3.

indicated staging positions (using real instruments if possible) and the number can be shot as a production sequence. In this case, the script should be used only as a guide. Each individual director should be encouraged to attempt some degree of variation in both staging and shot selection.

In an actual production, the director, assistant director, technical director, and possibly the audio operator will work with a copy of the blocking script. Quite frequently—depending upon the type of musical production—the director and/or A.D. will be using the actual musical score as the working script. Each camera operator will be given either a copy of the full script or a shot sheet, which lists only the shots for that particular camera.

14.3 Production of the Dramatic Sequence

Contemporary directors of television programming have developed a diversity of shooting techniques for both film and electronic cameras. Some have gone so far as to reverse traditional patterns and use multiple film cameras, and others have explored the use of the single electronic camera. During the 1980s a whole new generation of technology has begun to emerge that is based on improved electronic cameras and computer-based editing equipment. It is possible that several differently designed cameras will emerge, each suited to a particular type of production. This is already apparent with the development of the *mini* and *micro* electronic cameras and the camcorder, the introduction of the CCD camera, and the promise of high-definition (HDTV) technology.

While the 60-minute or 90-minute live dramatic production is probably a thing of the past, the return to the use of multiple electronic cameras on dramatic programs has been important. Soap operas, situation comedies, and even serious dramatic productions are increasingly using this production technique.[2]

Camera Blocking. The process whereby a television director plans the staging of actors borrows somewhat from both stage and single-camera motion picture techniques. The main difference between the older methods and those used for an ongoing television sequence lies in the fact that for television the director must continually relate the staging to three or more camera angles. The previously mentioned concept of the collective and particularized eye of

2. In 1984, the director of production system analysis for CBS pointed out that almost 90 percent of all situation comedies and variety shows were being produced not on film, but on videotape (*Broadcasting,* October 8, 1984, p. 54).

the camera again serves as the basis for shot framing and selection. The wide-angle shot encompasses the totality of the scene at given points in the action. With this shot, the director establishes and, at later points, re-establishes the relationships of the actors to one another and to the elements of the set. The wide-angle shot shows the choreography of the characters within the set.

The more important dramatic elements of the story line are, however, more often portrayed by tighter shots involving two people or single close-up shots. The eyes and facial expressions may be as important in the actor's communication process as the dialogue. In the use of the close-up, the director must be careful to position the camera and lights to reveal fully the expression of the face. The profile angle, unless specifically called for, usually is avoided.

The pattern of shots for a short, two-person sequence at the beginning of a longer scene could be as follows:

1. Camera 2. Wide-angle cover shot. Locates the actors within the set and establishes the set itself.
2. Camera 1. Closer two-shot, possibly over the shoulder of actor *A* into the face of actor *B*.
3. Camera 3. Close-up shot of actor *A*.
4. Camera 1. Close-up shot of actor *B*.
5. Camera 2. Medium two-shot.
6. Camera 3. Tight close-up of actor *A*.
7. Camera 1. Waist shot of actor *B*.
8. Camera 2. Medium wide shot. One or both actors move to new positions within the set.

The sequence of shots within a coherent scene usually is accomplished by means of an instantaneous camera cut or take. The director's decision to take to another camera and the framing of that subsequent shot is based

Figure 14-6 Rehearsal for a production of the script, "It's a Date."

on the structure of the dialogue and the related movements of the actors. A close-up shot points up the importance of any line or series of lines from an actor. A two-shot alerts the audience for some sort of verbal or even physical interaction between the actors. A wider shot allows for larger movements and can be used to permit the actors to physically express an emotional intensity. A widely framed two-shot can also be used to express an emotional separation or isolation.

The frequency of camera cuts in a scene is related to the sense of *pacing,* or intensity of action, communicated by that scene. To cut too often and without motivation can, however, create a cluttered look in a scene and actually disturb the continuity of the performance. A director often will avoid changing cameras and will instead have the performers move within the continuing frame of the camera. A side-by-side two-shot can flow into a close-up of one foreground actor as that person moves toward the camera. That actor can then turn his or her back to the camera for an over-the-shoulder two-shot. The actor

can then walk away from the camera, past the first actor, for what becomes a wide shot. The director has accomplished three differently framed shots all on the same camera.

Production Example

The short situation comedy script in appendix D-4 ("It's A Date?") was designed to present the kind of camera blocking problems common to most dramatic productions. The main difficulties are those that involve the handling of three or four performers. The staging of four people standing side by side should at all times be avoided. Whenever possible, actors should move both upstage and downstage, as well as in a line perpendicular to the camera. (See fig. 14-6.)

The script can be used as the basis of a single class production exercise or as a series of individual student productions. If the latter method is followed, each student should be encouraged to rewrite the lines to provide a variety of characterizations and actions.

Various interpretations and characterizations can lead to entirely different production treatments of the same basic script. The blank space under "Video" should be used to write in the director's notes—camera numbers and shot descriptions.

14.4 Full Facilities Production Project

Most live or live-to-tape video productions contain a substantial amount of material that has been previously recorded and pre-edited for insert into the studio-assembled production: film, live remote *feeds,* computer graphics, slides, music, announcer copy on cartridge, and—especially—videotape. Excluding anchor-desk lead-in and lead-out, over half of the average newscast, for example, may consist of videotaped material. And studio-based *magazine*-format programs usually contain a number of out-of-studio segments. One of the director's more demanding jobs is that of coordinating the timing of roll cues for these inserts.

Much of this material has to be set up with a 5-second cue period, so that picture breakup does not result from an insufficient tape speed; that is, the videotape insert must be rolled 5 seconds before it is to be put on the air. This means that the precision of any cue to roll tape is dependent upon the accuracy of the timing of the end of the preceding segment—whether it is live on-camera talent or another videotaped insert. Once

the pre-recorded videotape is rolling, the director is committed to putting it on the program line at the end of the 5-second roll period. This procedure requires complete confidence in accurate segment timings, as well as an ability (discipline) to make continual small adjustments in the timing of the transitions from segment to segment.

Some of this difficulty has been overcome by the development of quick-starting videotape equipment. Many professional playback machines can produce a fairly reliable tape speed within 1 or 2 seconds after rolling the tape. Anyone who has worked within the time pressures of a live newscast will appreciate the value of *instant roll* capability.

The scripted production model in appendix D-5 (Full Facilities Exercise) was designed to provide an introduction to the process of combining a series of short live and recorded production elements into an ongoing sequence. The format is that of an extra-long station break similar to the kind that might be viewed in the late afternoon hours. The techniques of production are much like those used in the production of a newscast.

Figure 14-7 shows the sequence of commands for the first part of the appendix D-5 exercise. Note the suggestion that the director reinforce the later videotape roll with an extra standby command prior to the beginning of the station break.

| DIRECTOR'S COMMANDS | | D-5 SCRIPT FOR FULL FACILITIES |

"READY TO FADE IN SLIDE"
"STANDBY MUSIC AND ANNOUNCER" —:10
"PREPARE VTR-2 WITH SOUND"

		VIDEO	AUDIO

"CUE MUSIC, FADE IN SLIDE"
"STANDBY TO TAKE MUSIC UNDER" :00 SLIDE, "FRAME OF REFERENCE" MUSIC: ESTABLISH, FIVE SECONDS AND

"MUSIC UNDER, CUE ANNOUNCER" :05 BOOTH ANNC (OFF CAMERA): Should the
"STANDBY TO ROLL TAPE"
"STANDBY TO TAKE MUSIC OUT" Government ban the sale and manufac

Kenneth Anderson is joined by exper

"ROLL VTR-2" :10 sides of this important question on

"MUSIC OUT" Reference," Saturday afternoon at f

"DISSOLVE TO VTR-2, SOUND UP" :15 VIDEOTAPE PUBLIC SERVICE SOUND ON TAPE
"STANDBY NEWS ANNOUNCER ON ONE"
"PREPARE A DISSOLVE TO CAMERA ONE" :30

"CUE NEWS ANNOUNCER, DISSOLVE TO ONE" :45 STUDIO NEWS PROMO NEWS ANNC: Tonight on the six o'cl

the latest statement by the Preside

availability of Middle Eastern oil.

from Washington that the plumbing i

Figure 14-7 Sequence of commands.

The verbal commands printed in the left-hand column are what might actually be said by the director for the "full facilities" production exercise

(appendix D–5). In practice, the director would probably mark his or her script with the symbols discussed in section 13.4 (see fig. 13-15).

In preparation for the *full facilities* station break production, each student should carefully plan a complete set of director's instructions (section 13.4) and write the commands in an abbreviated form on the left-hand side of the script, as in figure 14-7. The student should then mentally rehearse the whole sequence, using a watch or a stopwatch to approximate the pressures of the actual time frame. During class production of the exercise, it is suggested that the sequence of

materials in the script be rearranged to provide a variety of production experience.

Note: Artwork that can be used to produce the "Frame of Reference" slide is available in appendix D. Spare film and videotape inserts are available in most localities at no cost; television stations receive numerous public service and promotional spots that they, in turn, usually make available to teaching facilities.

14.5 A Wrap-Up and Summary

The traditional **wrap-up** is given to a performer about 15 seconds before he or she has to get off the air. It means that there is very little time left to wrap things up, quickly summarize, and say good-bye. Perhaps it is appropriate that we wrap up quickly at this point.

This text has been concerned with the production *techniques* of handling audio, lighting, camera, switcher, recorder, editor, staging, graphics, talent, floor crew positions, and directing. If it has been successful, it has also gotten into the *disciplines* of handling these various elements. Discipline has been defined as many things in this text. As much as anything, it can be considered a matter of attitude.

Attitude toward learning and improving is one major ingredient of discipline. If you truly want to learn as much as you can about the business of television, you will gain quite a bit from this course. You will observe intently. You will try conscientiously. One of the most important secrets of learning in a course such as this is the ability to admit areas of temporary ignorance and then ask questions or seek experiences to fill in those areas. If you are unsure about audio patching, ask to have it explained to you. If you are insecure with the switcher, get all the experience you can as technical director. Do not try to bluff your way through; no one gets very far in that manner.

Attitude toward communication is important. Unless you have a strong feeling for the pursuit of communication—unless you really have a deep desire to want to succeed in communicating a message—then you are in the wrong field. Television is not just a business of glamour, or money, or excitement. It is the business of communication. For example, every program starts with a specific purpose—a clear-cut idea of what is to be attained in the production. Until you begin program planning with this attitude, your productions may be slick and polished, but they most certainly will turn out to be meaningless.

Finally, *attitude toward a professional obligation* must be considered. The terms *professional attitude* and *professionalism* are bandied about with little thought as to their implications. We use the terms here to imply more than just a means of earning a livelihood (a profession is a vocation; a professional is one who gets paid—as opposed to an amateur). We also challenge the student to think of the designation *professional* as it applied in the original sense to the three learned professions (law, medicine, and theology), which carried strong societal obligations. The true professional is one who is dedicated to high principles and a sense of community benefit. If you are committed to this kind of altruistic professionalism, you certainly will be more likely to leave your mark upon the field.

Appendix A
Electromagnetic Waves

The principles employed in the transmission of television picture and sound are extensions of several important discoveries made more than 100 years ago involving the related phenomena of electricity and magnetism. In 1856 James Clerk Maxwell further developed Faraday's concept of magnetic lines of force and expressed the theory that electrical energy existed within the universe in the form of oscillating waves. He further suggested that not only did these electric waves travel at the same speed as light but also that the waves were physically related to light itself.

By 1887 Heinrich Hertz was able to prove the existence of waves of electrical force by developing the equipment with which to generate them. His experiments revealed that the waves had varying lengths and differing rates of oscillation. It was further seen that these two factors interact with each other in a mathematical relationship also involving the wave velocity.

Before proceeding, it should be pointed out that while the vibrations that constitute natural sound in some ways resemble the qualities of the waves of the **electromagnetic spectrum,** present-day scientific thinking considers each of these to be a separate phenomenon, existing side by side within the physical laws of the universe. (See chapter 2 and appendix B.) Pressure sound waves can be transmitted only through the media of the atoms and molecules of solids, liquids, and gases; whereas electromagnetic waves can move also through the vacuum of space.

The analogy to water waves has developed as a convenient way of expressing the very complex properties of both of these forms of energy transmission. While sound pressure waves are relatively well understood, most scientists confess an inability to comprehend totally the nature of electromagnetic energy.

In any case, let us use the water wave analogy as a means of understanding the properties of both types of oscillations. Think of a series of ocean waves as seen from a cutaway

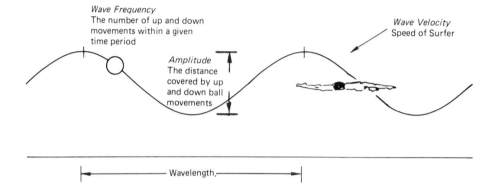

Figure A-1 Relationship of wavelength, frequency, amplitude, and velocity.

side view. In the water there is a rubber ball that floats up and down with the crests and troughs of the passing waves but remains stationary in relation to a fixed point on the sand beneath. Riding just in front of a wave crest is a body surfer. If the person moves in a straight line, he or she will indicate the speed at which the wave is traveling relative to the shoreline. In our hypothetical ocean, all of the waves come into the shore at the same speed. With this in mind, we can tell several important things by looking at the ball and the surfer. (See fig. A-1.)

First, we can measure the distance from crest to crest to determine the **wavelength.** We then notice that this wavelength has a definite relationship to the number of times the ball goes up and down in a certain period of time. This crest to trough and back to crest rate of oscillation is the measure of **frequency.** If the wavelength were shorter (distance between crests), the ball would go up and down more often in the same period of time. (Do not forget that our waves move through the water at a constant velocity.) This is an important quality of waves of electrical energy—*the greater the frequency, the shorter the wavelength.*

Watching the up-and-down movements of the ball over a long period of time may give us one more important piece of information. The ball may continue its same up-and-down

movement at a consistent number of oscillations per minute, but as the hours pass we may notice that it is not going as far up and down. As in a real ocean, the height of the wave is often the result of energy expended by a storm out at sea. The height of the wave will decrease as the energy creating it decreases. In electrical energy wave theory, the *amplitude* or amount of oscillation is the result of the amount of energy applied to the wave.

The *velocity* of the wave is simply a measure of how long it takes the crest of a single wave to move from one given point to another. In the case of electromagnetic energy, this speed is constant—the same as the speed of light, roughly 186,000 miles per second. As with light, the direction follows that of a straight line. The complex exceptions to this general rule are such that they need not draw our attention.

The basic wave cycle that measures one complete oscillation from crest to trough and back to crest again is usually called a *Hertz* in honor of Heinrich Hertz, who did so much of the preliminary research in this scientific area. Because the number of cycles per second is so large in most scientific measurements, figures are usually expressed in *kiloHertz,* or thousands of cycles, and *megaHertz,* or millions of cycles.

Looking at the AM radio, we see that the carrier frequencies utilized for transmission are those of 540 kiloHertz (540,000 cps) to 1,600

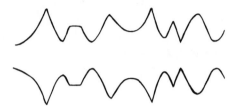

Electronic signal carrying audio information

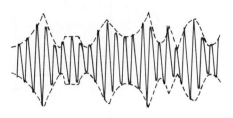

Carrier wave with amplitude modulated

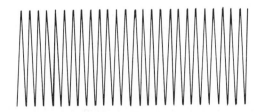

Unmodulated carrier wave

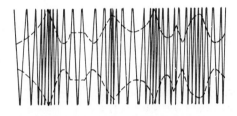

Carrier wave with frequency modulated

Top, the electronic signal coming from the microphone or recorder consists of electrical information that carries the original sound waves. *Bottom*, the unmodulated carrier wave is generated at a specific frequency in the electromagnetic spectrum.

Top, **AM Broadcasting.** The electronic signal can be superimposed onto the carrier wave by changing or *modulating the amplitude* of the carrier wave. (The dotted line indicates the original electronic signal). *Bottom*, **FM Broadcasting.** The electronic information also can be combined with the electromagnetic wave by varying or *modulating the frequency* of the carrier wave. Where the original electronic signal is strongest (indicated by the pattern of the dotted lines), the frequencies are relatively compressed.

Figure A-2   AM and FM modulation of a carrier wave.

kiloHertz. Each AM station occupies a band of frequencies 10 kiloHertz wide. The station's call letters are identified with the midpoint of these frequencies. For example, KNX in Los Angeles, 1070 on the dial, actually utilizes 1,065 to 1,075 kiloHertz for broadcast purposes.

In AM (amplitude modulation) radio the broadcast signal is, in effect, added onto the carrier frequency, and in the process variously alters the amplitude of the signal. It is this

modulation of the amplitude that the receiver translates back into sound. (See fig. A-2.)

FM (frequency modulation) radio uses much higher carrier frequencies, from 88 to 108 megaHertz. Here, it is the frequency of the carrier signal that is changed by the modulation process and, in turn, translated or demodulated back into sound. (See fig. A-2.)

As shown in figure A-3, radio and television occupy but a small part of the immense range of the known electromagnetic spectrum.

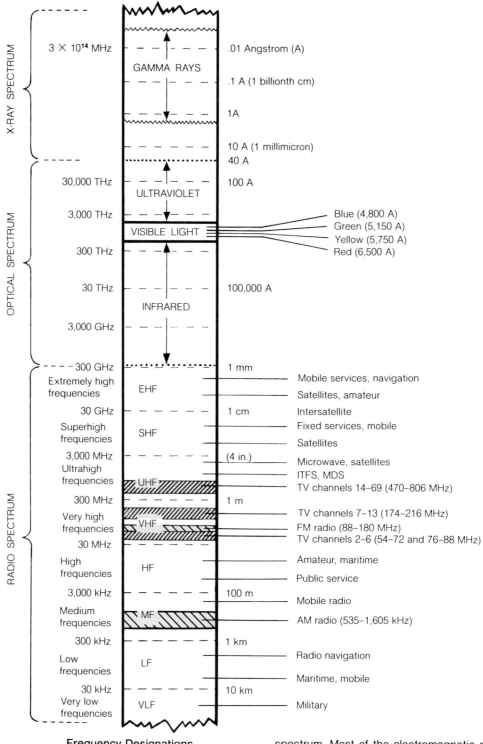

Frequency Designations

1 Hertz (Hz)	=	1 "cycle" per second
1 kiloHertz (kHz)	=	1,000 Hz
1 megaHertz (mHz)	=	1,000 kHz
1 gigaHertz (gHz)	=	1,000 mHz
1 teraHertz (tHz)	=	1,000 gHz

The entire electromagnetic spectrum includes waves that range from infinitesimally short X rays to light waves measured in *angstroms* (1 angstrom equals 1 ten-millionth of a millimeter) to radio waves that vary in length from 1 millimeter to several miles. Radio and television broadcast services occupy only a very small portion of the radio spectrum. Most of the electromagnetic space is assigned to hundreds of various services—military, navigational, satellite services; data transmissions, cellular radio, amateur (ham radio), public service, cable TV distribution; fire, police, emergency services; mobile radio (taxis, businesses), maritime, CB radio, aircraft, microwaves, remote telephones; forest services; medical, government, industrial, mobile paging; highway maintenance; short wave; civil air patrol; power utilities; transportation; and on and on.

Figure A-3
Electromagnetic spectrum.

Appendix B
The Overtone Series

In the early chapters of this text, we explained in rather simple terms the process whereby the wave form of natural sound, known as pressure waves, is transformed for broadcasting purposes into the very different electromagnetic energy wave. The production use of microphones, speakers, and other audio equipment depends largely upon a good understanding of the qualities of sound itself. The water wave analogy used in appendix A is of considerable help in examining these qualities.

The factor that distinguishes the tone of middle C on a piano from its higher neighbor, D, is its frequency. Whether it is the string on a violin, the reed on a clarinet, or the vocal cords of the human voice, each instrument has an element that is able to vibrate at varying rates of cycles per second. The relative size of the vibration is the measure of amplitude. If more force in terms of air pressure is applied to the reed, the vibration is bigger and the tone therefore is louder. The frequency, however, does not change. The pitch of the note stays the same—until the apparatus producing the tone (the clarinet's column of air or a violin string) is altered in shape or length to change the frequency of the vibration.

The velocity, or traveling speed, of a sound wave is relative to the density of the form of matter within which it moves. In the air, altitude and temperature can affect this speed. In fairly average conditions, the velocity of sound is 1,120 feet per second. With the increased density of water, the speed is 4,700 feet per second. In solid steel, for example, the velocity is sixteen times that which occurs in the air. Such velocities are a very minor consideration in broadcasting.

Our primary consideration is the effect of a vibrating instrument upon the molecules of the air. Let us take the example of a middle C tone struck on a piano. Actually, three middle C strings are set in motion when struck by the hammer, but let us follow just the action of one.

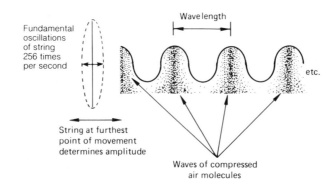

Figure B-1 Sound pressure waves.

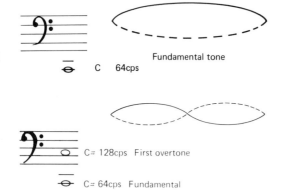

Figure B-2 Fundamental tone.

Figure B-3 First overtone.

The string is set in motion at the rate of 256 cycles per second. Each oscillation presses against the molecules of the air and creates a moving pressure wave. When 256 of these pressure waves strike the ear every second, we hear it as middle C. (See fig. B-1.)

This simple example of the back-and-forth movement of the string is not a complete description of what is happening to the agitated string. Actually, a vibrating string further subdivides itself into smaller vibrating lengths that produce additional pitches or *overtones* or *harmonics* at higher frequencies. The main tone we hear is called the *fundamental tone.*

As an example, we shall move two octaves down the piano keyboard to the low C just off the musical staff. As a fundamental tone, it vibrates at a frequency of sixty-four times a second. (See fig. B-2.)

Together with this main vibration of the string between its two endpoints, a series of smaller subdivisions occurs, each of which produces its own tone. The first subdivision divides the string in half and produces the first overtone. (See fig. B-3.) Each subsequent subdivision separates the vibrating string into quarters, eighths, sixteenths, and so forth. (See fig. B-4.)

The series of succeeding overtones are of far less intensity or loudness than the fundamental tone. Only the most discriminating ear even hears them as separate notes. Generally speaking, the lower overtones predominate, with the higher frequencies becoming almost inaudible. It is the resonating quality of each type of instrument that determines the presence or absence of overtones. The fundamental tone of A, at 440 cycles per second, on a violin will resonate and thereby reflect certain overtone frequencies better than others in the series as a result of the very design of the instrument. A metal flute playing the identical tone will resonate an entirely different series

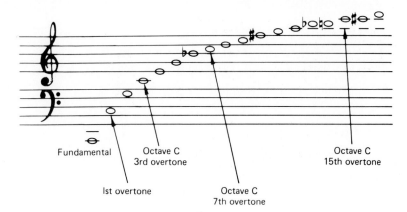

Fundamental

1st overtone

Octave C
3rd overtone

Octave C
7th overtone

Octave C
15th overtone

Figure B-4 Overtone series.

of overtones. It is this differing profile of selected overtones from among the entire series that determines the distinctive tonal quality of an instrument.[1] The electronic synthesizer artificially creates tones closely resembling real instruments by manipulating the overtone series. In the same manner, it can create tonal effects previously unattainable on conventional instruments.

1. The equal-tempered scale of the modern keyboard instruments such as the piano has made necessary some minute compromises in the tuning of such instruments. As a result, several of the overtones on the piano, notably the sixth, tenth, twelfth, and thirteenth, are at slight variance as to the exact number of cycles per second. A well-written description of the development of the modern keyboard scale is contained in the book *Science and Music,* written by Sir James Jeans (New York: Dover Publications, 1968).

Appendix C
Hand and Arm Signals

In a production situation, the hand and arm signals of the stage manager are simply a visual extension of the director's commands. Most of these gestures were developed during the early days of radio. A few have been altered somewhat for use in television production. The following examples show the signals most generally in use today.

TELEVISION HAND SIGNALS

CUE	MEANING	DESCRIPTION
STAND BY	Ready to start show Ready to record Quiet on the set	Stage Manager raises hand in air, with fingers pointing upward
YOU'RE ON TAKE YOUR CUE	Start talking Talent is on the air	Points to performer or live camera
GET CLOSER TOGETHER	Talent, performers or reporters too far apart Get closer together Get closer to object of interest	Stage Manager plays an invisible accordian, bringing palms together repeatedly

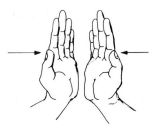

CUE	MEANING	DESCRIPTION
GET FURTHER APART	Talent too close together	Stage Manager moves hands together, back to back, then spreads them sharply apart

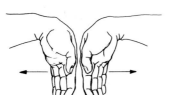

STOP **THAT'S FAR ENOUGH**	Close enough or far enough, stop moving together or apart	Traffic cop's signal, similar to stand-by signal
TALK TO THIS CAMERA **CAMERA CHANGE**	Changing cameras	Stage Manager swings hands through a wide arc from camera that is on the air to the camera that will be on the air

GET CLOSER TO THE **MICROPHONE OR** **SPEAK LOUDER**	Audio level too low Get closer to the mike	Stage Manager moves hands toward himself/ herself or toward the mike

GET FURTHER FROM **MICROPHONE OR** **SPEAK LOWER**	Opposite of above	Opposite of above
KEEP TALKING **STRETCH**	Too much time left Fill in	Extend thumb and forefinger horizon- tally, move them like the beak of a bird

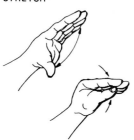

CUE	MEANING	DESCRIPTION
STRETCH IT OUT SLOW DOWN	Talking too fast	Move hands as if pulling taffy apart or stretching rubber bands.

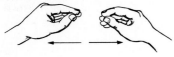

| SPEED IT UP | Talking too slow Running out of time | Move forefinger in circles |

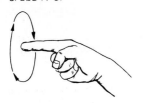

| ON THE NOSE PROGRAM ON TIME | Program is running right on time, no problems | Stage Manager touches nose with foreginger |

| O.K. ALL IS WELL YOUR POSITION IS FINE | Well done Stay right there | Form an "O" with thumb and forefinger with other three fingers raised |

CUE	MEANING	DESCRIPTION
FIVE MINUTES TO GO TWO MINUTES TO GO ONE MINUTE TO GO	Time cues to end of show	Raise hand with corresponding number of fingers spread apart or raise flash cards

| HALF A MINUTE TO GO | Time to end of segment or end of show | Cross forefingers or forearms at midpoint |

| WRAP IT UP | 10 seconds left
Come to a conclusion | Rocking or shaking of clenched fist |

| CUT
FINISH
OFF THE AIR | Segment or show is over | Stage Manager slashes own throat with fore-finger or edge of hand |

| STATION BREAK
(I.D.) | Commercial | The motion of break-ing a twig is made with clenched fists |

Appendix D
Production Projects

D–1 Class Audio Production Project (Chapter 3)

COPY: "INTEGRATED SOUND CORPORATION" COMMERCIAL

MUSIC: UP FULL FOR TEN SECONDS AND UNDER

ANNC #1   THE <u>INTEGRATED SOUND CORPORATION</u> OF MANHATTAN CORDIALLY

                   INVITES YOU TO A PREVIEW PRESENTATION OF THE NEWEST

                   DEVELOPMENTS FROM THE <u>OLYMPIA</u> LINE OF FINE SOUND

                   REPRODUCTION SYSTEMS. FOR THE NEXT WEEK, ALL TEN

                   <u>INTEGRATED</u> STORES IN NEW YORK CITY AND NEW JERSEY WILL BE

                   DEMONSTRATING STEREO COMPONENTS DESIGNED TO PRODUCE A

                   FULL FREQUENCY RESPONSE HERETOFORE HEARD ONLY IN

                   PROFESSIONAL SOUND RECORDING STUDIOS.

MUSIC: FADE UP FULL TEN SECONDS AND UNDER

ANNC #2   <u>OLYMPIA'S</u> GREATEST ADVANCE IN THE PAST TWENTY YEARS HAS

                   BEEN MADE POSSIBLE BY THE NEW HORIZONTAL FIELD EFFECT

                   TRANSISTOR, WHICH PRODUCES A CLEAN, UNCOLORED SOUND POWER

                   OF INCREDIBLE DIMENSION.

(CONTINUED)

MUSIC:	FADE UP FULL TEN SECONDS AND UNDER
ANNC #1	THE OLYMPIA T-E-A 850 STEREO AMPLIFIER, WITH 100 WATTS PER CHANNEL, REPRODUCES FREQUENCIES AS LOW AS 20 CYCLES PER SECOND UP TO 20,000 CYCLES PER SECOND. THESE RANGE FROM TONES THAT ARE LOWER THAN THE LOWEST NOTE ON THE PIANO KEYBOARD UP TO THE HIGHEST OVERTONE FREQUENCIES THAT ARE WITHIN THE RANGE OF HUMAN HEARING. THE RESULT IS A LIFELIKE "OPEN" SOUND QUALITY PRODUCED WITH SOLID STATE HIGH STABILITY AND RELIABILITY.
MUSIC:	FADE UP FULL TEN SECONDS AND UNDER
ANNC #2	SEE ALL OF THE COMPONENTS IN THE EXCITING NEW LINE FROM OLYMPIA THIS WEEK AT ANY OF YOUR INTEGRATED STORES IN NEW YORK CITY AND NEW JERSEY.
MUSIC:	UP FULL FIVE SECONDS AND OUT

D–2 *"The Magnificent Burden" Visual Materials (Chapter 7)*

VIDEO	AUDIO
CARD, CONVENTION	<u>MUSIC</u>: ESTABLISH THREE SECONDS AND UNDER <u>ANNC</u>: WHAT QUALITY OF MIND IS IT THAT WOULD MAKE A MAN OR WOMAN WANT TO BECOME PRESIDENT OF THE UNITED STATES? STATURE? . . . POWER? . . . OR WEALTH?
CARD, PARADE	MOST OF THE MEN WHO ARE SERIOUSLY CONSIDERED FOR THE OFFICE HAVE ALREADY ACHIEVED MORE THAN ENOUGH OF THESE TO LAST MOST OF A LIFETIME.
CARD, ROOSEVELT	FRANKLIN D. ROOSEVELT, WHO SERVED THROUGHOUT A MAJOR DEPRESSION AND A WORLD WAR, EXERCISED MORE POWER FOR THE GOOD OF HIS COUNTRY THAN ALMOST ANY OTHER PRESIDENT BEFORE HIM. HE LED WHILE FACING PHYSICAL HANDICAPS THAT WOULD HAVE EASILY DEFEATED A LESSER MAN.

(CONTINUED)

VIDEO	AUDIO

CARD, KENNEDY

MANY SENSED IN JOHN F. KENNEDY A DEEP FEELING OF RESPONSIBILITY TO THE PEOPLE OF ALL THE WORLD. AFTER EARLY ERRORS HE SHOWED INCREASING STRENGTH, AS WAS EVIDENCED BY HIS HANDLING OF THE CUBAN MISSILE CRISIS. HE WAS GIVEN ONLY A THOUSAND DAYS.

CARD, JOHNSON

POWER ALONE IS INADEQUATE TO COMPLETELY EXPLAIN THE EXERCISE OF AUTHORITY THAT CIRCUMSTANCES CAN PLACE UPON OUR NATIONAL LEADER. LYNDON B. JOHNSON, A MAN WHO HAD USED POWER LONG AND WELL IN THE CONGRESS, FOUND HIS STRENGTH DILUTED AND BLOCKED DURING HIS LAST MONTHS IN OFFICE.

CARD, NIXON

THERE ARE TIMES WHEN CIRCUMSTANCES APPEAR TO OVERWHELM THE MEN WHO HOLD THIS GREAT OFFICE. A FINAL FAIR AND MEANINGFUL JUDGMENT OF THE PRESIDENCY OF RICHARD M. NIXON WILL PROBABLY NOT BE COMPLETELY WRITTEN FOR AT LEAST A DECADE.

CARD, FORD AND CARTER

GERALD FORD AND JIMMY CARTER BOTH STARTED THEIR PRESIDENTIAL CAREERS ON A STRONG WAVE OF PERSONAL POPULARITY. ONE SUCCEEDED TO THE OFFICE FOLLOWING AN UNPRECEDENTED PRESIDENTIAL RESIGNATION. AND THE OTHER

VIDEO	AUDIO
	WAS INITIALLY ELECTED WITH A POPULAR MANDATE. YET NEITHER MAN WAS ABLE TO BUILD A SUCCESSFUL MEDIA IMAGE AS A POWERFUL AND EFFECTIVE LEADER. NEITHER MAN WAS ABLE TO GET ELECTED TO A SECOND TERM.
CARD, REAGAN AND GROUP	ONE OF THE MOST POPULAR PRESIDENTS OF THE LAST HALF-CENTURY, RONALD REAGAN ACHIEVED ECONOMIC REFORMS THAT ASTOUNDED BOTH SUPPORTERS AND OPPONENTS. YET HE LEFT OFFICE FRUSTRATED BY A NATIONAL DEBT OF TWO TRILLION DOLLARS AND TROUBLED BY THE LARGER CONCERNS OF WORLD PEACE.
CARD, CAPITOL	THE LONELINESS AND ISOLATION OF HIGH OFFICE, COUPLED WITH THE TREMENDOUS PRESSURES OF LEADERSHIP AND DECISION-MAKING, MAKE THE ACHIEVEMENTS OF THESE UNIQUE INDIVIDUALS SEEM TRULY REMARKABLE IN THE JUDGMENT OF HISTORY.
TITLE CARD, SUPERED OR KEYED OVER CAPITOL CARD	OUR SERIES, "THE MAGNIFICENT BURDEN," PROBES THEIR VICTORIES AND THEIR DISAPPOINTMENTS . . . SUNDAY EVENINGS AT NINE.
FADE TO BLACK	<u>MUSIC</u>: UP FULL FOR 3 SECONDS. FADE OUT.

D–3 *Production Project: Discussion Program (Chapter 13)*

OPENING AND CLOSING FORMAT

VIDEO	AUDIO

WIDE ESTAB. SHOT CAM 2

<u>MUSIC</u>: ESTABLISH FIVE SECONDS AND UNDER

<u>ANNC</u>: "Frame of Reference," an information service program designed to explore the multifaceted issues that affect us, both as individuals and as members of an increasingly complex society. Here with our guests is the "Frame of Reference" moderator, _____ .

<u>MUSIC</u>: OUT

MCU, CAM 1

<u>MODERATOR</u>: Our area of examination today is _____

_____ .

<u>MODERATOR</u>: (CONTINUED) To help us in gaining a greater understanding of the problems that are involved in this issue are three people who hold somewhat differing views on the solutions to

those problems. Seated next to me is

_____ from _____ .

```
VIDEO                AUDIO
```

CU CAM 3   Our second guest is _____

who represents _____ .

CU CAM 2   Our final guest, who is from _____ ,

is _____ .

WIDE-SHOT   As a way of establishing the background to today's issue,
CAM 1
I would like to ask my first question of

_____ .

(BODY OF PROGRAM)

CU MODERATOR CAM   MODERATOR: With that last point we must, for now,
1
conclude our discussion of _____ . The issue is a

large one and our program time is, unfortunately,

limited. I would like to thank our guests _____ ,

ZOOM OUT TO TIGHT   _____ , and _____ for joining us today and for
4 SHOT
measurably adding to our collective knowledge of this

controversial issue. This is _____ .

Good-bye until next week.

(CONTINUED)

VIDEO	AUDIO
EXTREME WIDE-SHOT CAM 2	MUSIC: ESTABLISH FIVE SECONDS AND UNDER
(SUPER CREDITS)	ANNC: As a program, "Frame of Reference" makes no attempt to establish any final solutions to the problems under discussion. Our goal is that of presenting well-informed opinion leaders to our viewing public so that each individual can come to his or her own conclusions. Next week our "Frame of Reference" will encompass the matter of _____ _____ . Be sure to join us then.
	MUSIC: UP FULL TO CONCLUSION
FADE TO BLACK	MUSIC: FADE OUT

D–4 *Production Exercise: "It's a Date?" (Chapter 14)*

VIDEO   AUDIO   (APPROX. 4:00 MIN.)

<u>HARRY:</u> (TALKING TO NANCY, WHO IS OFFSTAGE) I see where old Harold Osgood is fighting with the university again.

<u>NANCY:</u> (ENTERING FROM CAMERA RIGHT) What, dear?

<u>HARRY:</u> Councilman Osgood objects to the fact that taxpayers' money is being spent on a college course called "The Crisis in Human Sexuality." He says that it's part of a plot to destroy the morals of American youth.

<u>NANCY:</u> Oh, it's probably just one of those courses that teach people how to get along with one another.

<u>HARRY:</u> (SARCASTICALLY) Yeah, I'll <u>bet</u> it is.

<u>NANCY:</u> Oh, Harry, it's not <u>that</u>. Those kind of classes just help people to establish their personal identity . . . you know, who they really are.

(CONTINUED)

VIDEO	AUDIO

HARRY: Well, when I was in college no professor had to tell me who or what I was.

NANCY: I remember very well what kind of a guy you were. (KIDDING) You were a big <u>wolf</u>, that's what you were.

HARRY: (SMILING) Oh, come on, Nancy, I was just a normal red-blooded American boy.

NANCY: Well it just might have done <u>you</u> some good to have taken one of those courses. Things are different now with men and women, Harry. We're no longer in the Dark Ages.

HARRY: Yeh, a lot of good it's done . . . a bunch of so-called liberated females running around. . . .

NANCY: (INTERRUPTING) Harry, they don't run around. They do a lot of constructive things. Why only last week. . . .

KIM: (INTERRUPTING FROM OFFSTAGE) Daddy, what time is it? (ENTERING SOMEWHAT BREATHLESSLY) Richard will be here any minute.

VIDEO	AUDIO

HARRY: (STERN BUT FATHERLY) It's seven twenty-five, and who's Richard?

KIM: He's only a really neat guy, that's all. And don't be so uptight, Daddy.

NANCY: Kim, you know that your father always thinks of your dates as being direct descendants of Attila the Hun.

KIM: Well he's not. He's really nice. He writes on the school newspaper and he's really into broadcasting.

HARRY: If he has somehow made you suddenly aware of the discipline of time, he can't be all bad.

KIM: Well, he's very . . . you know, intellectual. He knows <u>all</u> about music and things.

HARRY: Yes, I can imagine. I remember that football player friend of yours. He spoke English like a second language.

MUSIC: ROCK AND ROLL MUSIC UNDER THE CONVERSATION AS IF FROM OUTSIDE THE HOUSE.

(CONTINUED)

VIDEO	AUDIO

HARRY: (CONTINUING) The only trouble was that he didn't have a first . . . . say what's that noise?

KIM: Oh, that must be Richard. Will you go to the door? I'm not ready! (EXITS)

NANCY: Well, we should be thankful that Richard at least comes to the door . . . not like the boy who sat in the driveway and honked. (SHE EXITS CAMERA RIGHT)

(HARRY PUTS DOWN THE NEWSPAPER AND SLOWLY STANDS UP SHAKING HIS HEAD.)

NANCY: (OFFSTAGE) Hello, I'm Kim's mother. You must be Richard. Won't you come in? She will be right out. (ENTERING FROM CAMERA RIGHT) Harry, this is Kim's friend, Richard. I'm afraid that Kim hasn't told us your last name.

RICHARD: Uh, Richard's O.K.

(THERE IS AN AWKWARD FIVE-SECOND PAUSE WHILE ALL TRY TO THINK OF SOMETHING TO SAY.)

VIDEO	AUDIO

NANCY: Well, it's so nice.

HARRY: (OVER NANCY'S LINE) Is that music coming from your car?

RICHARD: That's my van. It sleeps two.

(HARRY STARTS TO SAY SOMETHING, THINKS BETTER OF IT, AND QUICKLY TRIES TO COVER HIS STARTLED EXPRESSION.)

RICHARD: (CONTINUING) Like, I do a lot of camping. It's really great with my tape deck out in the woods.

HARRY: (STRAIGHT BUT WITH A TOUCH OF SARCASM) Yes, I guess you could really get back to nature.

(NANCY CROSSES TO HIM, TAKES HIS ARM AND GIVES IT A WARNING SQUEEZE.)

RICHARD: That's Wretched Yellow playing "Boogie 'Til Nineteen Ninety-five." It's their big hit. Great guitar. (HE MOVES SLIGHTLY WITH THE MUSIC)

(CONTINUED)

VIDEO	AUDIO

NANCY: Kim tells us that you write for the school newspaper.

RICHARD: Yeah, I write a column called "Diggin' the Discs." They wanted me to call it "Pickin' the Platters," but I thought it sounded kinda' corny.

HARRY: You're right, it just doesn't have the same ring to it.

(NANCY GIVES HARRY ANOTHER WARNING SQUEEZE.)

RICHARD: What do you do, Mr. Olmstead?

HARRY: Well, I . . . uh . . . I work at the bank.

RICHARD: Oh yeah, Kim told me. Well, I guess everybody has to do something.

HARRY: (REACTING) It may seem sort of quaint, but in today's society. . . .

KIM: (INTERRUPTING AS SHE ENTERS FROM CAMERA LEFT) Hi, Richard. (SHE CROSSES TO HIM.)

VIDEO	AUDIO

RICHARD: Wow, you are some kind o' looker.

KIM: Richie, I just love your jacket. It's really neat. Hey, we better go.

NANCY: Wait a minute. Where are you two going?

KIM: To the movies. We can either see a musical, <u>The Monster on Lead Guitar</u> or <u>My Secret Swedish Summer.</u> They say it's a beautiful, artistic movie about this couple in love. . . .

HARRY: I don't think I want to hear . . . I can already guess.

NANCY: Isn't there something else playing?

RICHARD: Yeah, but they're just like what's on television. Kim, let's go to the monster movie. They say that Lulu Bash is fantastic in the death scenes. She does karate moves while playing the love theme from the movie on her guitar.

(CONTINUED)

VIDEO	AUDIO

KIM: Super. Well, we better go. See you later. (EXITING) Everybody at school has seen it by now. We just have to go.

NANCY: Don't be too late, dear.

KIM: I won't. (OFFSTAGE) Bye-bye.

(WHEN THEY ARE GONE, THERE IS A PAUSE AS NANCY AND HARRY LOOK AT EACH OTHER.)

HARRY: (LAUGHING RUEFULLY) Where did we go wrong?

NANCY: Oh, he's a nice boy, Harry. He's just at that age.

HARRY: I guess you're right. I hope so anyway. Say . . . how would you like to sneak off and see <u>My Secret Swedish Summer?</u>

NANCY: (LAUGHING) Let me think about it.

MUSIC: Briefly fade rock music up full and out.

D–5　*Script for Full Facilities Production Exercise (Chapter 14)*

VIDEO	AUDIO

SLIDE, "FRAME OF REFERENCE"	<u>MUSIC</u>: ESTABLISH, FIVE SECONDS AND UNDER
	<u>BOOTH ANNC</u> (OFF CAMERA): Should the United States Government ban the sale and manufacture of DMSO? Kenneth Anderson is joined by experts on both sides of this important question on "Frame of Reference," Saturday afternoon at four.
VIDEOTAPE PUBLIC SERVICE :30	<u>SOUND ON TAPE</u>
STUDIO NEWS PROMO :30	NEWS ANNC: Tonight on the six o'clock news we have the latest statement by the President on the availability of Middle Eastern oil. . . . A report from Washington that the plumbing in the Watergate Hotel has sprung its own leak. . . News from Detroit that thousands of new cars have been recalled before they ever got off the assembly line . . . and sportscaster Stan Dilbeck has a report on the Matadors and their chance for a winning season.

(CONTINUED)

VIDEO	AUDIO
STUDIO HOST	<u>HOST (ON CAMERA)</u>: Tonight at nine our program series "The Magnificent Burden" presents an account of the triumphs and defeats of Lyndon B. Johnson. As a man forced to assume power in a time of crisis, he was often admired for the way in which he took over the responsibilities of leadership. Many of his proposed social reforms were, however, sacrificed to the demands of a war that seemingly could not be ended. "The Magnificent Burden" tonight at nine.
CARD: JOHNSON	
CARD: MATTE "THE MAGNIFICENT BURDEN"	
STUDIO	<u>HOST (ON CAMERA)</u>: Coming up in just a moment we have something in a lighter vein on "Campus Rock." Host, Charlie "Red" Stewart, presents The Grass Valley Boys singing "Pure Pleasure," Bonnie Street does her version of "The Sadness of My Life," and that new group, The Electric Car, performs their hit, "Turn on the Lights." They get it all together, next on _____ TV.
VTR	<u>SOUND ON TAPE</u>

The seven photographs and one super card included in this appendix are to be photographically enlarged and used in the class production projects for sections 7.6 and 14.4.

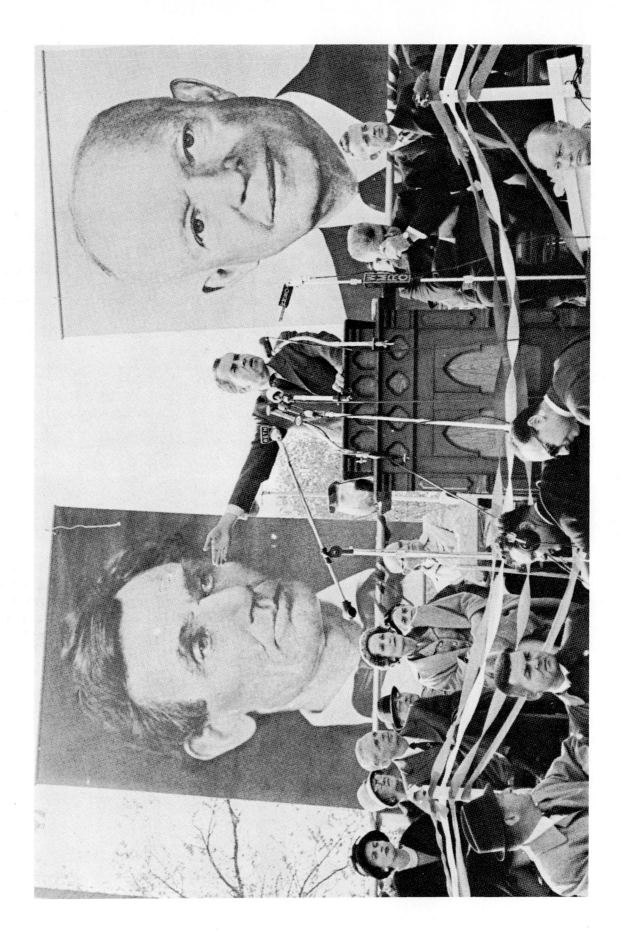

THE MAGNIFICENT BURDEN

Sundays, 9:00pm

Appendix E
The Rate Card

As introduced in chapter 11 (section 11.3), the unit manager (or production manager) is usually the chief budget supervisor on any professional production. It is his or her job to oversee all fiscal aspects of the production contract. To help you understand some of the details and concerns of the unit manager's position, the Rate Cards and associated materials in this appendix have been prepared for examination and utilization in production courses.[1]

It is suggested that these materials be removed (at the perforations) and used for actual studio productions. Students should be given the experience of working through these sheets and estimating actual production costs as part of their curricular training. These forms may be used as they are, or instructors may want to revise the figures in order to reflect actual dollar costs in a given locality.

Below-the-Line Costs

Each production house or network has a set of rates that it charges for its services. Essentially, these are the below-the-line costs as introduced in section 1.6. These rates are listed on the **rate card,** which is updated each year to reflect economic realities. As union contracts are negotiated periodically—increasing the salaries of those personnel assigned to the production—so the rate charged to the producer must be increased.

The charges listed on the rate card do not reflect the actual money paid to the listed engineer or production person. In fact, the salary of that person may be as little as one-third of the charge for that position levied against the show producer. The production studios and networks must maintain large staffs—management, clerical, maintenance, legal, janitorial, budget and personnel officers, support

1. Most of this appendix is based upon materials developed by Jay Roper, Director, NBC News West Coast, for use in production courses. The authors gratefully thank Mr. Roper for his permission to use the materials in this text.

staff, technical operations schedulers, and so forth—to support those production positions. Fringe benefits, medical insurance, taxes, and other deductions all are covered by the charges on the rate card; these costs all must be passed along to the contracting/producing agency.

Generally, the rate card can be broken down into three separate components:

(1) *The Technical Personnel Chart;* (2) *Facilities Rates Chart;* and (3) *Personnel Hourly Rate Chart.*

Technical Personnel Chart.

The size and complexity of any given production will obviously determine the staff needed for that show. Additionally, sometimes the contractual obligations will dictate the needs for a production. For example, some equipment—such as a crane—may require, according to the engineering contract, a certain number of people to operate it.

All engineering positions cost the same on the rate card—even though some individuals will actually receive more pay than others (due to seniority, expertise, responsibility, and so forth). The Technical Personnel Chart (fig. E-1) reflects costs on a quarter-hour basis, adjusted to a three-hour production period for training situations.

Engineers usually will be assigned to a production in eight-hour blocks—the standard work day defined by the union. (Of that eight hours, one is set aside for a meal. And if you, as a producer, are shooting on location at some distance from a restaurant, you will want to have the meals catered; otherwise the union contract states that travel time to the nearest restaurant is "on the clock.")

In case of overtime, the producer will have to pay an additional rate. Also, you are charged less per hour after a certain amount of time; this is done to discourage producers from renting facilities in short blocks of time. Therefore, it is most cost-efficient to plan your production within eight-hour periods.

Facilities Rates.

At most networks and production facilities, the charges for studio rental might vary from maybe $300 per hour to as much as $700 an hour for a large stage (for a six-hour minimum). This charge includes basically an empty studio with cyclorama, lighting instruments and controls, normal camera complement, and control rooms—no sets, no special electronic effects, no special lights, and, of course, no personnel.

The charge indicated on the Facilities Rates Chart (fig. E-2) for videotape facilities are for playback only. Charges for editing time usually would be much higher since editing would demand much more sophisticated equipment. Costs for 2-inch (quad) and 1-inch (type C) playback machines are higher than for ¾-inch format players because of both (a) higher initial costs and maintenance and (b) longer setup time.

The rental of the film chain includes the full facilities of the chain (slides, 16mm and 35mm film projectors) as well as the video control panel for that telecine chain and the patching necessary to deliver the feed to the studio control room or other destination.

A production may require additional engineering equipment and special effects such as frame storers, character generators, advanced SEG switchers, editing facilities, and so forth. These costs would have to be added to the basic Facilities Rates.

Although the additional production costs would appear to be quite steep for these added extras, it may be that the increased expenditures are worth the cost because of the time that can be saved; computer graphics capabilities or editing facilities may save you hours of preproduction, production, or postproduction work that you would otherwise be paying for in other ways. Therefore, the thorough producer must carefully "cost out" all possible production options.

Personnel Hourly Rates. Many different categories of nonengineering production personnel must also be considered. Depending upon the needs of the producer, many of these costs will be below-the-line expenses. These personnel also can be provided by the network or the production house. Again, the fees charged on the Personnel Hourly Rate Chart (fig. E-3) are not indicative of actual pay scales—as overhead costs must be covered by the production house or network.

Before the Show. Before the production moves near the studio, much work must be accomplished. Design, construction, acquisition, transportation, and placement of sets, set pieces, props, art work, costumes, drapes, and lights call for the "renting" (from the production house) of many different types of personnel—carpenters, set designers, wardrobe staff, graphic artists, stagehands, grips, prop handlers, drape constructionists, electricians, and so forth.

During the Production. The chief below-the-line positions would probably be the associate director and the stage manager(s). Other specialized positions may have to be considered—pages (to handle the studio audience), security guards (to stand over the game show prizes), makeup, production assistants, and so forth.

After the Production. Somebody must clean up. Sets must be struck. Props and costumes have to be returned. In effect, the studio must be returned to the condition that it was in prior to the production. Personnel must be retained to handle all this.

In summary, it should be realized that the rate card is a *guide* and that while these charges reflect an honest, competitive position, there is always room for negotiation—especially if you are planning on producing a number of productions at the same production facility. Nevertheless, the rate card is a basis for that negotiation and you, as a producer, must learn to use it in planning and determining your below-the-line costs.

Above-the-Line Costs

In addition to the below-the-line expenses, you must also plan on budgeting for above-the-line costs. These are the expenses that are incurred by the producer outside of the production house or network studio charges (section 1.6).

Many of the above-the-line budget items are for personnel and most of these are *negotiated fees*. The American Federation of Television and Radio Artists (AFTRA), the Writers Guild of America (WGA), the Directors Guild of America (DGA), and the American Federation of Musicians (AFM) all have contracts that specify the fee that the creative talent involved is to receive. In addition to these stated minimum guild and union (federation) fees, many artists of "star" caliber will, of course, negotiate much higher salaries. Special *perquisites* may also have to be provided—limousine service, personalized travel arrangements, private hairdressers, personal secretaries, and so forth.

In addition to the salaries paid to the talent and creative personnel, consideration must be given to other salaries (of production associates, secretaries, typists) and to other business expenses (rental of offices, telephones, office supplies, and similar items).

In the case of remotes or *location shoots,* other costs may involve housing, catering, transportation, telephone lines, microwave links, and possibly satellite time and uplink facilities. Other special services may involve standby firefighters (for any explosive or incendiary effects), ambulance and medical contingencies (for difficult stunt work), off-duty police officers (for security and traffic control), teachers (tutors for child actors), helicopter services, and any other extraordinary services the production may require.

The two contract forms (figs. E-4 and E-5) are variations of basic contracts that can be used for directors and for performing talent, respectively. (As with the three preceding below-the-line charts, these forms may be torn out and used as they are or may be modified to reflect specific university training situations.)

The final four sheets of this appendix comprise a "Production Cost Report," which can be used as a realistic exercise in working out detailed budget projections for a typical television production. It is suggested that student producers and/or unit managers be required to turn in an accurate budget estimate, following these forms. The first form is a summary cover sheet. The remaining forms are below-the-line and above-the-line worksheets.

This appendix has been but a cursory simplification of the business end of producing a television program. We have only briefly touched upon some of the complexities with which producers and networks must be involved—negotiating studio costs, union contracts, personnel services; scheduling crews; booking transportation; renting outside facilities; arranging for special police and medical services, communication utilities and hookups; and so forth. However, this should serve to familiarize the beginning student with some of the budget considerations that producers and unit managers must learn to juggle in managing any kind of production enterprise.

Technical Personnel Chart

Number of Engineers

Rate	Hour	1	2	3	4	5	6	7	8	9	10
$20	¼	20	40	60	80	100	120	140	160	180	200
$20	½	220	240	260	280	300	320	340	360	380	400
$20	¾	415	430	445	460	475	490	505	520	535	550
$20	1	565	580	595	610	625	640	655	670	685	700
$20	1¼	725	750	775	800	825	850	875	900	925	950
$20	1½	975	1000	1025	1050	1075	1100	1125	1150	1175	1200
$20	1¾	1230	1260	1290	1320	1350	1380	1410	1440	1470	1500
$20	2	1530	1560	1590	1620	1650	1680	1710	1740	1770	1800
$20	2¼	1830	1860	1890	1920	1950	1980	2010	2040	2070	2100
$20	2½	2130	2160	2190	2220	2250	2280	2310	2340	2370	2400
$20	2¾	2435	2470	2505	2540	2575	2610	2645	2680	2715	2750
$20	3	2790	2830	2870	2910	2950	2990	3030	3070	3110	3150

College Engineering Contract Provisions

1. In the event the engineers are scheduled for 15 minutes or less, the following provisions do not apply.
2. Engineers will be given a 5-minute break each half hour. These break times may be accumulative.
3. Engineers may be given their accumulated breaktime (up to 15 minutes of accumulated time) prior to their beginning work.
4. Engineers will be given a break of at least 5 minutes no later than 1½ hours into the schedule regardless of the accumulated time.

Figure E-1

Facilities Rates Chart

1. Minimum rental of studio is ½ hour with the charges being assessed at the rate of $50.00 per 15-minute period. This means a minimum rental of $100.00.
2. The rental of a film chain will be $15.00 per 15-minute period. Minimum rental is 15 minutes.
3. Videotape facilities will be $20.00 per 15-minute period with ½ hour being the minimum rental.
4. The following are miscellaneous studio costs:
   a. Graphics easels .... $10.00 per day each
   b. Slides* .... $ 5.00 per day each
   c. Matte cards* .... $ 5.00 per day each
   d. Full pictures* .... $ 5.00 per day each
   e. Film* .... $20.00 per 30 seconds
   f. Flats .... $10.00 per day each
   g. Desks .... $ 5.00 per day each
   h. Chairs .... $ 5.00 per day each
   i. Risers .... $10.00 per day each
   j. Any furniture brought from outside .... $20.00 transportation each item
   k. House piano .... $20.00 per day
   l. Musical instrument brought in .... $15.00 per day transportation

*Remember that if you had been working with a production house or a network, you would either have had to farm out services for matte cards and full pictures to the graphic arts department or you would have had to hire a photographer for your film. These are costs that you would have had to pick up. So you, as a student, must be billed for these services even though you may have done the graphics or the films yourself.

Figure E-2

Personnel Hourly Rate Chart

One-Hour Call Minimum

Associate Director	$25.00
Stage Manager	$25.00
Stagehands/Electricians	$20.00
Wardrobe[1]	$18.00
Makeup/Hair Stylist[2]	$18.00
Graphic Artist[3]	$22.00
Scenic Designer[4]	$25.00
Costume Handler[5]	$18.00
Prop Handler	$19.00
Scenic Carpenter[6]	$19.00
Scenic Artist[7]	$22.00
Drape Constructionist[8]	$25.00

1. If the performers use any clothes other than street clothes, even though it is their clothing, this charge must be assessed.
2. If the performers require any makeup, even though they may apply it themselves, this charge must be assessed.
3. If any full pictures or matte cards are used, this charge must be assessed.
4. If a set of any kind is used, this charge must be assessed.
5. If the performer uses any clothing that would be considered a costume (i.e., period clothing), this charge must be assessed.
6. If any of the flats or risers are used, this charge must be assessed.
7. If any artwork other than matte or full cards are used, then this charge must be assessed.
8. If drapes other than the cyclorama are used, then this charge must be assessed.

Realize—due to the structure of this class—that some of these costs will be "dummy" costs; that is, there will not be a person fulfilling each one of these tasks—unlike the assignment of a person to a camera. Nevertheless, if you were producing at a production house or a network, these would be real costs, and in order to familiarize you (as a student) with the real world, these costs should be figured into your production.

Figure E-3

Directors Contract

Directors working on production projects will be paid the following rates:

News and Documentary

0–5 min.	5–10 min.	10–15 min.	15–30 min.
$150.00	$175.00	$200.00	$400.00

Dramas

0–15 min	15–30 min.
$400.00	$750.00

Musicals

0–5 min.	5–15 min.	15–30 min.
$350.00	$500.00	$750.00

Each director may negotiate his or her own agreement but the above are the minimum salary rates that must be met. In the event a personal services contract is negotiated, a copy of the following must be attached to the Production Cost Report by the unit manager:

The minimum salary for a personal services contract will be 150% of the rate shown above.

Tear here

Date: _____

To: Business Affairs

From: _____ (Unit Manager)

This constitutes an agreement between the below-signed producer and the below-signed director that the director shall receive as compensation for services the figure shown below.

AMOUNT: $ _____

Director: _____ Producer: _____

Figure E-4

Artists Contract

Performers working on production projects will be paid the following rates:

Principle Performers (Dramatic, Nondramatic)

0–5 min.	5–10 min.	10–15 min.	15–30 min.
$100.00	$150.00	$200.00	$300.00

Performers—Five lines or less

0–5 min	5–10 min.	10–15 min.	15–30 min.
$50.00	$75.00	$100.00	$130.00

Off Camera—five lines or less (includes announcers)

0–5 min.	5–10 min.	10–15 min.	15–30 min.
$25.00	$37.00	$50.00	$65.00

Off Camera—six lines or more (includes announcers)

0–5 min.	5–10 min.	10–15 min.	15–30 min.
$50.00	$75.00	$100.00	$125.00

Groups/Chorus (includes musicians but not lead singers)

Three to Seven People (each)

0–15 min.	15–30 min.
$25.00	$45.00

Eight or More People (each)

0–15 min.	15–30 min.
$15.00	$30.00

Additional payment for stepping out as soloist or part of chorus for 8 bars or more but less than 16 bars:

150% of above rate

Additional payment for 16 bars or more:

200% of above rate

Sportscaster:

Each sportscaster shall receive $200 per event.

This fee is only for sports events . . . if in a news segment, the principle performer rate shall apply.

Extras/Walkons

0–5 min.	5–10 min.	10–15 min.	15–30 min.
$10.00	$15.00	$20.00	$30.00

Figure E-5

Production Cost Report

Show Name: _____

Producer: _____

Unit Manager: _____

Description	Estimate	Actual	Notes
Below-line Costs			
Above-line Costs			

Total Estimate: _____

Total Actual: _____

Comments:

Below-Line Costs Worksheet

Show Name: _____

Producer: _____

Unit Manager _____

Description	Estimate	Actual	Notes

*Scenic, Graphic, and
  Prop Charges*

Piano

Flats

Risers

Desks

Chairs

Matte cards

Full pictures

Graphics easels

Transportation

Slides

Film

Personnel Costs
Engineers

Associate director

Stage manager

Stagehands

(CONTINUED)

Electricians

_____

Wardrobe

_____

Makeup/Hair stylist

_____

Graphic artist

_____

Scenic designer

_____

Costume handlers

_____

Scenic carpenter

_____

Scenic artist

_____

Drape constructionist

_____

_____

_____

_____

_____

_____

Studio Facilities
Film chain

_____

Video tape

_____

Studio rental

_____

_____

_____

_____

_____

Estimated Total = _____

Actual Total = _____

Comments:

_____

Above-Line Costs Worksheet

Show Name: _____

Producer: _____

Unit Manager: _____

Description	Estimate	Actual	Notes
Personnel			
Talent			
Talent			
Talent			
Talent			
Talent			
Talent			
Talent			
Talent			
Director			
Musician			
Musician			
Musician			
Musician			
Musician			
Musician			
Musician			

Estimate Total: _____

Actual Total: _____

Comments: _____

Glossary

above-the-line costs Expenditures for creative and performing personnel (such as the producer, associate producers, writers, artists, musicians, actors, and others) and other administrative elements (such as office space, rehearsal halls, studio space, and so forth).

A.D. (associate director, assistant director) A key production assistant—usually responsible for timing of the program—who may be delegated any other key responsibilities by the director.

address system Those editing components with their numerical readout—based either upon the SMPTE time code or upon the vertical sync pulse on the control track—that allow for the precise location of each recorded picture frame on a given reel of videotape.

ad-lib Dialogue or action that is completely spontaneous and unrehearsed.

amplifier A device that can magnify an electrical signal—either audio or video—for mixing, distribution, and transducing purposes.

amplitude Measurement of the intensity of an electromagnetic wave.

aperture The opening in the camera lens that determines how much light will pass through.

arcing A combination trucking, panning, and dollying movement, in which the camera is moved in an arc around a subject while the camera head is always pointed towards the same subject.

aspect ratio The ratio of the height of the television screen (three units high) to its width (four units wide).

assemble editing Creation of a television production by adding various segments sequentially in the final program order.

asymmetrical balance An informal arrangement in which an important object placed close to the center of the picture is balanced by a lightweight object some distance from the center.

attenuator *See* Potentiometer.

audio The sound portion of a television production.

audio booth (audio control room) The room where all audio signals are controlled and mixed; all audio inputs (microphones, prerecorded tapes and records, and the like) are centrally controlled and then sent on to a master control room, video recorder, or transmitter.

audio compressor An electronic device used to bring weak audio levels up to an averaged volume.

audio signal flow The theoretical schematic model that sequentially traces every step of the audio path from the microphone (or other audio source) to the home radio or TV receiver.

automatic gain control (AGC) An internal control device, for either audio or video signals, that automatically increases and decreases (as needed) the strength of the incoming sound or picture in order to maintain optimum signal strength for recording, playback, editing, and other production purposes.

axis of action/conversation An imaginary line that (1) extends the path in which a character is moving or (2) connects two persons talking to each other; all cameras should remain on the same side of this line.

back focus *See* Tube Focus.

background light *See* Set Light.

back light A highly directional light coming from above and behind a subject, adding highlights, shape, and separation from the background.

backpack VTR *See* Portapak.

balance 1. In audio, the achievement of the correct ratio among several sound sources. 2. Visually, the relative composition and stability among elements in a picture.

bank *See* Bus, definition 2.

barn doors Movable metal shutters, attached to the front of a lighting instrument, that are used to limit the area of the projected light.

base light The basic lighting needed for adequate illumination to achieve a technically acceptable television picture.

beam splitter The optical device in a color camera, consisting of a prism and mirrors, that separates the incoming visual image into the primary colors of blue, red, and green.

below-the-line costs The technical and production personnel (such as the engineers, camera and audio operators, stagehands, and others) and other production equipment, facilities, and services.

black Technically, a synchronized video signal that contains no picture information—a blank screen.

blanking The process of momentarily turning off the scanning beam while it retraces its path before starting to scan another line.

blocking Careful planning and coordinating of all movement and positioning of talent and production equipment.

body time Time remaining in the body of the program—not including closing credits and titles—indicating the time signals that must be given to the talent.

boom (mike boom) Any device consisting of a movable base, an adjustable stand, and a long arm for suspending a microphone above and in front of a performer.

booming (craning) Moving the boom arm or tongue of a camera crane up or down. (*See* Crane, definition 2.)

brightness (lightness, value) 1. The intensity of the picture on a television tube. 2. An indication of where a color would fall on a scale from light (white) to dark (black); corresponds to the gray scale for monochrome television.

broad A floodlight with a large rectangular, pan-like reflector.

broadcasting *See* Open Circuit.

burn-in *See* Image Retention.

bus 1. A common audio circuit that collects signals from several audio sources and feeds them into one source (for example, a mix bus feeds the combined audio signal to the master potentiometer). 2. The row of buttons representing various video sources on the switcher (also called a *bank*).

butt edit The editing of two segments together so that the end of the first is immediately followed by the beginning of the second.

cameo lighting Lighting the foreground subject with carefully controlled, directional light; the background is kept dark.

camera chain The electronic camera plus associated equipment such as the sync generator, camera control unit, and so forth.

camera control unit (CCU) Electronic control equipment, usually located in the master control area, that regulates all of the engineering functions of each camera.

camera head (camera) The electronic picture pickup device, which includes the lens (or lenses), pickup tube (or tubes), and viewfinder; the camera serves as a video transducer that converts incoming light energy (pictures) into electrical signals.

camera mount The support arrangement that holds the camera mounting head and the camera itself—usually a movable tripod, pedestal, or crane.

camera mounting head (pan head) The mechanism that connects the camera itself to the camera mount; it allows the camera head to be tilted vertically and to be panned horizontally.

camera pattern The basic positioning and blocking of studio cameras and subsequent movement of the cameras for a particular program sequence.

cardioid pattern *See* Unidirectional.

carrier frequency A specific portion of the electromagnetic spectrum assigned, by the Federal Communications Commission, to a radio or television station for transmission of its modulated broadcast signal.

cartridge An audiotape or videotape recording and/or playback unit that uses a self-contained single-reel case that can be cued up automatically.

cassette An audiotape or videotape recording and/or playback unit that contains both a supply reel and take-up reel in a self-contained case.

catwalk A walkway, one in a system of walkways suspended below the studio ceiling, that allows lighting personnel easy access to lighting instruments.

CCD (charge-coupled device) A microchip that can be used to pick up picture information, replacing the conventional picture pickup tube.

C-clamp A metal clamp with a pivot adjustment for attaching lighting instruments to a lighting grid.

CCU *See* Camera Control Unit.

central processing unit *See* CPU.

channel selector key An audio channeling switch, usually located adjacent to a pot, that can send the audio signal out through either of two or more line-out channels.

character generator A special electronic effects device with a typewriterlike keyboard that can produce letters and numerals directly on the television screen.

cheat Make minor on-the-air adjustments that the audience will not notice: (1) adjust camera composition; (2) angle a performer toward a camera.

chip *See* Silicon Chip.

chroma key A special effects color matte whereby a specific color (usually green or blue) is used as a key to determine what picture information is to be cut out of the picture with the foreground image.

chrominance channel The color portion of a video signal, which contains hue and saturation information, as opposed to luminance information.

clip An SEG adjustment that can set a threshold level for a particular video variable—hue, chrominance, or luminance—for keying.

closed-circuit (CCTV) Television distribution between points connected by cable—anything from a simple two-room hookup to a multichannel statewide interconnection.

close-up (CU) View of a subject from a relatively short distance.

coaxial cable (coax) Standard camera and video cable with a central insulated conducting wire and a concentrically arranged outer wire.

collective shot A wide shot showing the collective effect or relationship of various elements—an establishing shot.

color bars An electronically generated pattern of vertical color strips, which, when sent through the switcher, can be used to standardize and calibrate the color values on all cameras, monitors, etc.

color burst A part of the composite video signal produced by a camera (or reproduced by a VTR) that serves as a reference point for the receiving tube. This pulse synchronizes the three incoming color signals.

colorization The use of a special color video synthesizer to produce abstract color effects.

color temperature The relative reddish or bluish quality of a light source, as measured in degrees Kelvin.

comet-tailing *See* Lag.

composite signal Electronic signal that contains both picture information and the sync pulse.

condenser microphone A high quality microphone whose transducer consists of a vibrating condenser plate and a fixed backplate.

console (audio board) The control panel or *mixing board* where all audio signals can be amplified, combined, shaped, and channeled.

continuity *See* Picture Continuity.

contrast ratio The ratio of the brightest area to the darkest area in a given camera shot, as determined by reflected light readings.

control room (video booth, studio control room) The room where all video signals are mixed; the director and T.D. control all program elements from this location; sometimes audio and lighting control will also be incorporated into the same area.

control track Portion of a videotape that is used to record the synchronizing pulse.

corner insert A split screen with one camera inserted into a specific quadrant of the picture.

cover shot *See* Establishing Shot.

CPU Central processing unit, the actual microprocessor that is the heart of any computer-based equipment (for graphics generation, editing, special effects) that does the actual "computing" or processing of digitalized information.

crabbing Moving the crane or crab dolly base sideways, similar to a *trucking* shot.

crab dolly A small studio crane, first developed for film camera movement.

crane (studio crane) 1. Large camera mount with an extended boom arm or tongue for the camera, with everything—including a seat for the camera operator—placed on a large, four-wheeled dolly or crane base. 2. To move the boom arm up or down.

crawl *See* Drum.

critical area *See* Essential Area.

cropping Cutting off the edges or border of a picture.

cross-fade 1. An audio transition in which one sound is faded out while another is simultaneously faded in (similar to a video dissolve). 2. A video transition in which one picture is faded out and another picture is immediately faded in from black (similar to an audio segue).

cucalorus (cookie, kook) 1. A special metal cutout pattern that can be inserted into an ellipsoidal spotlight to achieve definite shadow effects. 2. A cardboard or wooden cutout pattern that is placed in front of a spotlight to produce a shadow effect on a scenic background.

cue 1. To give a signal to a talent to start or to perform a certain action. 2. To prepare an audio source (record or audiotape) for a precise start at some predetermined point.

cue cards (idiot sheets) Large, lightweight cards, containing either script material or content outline, held next to the camera for the talent to read.

cue position (audition position) A position on most audio pots and faders that connects the audio source to a separate nonprogram *cue* amplifier and speaker to enable the audio operator to listen to the source without interfering with the program audio.

cue track Portion of a videotape that is used to record electronic or audio cues, the SMPTE time code, or similar information.

cut 1. To eliminate some program material, leave out part of the script. 2. To interrupt a rehearsal. 3. *See* Take, definition 1.

cutting ratio The relationship between the size of an object in two successive shots; ordinarily this ratio should not be more than three to one.

cyc (cyclorama) A large, continuous, smooth backing—usually made of cloth—that may cover two or three walls of a studio.

cycles per second (cps) *See* Hertz.

dailies The videotape or film footage shot during a day's production sessions.

debeaming Turning down the intensity of the scanning beam, resulting in a high-contrast picture that gradually deteriorates into a faded gray image.

decibel (Db) A unit of measurement of sound that compares the relative intensity of different sound sources.

decorative setting An abstract style of staging with nonrealistic elements added purely for artistic effect.

deflection magnets The wire coils at the rear of the video tube. They produce a constantly changing magnetic field that "pulls" the stream of electrons across and down the inside face of the tube. This sequentially energizes the individual pixels that make up the 525 lines of the two alternating picture fields.

defocus dissolve A camera transition in which the on-the-air camera defocuses and the switcher then dissolves to a similarly defocused camera, which then focuses after it is on the air.

depth of field The distance between the nearest point at which objects are in focus and the farthest point at which objects are in focus.

depth staging The use of foreground and background elements in order to give a feeling of depth to the television picture.

diaphragm 1. The vibrating element in a dynamic microphone that responds to the compressed air molecules of sound waves. 2. The adjustable mechanism that controls the size of the lens aperture.

digital recording An advanced form of video and/ or audio electromagnetic recording wherein picture and/or sound information is converted into computerlike off-and-on bits of data.

digital video manipulator (DVM) An electronic control device that can manipulate video signals—once they have been converted into digital information—to achieve a wide variety of pictorial effects.

dimmer board A lighting control unit, operated on the same principle as a rheostat, that determines the intensity of a light by controlling the amount of electric current flowing to the instrument.

director The person in charge of actual production and editing operations—everything that takes place in the studio or on a remote—directing all picture and sound elements to create a final program.

disciplines Those learned and acquired attitudes and habits, developed over a period of time, that comprise an internalized system of professional behavior—such as responsibility, self-control, respect, and initiative.

disk drive The input memory device, which may be either a "floppy disk" or a much larger (in terms of storage) hard disk, for a computer system that stores the programs or data for various tasks—generating graphics, manipulating images, editing, producing special effects, and so forth.

dissolve A simultaneous fading out of one picture while fading in another picture, thus effecting a gradual transition between shots with a momentary overlapping or *superimposition* of images as one strengthens while the other weakens.

dollying Moving the entire camera mount closer to (dollying in) or farther from (dollying out) the subject.

downcut During either production or editing, the loss of a small amount of audio and/or video material at the end of a segment—usually occuring at the point of transition between program elements from two different sources.

dress rehearsal Final, full rehearsal before the actual production take—using all sets, props, and costumes—designed to be conducted straight through without interruption.

drum (crawl) Large cylindrical graphics-mounting device (similar in appearance to a bass drum) that can roll a long vertical graphic up a television screen.

dry-run rehearsal Rehearsal—either in a rehearsal hall or in the studio—without any technical facilities.

dubbing The electronic duplication of a videotape onto a second tape.

dynamic microphone A rugged microphone whose transducer consists of a diaphragm connected to a movable coil.

editing Putting together pieces of program either by physically splicing film or tape or by arranging program elements by means of electronic transfer.

effects *See* Special Effects *and* Staging Effects.

effects bus The switcher bus that is used for special electronic effects such as inserts, keys, and wipes.

EFP (electronic field production) The use of a single video camera to record any kind of program in the field (on location) for later editing in the postproduction process.

electromagnetic spectrum The entire range of electromagnetic energy wavelengths (and frequencies), which includes everything from cosmic rays and visible light to broadcast waves.

electron gun The device, in the rear of the camera pickup tube, that shoots out the electron scanning beam.

electronic editing Joining together program elements on videotape by sequential signal transfer from an original (playback) tape to a second (record) tape.

ellipsoidal spotlight (leko) A specialized spotlight with a highly defined beam that can be further shaped by means of metal shutters and the insertion of a cucalorus pattern.

ENG (electronic news gathering) The use of a high-quality, portable broadcast camera to record news events and other actualities; it is a single-camera technique (replacing a film camera with an electronic camera), resulting in a fast and mobile professional operation.

equalizer An electronic device used to increase or decrease the levels of different audio frequencies.

essential area (critical area) That center portion of the *scanning area* of a graphic card that contains all of the critical or essential information that probably will be seen on the receiving set.

establishing shot (cover shot) An all-inclusive long shot that, by its collective nature, establishes the relationships of performers and other elements in a given scene.

extemporaneous Speaking from a semiscripted format or outline—broadly prepared but not written out word for word.

external key An electronic keying effect whereby a third camera furnishes the keying (or stenciling) image used in combining two other video signals.

fade 1. The gradual bringing in or taking out of an audio source. 2. The gradual transition from black to a picture (fade in) or from a picture to black (fade out).

fader (slide-fader) *See* Potentiometer.

fader arm On the switcher, a small lever—operating on the same principle as a rheostat—that controls the amount of video signal flowing to a specific bus.

feed A program signal, audio and/or video, brought into a mixer (audio console or switcher) from some outside (nonstudio) source, e.g., a remote location, satellite, or a network line.

feedback 1. In audio, a high-pitched squeal that results from accidentally feeding a program monitor into a live microphone, causing an instantaneous overamplification of the system. 2. A video effect caused by re-entry of a video signal into the switcher with subsequent over-amplification.

fidelity The ability to reproduce a given tone, with all of its overtones, accurately.

field One-half of a television picture, consisting of alternate scanning lines, lasting $1/60$ of a second.

field of view Size or scope of a shot, indicating how much is encompassed.

field synchronizer *See* Frame Synchronizer.

fill light An unfocused and diffused (nondirectional) light used to complement the key light, coming from the side opposite the key, filling in dark areas and softening the shadows.

film chain (telecine) A film island where various picture sources (16mm film, 8mm film, slides) can be mixed through a multiplexer and fed into a television pickup camera.

filter An audio device that can be used to eliminate selected low-frequency or high-frequency overtones.

fishpole A small, lightweight pole to which a microphone is attached, to be handheld by an audio assistant outside of the picture frame.

fixed-focal-length lens A simple lens that is one specific focal length.

flag A rectangular cloth-covered frame placed in front of a lighting instrument to produce a precise shadow on one side of the light beam.

flat A standard staging unit, constructed of a wooden frame covered with cloth or hardboard, often used to represent walls of a room or the exterior of a building.

floodlight A lighting instrument that produces a highly diffused, nondirectional source of light.

floor manager (floor director) *See* Stage Manager.

floor plan A scaled plan of the studio floor indicating where all scenery and staging units are to be placed.

focal length The distance from the optical center point of a lens, when it is set at infinity, to a point where the image is in focus (that is, the front surface of the camera pickup tube).

fold over A digital-based electronic transition in which one picture is squeezed and apparently flipped over (revealing a second picture) to simulate a turning page.

footcandle (ftc) A unit of light measurement equivalent to the amount of light falling upon a surface one foot away from a standard candle.

foundation makeup The makeup base upon which more detailed accent items are constructed.

frame 1. One complete television picture, consisting of two fields, lasting $1/30$ of a second. 2. To compose a picture artistically within the frame of the television screen.

frame store A unit which uses a computer disk drive to hold hundreds of still-frame visuals in a digital format—for the origination of sports and news graphics.

frame (field) synchronizer The electronic component which takes outside video sources (satellite, microwave, and other feeds), analyzes their sync pulses as compared with studio sync, converts the signals to a digital format, adjusts the differences, and thereby can route all signals through the same switcher.

freeze frame *See* Pause Mode.

frequency 1. The number of cycles per second of a given tone—which determines the basic pitch of that tone (the greater the frequency, the higher the pitch). 2. Measurement of the number of oscillations per second (hertz) of an electromagnetic wave of a given wavelength (the greater the frequency, the smaller the wavelength).

frequency range The total scope of frequencies or pitches (and overtones) that a microphone, ear, loudspeaker, or transmitter is able to discriminate and/or reproduce.

Fresnel lens A lightweight spotlight lens developed by Augustin Jean Fresnel that uses a system of concentric ring-shaped steps to achieve its focusing effect.

*f***-stop** A notation that indicates the size of the lens aperture; the higher the *f*-stop number, the smaller the opening; the lower the *f*-stop number, the larger the opening.

gain control *See* Potentiometer.

gel (gelatin) A thin, translucent, colored material such as gelatin or plastic that can be mounted in front of lighting instruments to produce specific color effects.

giraffe A medium-sized mike boom, consisting of a tripod base and a telescoping arm.

gobo A scenic cutout unit that is positioned several feet in front of a camera to provide foreground design, depth, and framing interest.

gopher An assistant who is asked to "go for" specific items—coffee, scripts, tape, paper, and so forth.

graphics Two-dimensional visuals specifically prepared for television presentation—charts, drawings, photographs, maps, slides, and the like.

graphics tablet An electronic pad which contains numerous X and Y (horizontal and vertical) coordinates buried beneath its surface so that when contact is made by a special electronic pen, the precise location of the spot can be transmitted to a monitor.

gray scale A theoretical scale, representing several shades of gray from TV white to TV black, that can be readily distinguished by a camera pickup tube; most good camera systems can be relied upon to reproduce only a seven-step gray scale.

grip A floor assistant or stagehand, especially one who is concerned with scenery and set dressing.

hanging mike A microphone suspended by its cord from a lighting grid or catwalk.

hanging units Any background pieces that are hung or flown in the studio—such as drapes, cloth drops, and the cyclorama.

harmonics *See* Overtones.

HDTV *See* High-Definition Television.

head The small electromagnet—on either a video recorder or an audio recorder—that puts the electromagnetic information on the tape (records), or erases the signal from the tape, or reads (plays back) the information that is on the tape.

headroom Space between the top of a subject's head and the upper edge of the camera frame.

headset The apparatus (worn over the head and consisting of an earphone and mouthpiece) that connects all production personnel on the intercom network.

helical-scan (slant-track) VTR A videotape recording format that lays down the video information in a long, slanted, helical pattern on the tape.

hertz (Hz) Basic unit of frequency measurement for electromagnetic waves—named after Heinrich Hertz—replacing the older term of *cycles per second;* broadcast frequencies are often measured in terms of kiloHertz (kHz) and megaHertz (mHz).

high-band recording High quality video recording, recorded in a high-frequency range, featured in most quality color recorders.

high-definition television (HDTV) A television system which uses 1100 or more scanning lines, resulting in an incredibly sharp picture; such systems also usually feature a wider screen ratio.

high-key lighting Overall intense illumination, with a fully lit background.

horizontal sync pulse The portion of the synchronizing pulse that controls the horizontal sweep of the scanning beam.

hue The actual color base, such as red, green, orange, and so forth.

iconoscope No longer used, this was the first practical electronic camera pickup tube.

image-orthicon (I-O) A particular type of camera pickup tube, long the standard of the broadcast industry for monochrome production.

image retention (burn-in, sticking) A phenomenon, characteristic of older I-O tubes, where the tube superimposes a negative image of a shot (especially a high contrast shot) over succeeding shots the tube picks up.

impedance Resistance to the flow of an audio signal in a microphone cable.

incandescent light The conventional lamp, housed in a glass bulb, that produces light by the glow of a heated filament.

incident light Light coming directly from the source of illumination.

input selector switch The switch found on many audio control boards (either a toggle switch or a push-button connector) that will connect a specific patch bay input to a particular microphone position on the console.

insert editing Electronically inserting a new program segment into the middle of a previously recorded production; the new material (video and/or audio) to be inserted is locked into the existing control track.

intercom network (P.L.) A closed-circuit intercommunication audio network connecting all production personnel with headsets.

interlacing The process of combining two picture fields to produce one full frame.

internal key An electronic keying effect whereby one of the two cameras involved also furnishes the key (or stenciling) signal.

I-O tube *See* Image-Orthicon.

isolated (iso) camera A camera that is patched directly to its separate video recorder—which can be used either for instant replay (in live productions) or for postproduction editing.

jack 1. A socket or receptacle (female) for an audio connection. 2. A hinged stage brace attached to the rear of a flat.

jump cut A take between two cameras—or a badly planned edit—that results in connecting two shots that have almost identical views of the same object; as a result the object appears to jump slightly for no apparent reason.

key A special electronic effect, where one camera cuts in with a solid image into the background picture produced by another camera.

key light The primary source of illumination falling upon a subject, highly directional, producing a definite modeling or shaping effect with well-defined shadows.

kicker Additional light, usually a spotlight, coming from the side and slightly to the rear of the subject.

kill To turn off equipment (such as microphones, lights).

kinescope recording The process of using a specially adapted film camera to record a television program from the face of the kinescope tube.

kinescope tube The television receiving tube.

kook (cookie) *See* Cucalorus, definition 1.

lag (smear, comet-tailing) A cometlike tail that follows a moving image across the screen, characteristic of the vidicon tube at low light levels.

lavaliere (chest mike, neck mike) A very small microphone that can be worn around the neck on a cord or clipped onto an article of clothing.

lead room (nose room, talk space) Additional framing space in a camera picture on the side toward which a subject is looking or moving.

leko *See* Ellipsoidal Spotlight.

lens 1. The optical glass disc, usually having one or both surfaces curved, used for focusing rays of light coming from a spotlight, for example, plano-convex or Fresnel. 2. The optical elements that make it possible to focus visual (light) images onto the face of a camera tube.

lens cap Protective covering that can be placed on the front of a camera lens.

lens turret A round metal plate on the front of a camera, holding three to five lenses, that can be rotated to place any one of the lenses into position in front of the pickup tube.

level Sound volume or intensity from a specific source or talent.

lighting grid A permanent arrangement of pipes suspended below the studio ceiling, upon which lighting instruments can be hung.

light meter A photoelectric device that measures the amount of light falling upon a specific area.

light plot A floor plan that indicates the lighting requirements—location, type, and function of each instrument—for every staging area in the studio.

limbo A neutral setting, often set against a plain backdrop with no staging elements in view.

limiter An electronic device used to cut off audio levels when the volume is too strong.

line monitor The master program monitor that displays the final program picture that is to be recorded or transmitted.

live-on-tape production Program that is recorded on videotape in its entirety, or in long complete segments; the viewing audience watches the performance, unedited, as it actually took place earlier.

live production Studio or remote production where the program is transmitted (either broadcast or closed-circuit) as the action takes place; the viewing audience watches the performance as it actually is happening.

long lens A long focal-length lens with a narrow viewing angle; it includes relatively little in the picture, but tends to compress distance.

long shot (LS) View of a subject from a relatively great distance.

looping An audio technique whereby a single loop of audiotape can be repeated endlessly on either a reel-to-reel recorder or on an audio cart machine.

loosen up (loosen a shot) To decrease the size of an object in a picture, either by dollying back or by zooming out.

low-key lighting Selective lighting, with an overall low level of intensity and a dark background.

luminance channel A monochrome signal, in color cameras, that is derived from the three color pictures; it is used to provide the correct contrast for the color signal as well as to produce the compatible black-and-white picture for monochrome receivers.

macro lens Special wide-angle lens designed for close-ups of small objects at short distances.

master control room Primary engineering control center where all video and audio signals are ultimately channeled; program input (both studio and network feeds), camera controls, video recording, and transmitter distribution usually are all handled from this location.

matte A special electronic effect whereby two cameras are electronically keyed together, with one furnishing a foreground image and the other the background.

medium shot (MS) View of a subject from a comfortable medium distance, between a long shot and a close-up.

microchip *See* Silicon Chip.

microphone (mike, mic) An audio transducer that converts sound pressure waves (sound energy) into electrical signals.

mix buses The switcher buses, with fader arms, that are used for on-the-air fading and mixing of video sources such as supers and dissolves.

mixer 1. An electronic control unit for selecting and combining audio or video signals from more than one source and forming a new program signal—such as the audio console or the video switcher. 2. *See* Potentiometer.

mixing 1. The combining and balancing of two or more audio sources through the audio console. 2. The combining of two or more video sources through the switcher.

modulation The alteration of a carrier frequency—either by amplitude modulation (AM) or by frequency modulation (FM)—in order to superimpose a video and/or audio signal for broadcast purposes.

moiré effect Distracting visual vibration caused by the interaction of a narrow striped pattern and the television scanning lines.

monitor 1. An audio speaker used to check the actual sounds being mixed. 2. A video display device that features a high quality television picture that has not been modulated to an RF signal; it is ordinarily used in studio and control room applications.

multiple-camera production Conventional television production situation—either in a studio or remote on-location origination—where several cameras are used simultaneously to pick up the action or performance; whether transmitted live or recorded, the pictures from the various cameras are edited instantaneously as the program progresses.

multiplexer A system of mirrors and prisms in the film chain designed to direct the various projected images into the television camera.

narrow-angle lens *See* Long Lens.

neutral setting (nonassociative style) A setting with no identifiable elements at all.

noise 1. Any interference that distracts from the communicative act. 2. Specific audio interference (unwanted sounds or static) or video interference (electronic disturbance or snow).

nondirectional *See* Omnidirectional.

normalled Having a certain output on an audio patch bay permanently wired to a given position on the console so that a patch cord is not needed to make the temporary connection.

nose room *See* Lead Room.

NTSC National Television System Committee, an industry body which developed the basic technical specifications (525 lines, 30 frames per second, FM audio) and color standards still in use today in North and South America and Japan.

objective perspective Use of a camera as an observer or eavesdropper; no one addresses the camera directly.

off-camera Any sound or action that takes place out of the camera's view.

off-line editing Any of several sophisticated electronic editing techniques involving intermediate steps such as first-stage trial assembly or production of special effects; the final editing is typically computer-controlled using the SMPTE time code.

off-mike The audio quality resulting from a sound source that is a great distance from the microphone or out of the pickup pattern of a unidirectional mike.

off-set graphics Graphics, such as title cards and slides, that are never seen in or on the set; the audience has no idea where they are originating.

omnidirectional (nondirectional) A microphone pickup pattern in which sounds are received equally well from all directions.

on-line editing Electronic editing technique involving the direct transfer of materials from an original tape to a final program master.

on-set graphics Large graphics and display devices designed to be integrated into the set.

open-circuit (broadcasting) Television distribution through open space; a specific carrier frequency is modulated with video and/or audio signals and then transmitted from an antenna to receivers that are not connected by wire or cable to the origination point.

oscilloscope Engineering evaluation instrument that displays various electronic patterns on a video screen.

outline script *See* Semiscripted Outline.

over-the-shoulder shot (O/S) Camera shot looking at one person framed by the back of the head and shoulder of another person in the foreground.

overtones (harmonics) Acoustical or electrical frequencies that are higher than the fundamental tone.

pad 1. Extra video material that is recorded before and after a program segment to facilitate a margin of judgment during editing. 2. Extra script material that may be used if the program begins to run short.

pan card A long horizontal graphic designed to be panned on the air.

pan head *See* Camera Mounting Head.

panning Turning the camera horizontally by rotating the camera mounting head.

panning handle (pan handle) The handle extending toward the rear of the camera with which the camera operator controls movement of the camera.

pantograph A scissors-like, spring, counterbalanced lighting mount that enables lights to be quickly pushed up or pulled down to any height.

particularized shot A close shot showing the important aspect of some specific object.

patch bay (patch board) A board with numerous terminals (inputs and outputs) through which various audio, video, or lighting signals can be connected by patch cords to other channels or circuits.

pause mode (still frame, freeze frame) Repeated scanning of a single video frame—while holding the videotape stationary—resulting in a still frame during playback.

pedestal 1. Heavy camera mount that facilitates easy raising or lowering of the camera head, usually with a counterweight system or with compressed air. 2. To move the camera head up or down with the pedestal mount.

perambulator boom A large boom on a dolly base, having a platform for the mike operator, with a long counterweighted boom arm.

performer Any talent who is addressing the audience directly, as opposed to an actor portraying a dramatic character.

perspective 1. In audio, the quality of matching visual and sound distance. 2. In scenery, the illusion of distance caused by several lines converging at one point on the horizon.

pickup tube The transducing element of the camera that receives the visual image and converts it into an electronic signal.

picture continuity The relationship of visual images from one shot to the next, involving flow of action, screen direction, composition, cutting ratio, type of transitions, motivation, and similar considerations.

pin Concentrating or narrowing the beam of a spotlight by moving the bulb-reflector unit away from the lens.

pixel The computer-derived term for "picture element" that designates the smallest addressable triad of phosphor dots on a picture tube that can be manipulated and illuminated for graphics display.

P.L. (private line) *See* Intercom Network.

plano-convex lens The basic, relatively heavy, spotlight lens—with one flat surface and one convex surface—from which the Fresnel lens was developed.

playback The process whereby the recorded magnetic information stored on the recording tape is picked up by the playback head to recreate the original video and/or audio electronic signals.

Plumbicon® A lead-oxide version of the vidicon tube, used extensively for color cameras. (The word *Plumbicon* is a registered trademark of N. V. Philips.)

polarity reversal Interchange of the black and white aspects of a picture, thus attaining a negative image.

pop filter A protective shield attached to a microphone that filters out air blasts from plosive consonants such as *p*'s and *t*'s.

portapak (backpack) Small, portable, battery-operated, lightweight video recorder—typically using ½-inch or ¼-inch tape—used for small-format television.

postproduction editing Electronic editing process that takes place after the individual program segments have been produced and recorded.

potentiometer (pot) A volume-control device that is manipulated by either a rotating knob or a sliding *fader*.

preamplifier An electronic device that can magnify the low signal output of microphones and other transducers before the signal is sent to a mixing board or to other amplifiers.

"prepare" (or "set up") The standard command of preparation preceding a fade, dissolve, super, or special effect that involves preparation of another bus.

preproduction editing Electronic editing process whereby individual program segments—especially in news and sports coverage—are edited in advance for later insertion or assembly editing into a finished production.

preproduction planning All of the preparation and careful planning that a director must complete before starting studio rehearsals.

presence The audio phenomenon of performing very close to a microphone, with a consequent intimate quality resulting from a lowered pitch, breathiness, and subdued tone.

preset 1. On a lighting board, to prearrange a given lighting setup so that it can be automatically executed when needed. 2. To adjust a zoom lens so that a given object is in focus at all focal lengths. 3. To use the switcher preview bus and preview monitor to set up a given effect before punching it up on the air.

pre-studio rehearsal Rehearsal with talent (e.g., actors) in a rehearsal hall or other location before coming into the studio.

preview bus The switcher bus, connected to the preview monitor, that is used for setting up any special effects or other picture before it is put on the air.

preview monitor A large monitor that can be used to look at any camera picture or video effect before putting it on the program line.

proc amp Process amplifier, the electronic component which takes the composite video signal from the switcher (chrominance, luminance, sync pulses, and blanking pulses), stabilizes the levels and removes unwanted elements (noise).

producer The creator and originator of a television program, usually in charge of all above-the-line elements such as writing, art, music, securing actors, and financial considerations.

program bus The switcher bank that controls the actual picture being sent out on the air.

program time Time remaining in the overall program until the program fades to black; this determines the time-remaining signals that must be given to the director.

props (properties) 1. Hand props, which include all items actually to be handled and used in a television production. 2. Stage props (*see* Set Dressings).

proscenium arch In the theater, the arch that separates the stage from the auditorium.

pull focus (rack focus) To change the focus of a camera from one extreme to the other—using a selective focus technique—in order to shift attention from one object to another (either in the foreground or background).

quadruplex (transverse) VTR (quad head) An older videotape recording format that uses four rotating heads in a pattern transverse to the movement of the videotape.

quartz light A highly efficient lamp with a high-intensity tungsten-halogen filament in a quartz or silica housing.

rack focus *See* Pull Focus.

racking 1. Rotating the lens turret in order to place a different lens in front of the pickup tube. 2. On monochrome cameras, moving the pickup tube closer to or farther from the lens (*see* Tube Focus).

raster The display of scanning lines on a cathode ray tube, covering the entire face of the tube.

rate card The printed list of prices charged by a production facility for its services and equipment; the rate card usually consists of three sections—the *technical personnel chart* for engineering costs; the *facilities rate chart* for all studio usage, telecine and videotape machines, furniture, and all other facilities; and the *personnel hourly rate chart* for all nonengineering below-the-line positions.

"ready" The standard command of preparation preceding a camera take or cut.

real-time editing Assembling a multiple-camera production by using a switcher or SEG during the continuing action of an event or performance.

rear focus *See* Tube Focus.

rear screen (R.P., rear projection) A translucent screen set up in the studio; slides or film are projected from the rear and photographed from the front.

receiver The device that receives the radio broadcast signal (radio set) or television signal (TV set) and demodulates the carrier wave to reproduce the original studio electrical signals.

recording The process whereby the audio and/or video electronic signal is used to arrange iron oxide particles on the magnetic recording tape to store a record of the electronic signal for later retrieval.

reel-to-reel Audiotape or videotape recording format that uses open reels (a supply reel and a take-up reel) and manual threading, as opposed to closed *cassette* or *cartridge* systems.

re-entry A switcher process which allows the operator to take a processed or mixed video signal and enter it into another processing circuit or mixing bus.

reflected light Light bounced back from the surface of an object.

remote production (on-location production) A television production, usually directed from a portable control room, that takes place outside of a regular studio.

reportorial perspective Use of a camera with the talent talking directly to the audience through the camera.

resolution Sharpness and detail of a television picture.

RF (radio frequency) Modulation of a specific radio frequency carrier wave with a video and audio signal—necessary for broadcasting and most closed-circuit distribution.

RGB The designation (referring to the primary colors of red, green, and blue) used to label the uncoded (non-composite) outputs of a color camera or computer.

rheostat A device that can control the amount of current or signal flowing to a specific control point or circuit—allowing a gradual increase or decrease in the amount of flow—such as the *pot* on the audio console, the *dimmer* handle on a lighting circuit, or the *fader arm* on a switcher bus.

ribbon microphone (velocity mike) A sensitive microphone whose transducing element consists of a ribbon suspended in a magnetic field.

riding gain (riding levels) Continually watching the VU meter and adjusting audio faders accordingly, in order to maintain proper volume levels throughout a program.

roll cue The exact words or actions that a talent will use at the precise point when a film or videotape insert is to be rolled a few seconds before it is actually put on the air.

rule of thirds Principle of composition that divides the television screen into thirds, horizontally and vertically, and places objects of interest at the points where the lines intersect.

rundown sheet (show format) Abbreviated scripting format that simply lists the various program segments in sequence.

run-through Usually, the first full facilities (start-and-stop) rehearsal.

saturation (chroma) The strength or intensity of a color—how far removed it is from a neutral or gray shade.

scanning The pattern of movement of the electron beam, in both the camera and the TV receiver, horizontally and from top to bottom.

scanning area The portion of a graphic card that actually can be seen by the camera pickup tube.

scanning beam The electron beam that is pulled back and forth, up and down, across the television tube to produce the scanning pattern.

scoop A rounded floodlight with a spherical diffusing reflector.

scrim A translucent filter, often made of fiberglass or fine screening, used in front of either a spotlight or floodlight to soften and diffuse the light quality.

segment timing sheet A list of all of the segments of a production with space for unit times and cumulative times (ideal and actual) for each segment.

segue An audio transition in which one sound is completely faded out and then a second source is immediately faded in (similar to a video cross-fade).

selective focus The technique of using a shallow depth of field to deliberately keep either foreground or background objects out of focus, in order to concentrate attention on a particular object that is in focus.

semiscripted outline A summarization of a program's content—with opening and closing material (and other crucial elements such as roll cues) written out in full while the remaining content is presented in outline form.

set dressings (stage props) Major items of furniture (desks, tables), large props (bicycles, tree stumps), and minor items (ashtrays, books), used to dress up a set.

set light (background light) General lighting of the set and background behind the talent.

set pieces Three-dimensional items, usually functional, that are integrated into the set—platforms, stairways, pillars, arches, lampposts, and so forth.

setting The major pieces that comprise the background and environment of a scene—set units, hanging units, and set pieces.

set units Staging units such as flats, two-folds, and other standing background pieces.

shading (video engineering) Operating the video controls of a CCU in order to maintain the best engineering quality control of the picture.

shaping The alteration of an audio signal by controlling volume, filtering out certain frequencies, emphasizing upper or lower pitches, creating an echo effect, and so forth.

shoot (Verb) To record program information on either film or videotape. (Noun) The entire enterprise of a remote, on-location television or film recording session, including all production operations of the non-studio, in-the-field, situation.

short lens (wide-angle lens) A short focal-length lens with a wide viewing angle; it includes quite a bit in the picture but tends to exaggerate distance.

shotgun microphone A highly directional microphone, used for picking up sounds from a great distance.

shot sheet A small sheet or card, attached to the rear of the camera, listing a summary of all shots the camera operator is to get during the production.

show format *See* Rundown Sheet.

silhouette A lighting effect where the foreground figures are dark and the background is fully lit.

silicon chip A tiny electronic component containing microscopic electrical circuits that amplify and in other ways control the flow of electromagnetic information, the heart of every computer operation.

single Shot of just one person.

single-camera production Television production situation in which a single electronic camera is used to record all of the action—similar to the traditional film-camera technique; one camera is repositioned for each shot, and the individual shots are then electronically edited together in the postproduction editing process.

slant-track recorder *See* Helical-Scan.

slate An identification procedure whereby date, scene, segment, and other information necessary to tape and film editing are recorded at the beginning of a designated camera sequence.

small-format television (video) Inexpensive, small, lightweight television gear (camera, microphone, and video recorder)—usually portable—that can be used for a variety of nonbroadcast (and nonprofessional) applications.

SMPTE time code A frame-location "address" system—developed by the Society of Motion Picture and Television Engineers—that can label and find any section of a videotape by hour, minute, second, and frame.

snoot A stovepipe-like attachment that can be put on the front of a spotlight to reduce the beam to a smaller clearly defined circle, without increasing the intensity of the spot.

SOF (sound-on-film) A designation used to denote a film soundtrack.

soft edge The line between two video signals (as in an insert or wipe), which can be blurred so that the two pictures dissolve or blend together.

speaker (loudspeaker) An electronic device, actually a transducer, that converts an electronic audio signal back into audible sound waves.

special effects Fancy electronic video transitions and methods of combining video sources, such as wipes, keys, mattes, inserts, and so forth.

special effects generator (SEG) Part of a sophisticated switcher that can produce a variety of special electronic effects.

speed up A signal to the talent to read faster or get through the script outline faster.

split screen A special effect with the screen split into two or more sections, with a picture from a different camera filling each portion of the screen.

spotlight A lighting instrument that produces a highly directional, controlled source of light.

spread To open up or enlarge the beam of a spotlight by moving the bulb-reflector unit closer to the lens.

sprocket holes Small, square holes on the side of film, used to guide the film and keep it moving at a constant speed.

squeeze zoom A digital-based electronic transition in which the picture is reduced in size and squeezed down to a pinpoint before disappearing from the screen.

stage manager (floor manager, floor director) The director's key assistant in charge of all production concerns on the studio floor.

staging effects Special optical and mechanical studio effects, such as smoke, wind, fog, rain, fire, and so forth.

"standby" General command of preparation.

start-and-stop rehearsal (stop-start, stop-and-go) Usually the first full facilities rehearsal with cameras operating—designed to be interrupted to work out problems as the production progresses.

still frame *See* Pause Mode.

stop-start (stop-and-go) rehearsal *See* Start-and-Stop Rehearsal.

stretch A signal to the talent to slow down, read slower, and stretch out the remaining script.

striking To remove specific set pieces or props; taking down and removing everything on the studio floor at the end of a production.

strip lights A series of broads (pan lights) or low-wattage bulbs mounted in a row of three to twelve lights in one housing, used as a specialized floodlight for lighting a cyclorama or other large background area.

studio The primary room devoted to television production, containing all of the paraphernalia for sets, lighting, cameras, microphones, and so forth—the space where all acting or performing takes place.

studio address (S.A., talkback) A public address loudspeaker system, allowing the control room to talk directly to the studio floor.

subjective perspective Use of a camera as an actual participant or actor in a dramatic sequence, viewing the scene from the standpoint of a person who is involved.

super (superimposition) A picture resulting from the simultaneous display of two complete images on the screen.

super card A graphics card with white lettering on a black background, used either to *super* or to *key* the printed information over a background picture.

sweep reversal Reversal of the scanning pattern of a camera (either horizontally or vertically) to attain either a mirror image or an upside-down image.

sweetening The process of augmenting an audio track during postproduction editing by adding prerecorded laughter and other audience reactions.

switcher 1. A video mixing panel, consisting of selection buttons and control levers (fader arms), that permits the selection and combining of incoming video signals to form the final program picture. 2. The person who operates the video switcher, usually the technical director.

symmetrical balance Formal arrangement with the most important element centered in the picture and other equal objects placed equidistant from the center.

sync generator The part of the video system that produces a synchronizing signal (sync pulse), based on the basic 60-cycle alternating current (in the U.S. and other countries using the NTSC color system), which serves as a timing pulse to coordinate the video elements of all components in the video system (cameras, switcher, recorders, and so forth).

sync pulse A complex signal (added to the picture information) consisting of electronic control information that keeps all video components synchronized.

take 1. An instantaneous change from one video source to another (cut). 2. The final production of a program as recorded or distributed live.

talent Any person who appears in front of a camera.

talkback system *See* Studio Address.

tally lights Small red indicator lights on each camera to let the talent and camera operator(s) know which camera is on the air.

target The electronic elements that form the light-sensitive (photoemissive) front surface of the pickup tube, which is read by the scanning beam.

technical director (T.D.) Engineer or production person who operates the switcher.

techniques Those learned and acquired skills utilized in operating various pieces of equipment and in performing specific crew assignments.

telecine 1. Same as film chain. 2. The room where the film chain is located.

telephoto lens A lens with a very long focal length, used for close-ups of objects from great distances.

teleprompter A mechanical device that projects the moving script, via mirrors, directly in front of the camera lens. (The word *TelePrompTer* is a registered trademark of the Teleprompter Corporation.)

telescope hanger A lighting mount, consisting of a system of telescoping pipes, that enables the lighting instrument to be positioned at varying heights.

three-point lighting The traditional arrangement of key, fill, and back lights.

tie lines Permanent audio lines connecting various control rooms or patch bays and engineering locations.

tighten a shot (tighten up) To increase the size of the object in a picture, either by zooming in or by dollying in.

tilt card A tall, vertical graphic card designed to be tilted on the air.

tilting Pivoting the camera vertically by pointing the camera mounting head up or down.

time-base corrector The electronic apparatus that takes the video feed from the videorecorder (which has been slightly altered by variations in the tape transport system), encodes that signal into a digital form, and then reconstructs an enhanced control track and video signal for distribution and playback.

title card A graphics card containing basic information about the program title, used at the open (and close) of a program.

tonguing Moving the tongue or boom arm of a camera crane laterally to the left or right.

transducer Any device (such as a microphone or camera) that receives energy in one form (sound waves or light energy) and converts it into another form of energy (electrical signals).

transfer edit The electronic re-recording (or dubbing) of video and audio information from an original videotape to a second tape for assembly in program sequence.

transmitter The broadcasting apparatus that modulates the audio and video signals onto a carrier frequency and, through an antenna, broadcasts the signals as electromagnetic waves.

transverse video recorder *See* Quadruplex.

trim 1. To adjust a lighting instrument by aiming the housing and focusing (pinning or spreading) the beam. 2. That part of the editing process whereby small amounts of program information at the head and/or tail of a video segment are added or deleted as the final editing decisions are perfected.

tripod Three-legged camera mount, usually with casters to facilitate camera movement.

trucking Moving the entire camera mount laterally to the left or right.

tube focus (back focus, rear focus, rack focus) To change focus, on monochrome cameras, by physically moving the pickup tube in relation to the lens.

turret *See* Lens Turret.

two-fold Two stage flats, hinged together to form a self-standing unit.

two-shot Camera shot that includes two people or a person and one other prominent object.

undercut To change one video source of a two-camera super or effect instantaneously while the effect is on the air.

unidirectional (cardioid) A microphone pickup pattern in which sounds are received best from one direction, in a heart-shaped or cardioid pattern.

upcut During either production or editing, the loss of a small amount of audio and/or video material at the beginning of a segment—usually occurring at the point of transition between program elements from two different sources.

variable-focal-length lens *See* Zoom Lens.

vectorscope A specialized electronic monitor that graphically displays the saturation levels for each of the three primary colors and complementary colors.

vertical sync pulse The portion of the synchronizing pulse that controls the vertical movement of the scanning beam between fields.

video 1. The visual portion of a television production. 2. An unmodulated electronic picture signal distributed over a closed-circuit system without converting to an RF signal, resulting in a higher quality picture. 3. *See* Small-Format Television.

video disc 1. A magnetic video recording format in which short segments can be recorded for instant playback, freeze frame, and slow-motion production applications. 2. A distribution medium in which lengthy programs are pressed onto discs for consumer retail.

video engineering *See* Shading.

video feedback Process of feeding a camera's signal into a floor monitor and then using the same camera to shoot the face of the monitor (*see* Feedback, definition 2).

video signal flow The theoretical schematic model that traces every step of the video path from the picture picked up by the camera to the home TV set.

videotape A plastic tape, coated with iron oxide, that can magnetically record various audio, video, and control track information.

videotape recorder (video recorder, VTR) A magnetic-electronic recording machine that records audio, video, and control signals on videotape.

vidicon A simple and inexpensive type of camera pickup tube used for many basic television purposes.

VU meter (volume unit meter) A display meter that shows the relative volume of program audio.

walk-through rehearsal An abbreviated rehearsal—conducted from the studio floor—to acquaint the talent and/or production crew with the major outline of the production.

waveform monitor A type of oscilloscope that displays the brightness of all picture elements on a video screen and that, like a VU meter, allows the operator to keep the elements with highest intensity from exceeding the capabilities of the equipment.

wavelength Measurement of the length of an electromagnetic wave from one theoretical crest to the next; since the velocity of all electromagnetic waves is constant (186,000 miles per second), the longer the wavelength, the lower the frequency.

white balance An adjustment process through which light reflected from a white card in a given lighting situation is used as a reference point. In this setup mode, the camera automatically balances the red and blue intensities with the available light.

wide-angle lens *See* Short Lens.

wildtrack A nonsynchronous audio recording made on a remote or location production to record actual background sounds, which can then be mixed with other audio (e.g., an in-studio, voice-over narration) during postproduction editing.

wipe A camera transition whereby one image is gradually pushed off the screen—horizontally, vertically, or diagonally—as another picture replaces it.

wireless mike A microphone with a self-contained miniature FM transmitter built in; the microphone-transmitter can send its signal several hundred feet to the control room, eliminating the use of mike cables.

wow The audible result of putting a record on the air before the turntable has reached full speed.

wrap-up (wind up) A cue to the talent that there are about fifteen seconds remaining in this program segment or in the total program.

zoom in To change a zoom lens to a narrow angle (long focal length) position.

zoom lens A variable-focal-length lens that, through a complicated optical system, can be smoothly changed from one focal length to another.

zoom out (zoom back) To change a zoom lens to a wide angle (short focal length) position.

Bibliography

The following list of additional sources is presented for the student who may want to pursue specific topics in more detail than has been possible in this text. The bibliography has been divided into seven sections.

General Background

Bermingham, Alan, et al. *The Small TV Studio: Equipment and Facilities.* New York: Hastings House, 1975.

Chester, Giraud; Garrison, Garnet R.; and Willis, Edgar E. *Television and Radio,* 4th ed. New York: Appleton-Century-Crofts, 1971.

Gross, Lynne S. *See/Hear: An Introduction to Broadcasting.* Dubuque, Iowa: Wm. C. Brown Company Publishers, 1979.

Head, Sydney W. *Broadcasting in America,* 3d ed. Boston: Houghton Mifflin Co., 1976.

————. *World Broadcasting Systems.* Belmont, Calif.: Wadsworth Publishing Co., 1985.

Seidle, Ronald J. *Air Time.* Boston: Holbrook Press, 1977.

Sterling, Christopher H., and Kittross, John M. *Stay Tuned: A Concise History of American Broadcasting.* Belmont, Calif.: Wadsworth Publishing Co., 1978.

Audio, Technical

Alten, Stanley R. *Audio in Media.* Belmont, Calif.: Wadsworth Publishing Co., 1981.

Burroughs, Lou. *Microphones: Design and Application.* Plainview, N.Y.: Sagamore Publishing Co., 1973.

Jeans, James. *Science and Music.* New York: Dover Publications, 1966.

Lowery, H. *A Guide to Musical Acoustics.* New York: Dover Publications, 1966.

Nisbett, Alec. *The Use of Microphones.* New York: Hastings House, 1974.

Oringel, Robert. *Audio Control Handbook.* New York: Hastings House, 1972.

Woram, John M. *The Recording Studio Handbook.* Plainview, N.Y.: Sagamore Publishing Co., 1976.

Video, Technical

Bensinger, Charles. *The Video Guide,* 3d ed. Santa Fe, New Mexico: Video-Info Publications, 1982.

Fink, Donald, and Lutyens, David. *The Physics of Television.* Garden City: Anchor Books, Doubleday & Co., 1960.

Hewish, A., ed. *Seeing Beyond the Visible*. New York: American Elsevier Publishing Corp., 1967.

Howorth, D., and Wharton, W. *Principles of Television Reception*. New York: Pitman Publishing Corp., 1967.

Marsh, Ken. *Independent Video: A Complete Guide to the Physics, Operation, and Application of the New Television*. San Francisco: Straight Arrow Books, 1974.

Video Freex. *Spaghetti City Video Manual*. New York: Praeger Publications, 1973.

Production, General

Anderson, Gary H. *Video Editing and Post-Production: A Professional Guide*. New York: Directors Guild of America, 1984.

Bensinger, Charles. *Peterson's Guide to Video Tape Recording*. Los Angeles: Peterson Publishing Co., 1973.

Browne, Steven E. *The Videotape Post Production Primer*. Burbank, Calif.: Wilton Place Communications, 1982.

Costa, Sylvia Allen. *How to Prepare a Production Budget for Film and Video Tape*. Blue Ridge Summit, Pa.: Tab Books, 1973.

Fuller, Barry J., Kanaba, Steve, and Brisch-Kanaba, Janyce. *Single-Camera Video Production*. Englewood Cliffs, N.J.: Prentice-Hall, Inc., 1982.

Gross, Lynne S. *Self Instruction in Radio Production*. Los Alamitos, Calif.: Hwong Publishing Co., 1977.

Jones, Gary William. *Electronic Film/Tape Post-Production Handbook*. Edmonton, Alberta, Canada: Jones Family Reunion, 1974.

Millerson, Gerald. *The Techniques of Television Production*, 9th ed. New York: Hastings House, 1972.

————. *TV Camera Operation*. New York: Hastings House, 1974.

Nisbett, Alec. *The Technique of the Sound Studio*, 3d ed. New York: Hastings House, 1972.

Shook, Frederick. *The Process of Electronic News Gathering*. Englewood, Colo.: Morton Publishing Company, 1982.

Wurtzel, Alan. *Television Production*. New York: McGraw-Hill, 1979.

Zettl, Herbert. *Television Production Handbook*, 4th ed. Belmont, Calif.: Wadsworth Publishing Co., 1984.

Directing and Aesthetics

Armer, Alan A. *Directing Television and Film*. Belmont, Calif.: Wadsworth Publishing Co., 1986.

Bretz, Rudy, and Stasheff, Edward. *Television Scripts for Staging and Study: With a Guide to Creative Camerawork*. New York: A. A. Wyn, 1953.

Davis, Desmond. *The Grammar of Television Production*, 3d ed. London: Barrie & Jenkins, 1974.

Lewis, Colby. *The TV Director/Interpreter*. New York: Hastings House, 1972.

Stasheff, Edward, and Bretz, Rudy. *The Television Program: Its Direction and Production*, 4th ed. New York: Hill & Wang, 1968.

Zettl, Herbert. *Sight-Sound-Motion: Applied Media Aesthetics*. Belmont, Calif.: Wadsworth Publishing Co., 1973.

Staging, Design, and Graphics

Bay, Howard. *Stage Design*. New York: Drama Book Specialists, 1974.

Bellman, Willard F. *Scenography and Stage Technology: An Introduction*. New York: Thomas Y. Crowell Co., 1977.

Clarke, Beverley. *Graphic Design in Educational Television*. New York: Watson-Guptill, 1974.

Hurrell, Ron. *Van Nostrand Reinhold Manual of Television Graphics*. New York: Van Nostrand Reinhold Co., 1974.

Millerson, Gerald. *Basic TV Staging*. New York: Hastings House, 1974.

————. *The Technique of Lighting for Television and Motion Pictures*. New York: Hastings House, 1974.

Parker, W. Oren, and Smith, Harvey K. *Scene Design and Stage Lighting*, 2d ed. New York: Holt, Rinehart & Winston, 1968.

Small Format Video

Compesi, Ronald J., and Sherriffs, Ronald E. *Small Format Television Production*. Boston: Allyn and Bacon, Inc., 1985.

Frederickson, H. Allen. *Community Access Video*. Santa Cruz, Calif.: Johnny Videotape, 1972.

Murray, Michael. *The Videotape Book*. New York: Bantam Books, 1975.

Robinson, Richard. *The Video Primer*. New York: Links Books, 1974.

Shamberg, Michael, and Raindance Corporation. *Guerrilla Television*. New York: Holt, Rinehart & Winston, 1971.

Index